OXFORD WORL

RIGHTS OF MAN,

AND

TOM PAINE was
ing he was appre
his hand various
age of 37, in 17
grated to Ameri
controversy with
ful pamphlets of *Common Sense* and *The American
Crisis*. After the Re   Europe ar
caught up in the
Rights of Man (1   st
Edmund Burke's *Refle*   , was
the most widely read pamphlet of the decade. Its success, coupled
with the rise of a popular movement for political reform in Britain
and Paine's unrepentant *Letter Addressed to the Addressers* (1792)
resulted in his being outlawed. A year later, as a deputy to the
National Convention in France, he fell foul of the Jacobins and
was imprisoned. He was released at the end of 1794 and went on
to write *Dissertation on the First Principles of Government* (1795)
and *Agrarian Justice* (1796), which develop still further his earlier
arguments for an egalitarian yet liberal democratic order. Paine
returned to America in 1802, to be vilified as an atheist by the
Federation party (primarily because of his *Age of Reason* (1794), an
attack on Christianity). He died in obscurity in 1809.

MARK PHILP is a Fellow and Tutor in Politics at Oriel College,
Oxford. He is the author of *Paine* (1989) in the Oxford Past Masters
Series, and *Godwin's Political Justice* (1986). He is the general editor
of the *Collected Novels and Memoirs of William Godwin* (1992) and
the *Political and Philosophical Writings of William Godwin* (1993). He
has written widely on late eighteenth-century political ideas and
movements and is the editor of *The French Revolution and British
Popular Politics* (1991).

OXFORD WORLD'S CLASSICS

*For almost 100 years Oxford World's Classics have brought
readers closer to the world's great literature. Now with over 700
titles—from the 4,000-year-old myths of Mesopotamia to the
twentieth century's greatest novels—the series makes available
lesser-known as well as celebrated writing.*

*The pocket-sized hardbacks of the early years contained
introductions by Virginia Woolf, T. S. Eliot, Graham Greene,
and other literary figures which enriched the experience of reading.
Today the series is recognized for its fine scholarship and
reliability in texts that span world literature, drama and poetry,
religion, philosophy and politics. Each edition includes perceptive
commentary and essential background information to meet the
changing needs of readers.*

OXFORD WORLD'S CLASSICS

THOMAS PAINE

Rights of Man
Common Sense
and Other Political Writings

Edited with an Introduction and Notes by
MARK PHILP

OXFORD

UNIVERSITY PRESS

OXFORD
UNIVERSITY PRESS

Great Clarendon Street, Oxford OX2 6DP

Oxford University Press is a department of the University of Oxford.
It furthers the University's objective of excellence in research, scholarship,
and education by publishing worldwide in

Oxford New York

Athens Auckland Bangkok Bogotá Buenos Aires Calcutta
Cape Town Chennai Dar es Salaam Delhi Florence Hong Kong Istanbul
Karachi Kuala Lumpur Madrid Melbourne Mexico City Mumbai
Nairobi Paris São Paulo Singapore Taipei Tokyo Toronto Warsaw

with associated companies in Berlin Ibadan

Oxford is a registered trade mark of Oxford University Press
in the UK and in certain other countries

Published in the United States
by Oxford University Press Inc., New York

Editorial matter © Mark Philp 1995

British Library Cataloguing in Publication Data

Data available

Library of Congress Cataloging in Publication Data

Paine, Thomas, 1737–1809.
[Works. 1995]
Rights of man; Common sense; and other writings /Thomas Paine;
edited with an introduction by Mark Philp.
p.   cm.—(Oxford world's classics)
Includes bibliographical references and index.
1. Political science—Early works to 1800.   I. Philp, Mark.
II. Title.   III. Series.
JC177.A3 1995 320—dc20   94–7288

ISBN 0–19–283557–2

3 5 7 9 10 8 6 4

Printed in Great Britain by
Cox & Wyman Ltd.
Reading, Berkshire

CONTENTS

ACKNOWLEDGEMENTS

My thanks are owed to those who have helped me chase some of Paine's more obscure references, especially Nigel Biggar, Selina Chen, David Eastwood, Martin Fitzpatrick, Simon Hornblower, Colin Lucas, Paul Langford, Leslie Mitchell, Sarah Turvey, and David Wootton.

This collection is for my children, Joe, Ruth, and Hannah. Their various contributions gave added resonance to Paine's insistence that 'every age and generation must be free to act for itself, *in all cases*, as the ages and generations which preceded it.' Given their ages, their sovereignty is still a long way off, although we already disagree about exactly how far. But when it comes, they could do a lot worse than to have Paine's work to hand.

INTRODUCTION

BETWEEN 1775 and 1815, from the beginning of the American Revolution to the end of the French, the meaning of the term 'revolution' changed dramatically. In the mid-eighteenth century, revolution involved a change in government, and in a more specialized sense, a return to the basic principles of the constitution: it had no connotations of progressive and permanent change. By the beginning of the nineteenth century, in the lexicon of reformers and radicals the term had come to mean a process of rapid, fundamental, and progressive social and political change. Reform efforts were no longer directed by a backward-looking concern with an original constitution or uncorrupted state; instead, they became linked to a belief in the advancement of mankind from barbarism to civilization, based on the spread of enlightenment and the recognition of the inalienable rights of man.

No individual's writing better exemplifies this transformation of the language of social and political change than that of Thomas Paine (1737–1809). And no individual has a better claim to be the world's first international revolutionary. Paine was a man of multiple citizenships: he played a major role in the American and French Revolutions, and did his best to ensure their imitation in Britain and Ireland. He had a wide circle of acquaintance among leading figures of this age of revolutions, including Franklin, Jefferson, Washington, Burke, Condorcet, Lafayette, Danton, and Napoleon. He also held office under the Continental Congress during the American Revolution, acted as unofficial ambassador for America in Britain in the late 1780s, and in 1792 was an elected member of the French National Convention. In Britain, he earned the double distinction of being the most widely read of the radical pamphleteers of the 1790s, and the one whose works were most often prosecuted. He was outlawed in Britain in 1792, nearly guillotined in France in 1794, and anathematized as a Jacobin and infidel in America on his return in 1802.

Unlike most of those with whom he worked, however, Paine was not born into a position of power and influence. His father was a stay-maker of modest means, able to provide only a basic education for his son at the local grammar school, together with a training in his craft. Neither the education nor the training was much appreciated: Paine ran off to sea while working for his father, and although he later practised as a stay-maker, he found alternative ways of making a living when he could. In the first thirty-seven years of his life, almost without exception, nothing to which he turned his hand succeeded. In 1774 he emigrated to America after failure as a stay-maker, excise officer, tobacconist, sometime teacher, and as a husband. He was a disillusioned and disappointed man, but he was still, as far as we know, reasonably orthodox in his political views.

The fever he contracted on the voyage to America nearly killed him, but once he had recovered he secured employment as an editorial assistant and writer for the *Pennsylvania Magazine*, based in Philadelphia. In this role, and through his developing contacts in coffee-house society in the city, he was introduced to American politics just as the first casualties of the conflict with Britain fell at Lexington and Concord in April 1775. In January 1776 he published his *Common Sense*, the most powerful and widely read of the early demands for American Independence from Britain. Within a year it sold over 150,000 copies and, according to many contemporaries, it did more than any other publication to persuade America of the justice and necessity of independence. Thereafter, Paine became a major figure in the pamphlet and newspaper controversies of the Revolution, and in both local and national politics. He brought his pen to bear whenever he felt the American cause needed upholding, and he wrote some of his finest prose in the bleakest days of the war. Most famously, as Washington's troops retreated again and again in the face of the British advance in December 1776, he provided the rallying cry his new countrymen needed:

These are the times that try men's souls. The summer soldier and the sunshine patriot will, in this crisis, shrink from the service of their country; but he that stands it *now*, deserves the love and thanks of every man and woman. Tyranny, like hell, is not easily conquered; yet we have this consolation with us, that the harder the conflict, the more glorious the triumph. (p. 63)

Paine's services to the cause of independence were recognized by the Continental Congress, who employed him as secretary to its Foreign Affairs committee. The appointment was short-lived: Paine leaked privileged information in an attempt to prove the untrustworthiness of Silas Deane, one of Congress's agents negotiating with France. Although widely attacked at the time, Paine was subsequently vindicated when Deane, in 1781, wrote a series of letters from Antwerp encouraging reunion with Britain. But Paine had already been rehabilitated, having been appointed clerk to the Pennsylvania Assembly in November 1779, and Congress acknowledged his value by paying him a salary from the secret service fund to write for the congressional cause as the war drew to an end. As the last of his *American Crisis* letters makes clear, he was convinced of the need for a federal power to act as a unifying force in what threatened to be a fragmented country.

Paine's commitment to America was unconditional; he fought for it with the passion of a convert. Yet, as John Quincy Adams later remarked, he had 'no country, no affections that constitute the pillars of patriotism'.[1] What Adams refused to acknowledge was that Paine's devotion was not to the country itself, but to the principles for which it stood: to liberty and equality, and to the prospect of realizing a political order based on representative government, unscarred by the European legacy of hereditary privilege and monarchical government. Paine took America to his heart in the same way as he later adopted the cause of revolution in Europe: for the principles it sought to realize, not because of some emotional attachment to place. In abandoning his native country in 1774, he left behind all particular attach-

[1] Cited in David Freeman Hawke, *Paine* (New York, 1974), 33.

ments. Although *Common Sense* is a clarion call to Americans to defend their patrimony, it is one which proclaims universal values of freedom and equality and which rests its appeal on reason, nature, and sentiment. In keeping with these commitments, Paine characterizes himself not as British, American, or French, but as a citizen of the world, and the cause he defends is similarly universal in scope: 'We have it in our power to begin the world over again.' (p. 53)

These were not, for Paine, mere theoretical claims. He was not an abstract political theorist, nor is it easy to identify those thinkers by whom he was influenced. He was wholly self-taught in political theory and he disclaimed any indebtedness to others, insisting, for example, that he had never read Locke. His political philosophy is less the product of a system and more a response to the polemical cut and thrust of contemporary political controversy. It is easy to see why commentators, such as J. G. A. Pocock, find him 'difficult to fit into any kind of category'.[2] Paine's political theory was forged in political conflict and hammered out in the midst of war and revolution. When writing he drew on the arguments of coffee-house political circles and on the cultural baggage he had accumulated on his travels. He had an astonishing memory, not least for his own writings, which contemporaries claimed he could and would recite in full at the drop of a hat. Comments by others also clearly stuck in his mind— such as a phrase from an obscure Italian political theorist, Dragonetti (pp. 33 and 359)—but, for the most part, he collected material from his discussions with others and from sources close to hand, and worked them up into his own distinctive style of argument. There is, however, a basic touchstone for Paine's thinking, namely his enduring intellectual and personal investment in his distinctive understanding of the American Revolution. In the translation of the American cause from a little local difficulty into the cause of all the world, Paine found a sense of purpose and a sense of himself which he had lacked in England. Paine's American Revolution was one which legitimated, and gave a focus for,

[2] J. G. A. Pocock, *Virtue, Commerce, and History* (Cambridge, 1985), 276.

the resentments, frustrations, and anger generated by his life in England. In embracing the new world he was repudiating the old; in beginning the world again he was starting his own life again; and when he returned to Europe and became involved in the reform movements of Britain and France, he sought to reform the old world in the light of the new.

In the five years after the end of the war, Paine more or less left politics behind, becoming absorbed in a series of scientific experiments—some on a design for a smokeless candle, but most concerning the design and construction of . a single-arched iron bridge. The bridge bore the trademark of its country of origin: made up of thirteen sections (the number of states), it was designed to span the rivers of America whose spring ice floes made bridges using piers unsuitable. Ever impatient, Paine balked at the long delays he met in Pennsylvania as the State Assembly debated whether to fund a bridge on his design to span the Schuylkill, and decided to try his luck with it in Europe. In April 1787 he embarked for France.

Paine travelled between England and France from 1787 to 1792, initially because of negotiations over financing and building a model of his bridge, but increasingly because of his involvement with the politics of the two countries. When in England he visited leading members of the opposition and acted as an informal source of information for Thomas Jefferson (then American Ambassador in Paris) about British attitudes to America and France. Through his contacts in Paris, first through Jefferson and Lafayette, and subsequently through the liberal intellectuals of the Girondins,[3] he kept in touch with the opening stages of the revolution and was soon drawn into it in a more practical way. In September 1792, despite being unable to speak French, Paine found himself nominated and elected as a representative to the National Convention in three constituencies. His

[3] The Girondins were a loosely organized political grouping in the early period of the French Revolution, named after the area of origin, the Gironde, of several of their deputies. The group was distinctive for its early republicanism and its advocacy of war. After a period of ascendancy in 1792 they fell from power in the late spring of 1793.

reputation in France was partly derived from his American writings (which, thus far, had been suitably edited in translation to remove the attacks on monarchy) and his *Letter to the Abbé Raynal* (1782), in which he sought to explain the nature and significance of the American Revolution to a European audience. But it had a more recent basis in his *Rights of Man* (1791 and 1792), written as a defence of the French Revolution and its principles in response to Edmund Burke's *Reflections on the Revolution in France* (1790).

Burke's *Reflections* was a double-edged attack aimed at both the French revolutionaries and their English sympathizers. It provoked a pamphlet war which began by challenging Burke's interpretation of events in France, but quickly became a polarizing controversy about the basic principles of politics. This controversy in turn prompted a revival of the extra-parliamentary movement for reform which had first appeared in the wake of the American war. By early 1792, organizations for political discussion and for promoting reform in Britain were spreading throughout the country; and the initiative for political reform began to move from the élite-dominated associations of the early 1780s to the democratically organized, mass-membership societies of the middling and artisan ranks. The political aspirations of these societies began moderately but many developed radical demands for annual parliaments, universal manhood suffrage, and the reform of the apportionment of parliamentary seats. As the government proved increasingly hostile to reform, attitudes hardened and the societies looked for new ways to exert pressure on parliament.

Paine's *Rights of Man*, issued in two parts (March 1791 and February 1792), was without doubt the single most successful response to Burke, selling in unprecedented numbers and circulated throughout the country by the radical societies. Moreover, it undoubtedly helped radicalize the aspirations of many in the societies. The pamphlet's success so alarmed the government that in May 1792 a Royal Proclamation against seditious writing was issued, together with a warrant against its author. By the time the case came to court, Paine was in France, helping to design a republican constitution. The hand-picked jury outlawed him, and he never returned to England. Thereafter, the radical movement in Britain was led into an ever more confrontational stance towards the government, spurred on both by Paine's *Letter Addressed to the Addressers* (1792), which called for a convention to be popularly elected to create a republican constitution, and by government prosecutions and the rise of popular loyalism. Early in 1794, Scottish courts handed out draconian sentences against radical activists attending a British convention for reform in Edinburgh; and in May 1794 the leading members of the two major English organizations, the Society for Constitutional Information and the London Corresponding Society, were arrested and held in the Tower. They were eventually acquitted at the end of the year but although their fortunes revived in the summer of 1795, when there was extensive popular protest against food shortages and the war, they were further constrained in their activities by acts passed at the end of 1795. Although radical societies continued to meet until the early 1800s, they were increasingly forced to do so clandestinely.

Meanwhile, Paine's involvement in France had become a more hazardous enterprise. He was denounced by Marat for speaking against the execution of Louis XVI, and was associated by Robespierre with the Girondins, who were arrested in June and executed in October 1793; as a result he was left increasingly exposed. He was finally arrested, in December 1793, a matter of days after completing the first part of his denunciation of Christianity and priestcraft, the *Age of Reason*. His ambiguous nationality did not help him: as a British national he could be imprisoned without trial; as an American, he could claim more consideration. But the American Minister, Gouverneur Morris, refused to claim him as a fellow national, thereby condemning him to continued imprisonment and probable death. Paine somehow avoided the summary trial to which victims of the Jacobin Terror were subjected, and he also narrowly escaped death from the diseases rife in the Luxembourg prison. Luckily—on his account, providentially—he survived both Robespierre's 'Reign of Terror' and Morris's indifference to his plight, and with the recall of Morris and the intervention of his replacement, James Monroe, he was released in November 1794.

Paine's involvement with the French Revolution continued after his recovery. He remained a member of the Convention, and was unanimously welcomed back by it in the winter of 1794–5. He also published two of his most important pamphlets in the following twenty-four months. In *Dissertations on First Principles of Government* (1795), he attacked the limitations on suffrage included in the Constitution of 1795 and made unequivocal his commitment to universal manhood suffrage. This was followed by *Agrarian Justice* (1797), in which he responded to the attempted coups by left and right against the Directory by elaborating a justification and a plan for a basic inheritance right for all citizens at the age of twenty-one, to be derived from taxation and provided as compensation for the private ownership of land. Although his *Rights of Man: Part Two* (1792) had advanced a plan for a redistributive element in taxation, it was only in *Agrarian Justice* that he justified such claims and linked them to a more general argument about the social responsibilities of legitimate government.

When Paine finally returned to America in 1802, fifteen years after leaving, the political atmosphere had changed dramatically and he found himself a ready target for Federalist attack. This was partly a result of his writings—his *Age of Reason* (1795 and 1796), with its assault on Christianity and the authority of the Bible, and his bitter invective in his *Letter to George Washington* (1795) against what he saw as his abandonment by America during his time in the Luxembourg, alienated many. So too did his public boasting of his friendship with Jefferson, who was now president. Jefferson stuck by his friend, and even had him to stay at the White House; and Paine continued to write, becoming increasingly vituperative in his attacks on the Federalists, but he never regained his former standing. His health gradually deteriorated and he became subject to fits. Never a temperate man, nor clean in his personal habits, he ended his life in squalid isolation, cared for by the wife of his friend Nicolas Bonneville, with whom he had lived in Paris. After his death, his one-time critic turned disciple, William Cobbett, had his bones dug up and returned to England, where they were promptly lost. The absence of a final resting place is not inappropriate. Paine's philosophy was universal: he was a better 'citizen of the world' than he could ever have been the subject of a state.

Paine's writings bear witness to his revolutionary activities, and provide us with a detailed picture of the evolving understanding of social and political change at the end of the eighteenth century. They also help us to see that Paine himself plays an important role in this process.

The changing understanding of revolutions in this period is attested by Paine's developing sense of the significance of the American Revolution. *Common Sense* insists on the exceptional character of the American case, seeing it as an asylum for mankind, the last uncorrupted country and resting place for freedom. The biblical parallel to Noah is explicit: 'The inhabitants of heaven long to see the ark finished in which all the liberty and true religion in the world are to be deposited'.[4] However, he also believes that Americans must seize the time or their liberty will be lost: 'Virtue is not hereditary, neither is it perpetual' (p. 52); if America remains under English rule she will succumb to the corruption which marks the states of Europe. Yet he does not represent America as a state of nature: 'Government, like dress, is the badge of lost innocence' (p. 5), and there is no attempt to claim that America retains its original state of innocence. His optimism about America's role rests on his view that the country is united by interest, reason, and sentiment—that is, by a common sense that the collective good can no longer be served by subservience to Britain. The very title of Paine's first revolutionary work appeals to the utterly obvious nature of Americans' shared interests and concerns, and to the naturalness and reasonableness of their common cause: 'as well can the lover forgive the ravisher of his mistress, as the

[4] Philip S. Foner, *The Life and Major Writings of Thomas Paine*, 2 vols. (Secaucus, NJ, 1948), ii. 93.

continent forgive the murders of Britain'. (p. 35) But Paine also appeals to virtue: his readers should not mistake 'a cold matter of interest' for the demands of their 'bounden duty'.[5] They must be prepared to pay the costs of their just resistance. They must try the case not solely by reference to their interests, but 'by those feelings and affections which nature justifies, and without which we should be incapable of discharging the social duties of life, or enjoying the felicities of it'. (p. 26)

As the revolution draws to a close a more general set of claims begins to emerge in his writings. The reconciliation of the liberty and property of the individual with the claims of the common good is achieved less by an appeal to virtue and more in terms of the triumph of reason. 'The mind once enlightened cannot again become dark ... There is no possibility, neither is there any term to express the supposition by; of the mind *un*knowing anything it already knows'.[6] In keeping with this new optimism, his *Rights of Man* and his other later works present America as setting the example which the rest of the world will follow. What was first seen as an exception now sets the rule: 'The independence of America ... (has) been accompanied by a revolution in the principles and practice of governments.' 'No sooner did the America governments display themselves to the world, than despotism felt a shock, and man began to contemplate redress.' (p. 210) Now that such revolutions have begun 'it is natural to expect that other revolutions will follow.' 'Reason, like time, will make its own way, and prejudice will fall in its combat with interest.' (p. 212) In these works Paine moves from a static conception of revolution to one which sees it as the product of the progress of reason and civilization through history. In place of the pre-political pastoral idyll indicated in the opening pages of *Common Sense*—'the palaces of kings are built on the ruins of the bowers of paradise' (p. 5)—the idyll is now projected into the future: 'the more perfect civilisation is, the less occasion it has for government.' (p. 216)

[5] Ibid. i. 205.
[6] Ibid. ii. 244.

As Paine generalizes the American case, he leaves behind the parochial conventions of much eighteenth-century political thought. The shibboleths of mixed government—the balanced constitution, the Revolution Settlement of 1688, and the rights of the free-born Englishman—are systematically jettisoned. In their place he advances a political theory based on the equal natural rights of man, which he subsequently develops into an argument for equal rights of citizenship and a degree of economic equality.

Although there is a clear egalitarianism throughout Paine's writing, such as his denunciation of hereditary orders in *Common Sense*, his debunking of titles in *Rights of Man*, and his arguments for some element of distributive equality in *Agrarian Justice*, he only gradually develops the distinctions between natural and civil rights which mark *Rights of Man*, and only later still does he link rights claims to questions of material equality. The earliest works do insist on the natural equality of men and their equal right to freedom: 'Whenever I use the words *freedom* or *rights*, I desire to be understood to mean a perfect equality of them. Let the rich man enjoy his riches, and the poor man comfort himself in his poverty. But the floor of freedom is as level as water.'[7] However, the equality of rights is largely implicit in *Common Sense*, and while there is an indication in his *Candid and Critical remarks on a Letter signed Ludlow* (1777) of the distinction between natural and civil rights which is explicitly drawn in *Rights of Man*, there is little sign in this earlier work of the equally important distinction between perfect and imperfect rights.

Remarks on Ludlow . . . suggests a view of natural rights as liberties appropriate to the state of nature which are exchanged for civil rights in a state of society. In the *Rights of Man*, written nearly fifteen years later, he insists that 'every civil right has for its foundation, some natural right pre-existing in the individual, but to the enjoyment of which his individual power is not, in all cases, sufficiently competent'. We can thus distinguish between those natural rights 'in which the power to execute is as perfect as the right itself'

[7] Ibid. ii. 287.

(p. 119)—as in the right of freedom of conscience—and those in which the power of the individual is imperfect. This distinction, however, is not the fruit of Paine's response to Burke, since it is foreshadowed in a letter written to Thomas Jefferson in February 1788—a letter prompted by a discussion the evening before (probably in the company of Lafayette and other French constitutional reformers) of a pamphlet by James Wilson on the new federal constitution. This letter is an important link between Paine's thinking on America and his later contributions to the reform movements in Europe.

The distinction between natural and civil rights was commonly, but loosely, drawn in the eighteenth century. Burke himself invokes the distinction in his *Reflections*. But what was at issue between Burke and Paine was the question of how far natural rights are surrendered for the rights of civil society. In 1788, Paine read Wilson as arguing that the more rights we entrust to civil society the better. Burke similarly insists that the advantages of civil society cannot be secured without the surrender of 'the first fundamental right of uncovenanted man, that is, the right to judge for himself, and to assert his own cause ... Man cannot enjoy the rights of an uncivil and of a civil state together.'[8] In contrast, the first part of *Rights of Man* argues that where our power to execute our natural right is perfect government has no legitimate jurisdiction. Thus freedom of conscience is a natural right which no government can curtail. Where we need the assistance of others to enforce our natural right, as in the right to redress, we 'deposit this right in the common stock of society'. We do not give up the right so much as entrust it, and society does not grant us anything we are not already owed by natural right. Our civil rights are simply those natural rights for which we require 'the arm of society'. (p. 120)

With hindsight we can recognize distinct currents of thought in the eighteenth century on these issues, but for

---

[8] Edmund Burke, *Reflections on the Revolution in France*, ed. L. G. Mitchell (Oxford, 1993), 60. See also Wks. 110; O'B. 150; p. 52 (these abbreviations refer to other editions as indicated on p. 435).

many of those who used rights arguments, not least Burke and Paine, it was often only in the heat of debate that their inchoate sense of these distinctions crystallized into clear doctrinal positions. Paine's settled view of the distinction between natural and civil rights emerges in his discussions with Jefferson on the Federal constitution. In the second part of his response to Burke, however, he extends his position to make a more general set of claims concerning social equality and the welfare of citizens, and he develops his argument still further in *Agrarian Justice*.

In *Agrarian Justice* the rights-based, rather Lockean, claims for formal equality of *Rights of Man* are expanded into a more substantive (un-Lockean) egalitarianism. Moreover, where Paine had once praised the pacific effects of commerce, he now doubts that either commerce, or civilization more generally, is inevitably beneficial. Civilization has operated in two ways: 'to make one part of society more affluent, and the other more wretched, than would have been the lot of either in a natural state'. (p. 416) To remedy the defects which arise from the inequality of property, Paine argues that each proprietor owes a ground rent to the community for the land he or she cultivates. There are limits to the amount of redistribution Paine believes is justified. He holds that the cultivator has a right to his or her produce while the claims of others are limited to a ground rent, based on their original common title to the earth. But he also begins to recognize that the distinctions between land and cultivation, and between the individual's efforts and the effects of society, are not easily drawn. Wages are not always just, not least in that they do not take into account the needs of a whole lifetime—so that many labourers become indigent when they are no longer able to work. By paying too little for labour, 'the working hand perishes in old age, and the employer abounds in affluence'. (p. 428) For these reasons, private property cannot be treated as wholly inviolable; society has a legitimate role in regulating it. Indeed, as he argues in his *Dissertation on First Principles of Government*, the right to property is but one right, 'and that not of the most essential kind. The protection of a man's person is more sacred than the protection of property . . .' (p. 400)

For Paine, the state of civilization which prevails in Europe is 'as unjust in its principle, as it is horrid in its effects; and it is the consciousness of this, and the apprehension that such a state cannot continue when once investigation begins in any country, that makes the possessors of property dread every idea of revolution'. (pp. 428–9) The solution is clear: each person must benefit from the system of private property which is established. To achieve this requires that the riches of one are seen to benefit the condition of the poorest: 'when the more riches a man acquires, the better it shall be for the general mass; it is then that antipathies will cease, and property be placed on the permanent basis of national interest and protection'. (p. 429). That is, 'to form a system, that, while it preserves one part of society from wretchedness, shall secure the other part from depredation'. (p. 429) Inequalities, when restrained by the principle of reciprocal benefit, will remove the social basis for revolution and will provide a firm foundation for government.

From a sense of the equality of mankind, and from a recognition that the proper end of government is the protection of those natural rights for which our natural power is deficient, Paine also develops a further extension of rights theory—namely, the right to self-government. In the second part of *Rights of Man* he uses the American example to show the appropriate relationships between the nation, its constitution and its government. Paine is a constitutionalist, not in the sense of favouring an intricate and balanced system for the division of constitutional powers, but in the sense of believing that a government can only be legitimate if it operates within a constitution established by a sovereign people. 'A constitution is a thing *antecedent* to a government, and a government is only the creature of a constitution.' (p. 122) The necessary complement to his account of natural rights is his assertion of the ultimate sovereignty of the people. It is first expressed tentatively in *Common Sense*—'A government of our own is our natural right'—and subsequently insisted on in *Rights of Man*: 'a nation has at all times an inherent, indefeasible right to abolish any form of Government it finds inconvenient, and establish such as accords with its interest, disposition, and happiness'. (p. 193) In his *Letter Addressed to the Addressers* and *Dissertation on First Principles*, he makes it clear that the sovereign people must retain their individual sovereignty through their right to vote for their representatives. 'The right of voting for representatives is the primary right by which other rights are protected. To take away this right is to reduce a man to a state of slavery . . .' (p. 398) (This view makes his lack of interest in women's suffrage seem strikingly myopic.)

From his starting point of the rights of man, Paine develops arguments for popular sovereignty, universal suffrage, representative government, and a citizenship based on formal equality and on the existence of a threshold of welfare below which individuals will not fall. It is these basic principles which he believes the revolutions of America and France have established, and which demonstrate their radically different character from their predecessors. The changes they have brought about are both progressive and permanent: 'Ignorance is of a peculiar nature; once dispelled, it is impossible to re-establish it . . . though man may be *kept* ignorant, he cannot be *made* ignorant.' (p. 169) The artifices by which monarchy, aristocracy, and hereditary government have retained their hold in Europe are being stripped away as the 'principles of universal reformation' inaugurated in the American Revolution spread irresistibly across the world. (p. 210) 'Government founded on a *moral theory, on a system of universal peace, on the indefeasible, hereditary rights of man*, is now revolving from West to East, by a stronger impulse than the government of the sword revolved from East to West. It . . . promises a new era to the human race.' (p. 213) As despotisms decline, and the representative system spreads, 'the animosities and prejudices fomented by the intrigues and artifice of courts will cease' as will the ruinous wars of Europe. 'The present age will hereafter merit to be called the Age of Reason, and the present generation will appear to the future as the Adam of a new world.' (p. 321)

Revolutions may invoke matters of principle, but they must be made by men and women. Modern revolutions, indeed, have been characterized by the involvement of the people—the masses, as they have been contemptuously referred to. In the nineteenth century, the espousal of revolutionary principles was coupled for the most part with attempts to harness the revolutionary agency of the working people. The roots of this mass-mobilization have been recognized in the activities of the Parisian *sansculottes* and in those of their artisan brethren in the radical societies of London. There have also been attempts to identify precursors in the radical artisan circles in which Paine mixed in Philadelphia. But to insist on the class credentials of these groups is of limited value. Modern historiography rightly encourages us to think less about some a-priori conception of class, and more about the processes by which groups come to be bound together by a common political lexicon and by common aspirations and objectives.

While it is possible to insist on Paine's class credentials, which are certainly closer to the artisan classes than most of his radical contemporaries, it is more instructive to focus on the part he plays in the formation of a populist, democratic political discourse levelled against the hierarchical and elitist orders of the *anciens régimes* of Europe. Paine is one of the first and most brilliant stylists of a vernacular prose, capable of reaching the ordinary reader and shattering the traditional attitudes of respect and deference for their social and political superiors. Although there was a growing movement in the print culture of the late eighteenth century which experimented with a more accessible prose style, Paine is undoubtedly one of its most strikingly successful exponents. Even today, readers find Paine's plain, unpretentious style both readable and powerful. Two hundred years ago, many found it a revelation. It is not difficult to imagine the impact of the first *Crisis* being read aloud to the dispirited troops of Washington's army; nor to doubt that Paine's words would have echoed in the minds of many after their subsequent triumph at Trenton. Similarly, it is easy to see the appeal of Paine's forthright iconoclasm when denouncing hereditary and monarchical institutions in the *Rights of Man*. An audience composed of 'those whom providence dooms to live on trust', as Burke put it,[9] would have had no difficulty in appreciating Paine's insistence on their rights as members of a sovereign people against the absurdities of the hereditary system: '... the idea of hereditary legislators is as inconsistent as that of hereditary judges, or hereditary juries; and as absurd as an hereditary mathematician, or an hereditary wise man; and as ridiculous as an hereditary poet-laureate.' (p. 134) The system is clearly risible, but it is also insulting: 'To inherit a government, is to inherit the people, as if they were flocks and herds.' (p. 224) This is angry, and powerfully assertive, prose: 'All that the noble asks of me is that I recognise his superiority because of his birth, while the king requires my submission: I am amused by the noble; I feel like setting my foot upon the King.'[10]

Because of the easy style of his writing and his knack of capturing the sentiments of his readers (and because he never sought to control the copyright of his work). Paine's pamphlets achieved phenomenally high sales and circulation. In America, *Common Sense* was the most widely sold pamphlets of the whole Revolution; in Britain, the *Rights of Man* outsold Burke three times over within two years; in ten years it probably did so thirtyfold. Indeed, he was prosecuted in Britain less for what he said than for the fact that it was not confined to 'the judicious reader' but was reaching those 'whose minds cannot be supposed to be conversant with subjects of this sort ... the ignorant, the credulous, the desperate'.[11] The sheer reach of his work indicates his importance in forcing a broadening of the political nation and the democratizing of national politics. If he did not succeed in undermining the frauds of hereditary and monarchical imposition and priestcraft, he forced them to defend their claims before a larger audience whose loyalty could no longer be assumed.

The success of the *Rights of Man* and its prosecution

⁹ *Reflections*, M. 97; Wks. 147; O'B. 195–6; P. 85.
¹⁰ Foner, ii. 545.
¹¹ *State Trials*, ed. T. B. Howell (London, 1812–20), xxii, case 574, 381–3.

further radicalized Paine and prompted him to offer his one-time countrymen an extra-parliamentary strategy for achieving reform. In his *Letter Addressed to the Addressers* (1792), which his contemporaries regarded as the third part of the *Rights of Man*, he drew again on his American experience to call for the formation of a British Convention to design a constitution for Britain. While conventionism had some history in England, Paine was willing to dispense with the niceties of petitions to parliament which had marked these precursors. For Paine, parliament had no right to reform itself, the right lay with the people as a whole: 'THE NATION WILL DECREE ITS OWN REFORMS.' (p. 376) Having been ignored in their petitions and appeals, the radical societies adopted something very like Paine's conventionist strategy. How far they saw this as a way of building up extra-parliamentary pressure, and how far they took this route in the spirit of Paine's insistence on the nation's right, remains unclear. They were tried for treason because the government believed the latter; they were acquitted because the jury believed the former. But for a critical period in the growth and development of British radicalism, Paine offered a non-violent strategy for achieving national reform. When this strategy failed, in the face of significant government repression and a loyalist backlash, the extra-parliamentary reform movement became smaller, more insular, and increasingly subversive in character and insurrectionary in ambition.

By invoking the American Revolution as the founding moment for a new order of European states, Paine was insisting on the radicalism of that revolution. This is not a characterization which America rushed to embrace. In the period of Federalist ascendancy and anti-Jacobinism at the end of the eighteenth century, and in continuing debates among American historians, there has been an insistence on the conservative, essentially political character of the Revolution and on its distance from events in France in the 1790s. The American Revolution, on this interpretation, was an attempt to resist the extension of the crown's prerogative power and to purify if possible, or resist if necessary, the corrupt constitution under which Americans laboured. Those who saw the Revolution in these terms were reluctant to concede a social dimension to the conflict, and at least some believed that America would develop its own aristocratic and hereditary institutions over time. From this perspective, Paine's espousal of egalitarian and redistributive commitments in his writings on France is anathema, and must be treated as wholly foreign to the American cause. But while Paine's views undoubtedly developed over time, there can be no doubt that his fundamental principles came from his initial act of commitment to what he saw as the American cause. Many of Paine's famous contemporaries in America were gentlemen, with an enlightened commitment to the equality of man in the sight of God. The Declaration drafted by Jefferson was not idiosyncratic:

We hold these truths to be self-evident: that all men are created equal; that they are endowed by their creator with *inherent and* inalienable rights; that among these are life, liberty, and the pursuit of happiness: that to secure these rights, governments are instituted among men, deriving their just powers from the consent of the governed; that whenever any form of government becomes destructive of these ends, it is the right of the people to alter or abolish it.[12]

It is not difficult to see why some believed the declaration to be Paine's work. But what Paine brought to these principles was first-hand experience of struggle and failure in a society divided by birth and title; what he read in them was an invitation to citizenship in a classless (and racially equal) society. His experience informed his interpretation of what America stood for, allowing him to give the rights claims of the Declaration an egalitarian and radical thrust which he developed further in his later works. From the beginning, however, he understood that the egalitarian sentiments of the Declaration, which he and his new countrymen espoused in the language of rights, could not be realised solely by a concern with equal liberties. These remain a central compo-

[12] 'A Declaration by the Representatives of the United States of America, in General Congress Assembled', in *Thomas Jefferson: Writings* (New York, 1984), 19.

nent of Paine's position, but they sit alongside the demands of duty and virtue and, in his later work, with a concern for the basic material conditions required to ensure that each citizen can claim equal standing and have a sense of the reciprocal interests which unite his or her society. When he wrote *Common Sense* he believed that his new country was sufficiently young and virtuous to win its cause—whereas the old European orders were too corrupted by long-standing inequalities in wealth and status to be able to change. After he returned to Europe this view gradually altered. The analysis of European degeneracy remained, but it is diagnosed as the fruit of ignorance, fostered by hereditary frauds and superstition. And for Paine ignorance was remediable. As a result, what America had achieved could be also be brought about in Europe, but to do so required both the elimination of political inequality and ignorance and the reduction in the extent of social and economic inequalities (to end exploitation and hardship). The equal rights of Americans are developed in the context of the Old World in terms of a broader conception of equal citizenship. This may not demonstrate the radicalism of the American revolution, but it does suggest that it fostered a spirit which was not radically distant from that which drove revolutionaries in France.

Looking back on the revolutionary era, de Tocqueville characterized the spirit of the age as democratization, but he glossed this as the demand for an equalization of condition. Like many of his contemporaries, he saw the French revolutionaries as having subverted liberty to the end of equality. There is no doubt much truth in this, with respect both to France and to the subsequent revolutions of the nineteenth and twentieth centuries, but it has limited validity for our understanding of Paine's position. Paine's sense that liberty must be secured was no less keen than de Tocqueville's. But, in contrast to de Tocqueville, his concern for liberty motivated his attention to economic hardship, his demand that there be a safety net for all, and his insistence that such provision is an essential element of government legitimacy. He believed that in the absence of a sense of reciprocal benefit between citizens, their sense of equal standing and of the justice of their lot would be destroyed. Representative democracy cannot exist in such a state, for those who are marginalized and excluded in this way must be ruled by force and fraud, not by consent. Without a degree of social and economic equality, liberty is also lost.

Paine believed that the states of Europe would be transformed into free republics as the growing political awareness of the people undermined the frauds of hereditary government and priestcraft. In 1776 he had sensed, and helped engender, a degree of unity of sentiment and commitment among his new countrymen against their treatment at the hands of the 'royal brute of Britain'. (p. 34) Over the subsequent twenty years, encouraged by the success of America, this unity came to be explained in terms of nature and reason, and was generalized from his fugitive people to the world as a whole. Paine found in America the seeds for a progressive social and political transformation of the world, and he sowed and sought to reap their harvest in revolutionary Europe in the 1790s. It is small wonder that John Adams should pay Paine the back-handed compliment of seeing him as the epitome of an age with which Adams had no wish to come to terms:

I am willing you should call this the Age of Frivolity as you do, and would not object if you had named it the Age of Folly, Vice, Frenzy, Brutality, Daemons, Buonaparte, Tom Paine, or the Age of the Burning Brand from the Bottomless Pit, or anything but the Age of Reason. I know not whether any man in the world has had more influence on its inhabitants or affairs for the last thirty years than Tom Paine. There can be no severer Satyr on the age. For such a mongrel between pig and puppy, begotten by a wild boar on a bitch wolf, never before in any age of the world was suffered the poltroonery of mankind, to run such a career of mischief. Call it then the Age of Paine.[13]

[13] Hawke, 7.

NOTE ON THE TEXTS

THERE are no established editions of Paine's work. Most of the pamphlets he wrote went through numerous reprintings, and it is impossible to tell which Paine regarded as authoritative. However, Paine did not change his writings significantly after publication, save for the addition of further Prefaces and Introductions. Accordingly, the earliest available edition of each text has been used, supplemented by the correction of typographical misprints and the addition of later Prefaces, Introductions, and Appendices. Double quotation marks have been changed to single, and full points removed from Dr, Mr, and St. With these exceptions, the variations and inconsistencies in the spelling and punctuation of the original have been preserved. Where Paine refers in the text to pages in the original edition these page numbers have been changed to refer to the present edition.

Paine's *Letter to Jefferson* is transcribed from the manuscript held in the Library of Congress.

Numbered footnotes are Paine's original notes; an asterisk signals an explanatory note to be found at the end of the volume.

SELECT BIBLIOGRAPHY

THE fullest edition of Paine's works is that edited by Philip S. Foner, *The Life and Major Writings of Thomas Paine* (Secaucus, NJ, 1948), 2 volumes. A. Owen Aldridge, author of *Man of Reason: The Life of Thomas Paine* (London, 1960) and *Thomas Paine's American Ideology* (Cranbury, NJ and London, 1984), has done more than any other scholar since Moncure Conway, who wrote in the 1890s, to identify new Paine material and reassess the status of previously attributed works.

Biographies and Studies

Aldridge, A. Owen, *Man of Reason: The Life of Thomas Paine*, (London, 1960).

Claeys, Gregory, *Thomas Paine: Social and Political Thought* (London, 1989).

Conway, Moncure, *The Life of Thomas Paine* (London, 1909).

Fruchtman, Jack, jr., *Thomas Paine and the Religion of Nature* (Baltimore, 1993).

Hawke, David Freeman, *Paine* (New York, 1974 and 1992).

Philp, Mark, *Paine* (Past Master, Oxford, 1989).

Articles

Bailyn, Bernard, 'Common Sense', in *Fundamental Testaments of the American Revolution* (Library of Congress, 1967); reprinted in Bailyn, *Faces of Revolution* (New York, 1990).

Dyck, Ian, 'Local attachments, national identities and world citizenship in the thought of Thomas Paine', *History Workshop Journal* 35 (1993), 117–35.

Kates, Gary, 'From Liberalism to Radicalism: Tom Paine's *Rights of Man*, *Journal of the History of Ideas* 1989, pp. 569–87.

Kramnick, Isaac, 'Tom Paine: Radical Liberal', in Kramnick, Isaac, *Republicanism and Bourgeois Radicalism: Political Ideology in late Eighteenth Century England and America* (Ithaca, NY, 1990).

Wootton, David, 'The Republican Tradition: from *Commonwealth* to *Common Sense*', in *Republicanism and Commercial Society: from the English Civil War to the American Revolution* (forthcoming).

American Background

Aldridge, A. Owen, *Thomas Paine's American Ideology* (Cranbury, NJ and London, 1984).

Bailyn, Bernard, *The Ideological Origins of the American Revolution* (Cambridge, Mass., 1967)

Foner, Eric, *Tom Paine and Revolutionary America* (Oxford, 1976).

Wood, Gordon, *The Creation of the American Republic 1776–1787* (New York, 1969).

——*The Radicalism of the American Revolution* (New York, 1992).

English and French Background

Butler, Marilyn, *Burke Paine and Godwin and the Revolution Controversy* (Cambridge, 1984).

Dickinson, H. T., *British Radicalism and the French Revolution, 1789–1815* (Oxford, 1985).

Fennessy, R. R., *Burke, Paine and the Rights of Man* (The Hague, 1963).

Goodwin, Albert, *The Friends of Liberty: The English Democratic Movement in the Age of the French Revolution* (London, 1979).

Philp, Mark, *The French Revolution and British Popular Politics* (Cambridge, 1992).

Thompson, E. P., *The Making of the English Working Class* (Harmondsworth, 1968).

A CHRONOLOGY OF
THOMAS PAINE

1737   Born 29 January at Thetford, Norfolk.

1742–51   Educated at a local school in Thetford.

1751–9   Apprenticed to his father in the stay-making trade, but on two occasions runs away to sea.

1759–60   Moves to Kent and sets up as a stay-maker. Marries, his wife dying less than twelve months later.

1764   Admitted into the Excise Service, accepts a post in Lincolnshire. Dismissed July 1765 for 'stamping' (approving cargo without checking its contents).

1767   Teaches in a school in London. Applies for re-admission into the Excise Service.

1768   Accepts a post as excise officer in Lewes, Sussex.

1771   Marries into a tobacconist business and combines his work there with his excise duties.

1772   Acts as the representative in London to the Excise Officers in their appeal for higher pay. Writes and circulates *The Case of the Offices of the Excise*.

1774   Discharged from Excise Service; marriage and business fail; secures letter of recommendation from Benjamin Franklin and, in October, emigrates to America.

1775   Settles in Philadelphia, works on *Pennsylvania Magazine*.

1776   Following the fighting in Lexington and Concord, April 1775, Paine becomes involved in the move to Independence for the colonies. In January his *Common Sense* is published, six months before the Declaration of Independence. First *Crisis* published December 1776.

1777–9   Serves in Congress as a Secretary to the Foreign Affairs Committee. Resigns following the Silas Deane affair—Paine using confidential information, embarassing to America's allies France, to argue that Deane had acted corruptly. November 1779, appointed Clerk to Pennsylvania Assembly.

1781   Visits France as secretary to John Laurens to secure aid for America.

1782   Accepts appointment to write in the interest of Congress, arranged by Robert Morris. Publishes *Letter to Abbé Raynal*.

1783   Seeks support from the Continental Congress and various states for his services to the Revolution.

1784-7 Principally involved in scientific interests, although he writes in support of a national bank in *Dissertations on Government* (1786).

1787   Sails for France to promote his design for a bridge. Visits London in September; meets leading Whigs, including Burke. Corresponds with Jefferson in Paris.

1788-90 In visits to France he becomes involved, mainly through Thomas Jefferson, American Ambassador, with the leaders of the constitutional wing of the French Revolution. Writes to Burke of events in France. His 'Letter to Jefferson' responds to developments in the debates on the constitution of the Federal Government in America.

1791   Publishes *Rights of Man*, his response to Burke's *Reflections on the Revolution in France* (November 1790). Joins in republican agitation in France in July 1791, arguing against retention of a monarchy.

1792   Publishes *Rights of Man, Part the Second, Combining Principal and Practice*. A Royal Proclamation against seditious writing is issued in May, along with a prosecution against Paine for seditious libel. The trial is deferred in July; Paine adds fuel to the fire with his *Letter Addressed to the Addressers* and leaves for France in September where he has been elected a member of the National Convention. In November, *in absentia* he is found guilty and outlawed.

1793   Opposes the execution of the King of France. He is associated with the Girondins, who fall from power and are executed in the summer; Paine is imprisoned in the Luxembourg at the end of the year, shortly after finishing his *Age of Reason*.

1794   His plight is ignored by the American Ambassador, Gouverneur Morris; he is released after the fall of Robespierre, only with the aid of Morris's replacement, James Monroe.

1795   Stays with Monroe and writes *Age of Reason, Part Two* (published 1796). Also publishes *Dissertations on first principles of Government* in response to the new French constitution of 1795.

1796   Writes *Letter to George Washington*, a bitter attack on the president for having abandoned him while in the Luxembourg.

1797   Publishes *Agrarian Justice*, his last major innovatory work in his arguments for distributive justice.

1798–1802   Attempts to advise Napoleon on an invasion of England, but becomes distrusted and seeks to return to America. Fearful that he is still pursued by the English, he waits until the Peace of Amiens before embarking for America.

1809   Dies 8 June.

COMMON SENSE;

ADDRESSED TO THE

INHABITANTS OF AMERICA,

ON THE FOLLOWING
INTERESTING SUBJECTS:

I. Of the Origin and Design of Government in general, with concise Remarks on the English Constitution.
II. Of Monarchy and Hereditary Succession.
III. Thoughts on the present State of American Affairs.
IV. Of the present ability of America, with some miscellaneous Reflections.

A NEW EDITION, with several Additions in the Body of the Work. To which is Added an APPENDIX; together with an Address to the People called QUAKERS.

Man knows no Master save creating HEAVEN,
Or those whom choice and common Good ordain.

THOMSON.*

INTRODUCTION

PERHAPS the sentiments contained in the following pages, are not yet sufficiently fashionable to procure them general favor; a long habit of not thinking a thing *wrong*, gives it a superficial appearance of being *right*, and raises at first a formidable outcry in defence of custom. But the tumult soon subsides. Time makes more converts than reason.

As a long and violent abuse of power, is generally the Means of calling the right of it in question (and in matters too which might never have been thought of, had not the Sufferers been aggravated into the inquiry) and as the King of England had undertaken in his *own Right*, to support the Parliament in what he calls *Theirs*, and as the good people of this country are grievously oppressed by the combination, they have an undoubted privilege to inquire into the pretensions of both, and equally to reject the usurpation of either.

In the following sheets, the author hath studiously avoided every thing which is personal among ourselves. Compliments as well as censure to individuals make no part thereof. The wise, and the worthy, need not the triumph of a pamphlet; and those whose sentiments are injudicious, or unfriendly, will cease of themselves unless too much pains are bestowed upon their conversion.

The cause of America is in a great measure the cause of all mankind. Many circumstances hath, and will arise, which are not local, but universal, and through which the principles of all Lovers of Mankind are affected, and in the Event of which, their Affections are interested. The laying a Country desolate with Fire and Sword,* declaring War against the natural rights of all Mankind, and extirpating the Defenders thereof from the Face of the Earth, is the Concern of every Man to whom Nature hath given the Power of feeling; of which Class, regardless of Party Censure, is the

AUTHOR

P.S. The Publication of this new Edition hath been delayed, with a View of taking notice (had it been necessary) of any Attempt to refute the Doctrine of Independance: As no Answer hath yet appeared, it is now presumed that none will, the Time needful for getting such a Performance ready for the Public being considerably past.

Who the Author of this Production is, is wholly unnecessary to the Public, as the Object for Attention is the *Doctrine itself*, not the *Man*. Yet it may not be unnecessary to say, That he is unconnected with any Party, and under no sort of Influence public or private, but the influence of reason and principle.

Philadelphia, February 14, 1776

COMMON SENSE

Of the Origin and Design of Government in General. With concise Remarks on the English Constitution.

SOME writers have so confounded society with government, as to leave little or no distinction between them; whereas they are not only different, but have different origins. Society is produced by our wants, and government by our wickedness; the former promotes our happiness *positively* by uniting our affections, the latter *negatively* by restraining our vices. The one encourages intercourse, the other creates distinctions. The first is a patron, the last a punisher.

Society in every state is a blessing, but government even in its best state is but a necessary evil; in its worst state an intolerable one; for when we suffer, or are exposed to the same miseries *by a government*, which we might expect in a country *without government*, our calamities is heightened by reflecting that we furnish the means by which we suffer. Government, like dress, is the badge of lost innocence; the palaces of kings are built on the ruins of the bowers of paradise. For were the impulses of conscience clear, uniform, and irresistibly obeyed, man would need no other lawgiver; but that not being the case, he finds it necessary to surrender up a part of his property to furnish means for the protection of the rest; and this he is induced to do by the same prudence which in every other case advises him out of two evils to choose the least. *Wherefore*, security being the true design and end of government, it unanswerably follows that whatever *form* thereof appears most likely to ensure it to us, with the least expence and greatest benefit, is preferable to all others.

In order to gain a clear and just idea of the design and end of government, let us suppose a small number of persons settled in some sequestered part of the earth, unconnected with the rest, they will then represent the first peopling of any country, or of the world. In this state of natural liberty, society will be their first thought. A thousand motives will excite them thereto, the strength of one man is so unequal to his wants, and his mind so unfitted for perpetual solitude, that he is soon obliged to seek assistance and relief of another, who in his turn requires the same. Four or five united would be able to raise a tolerable dwelling in the midst of a wilderness, but *one* man might labour out the common period of life without accomplishing any thing; when he had felled his timber he could not remove it, nor erect it after it was removed; hunger in the mean time would urge him from his work, and every different want call him a different way. Disease, nay even misfortune would be death, for though neither might be mortal, yet either would disable him from living, and reduce him to a state in which he might rather be said to perish than to die.

Thus necessity, like a gravitating power, would soon form our newly arrived emigrants into society, the reciprocal blessings of which, would supercede, and render the obligations of law and government unnecessary while they remained perfectly just to each other; but as nothing but heaven is impregnable to vice, it will unavoidably happen, that in proportion as they surmount the first difficulties of emigration, which bound them together in a common cause, they will begin to relax in their duty and attachment to each other; and this remissness, will point out the necessity, of establishing some form of government to supply the defect of moral virtue.

Some convenient tree will afford them a State-House, under the branches of which, the whole colony may assemble to deliberate on public matters. It is more than probable that their first laws will have the title only of REGULATIONS, and be enforced by no other penalty than public disesteem. In this first parliament every man, by natural right will have a feat.

But as the colony increases, the public concerns will increase likewise, and the distance at which the members may be separated, will render it too inconvenient for all of them to meet on every occasion as a first, when their number was small, their habitations near, and the public concerns few and trifling. This will point out the convenience of their consenting to leave the legislative part to be managed by a select number chosen from the whole body, who are supposed to have the same concerns at stake which those have who appointed them, and who will act in the same manner as the whole body would act were they present. If the colony continue increasing, it will become necessary to augment the number of the representatives, and that the interest of every part of the colony may be attended to, it will be found best to divide the whole into convenient parts, each part sending its proper number, and that the *elected* might never form to themselves an interest separate from the *electors*, prudence will point out the propriety of having elections often; because as the *elected* might by that means return and mix again with the general body of the *electors* in a few months, their fidelity to the public will be secured by the prudent reflexion of not making a rod for themselves. And as this frequent interchange will establish a common interest with every part of the community, they will mutually and naturally support each other, and on this (not on the unmeaning name of king) depends the *strength of government, and the happiness of the governed*.

Here then is the origin and rise of government; namely, a mode rendered necessary by the inability of moral virtue to govern the world; here too is the design and end of government, viz. freedom and security. And however our eyes may be dazzled with show, or our ears deceived by sound; however prejudice may warp our wills, or interest darken our understanding, the simple voice of nature and of reason will say, it is right.

I draw my idea of the form of government from a principle in nature, which no art can overturn, viz. that the more simple any thing is, the less liable it is to be disordered, and the easier repaired when disordered; and with this maxim in view, I offer a few remarks on the so much boasted constitution of England. That it was noble for the dark and slavish times in which it was erected is granted. When the world was over-run with tyranny the least remove therefrom was a glorious rescue. But that it is imperfect, subject to convulsions, and incapable of producing what it seems to promise, is easily demonstrated.

Absolute governments (tho' the disgrace of human nature) have this advantage with them, that they are simple; if the people suffer, they know the head from which their suffering springs, know likewise the remedy, and are not bewildered by a variety of causes and cures. But the constitution of England is so exceedingly complex, that the nation may suffer for years together without being able to discover in which part the fault lies, some will say in one and some in another, and every political physician will advise a different medicine.

I know it is difficult to get over local or long standing prejudices, yet if we will suffer ourselves to examine the component parts of the English constitution, we shall find them to be the base remains of two ancient tyrannies, compounded with some new republican materials.

First.—The remains of monarchical tyranny in the person of the king.

Secondly.—The remains of aristocratical tyranny in the persons of the peers.

Thirdly.—The new republican materials, in the persons of the commons, on whose virtue depends the freedom of England.

The two first, by being hereditary, are independent of the people; wherefore in a *constitutional sense* they contribute nothing towards the freedom of the state.

To say that the constitution of England is a *union* of three powers reciprocally *checking* each other, is farcical, either the words have no meaning, or they are flat contradictions.

To say that the commons is a check upon the king, presupposes two things.

First.—That the king is not to be trusted without being looked after, or in other words, that a thirst for absolute power is the natural disease of monarchy.

Secondly.—That the commons, by being appointed for

that purpose, are either wiser or more worthy of confidence than the crown.

But as the same constitution which gives the commons a power to check the king by withholding the supplies, gives afterwards the king a power to check the commons, by empowering him to reject their other bills; it again supposes that the king is wiser than those whom it has already supposed to be wiser than him. A mere absurdity!

There is something exceedingly ridiculous in the composition of monarchy; it first excludes a man from the means of information, yet empowers him to act in cases where the highest judgment is required. The state of a king shuts him from the world, yet the business of a king requires him to know it thoroughly; wherefore the different parts, unnaturally opposing and destroying each other, prove the whole character to be absurd and useless.

Some writers have explained the English constitution thus; the king, say they, is one, the people another; the peers are an house in behalf of the king; the commons in behalf of the people; but this hath all the distinctions of an house divided against itself; and though the expressions be pleasantly arranged, yet when examined they appear idle and ambiguous; and it will always happen, that the nicest construction that words are capable of, when applied to the description of some thing which either cannot exist, or is too incomprehensible to be within the compass of description, will be words of sound only, and though they may amuse the ear, they cannot inform the mind, for this explanation includes a previous question, viz. *How came the king by a power which the people are afraid to trust, and always obliged to check?* Such a power could not be the gift of a wise people, neither can any power, *which needs checking*, be from God; yet the provision, which the constitution makes, supposes such a power to exist.

But the provision is unequal to the task; the means either cannot or will not accomplish the end, and the whole affair is a *felo de se*;* for as the greater weight will always carry up the less, and as all the wheels of a machine are put in motion by one, it only remains to know which power in the constitution has the most weight, for that will govern; and though the others, or a part of them, may clog, or, as the phrase is, check the rapidity of its motion, yet so long as they cannot stop it, their endeavours will be ineffectual, the first moving power will at last have its way, and what it wants in speed is supplied by time.

That the crown is this overbearing part in the English constitution needs not be mentioned, and that it derives its whole consequence merely from being the giver of places and pensions is self-evident, wherefore, though we have been wise enough to shut and lock a door against absolute monarchy, we at the same time have been foolish enough to put the crown in possession of the key.

The prejudice of Englishmen, in favour of their own government by king, lords, and commons, arises as much or more from national pride than reason. Individuals are undoubtedly safer in England than in some other countries, but the *will* of the king is as much the *law* of the land in Britain as in France, with this difference, that instead of proceeding directly from his mouth, it is handed to the people under the most formidable shape of an act of parliament. For the fate of Charles the First,* hath only made kings more subtle—not more just.

Wherefore, laying aside all national pride and prejudice infavour of modes and forms, the plain truth is, that *it is wholly owing to the constitution of the people, and not to the constitution of the governement* that the crown is not as oppressive in England as in Turkey.*

An inquiry into the *constitutional errors* in the English form of government is at this time highly necessary; for as we are never in a proper condition of doing justice to others, while we continue under the influence of some leading partiality, so neither are we capable of doing it to ourselves while we remain fettered by any obstinate prejudice. And as a man, who is attached to a prostitute, is unfitted to choose or judge of a wife, so any prepossession in favour of a rotten constitution of government will disable us from discerning a good one.

Of MONARCHY *and* HEREDITARY SUCCESSION.

MANKIND being originally equals in the order of creation, the equality could only be destroyed by some subsequent circumstance; the distinctions of rich, and poor, may in a great measure be accounted for, and that without having recourse to the harsh, ill-sounding names of oppression and avarice. Oppression is often the *consequence*, but seldom or never the *means* of riches; and though avarice will preserve a man from being necessitously poor, it generally makes him too timorous to be wealthy.

But there is another and greater distinction for which no truly natural or religious reason can be assigned, and that is, the distinction of men into KINGS and SUBJECTS. Male and female are the distinctions of nature, good and bad the distinctions of heaven; but how a race of men came into the world so exalted above the rest, and distinguished like some new species, is worth enquiring into, and whether they are the means of happiness or of misery to mankind.

In the early ages of the world, according to the scripture chronology, there were no kings; the consequence of which was there were no wars; it is the pride of kings which throw mankind into confusion. Holland without a king hath enjoyed more peace for this last century than any of the monarchial governments in Europe. Antiquity favors the same remark; for the quiet and rural lives of the first patriarchs hath a happy something in them, which vanishes away when we come to the history of Jewish royalty.

Government by kings was first introduced into the world by the Heathens, from whom the children of Israel copied the custom.* It was the most prosperous invention the Devil ever set on foot for the promotion of idolatry. The Heathens paid divine honors to their deceased kings, and the christian world hath improved on the plan by doing the fame to their living ones. How impious is the title of *sacred majesty* applied to a worm, who in the midst of his splendor is crumbling into dust.

As the exalting one man so greatly above the rest cannot be justified on the equal rights of nature, so neither can it be defended on the authority of scripture; for the will of the Almighty, as declared by Gideon and the prophet Samuel, expressly disapproves of government by kings.* All anti-monarchial parts of scripture have been very smoothly glossed over in monarchial governments, but they undoubtedly merit the attention of countries which have their governments yet to form. 'Render unto Caesar the things which are Caesar's'* is the scriptural doctrine of courts, yet it is no support of monarchial government, for the Jews at that time were without a king, and in a state of vassalage to the Romans.

Near three thousand years passed away from the Mosaic account of the creation, till the Jews under a national delusion requested a king. Till then their form of government (except in extraordinary cases, where the Almighty interposed) was a kind of republic administered by a judge and the elders of the tribes. Kings they had none, and it was held sinful to acknowledge any being under that title but the Lord of Hosts. And when a man seriously reflects on the idolatrous homage which is paid to the persons of Kings, he need not wonder, that the Almighty, ever jealous of his honor, should disapprove of a form of government which so impiously invades the prerogative of heaven.

Monarchy is ranked in scripture as one of the sins of the Jews, for which a curse in reserve is denounced against them. The history of that transaction is worth attending to.

The children of Israel being oppressed by the Midianites, Gideon marched against them with a small army, and victory, thro' the divine interposition, decided in his favour. The Jews elate with success, and attributing it to the generalship of Gideon, proposed making him a king, saying, Rule thou over us, thou and thy son and thy son's son.* Here was temptation in its fullest extent; not a kingdom only, but an hereditary one, but Gideon in the piety of his foul replied, I will not rule over you, neither shall my son rule over you, THE LORD SHALL RULE OVER YOU.* Words need not be more explicit; Gideon doth not decline the honor but denieth their right to give it; neither doth he compliment them with invented declarations of his thanks, but in the positive stile of a prophet charges them with disaffection to their proper sovereign, the King of Heaven.

About one hundred and thirty years after this, they fell again into the same error. The hankering which the Jews had for the idolatrous customs of the Heathens, is something exceedingly unaccountable; but so it was, that laying hold of the misconduct of Samuel's two sons, who were entrusted with some secular concerns, they came in an abrupt and clamourous manner to Samuel, saying, *Behold thou art old, and thy sons walk not in thy ways, now make us a king to judge us like all the other nations.** And here we cannot but observe that their motives were bad, viz. that they might be *like* unto other nations, i.e. the Heathens, whereas their true glory laid in being as much *unlike* them as possible. *But the thing displeased Samuel when they said, give us a king to judge us; and Samuel prayed unto the Lord, and the Lord said unto Samuel, Hearken unto the voice of the people in all that they say unto thee, for they have not rejected thee, but they have rejected me,* THAT I SHOULD NOT REIGN OVER THEM. *According to all the works which they have done since the day that I brought them up out of Egypt, even unto this day; wherewith they have forsaken me and served other Gods; so do they also unto thee. Now therefore hearken unto their voice, howbeit, protest solemnly unto them and shew them the manner of the king that shall reign over them,** i.e. not of any particular king, but the general manner of the kings of the earth, whom Israel was so eagerly copying after. And notwithstanding the great distance of time and difference of manners, the character is still in fashion, *And Samuel told all the words of the Lord unto the people, that asked of him a king. And he said, This shall be the manner of the king that shall reign over you; he will take your sons and appoint them for himself for his chariots, and to be his horsemen, and some shall run before his chariots* (this description agrees with the present mode of impressing men) *and he will appoint him captains over thousands and captains over fifties, and will set them to ear his ground and to reap his harvest, and to make his instruments of war, and instruments of his chariots; and he will take your daughters to be confectionaries and to be cooks and to be bakers* (this describes the expence and luxury as well as the oppression of kings) *and he will take your fields and your olive yards, even the best of them, and give them to his servants; and he will take the tenth of your feed, and of your vineyards, and give them to his officers and to his servants* (by which we see that bribery, corruption, and favoritism are the standing vices of kings) *and he will take the tenth of your men servants, and your maid servants, and your goodliest young men and your asses, and put them to his work; and he will take the tenth of your sheep, and ye shall be his servants, and ye shall cry out in that day because of your king which ye shall have chosen,* AND THE LORD WILL NOT HEAR YOU IN THAT DAY.* This accounts for the continuation of monarchy; neither do the characters of the few good kings which have lived since, either sanctify the title, or blot out the sinfulness of the origin; the high encomium given of David takes no notice of him *officially as a king*, but only as a *man* after God's own heart. *Nevertheless the People refused to obey the voice of Samuel, and they said, Nay, but we will have a king over us, that we may be like all the nations, and that our king may judge us, and go out before us and fight our battles.* Samuel continued to reason with them, but to no purpose; he set before them their ingratitude, but all would not avail; and seeing them fully bent on their folly, he cried out, *I will call unto the Lord, and he shall send thunder and rain* (which then was a punishment, being in the time of wheat harvest) *that ye may perceive and see that your wickedness is great which ye have done in the sight of the Lord,* IN ASKING YOU A KING. *So Samuel called unto the Lord, and the Lord sent thunder and rain that day, and all the people greatly feared the Lord and Samuel. And all the people said unto Samuel, Pray for thy servants unto the Lord thy God that we die not, for* WE HAVE ADDED UNTO OUR SINS THIS EVIL, TO ASK A KING.* These portions of scripture are direct and positive. They admit of no equivocal construction. That the Almighty hath here entered his protest against monarchial government is true, or the scripture is false. And a man hath good reason to believe that there is as much of king-craft, as priest-craft in withholding the scripture from the public in Popish countries. For monarchy in every instance is the Popery of government.

To the evil of monarchy we have added that of hereditary succession; and as the first is a degradation and lessening of ourselves, so the second, claimed as a matter of right, is an insult and an imposition on posterity. For all men being originally equals, no *one* by *birth* could have a right to set up his own family in perpetual preference to all others for ever, and though himself might deserve *some* decent degree of honors of his contemporaries, yet his descendants might be far too unworthy to inherit them. One of the strongest *natural* proofs of the folly of hereditary right in kings, is, that nature disapproves it, otherwise she would not so frequently turn it into ridicule by giving mankind an *ass for a lion.**

Secondly, as no man at first could possess any other public honors than were bestowed upon him, so the givers of those honors could have no power to give away the right of posterity, and though they might say 'We choose you for *our* head,' they could not, without manifest injustice to their children, say 'that your children and your children's children shall reign over *ours* for ever.'* Because such an unwise, unjust, unnatural compact might (perhaps) in the next succession put them under the government of a rogue or a fool. Most wise men, in their private sentiments, have ever treated hereditary right with contempt; yet it is one of those evils, which when once established is not easily removed; many submit from fear, others from superstition, and the more powerful part shares with the king the plunder of the rest.

This is supposing the present race of kings in the world to have had an honourable origin; whereas it is more than probable, that could we take off the dark covering of antiquity, and trace them to their first rise, that we should find the first of them nothing better than the principal ruffian of some restless gang, whose savage manners or pre-eminence in subtilty obtained him the title of chief among plunderers; and who by increasing in power, and extending his depredations, over-awed the quiet and defenceless to purchase their safety by frequent contributions. Yet his electors could have no idea of giving hereditary right to his descendants, because such a perpetual exclusion of themselves was incompatible with the free and unrestrained principles they professed to live by. Wherefore, hereditary succession in the early ages of monarchy could not take place as a matter of claim, but as something casual or complimental; but as few or no records were extant in those days, and traditionary history stuffed with fables, it was very easy, after the lapse of a few generations, to trump up some superstitious tale, conveniently timed, Mahomet like,* to cram hereditary right down the throats of the vulgar. Perhaps the disorders which threatened, or seemed to threaten on the decease of a leader and the choice of a new one (for elections among ruffians could not be very orderly) induced many at first to favor hereditary pretensions; by which means it happened, as it hath happened since, that what at first was submitted to as a convenience, was afterwards claimed as a right.

England, since the conquest, hath known some few good monarchs, but groaned beneath a much larger number of bad ones, yet no man in his senses can say that their claim under William the Conqueror is a very honorable one.* A French bastard landing with an armed banditti, and establishing himself king of England against the consent of the natives, is in plain terms a very paltry rascally original.—It certainly hath no divinity in it. However, it is needless to spend much time in exposing the folly of hereditary right, if there are any so weak as to believe it, let them promiscuously worship the ass and lion, and welcome. I shall neither copy their humility, nor disturb their devotion.

Yet I should be glad to ask how they suppose kings came at first? The question admits but of three answers, viz. either by lot, by election, or by usurpation. If the first king was taken by lot, it establishes a precedent for the next, which excludes hereditary succession. Saul was by lot* yet the succession was not hereditary, neither does it appear from that transaction there was any intention it ever should. If the first king of any country was by election, that likewise establishes a precedent for the next; for to say, that the *right* of all future generations is taken away, by the act of the first electors, in their choice not only of a king, but of a family of kings for ever, hath no parallel in or out of scripture but the doctrine of original sin, which supposes the free will of all men lost in Adam; and from such comparison, and it will admit of no other, hereditary succession can derive no glory. For as in Adam all sinned, and as in the first electors all men obeyed; as in the one all mankind were subjected to Satan, and in the other to Sovereignty; as our innocence was lost in the first, and our authority in the last; and as both disable us from re-assuming some former state and privilege, it unanswerably follows that original sin and hereditary succession are parallels. Dishonourable rank! Inglorious connexion! Yet the most subtile sophist cannot produce a juster simile.

As to usurpation, no man will be so hardy as to defend it; and that William the Conqueror was an usurper is a fact not to be contradicted. The plain truth is, that the antiquity of English monarchy will not bear looking into.

But it is not so much the absurdity as the evil of hereditary succession which concerns mankind. Did it ensure a race of good and wise men it would have the seal of divine authority, but as it opens a door to the *foolish*, the *wicked*, and the *improper*, it hath in it the nature of oppression. Men who look upon themselves born to reign, and others to obey, soon grow insolent; selected from the rest of mankind their minds are early poisoned by importance; and the world they act in differs so materially from the world at large, that they have but little opportunity of knowing its true interests, and when they succeed to the government are frequently the most ignorant and unfit of any throughout the dominions.

Another evil which attends hereditary succession is, that the throne is subject to be possessed by a minor at any age; all which time the regency, acting under the cover of a king, have every opportunity and inducement to betray their trust. The same national misfortune happens, when a king worn out with age and infirmity, enters the last stage of human weakness. In both these cases the public becomes a prey to every miscreant, who can tamper successfully with the follies either of age or infancy.

The most plausible plea, which hath ever been offered in

favour of hereditary succession, is, that it preserves a nation from civil wars; and were this true, it would be weighty; whereas, it is the most barefaced falsity ever imposed upon mankind. The whole history of England disowns the fact. Thirty kings and two minors have reigned in that distracted kingdom since the conquest, in which time there have been (including the Revolution) no less than eight civil wars and nineteen rebellions. Wherefore instead of making for peace, it makes against it, and destroys the very foundation it seems to stand on.

The contest for monarchy and succession, between the houses of York and Lancaster, laid England in a scene of blood for many years.* Twelve pitched battles, besides skirmishes and sieges, were fought between Henry and Edward. Twice was Henry prisoner to Edward, who in his turn was prisoner to Henry. And so uncertain is the fate of war and the temper of a nation, when nothing but personal matters are the ground of a quarrel, that Henry was taken in triumph from a prison to a palace, and Edward obliged to fly from a palace to a foreign land; yet, as sudden transitions of temper are seldom lasting, Henry in his turn was driven from the throne, and Edward recalled to succeed him.* The parliament always following the strongest side.

This contest began in the reign of Henry the Sixth, and was not entirely extinguished till Henry the Seventh, in whom the families were united. Including a period of 67 years, viz. from 1422 to 1489.*

In short, monarchy and succession have laid (not this or that kingdom only) but the world in blood and ashes. 'Tis a form of government which the word of God bears testimony against, and blood will attend it.

If we inquire into the business of a king, we shall find that in some countries they have none; and after sauntering away their lives without pleasure to themselves or advantage to the nation, withdraw from the scene, and leave their successors to tread the same idle round. In absolute monarchies the whole weight of business civil and military, lies on the king; the children of Israel in their request for a king, urged this plea 'that he may judge us, and go out before us and

fight our battles.'* But in countries where he is neither a
judge nor a general, as in England, a man would be puzzled
to know what *is* his business.

The nearer any government approaches to a republic the
less business there is for a king. It is somewhat difficult to
find a proper name for the government of England. Sir
William Meredith* calls it a republic; but in its present state
it is unworthy of the name, because the corrupt influence of
the crown, by having all the places in its disposal, hath so
effectually swallowed up the power, and eaten out the virtue
of the house of commons (the republican part in the constitution) that the government of England is nearly as monarchical as that of France or Spain. Men fall out with names
without understanding them. For it is the republican and
not the monarchial part of the constitution of England which
Englishmen glory in, viz. the liberty of choosing an house of
commons from out of their own body—and it is easy to see
that when the republican virtue fails, slavery ensues. Why is
the constitution of England fickly, but because monarchy
hath poisoned the republic, the crown hath engrossed the
commons?

In England a king hath little more to do than to make war
and give away places; which in plain terms, is to impoverish
the nation and set it together by the ears. A pretty business
indeed for a man to be allowed eight hundred thousand
sterling* a year for, and worshipped into the bargain! Of
more worth is one honest man to society, and in the sight of
God, than all the crowned ruffians that ever lived.

Thoughts on the present State of American Affairs

I N the following pages I offer nothing more than simple facts,
plain arguments, and common sense; and have no other
preliminaries to settle with the reader, than that he will divest
himself of prejudice and prepossession, and suffer his reason
and his feelings to determine for themselves; that he will put
on, or rather that he will not put *off*, the true character of a man,
and generously enlarge his views beyond the present day.

Volumes have been written on the subject of the struggle between England and America. Men of all ranks have embarked in the controversy, from different motives, and with various designs; but all have been ineffectual, and the period of debate is closed. Arms, as the least resource, decide the contest; the appeal was the choice of the king, and the continent hath accepted the challenge.

It hath been reported of the late Mr Pelham (who tho' an able minister was not without his faults) that on his being attacked in the house of commons, on the score, that his measures were only of a temporary kind, replied, '*they will last my time.*'* Should a thought so fatal and unmanly possess the colonies in the present contest, the name of ancestors will be remembered by future generations with detestation.

The sun never shined on a cause of greater worth. 'Tis not the affair of a city, a county, a province, or a kingdom, but of a continent—of at least one eighth part of the habitable globe. 'Tis not the concern of a day, a year, or an age; posterity are virtually involved in the contest, and will be more or less affected, even to the end of time, by the proceedings now. Now is the seed time of continental union, faith and honor. The least fracture now will be like a name engraved with the point of a pin on the tender rind of a young oak; the wound will enlarge with the tree, and posterity read it in full grown characters.

By referring the matter from argument to arms, a new æra for politics is struck; a new method of thinking hath arisen. All plans, proposals, &c. prior to the nineteenth of April, *i.e.* to the commencement of hostilities,* are like the almanacks of the last year; which, though proper then, are superceded and useless now. Whatever was advanced by the advocates on either side of the question then, terminated in one and the same point, viz. a union with Great Britain; the only difference between the parties was the method of effecting it; the one proposing force, the other friendship; but it hath so far happened that the first hath failed, and the second hath withdrawn her influence.

As much hath been said of the advantages of reconciliation, which, like an agreeable dream, hath passed away and left us as we were, it is but right, that we should examine the contrary side of the argument, and inquire into some of the many material injuries which these colonies sustain, and always will sustain, by being connected with, and dependant on Great Britain. To examine that connexion and dependance, on the principles of nature and common sense, to see what we have to trust to, if separated, and what we are to expect, if dependant.

I have heard it asserted by some, that as America hath flourished under her former connexion with Great-Britain, that the same connexion is necessary towards her future-happiness, and will always have the same effect. Nothing can be more fallacious than this kind of argument. We may as well assert, that because a child has thrived upon milk, that it is never to have meat; or that the first twenty years of our lives is to become a precedent for the next twenty. But even this is admitting more than is true, for I answer roundly, that America would have flourished as much, and probably much more, had no European power had any thing to do with her. The commerce by which she hath enriched herself are the necessaries of life, and will always have a market while eating is the custom of Europe.

But she has protected us, say some. That she hath engrossed us is true, and defended the continent at our expence as well as her own is admitted, and she would have defended Turkey from the same motive, viz. the sake of trade and dominion.

Alas, we have been long led away by ancient prejudices, and made large sacrifices to superstition. We have boasted the protection of Great-Britain, without considering, that her motive was *interest* not *attachment*; that she did not protect us from *our enemies* on *our account*, but from *her enemies* on *her own account*, from those who had no quarrel with us on any *other account*, and who will always be our enemies on the *same account*. Let Britain wave her pretensions to the continent, or the continent throw off the dependance, and we should be at peace with France and Spain were they at war with Britain. The miseries of Hanover's last war ought to warn us against connexions.*

It hath lately been asserted in parliament, that the colonies have no relation to each other* but through the parent country, *i.e.* that Pensylvainia and the Jerseys, and so on for the rest, are sister colonies by the way of England; this is certainly a very round-about way of proving relationship, but it is the nearest and only true way of proving enemyship, if I may so call it. France and Spain never were, nor perhaps ever will be our enemies as *Americans*, but as our being the *subjects of Great Britain*.

But Britain is the parent country, say some. Then the more shame upon her conduct. Even brutes do not devour their young, nor savages make war upon their families; wherefore the assertion, if true, turns to her reproach; but it happens not to be true, or only partly so, and the phrase *parent* or *mother country* hath been jesuitically adopted by the King and his parasites, with a low papistical design of gaining an unfair bias on the credulous weakness of our minds. Europe, and not England, is the parent country of America. This new world hath been the asylum for the persecuted lovers of civil and religious liberty from *every part* of Europe. Hither have they fled, not from the tender embraces of the mother, but from the cruelty of the monster; and it is so far true of England, that the same tyranny which drove the first emigrants from home, pursues their descendants still.

In this extensive quarter of the globe, we forget the narrow limits of three hundred and sixty miles (the extent of England) and carry our friendship on a larger scale; we claim brotherhood with every European christian, and triumph in the generosity of the sentiment.

It is pleasant to observe by what regular gradations we surmount the force of local prejudice, as we enlarge our acquaintance with the world. A man born in any town in England divided into parishes, will naturally associate most with his fellow parishioners (because their interests in many cases will be common) and distinguish him by the name of *neighbour*; if he meet him but a few miles from home, he drops the narrow idea of a street, and salutes him by the name of *townsman*; if he travels out of the county, and meet him in any other, he forgets the minor divisions of street and town, and calls him *countryman*, i.e. *countyman*; but if in their foreign excursions they should associate in France or any other part of *Europe*, their local remembrance would be enlarged into that of *Englishmen*. And by a just parity of reasoning, all Europeans meeting in America, or any other quarter of the globe, are *countrymen*; for England, Holland, Germany, or Sweden, when compared with the whole, stand in the same places on the larger scale, which the divisions of street, town, and county do on the smaller ones; distinctions too limited for continental minds. Not one third of the inhabitants, even of this province, are of English descent. Wherefore I reprobate the phrase of parent or mother country applied to England only, as being false, selfish, narrow and ungenerous.

But admitting that we were all of English descent, what does it amount to? Nothing. Britain, being now an open enemy, extinguishes every other name and title: And to say that reconciliation is our duty, is truly farcical. The first king of England, of the present line (William the Conqueror) was a Frenchman, and half the peers of England are descendants from the same country; wherefore by the same method of reasoning, England ought to be governed by France.

Much hath been said of the united strength of Britain and the colonies, that in conjunction they might bid defiance to the world. But this is mere presumption; the fate of war is uncertain, neither do the expressions mean any thing; for this continent would never suffer itself to be drained of inhabitants to support the British arms in either Asia, Africa, or Europe.

Besides, what have we to do with setting the world at defiance? Our plan is commerce, and that, well attended to, will secure us the peace and friendship of all Europe; because it is the interest of all Europe to have America a *free port*.* Her trade will always be a protection, and her barrenness of gold and silver secure her from invaders.

I challenge the warmest advocate for reconciliation, to shew, a single advantage that this continent can reap, by being connected with Great Britain. I repeat the challenge, not a single advantage is derived. Our corn will fetch its price in any market in Europe, and our imported goods must be paid for buy them where we will.

But the injuries and disadvantages we sustain by that connection, are without number; and our duty to mankind at large, as well as to ourselves, instruct us to renounce the alliance: Because, any submission to, or dependance on Great Britain, tends directly to involve this continent in European wars and quarrels; and sets us at variance with nations, who would otherwise seek our friendship, and against whom, we have neither anger nor complaint. As Europe is our market for trade, we ought to form no partial connection with any part of it. It is the true interest of America to steer clear of European contentions, which she never can do, while by her dependance on Britain, she is made the make-weight in the scale of British politics.

Europe is too thickly planted with kingdoms to be long at peace, and whenever a war breaks out between England and any foreign power, the trade of America goes to ruin, *because of her connection with Britain*. The next war may not turn out like the last, and should it not, the advocates for reconciliation now will be wishing for separation then, because, neutrality in that case, would be a safer convoy than a man of war. Every thing that is right or natural pleads for separation. The blood of the slain, the weeping voice of nature cries, 'TIS TIME TO PART. Even the distance at which the Almighty hath placed England and America, is a strong and natural proof, that the authority of the one, over the other, was never the design of Heaven. The time likewise at which the continent was discovered, adds weight to the argument, and the manner in which it was peopled encreases the force of it. The reformation was preceded by the discovery of America, as if the Almighty graciously meant to open a sanctuary to the persecuted in future years, when home should afford neither friendship nor safety.

The authority of Great Britain over this continent, is a form of government, which sooner or later must have an end: And a serious mind can draw no true pleasure by looking forward, under the painful and positive conviction,

that what he calls 'the present constitution' is merely temporary. As parents, we can have no joy, knowing that *this
government* is not sufficiently lasting to ensure any thing
which we may bequeath to posterity: And by a plain method
of argument, as we are running the next generation into
debt, we ought to do the work of it, otherwise we use them
meanly and pitifully. In order to discover the line of our
duty rightly, we should take our children in our hand, and
fix our station a few years farther into life; that eminence
will present a prospect, which a few present fears and prejudices conceal from our sight.

Though I would carefully avoid giving unnecessary offence, yet I am inclined to believe, that all those who
espouse the doctrine of reconciliation, may be included
within the following descriptions. Interested men, who are
not to be trusted; weak men who *cannot* see; prejudiced men
who *will not* see; and a certain set of moderate men, who
think better of the European world than it deserves; and this
last class by an ill-judged deliberation, will be the cause of
more calamities to this continent than all the other three.

It is the good fortune of many to live distant from the
scene of sorrow; the evil is not sufficiently brought to *their*
doors to make *them* feel the precariousness with which all
American property is possessed. But let our imaginations
transport us for a few moments to Boston, that seat of
wretchedness will teach us wisdom, and instruct us for ever
to renounce a power in whom we can have no trust. The
inhabitants of that unfortunate city, who but a few months
ago were in ease and affluence, have now no other alternative
than to stay and starve, or turn out to beg. Endangered by
the fire of their friends if they continue within the city, and
plundered by the soldiery if they leave it. In their present
condition they are prisoners without the hope of redemption,
and in a general attack for their relief, they would be exposed
to the fury of both armies.*

Men of passive tempers look somewhat lightly over the
offences of Britain, and, still hoping for the best, are apt to
call out, '*Come we shall be friends again for all this.*' But
examine the passions and feelings of mankind. Bring the

doctrine of reconciliation to the touchstone of nature, and then tell me, whether you can, hereafter love, honour, and faithfully serve the power that hath carried fire and sword into your land? If you cannot do all these, then are you only deceiving yourselves, and by your delay bringing ruin upon posterity. Your future connection with Britain, whom you can neither love nor honour, will be forced and unnatural, and being formed only on the plan of present convenience, will in a little time fall into a relapse more wretched than the first. But if you say, you can still pass the violations over, then I ask, Hath your house been burnt? Hath your property been destroyed before your face? Are your wife and children destitute of a bed to lie on, or bread to live on? Have you lost a parent or a child by their hands, and yourself the ruined and wretched survivor? If you have not, then are you not a judge of those who have. But if you have, and can still shake hands with the murderers, then are you unworthy the name of husband, father, friend, or lover, and whatever may be your rank or title in life, you have the heart of a coward, and the spirit of a sycophant.

This is not inflaming or exaggerating matters, but trying them by those feelings and affections which nature justifies, and without which, we should be incapable of discharging the social duties of life, or enjoying the felicities of it (I mean not to exhibit horror for the purpose of provoking revenge, but to awaken us from fatal and unmanly slumbers, that we may pursue determinately some fixed object. It is not in the power of Britain or of Europe to conquer America, if she do not conquer herself by *delay* and *timidity*. The present winter is worth an age if rightly employed, but if lost or neglected, the whole continent will partake of the misfortune; and there is no punishment which that man will not deserve, be he who, or what, or where he will, that may be the means of sacrificing a season so precious and useful.

It is repugnant to reason, to the universal order of things, to all examples from the former ages, to suppose, that this continent can longer remain subject to any external power. The most sanguine in Britain does not think so. The utmost stretch of human wisdom cannot, at this time compass a plan short of separation, which can promise the continent even a year's security. Reconciliation is *now* a falacious dream. Nature hath deserted the connexion, and Art cannot supply her place. For, as Milton wisely expresses, 'never can true reconcilement grow where wounds of deadly hate have pierced so deep.'*

Every quiet method for peace hath been ineffectual. Our prayers have been rejected with disdain; and only tended to convince us, that nothing flatters vanity, or confirms obstinancy in Kings more than repeated petitioning—and nothing hath contributed more than that very measure to make the Kings of Europe absolute: Witness Denmark and Sweden.* Wherefore since nothing but blows will do, for God's sake, let us come to a final separation, and not leave the next generation to be cutting throats, under the violated unmeaning names of parent and child.

To say, they will never attempt it again is idle and visionary, we thought so at the repeal of the stamp-act,* yet a year or two undeceived us; as well may we suppose that nations, which have been once defeated, will never renew the quarrel.

As to government matters, it is not in the power of Britain to do this continent justice: The business of it will soon be too weight, and intricate, to be managed with any tolerable degree of convenience, by a power, so distant from us, and so very ignorant of us; for if they cannot conquer us, they cannot govern us. To be always running three or four thousand miles with a tale or a petition, waiting four or five months for an answer, which when obtained requires five or six more to explain it in, will in a few years be looked upon as folly and childishness—. There was a time when it was proper, and there is a proper time for it to cease.

Small islands not capable of protecting themselves, are the proper objects for kingdoms to take under their care; but there is something very absurd, in supposing a continent to be perpetually governed by an island. In no instance hath nature made the satellite larger than its primary planet, and as England and America, with respect to each other, reverses the common order of nature, it is evident they belong to different systems: England to Europe, America to itself.

I am not induced by motives of pride, party, or resentment to espouse the doctrine of separation and independance; I am clearly, positively, and conscientiously persuaded that it is the true interest of this continent to be so; that every thing short of *that* is mere patchwork, that it can afford no lasting felicity,—that it is leaving the sword to our children, and shrinking back at a time, when, a little more, a little farther, would have rendered this continent the glory of the earth.

As Britain hath not manifested the least inclination towards a compromise, we may be assured that no terms can be obtained worthy the acceptance of the continent, or any ways equal to the expence of blood and treasure we have been already put to.

The object contended for, ought always to bear some just proportion to the expence. The removal of North,* or the whole detestable junto, is a matter unworthy the millions we have expended. A temporary stoppage of trade, was an inconvenience, which would have sufficiently ballanced the repeal of all the acts complained of, had such repeals been obtained; but if the whole continent must take up arms, if every man must be a soldier, it is scarcely worth our while to fight against a contemptible ministry only. Dearly, dearly, do we pay for the repeal of the acts, if that is all we fight for; for in a just estimation, it is as great a folly to pay a Bunker-hill price for law, as for land.* As I have always considered the independancy of this continent, as an event, which sooner or later must arrive, so from the late rapid progress of the continent to maturity, the event could not be far off. Wherefore, on the breaking out of hostilities, it was not worth the while to have disputed a matter, which time would have finally redressed, unless we meant to be in earnest; otherwise, it is like wasting an estate on a suit at law, to regulate the trespasses of a tenant, whose lease is just expiring. No man was a warmer wisher for reconciliation than myself, before the fatal nineteenth of April 1775,[1] but the moment the event of that day was made known, I rejected the hardened, sullen tempered Pharoah of England

---

[1] *Massacre at Lexington.*

for ever; and disdain the wretch, that with the pretended title of FATHER OF HIS PEOPLE can unfeelingly hear of their slaughter, and composedly sleep with their blood upon his soul.

But admitting that matters were now made up, what would be the event? I answer, the ruin of the continent. And that for several reasons.

First. The powers of governing still remaining in the hands of the king, he will have a negative over the whole legislation of this continent. And as he hath shewn himself such an inveterate enemy to liberty, and discovered such a thirst for arbitrary power; is he, or is he not, a proper man to say to these colonies, '*You shall make no laws but what I please.*' And is there any inhabitants in America so ignorant, as not to know, that according to what is called the *present constitution*, that this continent can make no laws but what the king gives leave to; and is there any man so unwise, as not to see, that (considering what has happened) he will suffer no Law to be made here, but such as suit his purpose. We may be as effectually enslaved by the want of laws in America, as by submitting to laws made for us in England. After matters are made up (as it is called) can there be any doubt but the whole power of the crown will be exerted, to keep this continent as low and humble as possible? Instead of going forward we shall go backward, or be perpetually quarrelling or ridiculously petitioning.—We are already greater than the king wishes us to be, and will he not hereafter endeavour to make us less? To bring the matter to one point. Is the power who is jealous of our prosperity, a proper power to govern us? Whoever says *No* to this question is an *independant*, for independancy means no more, than, whether we shall make our own laws, or, whether the king, the greatest enemy this continent hath, or can have, shall tell us '*there shall be no laws but such as I like.*'

But the king you will say has a negative in England; the people there can make no laws without his consent. In point of right and good order, there is something very ridiculous, that a youth of twenty-one (which hath often happened) shall say to several millions of people, older and wiser than himself, I forbid this or that act of yours to be law. But in this place I decline this sort of reply, tho' I will never cease to expose the absurdity of it, and only answer, that England being the king's residence, and America not so, makes quite another case. The king's negative *here* is ten times more dangerous and fatal than it can be in England, for *there* he will scarcely refuse his consent to a bill for putting England into as strong a state of defence as possible, and in America he would never suffer such a bill to be passed.

America is only a secondary object in the system of British politics. England consults the good of *this* country, no farther than it answers her *own* purpose. Wherefore, her own interest leads her to suppress the growth of *ours* in every case which doth not promote her advantage, or in the least interfere with it. A pretty state we should soon be in under such a second-hand government, considering what has happened! Men do not change from enemies to friends by the alteration of a name: And in order to shew that reconciliation *now* is a dangerous doctrine, I affirm, *that it would be policy in the king at this time, to repeal the acts for the sake of reinstating himself in the government of the provinces*; in order, that HE MAY ACCOMPLISH BY CRAFT AND SUBTILTY, IN THE LONG RUN, WHAT HE CANNOT DO BY FORCE AND VIO- LENCE IN THE SHORT ONE. Reconciliation and ruin are nearly related.

Secondly, That as even the best terms, which we can expect to obtain, can amount to no more than a temporary expedi- ent, or a kind of government by guardianship, which can last no longer than till the colonies come of age, so the general face and state of things, in the interim, will be unsettled and unpromising. Emigrants of property will not choose to come to a country whose form of government hangs but by a thread, and who is every day tottering on the brink of commotion and disturbance; and numbers of the present inhabitants would lay hold of the interval, to dispose of their effects, and quit the continent.

But the most powerful of all arguments, is, that nothing

but independance, i.e. a continental form of government, can keep the peace of the continent and preserve it inviolate from civil wars. I dread the event of a reconciliation with Britain now, as it is more than probable, that it will be followed by a revolt somewhere or other, the consequences of which may be far more fatal than all the malice of Britain.

Thousands are already ruined by British barbarity; (thousands more will probably suffer the same fate.) Those men have other feelings than us who have nothing suffered. All they *now* possess is liberty, what they before enjoyed is sacrificed to its service, and having nothing more to lose, they disdain submission. Besides, the general temper of the colonies, towards a British government, will be like that of a youth, who is nearly out of his time; they will care very little about her. And a government which cannot preserve the peace, is no government at all, and in that case we pay our money for nothing; and pray what is it that Britain can do, whose power will be wholly on paper, should a civil tumult break out the very day after reconciliation? I have heard some men say, many of whom I believe spoke without thinking, that they dreaded an independance, fearing that it would produce civil wars. It is but seldom that our first thoughts are truly correct, and that is the case here; for there are ten times more to dread from a patched up connexion than from independance. I make the sufferers case my own, and I protest, that were I driven from house and home, my property destroyed, and my circumstances ruined, that as man, sensible of injuries, I could never relish the doctrine of reconciliation, or consider myself bound thereby.

The colonies have manifested such a spirit of good order and obedience to continental government, as is sufficient to make every reasonable person easy and happy on that head. No man can assign the least pretence for his fears, on any other grounds, than such as are truly childish and ridiculous, that one colony will be striving for superiority over another.

Where there are no distinctions there can be no superiority, perfect equality affords no temptation. The republics of Europe are all (and we may say always) in peace. Holland and Swisserland are without wars, foreign or domestic:

Monarchical governments, it is true, are never long at rest; the crown itself is a temptation to enterprizing ruffians at *home*; and that degree of pride and insolence ever attendant on regal authority, swells into a rupture with foreign powers, in instances, where a republican government, by being formed on more natural principles, would negociate the mistake.

If there is any true cause of fear respecting independance, it is because no plan is yet laid down. Men do not see their way out—Wherefore, as an opening into that business, I offer the following hints; at the same time modestly affirm- ing, that I have no other opinion of them myself, than that they may be the means of giving rise to something better. Could the straggling thoughts of individuals be collected, they would frequently form materials for wise and able men to improve to useful matter.

LET the assemblies be annual, with a President only. The representation more equal. Their business wholly domestic, and subject to the authority of a Continental Congress.

Let each colony be divided into six, eight, or ten, con- venient districts, each district to send a proper number of delegates to Congress, so that each colony send at least thirty. The whole number in Congress will be at least 390. Each Congress to sit   * and to choose a president by the following method. When the delegates are met, let a colony be taken from the whole thirteen colonies by lot, after which let the whole Congress choose (by ballot) a president from out of the delegates of *that* province. In the next Congress, let a colony be taken by lot from twelve only, omitting that colony from which the president was taken in the former Congress, and so proceeding on till the whole thirteen shall have had their proper rotation. And in order that nothing may pass into a law but what is satisfactorily just, not less than three fifths of the Congress to be called a majority.—He that will promote discord, under a government so equally formed as this, would join Lucifer in his revolt.*

But as there is a peculiar delicacy, from whom, or in what manner, this business must first arise, and as it seems most agreeable and consistent, that it should come from some intermediate body between the governed and the governors,

that is between the Congress and the people, let a CONTI-
NENTAL CONFERENCE be held, in the following manner,
and for the following purpose.

A committee of twenty-six members of Congress, viz. two
for each colony. Two members for each house of assembly,
or Provincial convention; and five representatives of the
people at large, to be chosen in the capital city or town of
each province, for, and in behalf of the whole province, by
as many qualified voters as shall think proper to attend from
all parts of the province for that purpose; or, if more convenient, the representatives may be chosen in two or three
of the most populous parts thereof. In this conference, thus
assembled, will be united, the two grand principles of business, *knowledge* and *power*. The members of Congress, Assemblies, or Conventions, by having had experience in national concerns, will be able and useful counsellors, and the
whole, being impowered by the people will have a truly legal
authority.

The conferring members being met, let their business be
to frame a CONTINENTAL CHARTER, or Charter of the
United Colonies; (answering to what is called the Magna
Charta of England)* fixing the number and manner of
choosing members of Congress, members of Assembly, with
their date of sitting, and drawing the line of business and
jurisdiction between them: (Always remembering, that our
strength is continental, not provincial:) Securing freedom
and property to all men, and above all things the free
exercise of religion, according to the dictates of conscience;
with such other matter as is necessary for a charter to
contain. Immediately after which, the said conference to
dissolve, and the bodies which shall be chosen conformable
to the said charter, to be the legislators and governors of this
continent for the time being: Whose peace and happiness,
may God preserve, Amen.

Should any body of men be hereafter delegated for this or
some similar purpose, I offer them the following extracts
from that wife observer on governments *Dragonetti*. 'The
science' says he, 'of the politician consists in fixing the true
point of happiness and freedom. Those men would deserve

the gratitude of ages, who should discover a mode of government that contained the greatest sum of individual happiness, with the least national expence.'

*Dragonetti on Virtue and Rewards.**

But where says some is the King of America? I'll tell you Friend, he reigns above, and doth not make havock of mankind like the Royal Brute of Britain. Yet that we may not appear to be defective even in earthly honors, let a day be solemnly set apart for proclaiming the charter; let it be brought forth placed on the divine law, the word of God; let a crown be placed thereon, by which the world may know, that so far as we approve of monarchy, that in America THE LAW IS KING. For as in absolute governments the King is law, so in free countries the law *ought* to be King; and there ought to be no other. But left any ill use should afterwards arise, let the crown at the conclusion of the ceremony be demolished, and scattered among the people whose right it is.

A government of our own is our natural right: And when a man seriously reflects on the precariousness of human affairs, he will become convinced, that it is infinitely wiser and safer, to form a constitution of our own in a cool deliberate manner, while we have it in our power, than to trust such an interesting event to time and chance. If we omit it now, some[1] Massenello* may hereafter arise, who laying hold of popular disquietudes, may collect together the desperate and the discontented, and by assuming to themselves the powers of government, may sweep away the liberties of the continent like a deluge. Should the government of America return again into the hands of Britain, the tottering situation of things, will be a temptation for some desperate adventurer to try his fortune; and in such a case, what relief can Britain give? Ere she could hear the news the fatal business might be done, and ourselves suffering like the wretched Britons under the oppression of the Conqueror.

---

[1] 'Thomas Anello, otherwise Massanello, a fisherman of Naples, who after spiriting up his countrymen in the public market place, against the oppression of the Spaniards, to whom the place was then subject, prompted them to revolt, and in the space of a day became King.

Ye that oppose independance now, ye know not what ye do; ye are opening a door to eternal tyranny, by keeping vacant the seat of government. There are thousands and tens of thousands, who would think it glorious to expel from the continent, that barbarous and hellish power, which hath stirred up the Indians and Negroes* to destroy us, the cruelty hath a double guilt, it is dealing brutally by us, and treacherously by them.

To talk of friendship with those in whom our reason forbids us to have faith, and our affections wounded through a thousand pores instruct us to detest, is madness and folly. Every day wears out the little remains of kindred between us and them, and can there be any reason to hope, that as the relationship expires, the affection will increase, or that we shall agree better, when we have ten times more and greater concerns to quarrel over than ever?

Ye that tell us of harmony and reconciliation, can ye restore to us the time that is past? Can ye give to prostitution its former innocence? Neither can ye reconcile Britain and America. The last cord now is broken, the people of England are presenting addresses against us. There are injuries which nature cannot forgive; she would cease to be nature if she did. As well can the lover forgive the ravisher of his mistress, as the continent forgive the murders of Britain. The Almighty hath implanted in us these unextinguishable feelings for good and wise purposes. They are the guardians of his image in our hearts. They distinguish us from the herd of common animals. The social compact would dissolve, and justice be extirpated the earth, or have only a casual existence were we callous to the touches of affection. The robber and the murderer, would often escape unpunished, did not the injuries which our tempers sustain, provoke us into justice.

O ye that love mankind! Ye that dare oppose, not only the tyranny, but the tyrant, stand forth! Every spot of the old world is over-run with oppression. Freedom hath been hunted round the globe. Asia, and Africa, have long expelled her.—Europe regards her like a stranger, and England hath given her warning to depart. O! receive the fugitive, and prepare in time an asylum for mankind.

Of the present ABILITY *of* AMERICA, *with some miscellaneous* REFLEXIONS

I HAVE never met with a man, either in England or, America, who hath not confessed his opinion, that a separation between the countries, would take place one time or other. And there is no instance in which we have shewn less judgment, than in endeavouring to describe, what we call, the ripeness or fitness of the Continent for independance.

As all men allow the measure, and vary only in their opinion of the time, let us, in order to remove mistakes, take a general survey of things and endeavour if possible, to find out the *very* time. But we need not go far, the inquiry ceases at once, for the *time hath found us*. The general concurrence, the glorious union of all things prove the fact.

It is not in numbers but in unity, that our great strength lies; yet our present numbers are sufficient to repel the force of all the world. The Continent hath, at this time, the largest body of armed and disciplined men of any power under Heaven; and is just arrived at that pitch of strength, in which no single colony is able to support itself, and the whole, when united can accomplish the matter, and either more, or, less than this, might be fatal in its effects. Our land force is already sufficient, and as to naval affairs, we cannot be insensible, that Britain would never suffer an American man of war to be built while the continent remained in her hands.* Wherefore we should be no forwarder an hundred years hence in that branch, than we are now; but the truth is, we should be less so, because the timber of the country is every day diminishing, and that which will remain at last, will be far off and difficult to procure.

Were the continent crowded with inhabitants, her sufferings under the present circumstances would be intolerable. The more sea port towns we had, the more should we have both to defend and to loose. Our present numbers are so happily proportioned to our wants, that no man need be idle. The diminution of trade affords an army, and the necessities of an army create a new trade.

Debts we have none; and whatever we may contract on

this account will serve as a glorious momento of our virtue. Can we but leave posterity with a settled form of government, an independant constitution of its own, the purchase at any price will be cheap. But to expend millions for the sake of getting a few vile acts repealed, and routing the present ministry only, is unworthy the charge, and is using posterity with the utmost cruelty; because it is leaving them the great work to do, and a debt upon their backs, from which they derive no advantage. Such a thought is unworthy a man of honor, and is the true characteristic of a narrow heart and a pedling politician.

The debt we may contract doth not deserve our regard if the work be but accomplished. No nation ought to be without a debt. A national debt is a national bond; and when it bears no interest, is in no case a grievance. Britain is oppressed with a debt of upwards of one hundred and forty millions sterling, for which she pays upwards of four millions interest.* And as a compensation for her debt, she has a large navy; America is without a debt, and without a navy; yet for the twentieth part of the English national debt, could have a navy as large again. The navy of England is not worth, at this time, more than three millions and an half sterling.

The first and second editions* of this pamphlet were published without the following calculations, which are now given as a proof that the above estimation of the navy is a just one. *See Entic's naval history, intro.* page 36.*

The charge of building a ship of each rate, and furnishing her with masts, yards, sails and rigging, together with a

	£
For a ship of 100 guns —	35,553
90 —	29,886
80 —	23,638
70 —	17,785
60 —	14,197
50 —	10,606
40 —	7,558
30 —	5,846
20 —	3,710

proportion of eight months boatswain's and carpenter's sea-stores, as calculated by Mr Burchett, Secretary to the navy.*

And from hence it is easy to sum up the value, or cost rather, of the whole British navy, which in the year 1757, when it was at its greatest glory consisted of the following ships and guns:

Ships	Guns	Cost of one	Cost of all
6 —	100 —	35,553 *l.* —	213,318 *l.*
12 —	90 —	29,886 —	358,632
12 —	80 —	23,638 —	283,656
43 —	70 —	17,785 —	764,755
35 —	60 —	14,197 —	496,895
40 —	50 —	10,606 —	424,240
45 —	40 —	7,558 —	340,110
58 —	20 —	3,710 —	215,180
85 Sloops, bombs, and fireships, one with another, at		2,000	170,000

Cost 3,266,786

Remains for guns, — 233,214

Total, 3,500,000

No country on the globe is so happily situated, so internally capable of raising a fleet as America. Tar, timber, iron, and cordage are her natural produce. We need go abroad for nothing. Whereas the Dutch, who make large profits by hiring out their ships of war to the Spaniards and Portuguese, are obliged to import most of the materials they use. We ought to view the building a fleet as an article of commerce, it being the natural manufactory of this country. It is the best money we can lay out. A navy when finished is worth more than it cost. And is that nice point in national policy, in which commerce and protection are united. Let us build; if we want them not, we can sell; and by that means replace our paper currency with ready gold and silver.

In point of manning a fleet, people in general run into great errors; it is not necessary that one-fourth part should be sailors. The Terrible privateer, Captain Death,* stood the hottest engagement of any ship last war, yet had not twenty sailors on board, though her complement of men was upwards of two hundred. A few able and social sailors will soon instruct a sufficient number of active land-men in the common work of a ship. Wherefore, we never can be more capable to begin on maritime matters than now, while our timber is standing, our fisheries blocked up, and our sailors and shipwrights out of employ. Men of war of seventy and 80 guns were built forty years ago in New-England, and why not the fame now? Ship-building is America's greatest pride,* and in which, she will in time excel the whole world. The great empires of the east are mostly inland, and consequently excluded from the possibility of rivalling her. Africa is in a state of barbarism; and no power in Europe, hath either such an extent of coast, or such an internal supply of materials. Where nature hath given the one, she has withheld the other; to America only hath she been liberal of both. The vast empire of Russia is almost shut out from the sea; wherefore, her boundless forests, her tar, iron, and cordage are only articles of commerce.

In point of safety, ought we to be without a fleet? We are not the little people now, which we were sixty years ago; at that time we might have trusted our property in the streets, or fields rather; and slept securely without locks or bolts to our doors or windows. The case now is altered, and our methods of defence ought to improve with our increase of property. A common pirate, twelve months ago, might have come up the Delaware, and laid the city of Philadelphia under instant contribution, for what sum he pleased; and the same might have happened to other places. Nay, any daring fellow, in a brig of fourteen or sixteen guns, might have robbed the whole Continent, and carried off half a million of money. These are circumstances which demand our attention, and point out the necessity of naval protection.

Some, perhaps, will say, that after we have made it up with Britain, she will protect us. Can we be so unwise as to mean, that she shall keep a navy in our harbours for that purpose? Common sense will tell us, that the power which hath endeavoured to subdue us, is of all others the most improper to defend us. Conquest may be effected under the pretence of friendship; and ourselves, after a long and brave resistance, be at last cheated into slavery. And if her ships are not to be admitted into our harbours, I would ask, how is she to protect us? A navy three or four thousand miles off can be of little use, and on sudden emergencies, none at all. Wherefore, if we must hereafter protect ourselves, why not do it for ourselves? Why do it for another?

The English list of ships of war is long and formidable, but not a tenth part of them are at any one time fit for service, numbers of them not in being; yet their names are pompously continued in the list, if only a plank be left of the ship: and not a fifth part, of such as are fit for service, can be spared on any one station at one time. The East, and West Indies, Mediterranean, Africa, and other parts over which Britain extends her claim, make large demands upon her navy. From a mixture of prejudice and inattention, we have contracted a false notion respecting the navy of England, and have talked as if we should have the whole of it to encounter at once, and for that reason, supposed that we must have one as large; which not being instantly practicable, have been made use of by a set of disguised Tories* to discourage our beginning thereon. Nothing can be farther from truth than this; for if America had only a twentieth part of the naval force of Britain, she would be by far an over match for her; because, as we neither have, nor claim any foreign dominion, our whole force would be employed on our own coast, where we should, in the long run, have two to one the advantage of those who had three or four thousand miles to sail over, before they could attack us, and the same distance to return in order to refit and recruit. And although Britain by her fleet, hath a check over our trade to Europe, we have as large a one over her trade to the West-Indies, which, by laying in the neighbourhood of the Continent, is entirely at its mercy.

Some method might be fallen on to keep up a naval force in time of peace, if we should not judge it necessary to support a constant navy. If premiums were to be given to merchants, to build and employ in their service, ships mounted with twenty, thirty, forty, or fifty guns, (the premiums to be in proportion to the loss of bulk to the merchants) fifty or sixty of those ships, with a few guard ships on constant duty, would keep up a sufficient navy, and that without burdening ourselves with the evil so loudly complained of in England, of suffering their fleet, in time of peace to lie rotting in the docks. To unite the sinews of commerce and defence is sound policy; for when our strength and our riches, play into each other's hand, we need fear no external enemy.

In almost every article of defence we abound. Hemp flourishes even to rankness, so that we need not want cordage. Our iron is superior to that of other countries. Our small arms equal to any in the world. Cannon we can cast at pleasure. Saltpetre and gunpowder we are every day producing. Our knowledge is hourly improving. Resolution is our inherent character, and courage hath never yet forsaken us. Wherefore, what is it that we want? Why is it that we hesitate? From Britain we can expect nothing but ruin. If she is once admitted to the government of America again, this Continent will not be worth living in. Jealousies will be always arising, insurrections will be constantly happening; and who will go forth to quell them? Who will venture his life to reduce his own countrymen to a foreign obedience? The difference between Pennsylvania and Connecticut, respecting some unlocated lands, shews the insignificance of a British government, and fully proves, that nothing but Continental authority can regulate Continental matters.

Another reason why the present time is preferable to all others, is, that the fewer our numbers are, the more land there is yet unoccupied, which instead of being lavished by the king on his worthless dependants, may be hereafter applied, not only to the discharge of the present debt, but to the constant support of government. No nation under heaven hath such an advantage as this.

The infant state of the Colonies, as it is called, so far from being against, is an argument in favor of independance.

We are sufficiently numerous, and were we more so, we might be less united. It is a matter worthy of observation, that the more a country is peopled, the smaller their armies are. In military numbers, the ancients far exceeded the moderns: and the reason is evident, for trade being the consequence of population, men become too much absorbed thereby to attend to any thing else. Commerce diminishes the spirit, both of patriotism and military defence. And history sufficiently informs us, that the bravest achievements were always accomplished in the non-age* of a nation. With the increase of commerce, England hath lost its spirit. The city of London, notwithstanding its numbers, submits to continued insults with the patience of a coward. The more men have to lose, the less willing are they to venture. The rich are in general slaves to fear, and submit to courtly power with the trembling duplicity of a spaniel.

Youth is the seed time of good habits, as well in nations as in individuals. It might be difficult, if not impossible, to form the Continent into one government half a century hence. The vast variety of interests, occasioned by an increase of trade and population, would create confusion. Colony would be against colony. Each being able might scorn each other's assistance: and while the proud and foolish gloried in their little distinctions, the wise would lament that the union had not been formed before. Wherefore, the *present time* is the *true time* for establishing it. The intimacy which is contracted in infancy, and the friendship which is formed in misfortune, are, of all others, the most lasting and unalterable. Our present union is marked with both these characters: we are young, and we have been distressed; but our concord hath withstood our troubles, and fixes a memorable æra for posterity to glory in.

The present time, likewise, is that peculiar time, which never happens to a nation but once, *viz.* the time of forming itself into a government. Most nations have let slip the opportunity, and by that means have been compelled to receive laws from their conquerors, instead of making laws for themselves. First, they had a king, and then a form of government; whereas, the articles or charter of government, should be formed first, and men delegated to execute them afterward: but from the errors of other nations, let us learn wisdom, and lay hold of the present opportunity—*To begin government at the right end*.

When William the conqueror subdued England he gave them law at the point of the sword; and until we consent that the seat of government in America, be legally and authoritatively occupied, we shall be in danger of having it filled by some fortunate ruffian, who may treat us in the same manner, and then, where will be our freedom? where our property?

As to religion, I hold it to be the indispensible duty of all government, to protect all conscientious professors thereof, and I know of no other business which government hath to do therewith. Let a man throw aside that narrowness of soul, that selfishness of principle, which the niggards of all professions are so unwilling to part with, and he will be at once delivered of his fears on that head. Suspicion is the companion of mean souls, and the bane of all good society. For myself I fully and conscientiously believe, that it is the will of the Almighty, that there should be diversity of religious opinions among us: It affords a larger field for our christian kindness. Were we all of one way of thinking, our religious dispositions would want matter for probation; and on this liberal principle, I look on the various denominations among us, to be like children of the same family, differing only, in what is called their Christian names.

In page 33, I threw out a few thoughts on the propriety of a Continental Charter,* (for I only presume to offer hints, not plans) and in this place, I take the liberty of rementioning the subject, by observing, that a charter is to be understood as a bond of solemn obligation, which the whole enters into, to support the right of every separate part, whether of religion, personal freedom, or property, A firm bargain and a right reckoning make long friends.

In a former page I likewise mentioned the necessity of a large and equal representation; and there is no political matter which more deserves our attention. A small number of electors, or a small number of representatives, are equally dangerous. But if the number of the representatives be not only small, but unequal, the danger is increased. As an instance of this, I mention the following; when the Associators petition was before the House of Assembly of Pennsylvania;* twenty-eight members only were present, all the Bucks county members, being eight, voted against it, and had seven of the Chester members done the same, this whole province had been governed by two counties only, and this danger it is always exposed to. The unwarrantable stretch likewise, which that house made in their last sitting, to gain an undue authority over the Delegates of that province, ought to warn the people at large, how they trust power out of their own hands. A set of instructions for the Delegates were put together, which in point of sense and business would have dishonored a school-boy, and after being approved by a *few*, a *very few* without doors, were carried into the House, and there passed *in behalf of the whole colony*; whereas, did the whole colony know, with what ill-will that House hath entered on some necessary public measures, they would not hesitate a moment to think them unworthy of such a trust.

Immediate necessity makes many things convenient, which if continued would grow into oppressions. Expedience and right are different things. When the calamities of America required a consultation, there was no method so ready, or at that time so proper, as to appoint persons from the several Houses of Assembly for that purpose and the wisdom with which they have proceeded hath preserved this continent from ruin. But as it is more than probable that we shall never be without a CONGRESS, every well wisher to good order, must own, that the mode for choosing members of that body, deserves consideration. And I put it as a question to those, who make a study of mankind, whether *representation and election* is not too great a power for one and the same body of men to possess? When we are planning for posterity, we ought to remember that virtue is not hereditary.

It is from our enemies that we often gain excellent maxims, and are frequently surprised into reason by their mistakes. Mr Cornwall* (one of the Lords of the Treasury) treated the petition of the New-York Assembly with contempt, because *that* House, he said, consisted but of twenty-six members, which trifling number, he argued, could not with decency be put for the whole. We thank him for his involuntary honesty.[1]

TO CONCLUDE, however strange it may appear to some, or however unwilling they may be to think so, matters not, but many strong and striking reasons may be given, to shew, that nothing can settle our affairs so expeditiously as an open and determined declaration for independance. Some of which are,

First.—It is the custom of nations, when any two are at war, for some other powers, not engaged in the quarrel, to step in as mediators, and bring about the preliminaries of a peace: but while America calls herself the subject of Great Britain, no power, however well disposed she may be, can offer her mediation. Wherefore, in our present state we may quarrel on for ever.

Secondly.—It is unreasonable to suppose, that France or Spain will give us any kind of assistance, if we mean only to make use of that assistance for the purpose of repairing the breach, and strengthening the connection between Britain and America, because, those powers would be sufferers by the consequences.

Thirdly.—While we profess ourselves the subjects of Britain, we must, in the eye of foreign nations, be considered as rebels. The precedent is somewhat dangerous to *their peace*, for men to be in arms under the name of subjects; we on the spot, can solve the paradox: but to unite resistance and subjection, requires an idea much too refined for common understanding.

Fourthly.—Were a manifesto to be published, and despatched to foreign courts, setting forth the miseries we have endured, and the peaceable methods we have ineffectually

---

[1] *Those who would fully understand of what great consequence a large and equal representation is to a state, should read Burgh's Political Disquisitions.**

used for redress; declaring, at the same time, that not being able, any longer to live happily or safely under the cruel disposition of the British court, we had been driven to the necessity of breaking off all connection with her; at the same time assuring all such courts of our peaceable disposition towards them, and of our desire of entering into trade with them: Such a memorial would produce more good effects to this Continent, than if a ship were freighted with petitions to Britain.

Under our present denomination of British subjects we can neither be received nor heard abroad: The custom of all courts is against us, and will be so, until, by an independance, we take rank with other nations.

These proceedings may at first appear strange and difficult; but, like all other steps which we have already passed over, will in a little time become familiar and agreeable; and, until an independance is declared, the Continent will feel itself like a man who continues putting off some unpleasant business from day to day, yet knows it must be done, hates to set about it, wishes it over, and is continually haunted with the thoughts of its necessity.

APPENDIX

SINCE the publication of the first edition of this pamphlet, or rather, on the same day on which it came out, the King's Speech made its appearance in this city.* Had the spirit of prophecy directed the birth of this production, it could not have brought it forth, at a more seasonable juncture, or a more necessary time. The bloody mindedness of the one, shew the necessity of pursuing the doctrine of the other. Men read by way of revenge. And the speech instead of terrifying, prepared a way for the manly principles of Independance.

Ceremony, and even, silence, from whatever motive they may arise, have a hurtful tendency, when they give the least degree of countenance to base and wicked performances; wherefore, if this maxim be admitted, it naturally follows, that the King's Speech, as being a piece of finished villainy, deserved, and still deserves, a general execration both by the Congress and the people. Yet as the domestic tranquility of a nation, depends greatly on the *chastity* of what may properly be called NATIONAL MANNERS, it is often better, to pass some things over in silent disdain, than to make use of such new methods of dislike, as might introduce the least innovation, on that guardian of our peace and safety. And perhaps, it is chiefly owing to this prudent delicacy, that the King's Speech, hath not before now, suffered a public execution. The Speech if it may be called one, is nothing better than a wilful audacious libel against the truth, the common good, and the existence of mankind; and is a formal and pompous method of offering up human sacrifices to the pride of tyrants. But this general massacre of mankind, is one of the privileges, and the certain consequences of Kings; for as nature knows them *not*, they know *not her*, and although they are beings of our *own* creating, they know not *us*, and are become the gods of their creators. The speech hath one good quality, which is, that it is not calculated to deceive, neither can we, even if we would, be deceived by it. Brutality and tyranny appear on the face of it. It leaves us at no loss: And every line convinces, even in the moment of reading, that He, who hunts the woods for prey, the naked and untutored Indian, is less a Savage than the King of Britain.

Sir J——n D———e,* the putative father of a whining jesuiti-
cal piece, fallaciously called, '*The Address of the people of* ENG-
LAND *to the inhabitants of* AMERICA,' hath, perhaps from a vain
supposition, that the people *here* were to be frightened at the
pomp and description of a king, given, (though very unwisely
on his part) the real character of the present one: 'But,' says this
writer, 'if you are inclined to pay compliments to an administration, which we do not complain of,' (meaning the Marquis of
Rockingham's at the repeal of the Stamp Act*) 'it is very unfair
in you to withold them from that prince, *by whose* NOD ALONE
they were permitted to do any thing.'* This is toryism with a
witness! Here is idolatry even without a mask: And he who can
calmly hear, and digest such doctrine, hath forfeited his claim
to rationality—an apostate from the order of manhood; and
ought to be considered—as one, who hath, not only given up
the proper dignity of a man, but sunk himself beneath the rank
of animals, and contemptibly crawl through the world like a
worm.

However, it matters very little now, what the King of England
either says or does; he hath wickedly broken through every
moral and human obligation, trampled nature and conscience
beneath his feet; and by a steady and constitutional spirit of
insolence and cruelty, procured for himself an universal hatred.
It is *now* the interest of America to provide for herself. She hath
already a large and young family, whom it is more her duty to
take care of, than to be granting away her property, to support
a power who is become a reproach to the names of men
and christians—YE, whose office it is to watch over the morals
of a nation, of whatsoever sect or denomination ye are of, as
well as ye, who are more immediately the guardians of the
public liberty, if ye wish to preserve your native country uncon-
taminated by European corruption, ye must in secret with a
separation—But leaving the moral part to private reflection, I
shall chiefly confine my farther remarks to the following heads.

First, That it is the interest of America to be separated from
Britain.

Secondly. Which is the earliest and most practicable plan,
RECONCILIATION or INDEPENDANCE? with some occasional
remarks.

In support of the first, I could, if I judged it proper, produce
the opinion of some of the ablest and most experienced men on

this continent; and whose sentiments, on that head, are not yet publickly known. It is in reality a self-evident position: For no nation in a state of foreign dependance, limited in its commerce, and cramped and fettered in its legislative powers, can ever arrive at any material eminence. America doth not yet know what opulence is, and although the progress which she hath made stands unparalleled in the history of other nations, it is but childhood, compared with what she would be capable of arriving at, had she, as she ought to have, the legislative powers in her own hands. England is, at this time, proudly coveting what would do her no good, were she to accomplish it; and the Continent hesitating on a matter, which will be her final ruin if neglected. It is the commerce and not the conquest of America, by which England is to be benefited, and that would in a great measure continue, were the countries as independant of each other as France and Spain; because in many articles, neither can go to a better market. But it is the independance of this country on Britain or any other, which is now the main and only object worthy of contention, and which, like all other truths discovered by necessity, will appear clearer and stronger every day.

First. Because it will come to that one time or other.

Secondly. Because the longer it is delayed the harder it will be to accomplish.

I have frequently amused myself both in public and private companies, with silently remarking the spacious errors of those who speak without reflecting. And among the many which I have heard, the following seems the most general, viz. that had this rupture happened forty or fifty years hence, instead of *now*, the Continent would have been more able to have shaken off the dependance. To which I reply, that our military ability, *at this time*, arises from the experience gained in the last war,* and which in forty or fifty years time, would have been totally extinct. The Continent, would not, by that time, have had a General, or even a military officer left; and we, or those who may succeed us, would have been as ignorant of martial matters as the ancient Indians: And this single position, closely attended to, will unanswerably prove, that the present time is preferable to all others. The argument turns thus—at the conclusion of the last war, we had experience, but wanted numbers; and forty or fifty years hence, we should have numbers, without experience;

wherefore, the proper point of time, must be some particular point between the two extremes, in which a sufficiency of the former remains, and a proper increase of the latter is obtained: And that point of time is the present time.

The reader will pardon this digression, as it does not properly come under the head I first set out with, and to which I again return by the following position, viz.

Should affairs be patched up with Britain, and she to remain the governing and sovereign power of America, (which as matters are now circumstanced, is giving up the point entirely) we shall deprive ourselves of the very means of sinking the debt we have or may contract. The value of the back lands* which some of the provinces are clandestinely deprived of, by the unjust extention of the limits of Canada, valued only at five pounds sterling per hundred acres, amount to upwards of twenty-five millions, Pennsylvania currency; and the quit-rents at one penny sterling per acre, to two millions yearly.

It is by the sale of those lands that the debt may be sunk, without burthen to any, and the quit-rent reserved thereon, will always lessen, and in time, will wholly support the yearly expence of government. It matters not how long the debt is in paying, so that the lands when sold be applied to the discharge of it, and for the execution of which, the Congress for the time being, will be the continental trustees.

I proceed now to the second head, viz. Which is the easiest and most practicable plan, RECONCILIATION or INDEPENDANCE? with some occasional remarks.

He who takes nature for his guide is not easily beaten out of his argument, and on that ground, I answer generally—*That* INDEPENDANCE *being a* SINGLE SIMPLE LINE, *contained within ourselves; and reconciliation, a matter exceedingly perplexed and complicated, and in which, a treacherous capricious court is to interfere, gives the answer without a doubt.*

The present state of America is truly alarming to every man who is capable of reflexion. Without law, without government, without any other mode of power than what is founded on, and granted by courtesy. Held together by an unexampled concurrence of sentiment, which is nevertheless subject to change, and which every secret enemy is endeavouring to dissolve. Our present condition, is, Legislation without law; wisdom without a plan; a constitution without a name; and, what is strangely astonishing, perfect Independance contending for Dependance. The instance is without a precedent; the case never existed before; and who can tell what may be the event? The property of no man is secure in the present unbraced system of things. The mind of the multitude is left at random, and seeing no fixed object before them, they pursue such as fancy or opinion starts. Nothing is criminal; there is no such thing as treason; wherefore, every one thinks himself at liberty to act as he pleases. The Tories dared not to have assembled offensively, had they known that their lives, by that act were forfeited to the laws of the state. A line of distinction should be drawn, between English soldiers taken in battle, and inhabitants of America taken in arms. The first are prisoners, but the latter traitors. The one forfeits his liberty the other his head.

Notwithstanding our wisdom, there is a visible feebleness in some of our proceedings which gives encouragement to dissentions. The Continental belt is too loosely buckled. And if something is not done in time, it will be too late to do any thing, and we shall fall into a state, in which, neither *reconciliation* nor *independance* will be practicable. The King and his worthless adherents are got at their old game of dividing the Continent, and there are not wanting among us, Printers, who will be busy in spreading specious falsehoods. The artful and hypocritical letter which appeared a few months ago in two of the New-York papers,* and likewise in two others, is an evidence that there are men who want either judgement or honesty.

It is easy getting into holes and corners and talking of reconciliation: But do such men seriously consider, how difficult the talk is, and how dangerous it may prove, should the Continent divide thereon. Do they take within their view, all the various orders of men whose situation and circumstances, as well as their own, are to be considered therein. Do they put themselves in the place of the sufferer whose *all* is *already* gone, and of the soldier, who hath quitted *all* for the defence of his country. If their ill-judged moderation be suited to their own private situations *only*, regardless of others, the event will convince them, that 'they are reckoning without their Host.'*

Put us, say some, on the footing we were on in sixty-three.* To which I answer, the request is not *now* in the power of Britain to comply with, neither will she propose it; but if it were, and even should be granted, I ask, as a reasonable question, By what means is such a corrupt and faithless court to be kept to its engagements? Another parliament, nay, even the present, may hereafter repeal the obligation, on the pretence of its being violently obtained, or unwisely granted; and in that case, Where is our redress?—No going to law with nations; cannon are the barristers of crowns; and the sword, not of justice, but of war, decides the suit. To be on the footing of sixty-three, it is not sufficient, that the laws only be put on the same state, but, that our circumstances, likewise, be put on the same state; Our burnt and destroyed towns repaired or built up, our private losses made good, our public debts (contracted for defence) discharged; otherwise, we shall be millions worse than we were at that enviable period. Such a request had it been complied with a year ago, would have won the heart and soul of the Continent—but now it is too late, 'The Rubicon is passed.'*

Besides the taking up arms, merely to enforce the repeal of a pecuniary law, seems as unwarrantable by the divine law, and as repugnant to human feelings, as the taking up arms to enforce obedience thereto. The object, on either side, doth not justify the ways and means; for the lives of men are too valuable to be cast away on such trifles. It is the violence which is done and threatened to our persons; the destruction of our property by an armed force; the invasion of our country by fire and sword, which conscientiously qualifies the use of arms: And the instant, in which such a mode of defence became necessary, all subjection to Britain ought to have ceased; and the independancy of America should have been considered, as dating its æra from, and published by, *the first musket that was fired against her*. This line is a line of consistency; neither drawn by caprice, nor extended by ambition; but produced by a chain of events, of which the colonies were not the authors.

I shall conclude these remarks, with the following timely and well intended hints. We ought to reflect, that there are three different ways by which an independancy may hereafter be effected; and that *one* of those *three*, will one day or other, be the fate of America, viz. By the legal voice of the people in Congress; by a military power; or by a mob: It may not always happen that our soldiers are citizens, and the multitude a body of reasonable men; virtue, as I have already remarked, is not hereditary, neither is it perpetual. Should an independancy be brought about by the first of those means, we have every opportunity and every encouragement before us, to form the noblest, purest constitution on the face of the earth. We have it in our power to begin the world over again. A situation, similar to the present, hath not happened since the days of Noah until now. The birth-day of a new world is at hand, and a race of men perhaps as numerous as all Europe contains, are to receive their portion of freedom from the event of a few months. The Reflexion is awful—and in this point of view, How trifling, how ridiculous, do the little, paltry cavellings, of a few weak or interested men appear, when weighed against the business of a world.

Should we neglect the present favorable and inviting period, and an independance be hereafter effected by any other means, we must charge the consequence to ourselves, or to those rather, whose narrow and prejudiced souls, are habitually opposing the measure, without either inquiring or reflecting. There are reasons to be given in support of Independance, which men should rather privately think of, than be publicly told of. We ought not now to be debating whether we shall be independant or not, but, anxious to accomplish it on a firm, secure, and honorable basis, and uneasy rather that it is not yet began upon. Every day convinces us of its necessity. Even the Tories (if such beings yet remain among us) should, of all men, be the most solicitous to promote it; for, as the appointment of committees at first, protected them from popular rage, so, a wise and well established form of government, will be the only certain means of continuing it securely to them. *Wherefore*, if they have not virtue enough to be WHIGS, they ought to have prudence enough to wish for Independance.

In short, Independance is the only BOND that can tye and keep us together. We shall then see our object, and our ears will be legally shut against the schemes of an intriguing, as well as a cruel enemy. We shall then too, be on a proper footing, to treat with Britain; for there is reason to conclude, that the pride of that court, will be less hurt by treating with the American states for terms of peace, than with those, whom she denominates, 'rebellious subjects,' for terms of accommodation. It is our delaying it that encourages her to hope for conquest, and our backwardness tends only to prolong the war. As we have, without any good effect, therefrom, with-held our trade to obtain a redress of our grievances, let us *now* try the alternative, by *independantly* redressing them ourselves, and then offering to open the trade. The mercantile and reasonable part of England will be still with us; because, peace *with* trade, is preferable to war *without* it. And if this offer be not accepted, other courts may be applied to.

On these grounds I rest the matter. And as no offer hath yet been made to refute the doctrine contained in the former editions of this pamphlet, it is a negative proof, that either the doctrine cannot be refuted, or, that the party in favour of it are too numerous to be opposed. WHEREFORE, instead of gazing at each other with suspicious or doubtful curiosity, let each of us, hold out to his neighbour the hearty hand of friendship, and unite in drawing a line, which, like an act of oblivion, shall bury in forgetfulness every former dissention. Let the names of Whig and Tory be extinct; and let none other be heard among us, than those of *a good citizen, an open and resolute friend, and a virtuous supporter of the* RIGHTS *of* MANKIND *and of the* FREE AND INDEPENDANT STATES OF AMERICA.

To the Representatives of the Religious Society of the People called Quakers, or to so many of them as were concerned in publishing a late piece, entitled 'The ANCIENT TESTIMONY and PRINCIPLES of the People called QUAKERS renewed, with respect to the KING and GOVERNMENT, and touching the COMMOTIONS now prevailing in these and other parts of AMERICA, addressed to the PEOPLE IN GENERAL.'*

THE Writer of this, is one of those few, who never dishonors religion either by ridiculing, or cavilling at any denomination whatsoever. To God, and not to man, are all men accountable on the score of religion. Wherefore, this epistle is not so properly addressed to you as a religious, but as a political body, dabbling in matters, which the professed Quietude of your Principles instruct you not to meddle with.

'As you have, without a proper authority for so doing, put yourselves in the place of the whole body of the Quakers, so, the writer of this, in order to be on an equal rank with yourselves, is under the necessity, of putting himself in the place of all those who approve the very writings and principles, against which your testimony is directed: And he hath chosen their singular situation, in order that you might discover in him, that presumption of character which you cannot see in yourselves. For neither he nor you have any claim or title to *Political Representation*.

When men have departed from the right way, it is no wonder that they stumble and fall. And it is evident from the manner in which ye have managed your testimony, that politics, (as a religious body of men) is not your proper Walk; for however well adapted it might appear to you, it is, nevertheless, a jumble of good and bad put unwisely together, and the conclusion drawn therefrom, both unnatural and unjust.

The two first pages, (and the whole doth not make four) we give you credit for, and expect the same civility from you, because the love and desire of peace is not confined to Quakerism, it is the *natural*, as well as the religious wish of all denominations of men. And on this ground, as men labouring to establish an Independant Constitution of our own, do we exceed all others in our hope, end, and aim. *Our plan is peace for ever*. We are tired of contention with Britain, and can see no real end to it but in a final separation. We act consistently, because for the sake of introducing an endless and uninterrupted peace, do we bear the evils and burthens of the present day. We are endeavouring, and will steadily continue to endeavor, to separate and dissolve a connexion which hath already filled our land with blood; and which, while the name of it remains, will be the fatal cause of future mischiefs to both countries.

We fight neither for revenge nor conquest; neither from pride nor passion; we are not insulting the world with our fleets and armies, nor ravaging the globe for plunder. Beneath the shade of our own vines are we attacked; in our own houses, and on our own lands, is the violence committed against us. We view our enemies in the characters of Highwaymen and Housebreakers, and having no defence for ourselves in the civil law, are obliged to punish them by the military one, and apply the sword, in the very case, where you have before now, applied the halter—Perhaps we feel for the ruined and insulted sufferers in all and every part of the continent, with a degree of tenderness which hath not yet made its way into some of your bosoms. But be ye sure that ye mistake not the cause and ground of your

Testimony. Call not coldness of soul, religion; nor put the *Bigot* in the place of the *Christian*.

O ye partial ministers of your own acknowledged principles. If the bearing arms be sinful, the first going to war must be more so, by all the difference between wilful attack and unavoidable defence. Wherefore, if ye really preach from conscience, and mean not to make a political hobby-horse of your religion, convince the world thereof, by proclaiming your doctrine to our enemies, *for they likewise bear* ARMS. Give us proof of your sincerity by publishing it at St James's, to the commanders in chief at Boston, to the Admirals and Captains who are piratically ravaging our coasts, and to all the murdering miscreants who are acting in authority under HIM whom ye profess to serve. Had ye the honest soul of[1] *Barclay** ye would preach repentance to *your* king; Ye would tell the Royal   his sins, and warn him of eternal ruin. Ye would not spend your partial invectives against the injured and the insulted only, but like faithful ministers, would cry aloud and *spare none*. Say not that ye are persecuted, neither endeavour to make us the authors of that reproach, which, ye are bringing upon yourselves; for we testify unto all men, that we do not complain against you because ye are *Quakers*, but because ye pretend to *be* and are NOT Quakers.

Alas! it seems by the particular tendency of some part of your testimony, and other parts of your conduct, as if all sin was reduced to, and comprehended in *the act of bearing arms*, and that by the *people only*. Ye appear to us, to have mistaken party for conscience; because the general tenor of your actions wants uniformity: And it is exceedingly difficult to us to give credit to many of your pretended scruples; because we see them made by the same men, who, in the very instant that they are exclaiming against the mammon of this world, are nevertheless, hunting

[1] '*Thou hast tasted of prosperity and adversity; thou knowest what it is to be banished thy native country, to be over-ruled as well as to rule, and set upon the throne; and being* oppressed *thou hast reason to know how* hateful *the* oppressor *is both to God and man: If after all these warnings and advertisements, thou dost not turn unto the Lord with all thy heart, but forget him who remembered thee in thy distress, and give up thyself to follow lust and vanity, surely great will be thy condemnation.—Against which snare, as well as the temptation of those who may or do feed thee, and prompt thee to evil, the most excellent and prevalent remedy will be, to apply thyself to that light of Christ which shineth in thy conscience and which neither can, nor will flatter thee, nor suffer thee to be at ease in thy sins.*'
Barclay's Address to Charles II.

after it with a step as steady as Time, and an appetite as keen as Death.

The quotation which ye have made from Proverbs, in the third page of your testimony, that, 'when a man's ways please the Lord, he maketh even his enemies to be at peace with him';* is very unwisely chosen on your part; because it amounts to a proof, that the king's ways (whom ye are so desirous of supporting) do *not* please the Lord, otherwise, his reign would be in peace.

I now proceed to the latter part of your testimony, and that, for which all the foregoing seems only an introduction, viz.

'It hath ever been our judgement and principle, since we were called to profess the light of Christ Jesus, manifested in our consciences unto this day, that the setting up and putting down kings and governments, is God's peculiar prerogative; for causes best known to himself: And that it is not our business to have any hand or contrivance therein; not to be busy bodies above our station, much less to plot and contrive the ruin, or overturn any of them, but to pray for the king, and safety of our nation, and good of all men: That we may live a peaceable and quiet life, in all goodliness and honesty; *under the government which God is pleased to set over us.*'—If these are *really* your principles why do ye not abide by them? Why do ye not leave that, which ye call God's Work, to be managed by himself? These very principles instruct you to wait with patience and humility, for the event of all public measures, and to receive *that event* as the divine will towards you. *Wherefore*, what occasion is there for your *political testimony* if you fully believe what it contains? And the very publishing it proves, that either, ye do not believe what ye profess, or have not virtue enough to practise what ye believe.

The principles of Quakerism have a direct tendency to make a man the quiet and inoffensive subject of any, and every government *which is set over him*. And if the setting up and putting down of kings and governments is God's peculiar prerogative, he most certainly will not be robbed thereof by us; wherefore, the principle itself leads you to approve of every thing, which ever happened, or may happen to kings as being his work. OLIVER CROMWELL thanks you.—CHARLES, then, died not by the hands of man;* and should the present Proud Imitator of him, come to the same untimely end, the writers and publishers of the testimony, are bound by the doctrine it contains, to applaud the fact. Kings are not taken away by miracles, neither are changes in governments brought about by any other means than such as are common and human; and such as we are now using. Even the dispersing of the Jews, though foretold by our Saviour,* was effected by arms. Wherefore, as ye refuse to be the means on one side, ye ought not to be meddlers on the other; but to wait the issue in silence; and unless you can produce divine authority, to prove, that the Almighty who hath created and placed this *new* world, at the greatest distance it could prossibly stand, east and west, from every part of the old, doth, nevertheless, disapprove of its being independant of the corrupt and abandoned court of Britain, unless I say, ye can show this, how can ye, on the ground of your principles, justify the exciting and stirring up the people 'firmly to unite in the *abhorrence* of all such *writings*, and *measures*, as evidence a desire and design to break off the *happy* connexion we have hitherto enjoyed, with the kingdom of Great-Britain, and our just and necessary subordination to the king, and those who are lawfully placed in authority under him.' What a slap in the face is here! the men, who, in the very paragraph before, have quietly and passively resigned up the ordering, altering, and disposal of kings and governments, into the hands of God, are now recalling their principles, and putting in for a share of the business. It is possible, that the conclusion, which is here justly quoted, can any ways follow from the doctrine laid down? The inconsistency is too glaring not to be seen; the absurdity too great not to be laughed at; and such as could only have been made by those, whose understandings were darkened by the narrow and crabby spirit of a despairing political party; for ye are not to be considered as the whole body of the Quakers but only as a factional and fractional part thereof.

Here ends the examination of your testimony; (which I call upon no man to abhor, as ye have done, but only to read and judge of fairly) to which I subjoin the following remark; 'That the setting up and putting down of kings,' most certainly mean, the making him a king, who is yet not so, and the making him no king who is already one. And pray what hath this to do in the present case? We neither mean to *set up* nor to *put down*, neither to *make* nor to *unmake*, but to have nothing to *do* with them. Wherefore, your testimony in whatever light it is viewed serves only to dishonour your judgment, and for many other reasons had better have been let alone than published.

First. Because it tends to the decrease and reproach of all religion whatever, and is of the utmost danger to society, to make it a party in political disputes.

Secondly. Because it exhibits a body of men, numbers of whom disavow the publishing of political testimonies, as being concerned therein and approvers thereof.

Thirdly. Because it hath a tendency to undo that continental harmony and friendship which yourselves by your late liberal and charitable donations hath lent a hand to establish; and the preservation of which, is of the utmost consequence to us all.

And here without anger or resentment I bid you farewell. Sincerely wishing, that as men and christians, ye may always fully and uninterruptedly enjoy every civil and religious right; and be, in your turn, the means of securing it to others; but that the example which ye have unwisely set, of mingling religion with politics, *may be disavowed and reprabated by every inhabitant* of AMERICA.

AMERICAN CRISIS

I & XIII

AMERICAN CRISIS

I

THESE are the times that try men's souls. The summer soldier and the sun-shine patriot will, in this crisis, shrink from the service of his country: but he that stands it *now*, deserves the thanks of man and woman. Tyranny, like hell, is not easily conquered: yet we have this consolation with us, that the harder the conflict, the more glorious the triumph. What we obtain too cheap, we esteem too lightly: 'tis dearness only that gives every thing its value. Heaven knows how to set a proper price upon its goods; and it would be strange, indeed, if so celestial an article as freedom should not be highly rated. Britain, with an army to enforce her tyranny, has declared that she has a right, not only to tax, but 'to bind us in all cases whatsoever:'* and if being bound in that manner is not slavery, there is not such a thing as slavery upon earth. Even the expression is impious: for so unlimited a power can belong only to God.

Whether the independence of the continent was declared too soon, or delayed too long, I will not now enter into as an argument: my own simple opinion is, that had it been eight months earlier, it would have been much better. We did not make a proper use of last winter; neither could we, while we were in a dependent situation. However, the fault, if it were one, was all our own: we have none to blame but ourselves.[1] But no great deal is lost yet: all that Howe has been doing for this month past, is rather a ravage than a conquest, which the spirit of the Jerseys a year ago, would have quickly repulsed, and which time and a little resolution will soon recover.*

I have as little superstition in me as any man living: but

---

[1] The present winter is worth an age, if rightly employed: but if lost, or neglected, the whole continent will partake of the evil: and there is no punishment that man does not deserve, be he who, or what, or where he will, that may be the means of sacrificing a season so precious and useful.

my secret opinion has ever been, and still is, that God will not give up a people to military destruction, or leave them unsupportedly to perish, who had so earnestly and so repeatedly fought to avoid the calamities of war, by every decent method which wisdom could invent. Neither have I so much of the infidel in me, as to suppose that he has relinquished the government of the world, and given us up to the care of devils: and as I do not, I cannot see on what grounds the king can look up to heaven for help against us. A common murderer, a highwayman, or a housebreaker, has as good a pretence as he.

'Tis surprising to see how rapidly a panic will sometimes run through a country. All nations and ages have been subject to them. Britain has trembled like an ague,* at the report of a French fleet of flat-bottomed boats,* and in the fourteenth century, the whole English army, after ravaging the kingdom of France, was driven back, like men petrified with fear: and this brave exploit was performed by a few broken forces, collected and headed by a woman, Joan of Arc.* Would that heaven might inspire some Jersey maid to spirit up her countrymen, and save her fair fellow sufferers from ravage and ravishment! Yet panics, in some cases, have their uses: they produce as much good as hurt. Their duration is always short: the mind soon grows through them, and acquires a firmer habit than before. But their peculiar advantage is, that they are the touchstones of sincerity and hypocrisy, and bring things and men to light, which might otherwise have lain for ever undiscovered. In fact, they have the same effect upon secret traitors, which an imaginary apparition would upon a private murderer. They sift out the private thoughts of man, and hold them up in public to the world. Many a disguised tory has lately shown his head, that shall penitentially solemnize with curses the day on which Howe arrived upon the Delaware.*

As I was with the troops at Fort Lee, and marched with them to the edge of Pennsylvania, I am well acquainted with many circumstances, which those, who lived at a distance, know but little or nothing of. Our situation there was exceedingly cramped, the place being on a narrow neck of land, between the North river and the Hackinsack. Our force was inconsiderable, being not one fourth so great as Howe could bring against us. We had no army at hand to have relieved the garrison, had we shut ourselves up, and stood on the defence. Our ammunition, light artillery, and the best part of our stores, had been removed, upon the apprehension that Howe would endeavour to penetrate the Jerseys, in which case Fort Lee could have been of no use to us: for it must occur to every thinking man, whether in the army or not, that these kinds of field-forts are only fit for temporary purposes, and last in use no longer than the enemy directs his force against the particular object which such forts were raised to defend. Such was our situation and condition at Fort Lee, on the morning of the twentieth of November,* when an officer arrived with information, that the enemy, with two hundred boats, had landed about seven or eight miles above. Major-general Green,* who commanded the garrison, immediately ordered them under arms, and sent express to his Excellency General Washington, at the town of Hackinsack, distant, by way of the ferry, six miles. Our first object was to secure the bridge over the Hackinsack, which lay up the river, between the enemy and us, about six miles from us, and three from them. General Washington* arrived in about three quarters of an hour, and marched at the head of the troops to the bridge, which place I expected we should have a brush for: however, they did not choose to dispute it with us: and the greatest part of our troops went over the bridge, the rest over the ferry, except some which passed at a mill, on a small creek, between the bridge and the ferry, and made their way through some marshy grounds, up to the town of Hackinsack, and there passed the river. We brought off as much baggage as the waggons could contain: the rest was lost. The simple object was to bring off the garrison, and to march them on till they could be strengthened by the Jersey or Pennysylvania militia, so as to be enabled to make a stand. We staid four days at Newark, collected in our out-posts, with some of the Jersey militia, and marched out twice to meet the enemy, on information of their being advancing, though our numbers were greatly inferior to theirs. General Howe, in my opinion, committed a great error in generalship, in not throwing a body of forces off from Staten Island through Amboy, by which means he might have seized all our stores at Brunswick, and intercepted our march into Pennsylvania. But if we believe the power of hell to be limited, we must likewise believe that their agents are under some providential controul.

I shall not now attempt to give all the particulars of our retreat to the Delaware. Suffice it for the present to say, that both officers and men, though greatly harrassed and fatigued, frequently without rest, covering, or provision, the inevitable consequences of a long retreat, bore it with a manly and a martial spirit. All their wishes were one; which was, that the country would turn out, and help them to drive the enemy back. Voltaire has remarked, that king William never appeared to full advantage, but in difficulties and in action.* The same remark may be made on General Washington, for the character fits him. There is a natural firmness in some minds, which cannot be unlocked by trifles; but which, when unlocked, discovers a cabinet of fortitude: and I reckon it among those kind of public blessings which we do not immediately see, that God hath blessed him with uninterrupted health, and given him a mind that can even flourish upon care.

I shall conclude this paper with some miscellaneous remarks on the state of our affairs; and shall begin with asking the following question: Why is it that the enemy hath left the New England provinces, and made these middle ones the seat of war? The answer is easy: New England is not infected with Tories, and we are. I have been tender in raising the cry against these men, and used numberless arguments to show them their danges: but it will not do to sacrifice a world to either their folly or their baseness. The period is now arrived, in which either they or we must change our sentiments, or one or both must fall. And what is a tory? Good God! what is he? I should not be afraid to go with an hundred Whigs against a thousand Tories, were they to attempt to get into arms. Every Tory is a coward; for a servile, slavish, self-interested fear is the foundation of toryism; and a man under such influence, though he may be cruel, never can be brave.

But before the line of irrecoverable separation may be drawn between us, let us reason the matter together: your conduct is an invitation to the enemy; yet not one in a thousand of you has heart enough to join him. Howe is as much deceived by you, as the American cause is injured by you. He expects you will all take up arms, and flock to his standard with muskets on your shoulders. Your opinions are of no use to him, unless you support him personally; for it is soldiers, and not tories, that he wants.

I once felt all that kind of anger, which a man ought to feel, against the mean principles that are held by the Tories. A noted one, who kept a tavern at Amboy, was standing at his door, with as pretty a child in his hand, about eight or nine years old, as most I ever saw; and after speaking his mind as freely as he thought was prudent, finished with this unfatherly expression, 'Well, give me peace in my days.' Not a man lives on the continent, but fully believes that separation must some time ór other finally take place, and a generous parent would have said, 'if there must be trouble, let it be in my days, that my child may have peace;' and this single reflection, well applied, is sufficient to awaken every man to duty. Not a place upon earth might be so happy as America. Her situation is remote from all the wrangling world, and she has nothing to do but to trade with them. A man may easily distinguish in himself between temper and principle, and I am as confident as I am that God governs the world, that America will never be happy till she gets clear of foreign dominion. Wars, without ceasing, will break out till that period arrives, and the continent must, in the end be conqueror; for, though the flame of liberty may sometimes cease to shine, the coal never can expire.

America did not, nor does not want force; but she wanted a proper application of that force. Wisdom is not the purchase of a day, and it is no wonder we should err at first setting off. From an excess of tenderness, we were unwilling to raise an army, and trusted our cause to the temporary defence of a well meaning militia. A summer's experience has now taught us better; yet with those troops, while they were collected, we were able to set bounds to the progress of the enemy; and, thank God! they are again assembling. I always considered a militia as the best troops in the world for a sudden exertion, but they will not do for a long campaign. Howe, it is probable, will make an attempt on this city; should he fail on this side the Delaware, he is ruined; if he succeeds, our cause is not ruined. He stakes all on his side against a part on ours; admitting he succeeds, the consequence will be, that armies from both ends of the continent will march to assist their suffering friends in the middle states; for he cannot go everywhere: it is impossible. I consider Howe as the greatest enemy the tories have; he is bringing a war into their own country, which, had it not been for him and partly for themselves, they had been clear of. Should he now be expelled, I wish, with all the devotion of a christian, that the names of whig and tory may never more be mentioned; but should the tories give him encouragement to come, or assistance if he come, I as sincerely wish that our next year's arms may expel them from the continent, and the congress appropriate their possessions to the relief of those who have suffered in well-doing. A single successful battle next year will settle the whole. America will carry on a two-years war by the confiscation of the property of disaffected persons, and be made happy by their expulsion. Say not that this is revenge: call it rather the soft resentment of a suffering people, who, having no object in view but the good of all, have staked their own all upon a seemingly doubtful event. Yet it is folly to argue against determined hardness: eloquence may strike the ear, and the language of sorrow draw forth the tear of compassion, but nothing can reach the heart that is steeled with prejudice.

Quitting this class of men, I turn, with the warm ardour of a friend, to those who have nobly stood, and are yet determined to stand the matter out. I call not upon a few, but upon all; not on this state, or that state, but on every state. Up and help us. Lay your shoulders to the wheel. Better have too much force than too little, when so great an object is at stake. Let it be told to the future world, that in the depth of winter, when nothing but hope and virtue could survive, that the city and the country, alarmed at one common danger, came forth to meet and to repulse it. Say not that thousands are gone: turn out your tens of thousands: throw not the burden of the day upon providence, but show your faith by your good works, that God may bless you. It matters not where you live, or what rank of life you hold; the evil or the blessing will reach you all. The far and the near, the home counties and the back, the rich and the poor, shall suffer or rejoice alike. The heart that feels not now, is dead. The blood of his children shall curse his cowardice, who shrinks back at a time when a little might have saved the whole and made them happy. I love the man that can smile in trouble—that can gather strength from distress, and grow brave by reflection. It is the business of little minds to shrink; but he, whose heart is firm, and whose conscience approves his conduct, will pursue his principles unto death. My own line of reasoning is to myself, as strait and clear as a ray of light. Not all the treasures of the world, so far as I believe, could have induced me to support an offensive war; for I think it murder: but if a thief break into my house— burn and destroy my property, and kill, or threaten to kill me and those that are in it, and to 'bind me in all cases whatsoever,' to his absolute will, am I to suffer it? What signifies it to me, whether he who does it, is a king or a common man; my countryman, or not my countryman; whether it is done by an individual, villain, or an army of them? If we reason to the root of things we shall find no difference; neither can any just cause be assigned, why we should punish in the one case and pardon in the other. Let them call me rebel, and welcome; I feel no concern from it; but I should suffer the misery of devils, were I to make a whore of my soul, by swearing allegiance to one whose character is that of a sottish, stupid, stubborn, worthless, brutish man. I conceive likewise, a horrid idea in receiving mercy from a being, who at the last day, shall be shrieking to the rocks and mountains to cover him, and fleeing with terror from the orphan, the widow, and the slain of America.

There are cases which cannot be overdone by language;

and this is one. There are persons too, who see not the full extent of the evil that threatens them. They solace themselves with hopes, that the enemy, if they succeed, will be merciful. It is the madness of folly, to expect mercy from those who have refused to do justice: and even mercy, where conquest is the object, is only a trick of war. The cunning of the fox is as murderous as the violence of the wolf, and we ought to be equally on our guard against both. Howe's first object is partly by threats, and partly by promises, to terrify or seduce the people to give up their arms, and receive mercy. The ministry recommended the same plan to Gage:* and this is what the tories call making their peace—'a peace which passeth all understanding,' indeed.* A peace which would be the immediate forerunner o' a worse ruin than any we have yet thought of. Ye men of Pennsylvania, do reason upon those things! Were the back counties to give up their arms, they would fall an easy prey to the Indians, who are all armed. This, perhaps, is what some tories would not be sorry for. Were the home counties to deliver up their arms, they would be exposed to the resentment of the back counties, who would then have it in their power to chastise their defection at pleasure. And were any one state to give up its arms, that state must be garrisoned by all Howe's army of Britons and Hessians, to preserve it from the anger of the rest. Mutual fear is a principal link in the chain of mutual love, and woe be to that state that breaks the compact. Howe is mercifully inviting you to a barbarous destruction, and men must be either rogues or fools that will not see it. I dwell not upon the vapours of imagination, I bring reason to your ears; and in language as plain as A, B, C, hold up truth to your eyes.

I thank God, that I fear not. I see no real cause for fear. I know our situation well, and can see the way out of it. While our army was collected, Howe dared not risk a battle: and it is no credit to him, that he decamped from the White Plains, and waited a mean opportunity to ravage the defenceless Jerseys:* but it is great credit to us, that, with an handful of men, we sustained an orderly retreat for near an hundred miles, brought off our ammunition, all our field pieces, the greatest part of our stores, and had four rivers to pass. None can say, that our retreat was precipitate, for we were near three weeks in performing it, that the country might have time to come in. Twice we marched back to meet the enemy, and remained out till dark. The sign of fear was not seen in our camp: and had not some of the cowardly and disaffected inhabitants spread false alarms through the country, the Jerseys had never been ravaged. Once more, we are again collected and collecting. Our new army, at both ends of the continent, is recruiting fast; and we shall be able to open the next campaign with sixty thousand men, well armed and cloathed. This is our situation—and who will, may know it. By perseverance and fortitude, we have the prospect of a glorious issue; by cowardice and submission, the sad choice of a variety of evils—a ravaged country—a depopulated city—habitations without safety—and slavery without hope—our homes turned into barracks and bawdy-houses for Hessians*—and a future race to provide for, whose fathers we shall doubt of! Look on this picture, and weep over it! and if there yet remains one thoughtless wretch, who believes it not, let him suffer it unlamented.

December, 1776

AMERICAN CRISIS
XIII

THOUGHTS ON THE PEACE, AND THE PROBABLE ADVANTAGES THEREOF

THE times that tried men souls,[1] are over—and the greatest and completest revolution the world ever knew, gloriously and happily accomplished.*

But to pass from the extremes of danger to safety—from the tumult of war to the tranquillity of peace, though sweet in contemplation, requires a gradual composure of the senses to receive it. Even calmness has the power of stunning, when it opens too instantly upon us. The long and raging hurricane that should cease in a moment, would leave us in a state rather of wonder than enjoyment; and some moments of recollection must pass, before we could be capable of tasting the felicity of repose. There are but few instances, in which the mind is fitted for sudden transitions: it takes in its pleasures by reflection and comparison and those must have time to act, before the relish for new scenes is complete.

In the present case—the mighty magnitude of the object—the various uncertainties of fate it has undergone—the numerous and complicated dangers we have suffered or escaped—the eminence we now stand on, and the vast prospect before us, must all conspire to impress us with contemplation.

To see it in our power to make a world happy—to teach mankind the art of being so—to exhibit, on the theatre of the universe a character hitherto unknown—and to have, as it were, a new creation intrusted to our hands, are honors that command reflection, and can neither be too highly estimated, nor too gratefully received.

In this pause then of recollection—while the storm is ceasing, and the long agitated mind vibrating to a rest, let us

[1] 'These are the times that try men's souls,' The Crisis No. I. published December, 1776.—*Author.*

look back on the scenes we have passed, and learn from experience what is yet to be done.

Never, I say, had a country so many openings to happiness as this. Her setting out in life, like the rising of a fair morning, was unclouded and promising. Her cause was good. Her principles just and liberal. Her temper serene and firm. Her conduct regulated by the nicest steps, and everything about her wore the mark of honor. It is not every country (perhaps there is not another in the world) that can boast so fair an origin. Even the first settlement of America corresponds with the character of the revolution. Rome, once the proud mistress of the universe, was originally a band of ruffians. Plunder and rapine made her rich, and her oppression of millions made her great. But America need never be ashamed to tell her birth, nor relate the stages by which she rose to empire.

The remembrance, then, of what is past, if it operates rightly, must inspire her with the most laudable of all ambition, that of adding to the fair fame she began with. The world has seen her great in adversity; struggling, without a thought of yielding, beneath accumulated difficulties, bravely, nay proudly, encountering distress, and rising in resolution as the storm increased. All this is justly due to her, for her fortitude has merited the character. Let, then, the world see that she can bear prosperity: and that her honest virtue in time of peace, is equal to the bravest virtue in time of war.

She is now descending to the scenes of quiet and domestic life. Not beneath the cypress shade of disappointement,* but to enjoy in her own land, and under her own vine, the sweet of her labors, and the reward of her toil.—In this situation, may she never forget that a fair national reputation is of as much importance as independence. That it possesses a charm that wins upon the world, and makes even enemies civil. That it gives a dignity which is often superior to power, and commands reverence where pomp and splendor fail.

It would be a circumstance ever to be lamented and never to be forgotten, were a single blot, from any cause whatever, suffered to fall on a revolution, which to the end of time must be an honor to the age that accomplished it: and which has contributed more to enlighten the world, and diffuse a spirit of freedom and liberality among mankind, than any human event (if this may be called one) that ever preceded it.

It is not among the least of the calamities of a long continued war, that it unhinges the mind from those nice sensations which at other times appear so amiable. The continual spectacle of woe blunts the finer feelings, and the necessity of bearing with the sight, renders it familiar. In like manner, are many of the moral obligations of society weakened, till the custom of acting by necessity becomes an apology, where it is truly a crime. Yet let but a nation conceive rightly of its character, and it will be chastely just in protecting it. None ever began with a fairer than America and none can be under a greater obligation to preserve it.

The debt which America has contracted, compared with the cause she has gained, and the advantages to flow from it, ought scarcely to be mentioned. She has it in her choice to do, and to live as happily as she pleases. The world is in her hands. She has no foreign power to monopolize her commerce, perplex her legislation, or control her prosperity. The struggle is over, which must one day have happened, and, perhaps, never could have happened at a better time.[1]

---

[1] That the revolution began at the exact period of time best fitted to the purpose, is sufficiently proved by the event.—But the great hinge on which the whole machine turned, is the *Union of the States*: and this union was naturally produced by the inability of any one state to support itself against any foreign enemy without the assistance of the rest.

Had the states severally been less able than they were when the war began, their united strength would not have been equal to the undertaking, and they must in all human probability have failed.—And, on the other hand, had they severally been more able, they might not have seen, or, what is more, might not have felt, the necessity of uniting: and, either by attempting to stand alone or in small confederacies, would have been separately conquered.

Now, as we cannot see a time (and many years must pass away before it can arrive) when the strength of any one state, or several united, can be equal to the whole of the present United States, and as we have seen the extreme difficulty of collectively prosecuting the war to a successful issue, and preserving our national importance in the world, therefore, from the experience we have had, and the knowledge we have gained, we must, unless we make a waste of wisdom, be strongly impressed with the advantage, as well as the necessity of strengthening that happy union which had been our salvation, and without which we should have been a ruined people.

And instead of a domineering master, she has gained an *ally* whose exemplary greatness, and universal liberality, have extorted a confession even from her enemies.

With the blessings of peace, independence, and an universal commerce, the states, individually and collectively, will have leisure and opportunity to regulate and establish their domestic concerns, and to put it beyond the power of calumny to throw the least reflection on their honor. Character is much easier kept than recovered, and that man, if any such there be, who, from sinister views, or littleness of soul, lends unseen his hand to injure it, contrives a wound it will never be in his power to heal.

As we have established an inheritance for posterity, let that inheritance descend, with every mark of an honorable conveyance. The little it will cost, compared with the worth of the states, the greatness of the object, and the value of the national character, will be a profitable exchange.

But that which must more forcibly strike a thoughtful, penetrating mind, and which includes and renders easy all inferior concerns, is the UNION OF THE STATES. On this our great national character depends. It is this which must give us importance abroad and security at home. It is through this only that we are, or can be, nationally known in the world; it is the flag of the United States which renders our ships and commerce safe on the seas, or in a foreign port. Our Mediterranean passes must be obtained under the

While I was writing this note, I cast my eye on the pamphlet, Common Sense, from which I shall make an extract, as it exactly applies to the case. It is as follows:*

'I have never met with a man, either in England or America, who has not confessed it as his opinion that a separation between the countries would take place one time or other; and there is no instance in which we have shown less judgment, than in endeavoring to describe what we call the ripeness or fitness of the continent for independence.

'As all men allow the measure, and differ only in their opinion of the time, let us, in order to remove mistakes, take a general survey of things, and endeavor, if possible, to find out the *very time*. But we need not to go far, the inquiry ceases at once, for, *the time has found us*. The general concurrence, the glorious union of all things prove the fact.

'It is not in numbers, but in a union, that our great strength lies. The continent is just arrived at that pitch of strength, in which no single colony is able to support itself, and the whole, when united, can accomplish the matter; and either more or less than this, might be fatal in its effects.'—*Author*.

same style. All our treaties, whether of alliance, peace, or commerce, are formed under the sovereignty of the United States, and Europe knows us by no other name or title.

The division of the empire into states is for our own convenience, but abroad this distinction ceases. The affairs of each state are local. They can go no further than to itself. And were the whole worth of even the richest of them expended in revenue, it would not be sufficient to support sovereignty against a foreign attack. *In short, we have no other national sovereignty than as United States.* It would even be fatal for us if we had—too expensive to be maintained, and impossible to be supported. Individuals, or individual states, may call themselves what they please; but the world, and especially the world of enemies, is not to be held in awe by the whistling of a name. *Sovereignty must have power to protect all the parts that compose and constitute it*: and as UNITED STATES we are equal to the importance of the title, but otherwise we are not. Our union, well and wisely regulated and cemented, is the cheapest way of being great—the easiest way of being powerful, and the happiest invention in government which the circumstances of America can admit of.—Because it collects from each state, that which, by being inadequate, can be of no use to it, and forms an aggregate that serves for all.

The states of Holland are an unfortunate instance of the effects of individual sovereignty.* Their disjointed condition exposes them to numerous intrigues, losses, calamities, and enemies; and the almost impossibility of bringing their measures to a decision, and that decision into execution, is to them, and would be to us, a source of endless misfortune.

It is with confederated states as with individuals in society; something must be yielded up to make the whole secure. In this view of things we gain by what we give, and draw an annual interest greater than the capital.—I ever feel myself hurt when I hear the union, that great palladium of our liberty and safety, the least irreverently spoken of. It is the most sacred thing in the constitution of America, and that which every man should be most proud and tender of. *Our citizenship in the United States is our national character. Our citizen-*

ship in any particular state is only our local distinction. By the latter we are known at home, by the former to the world. Our great title is AMERICANS—our inferior one varies with the place.

So far as my endeavors could go, they have all been directed to conciliate the affections, unite the interests, and draw and keep the mind of the country together; and the better to assist in this foundation work of the revolution, I have avoided all places of profit or office, either in the state I live in, or in the United States,* kept myself at a distance from all parties and party connections, and even disregarded all private and inferior concerns: and when we take into view the great work which we have gone through, and feel, as we ought to feel, the just importance of it, we shall then see, that the little wranglings and indecent contentions of personal parley, are as dishonorable to our characters, as they are injurious to our repose.

It was the cause of America that made me an author. The force with which it struck my mind, and the dangerous condition the country appeared to me in, by courting an impossible and an unnatural reconciliation with those who were determined to reduce her, instead of striking out into the only line that could cement and save her, A DECLARATION OF INDEPENDENCE, made it impossible for me, feeling as I did, to be silent: and if, in the course of more than seven years, I have rendered her any service, I have likewise added something to the reputation of literature, by freely and disinterestedly employing it in the great cause of mankind, and showing that there may be genius without prostitution.

Independence always appeared to me practicable and probable, provided the sentiment of the country could be formed and held to the object: and there is no instance in the world, where a people so extended, and wedded to former habits of thinking, and under such a variety of circumstances, were so instantly and effectually pervaded, by a turn in politics, as in the case of independence; and who supported their opinion, undiminished, through such a succession of good and ill fortune, till they crowned it with success.

But as the scenes of war are closed, and every man preparing for home and happier times, I therefore take my leave of the subject. I have most sincerely followed it from beginning to end, and through all its turns and windings: and whatever country I may hereafter be in, I shall always feel an honest pride at the part I have taken and acted, and a gratitude to nature and providence for putting it in my power to be of some use to mankind.

Philadelphia, April 19, 1783*

LETTER TO JEFFERSON

AFTER I got home, being alone and wanting amusement I sat down to explain to myself (for there is such a thing) my Ideas of natural and civil rights and the distinction between them—I send them to you to see how nearly we agree.

Suppose 20 persons, strangers to each other, to meet in a country not before inhabited. Each would be a Sovereign in his own natural right. His will would be his Law, but his power, in many cases, inadequate to his right, and the consequence would be that each might be exposed, not only to each other, but to the other nineteen.

It would then occur to them that their condition would be much improved, if a way could be devised to exchange that quantity of danger into so much protection, so that each individual should possess the strength of the whole number.

As all their rights, in the first case, are natural rights, and the exercise of those rights supposed only by their own natural individual power, they would begin by distinguishing between those rights they could individually exercise fully and perfectly and those they could not.

Of the first kind are the rights of thinking, speaking, forming and giving opinions, and perhaps all those which can be fully exercised by the individual without the aid of exterior assistance—or in other words, rights of personal competency.—Of the second kind are those of personal protection, or acquiring and possessing property, in the exercise of which the individual natural power is less than the natural right.

Having drawn this line they agree to retain individually the first Class of Rights, or those of personal competency; and so detach from their personal possession the second class, or those of defective power and to accept in lieu thereof a right to the whole power produced by a condensation of all the parts. These I conceive to be civil rights or rights of Compact, and are distinguishable from Natural rights, because in the one we act wholly in our own person, in the other we agree not to do so, but act under the guarantee of society.

It therefore follows that the more of those imperfect natural rights, or rights of imperfect power we give up and thus exchange the more security we possess, and as the word liberty is often mistakenly put for security Mr Wilson has confused his argument by confounding his terms.*

But it does not follow that the more natural rights of *every kind* we resign the more security we possess, because if we resign those of the first class we may suffer much by the exchange, for where the right and the power are equal with each other in the individual naturally they ought to rest there.

Mr Wilson must have some allusion to this Distinction or his position would be subject to the inference you draw from it.

I consider the individual sovereignty of the states retained under the Act of Confederation to be the second Class of rights. It becomes dangerous because it is defective in the power necessary to support it. It answers the pride and purpose of a few men in each state—but the State collectively is injured by it.

RIGHTS OF MAN:

BEING AN

ANSWER to MR BURKE'S ATTACK

ON THE

FRENCH REVOLUTION.*

TO GEORGE WASHINGTON,
PRESIDENT OF THE UNITED STATES OF AMERICA.*

SIR,

I PRESENT you a small Treatise in defence of those Principles of Freedom which your exemplary Virtue hath so eminently contributed to establish.—That the Rights of Man may become as universal as your Benevolence can wish, and that you may enjoy the Happiness of seeing the New World regenerate the Old, is the Prayer of

      SIR,

             Your much obliged, and

                Obedient humble Servant,

                  THOMAS PAINE.

PREFACE TO THE
ENGLISH EDITION

FROM the part Mr Burke took in the American Revolution,*
it was natural that I should consider him a friend to mankind;
and as our acquaintance commenced on that ground, it
would have been more agreeable to me to have had cause to
continue in that opinion, than to change it.

At the time Mr Burke made his violent speech last winter*
in the English Parliament against the French Revolution
and the National Assembly, I was in Paris, and had written
him, but a short time before,* to inform him how prosperously matters were going on. Soon after this, I saw his
advertisement of the Pamphlet he intended to publish: As
the attack was to be made in a language but little studied,
and less understood, in France, and as every thing suffers by
translation, I promised some of the friends of the Revolution
in that country, that whenever Mr Burke's Pamphlet came
forth, I would answer it. This appeared to me the more
necessary to be done, when I saw the flagrant misrepresenta-
tions which Mr Burke's Pamphlet contains; and that while it
is an outrageous abuse on the French Revolution, and the
principles of Liberty, it is an imposition on the rest of the
world.

I am the more astonished and disappointed at this conduct
in Mr Burke, as (from the circumstance I am going to
mention), I had formed other expectations.

I had seen enough of the miseries of war, to wish it might
never more have existence in the world, and that some other
mode might be found out to settle the differences that
should occasionally arise in the neighbourhood of nations.
This certainly might be done if Courts were disposed to set
honestly about it, or if countries were enlightened enough
not to be made the dupes of Courts. The people of America
had been bred up in the same prejudices against France,
which at that time characterized the people of England; but
experience and an acquaintance with the French Nation*

have most effectually shown to the Americans the falsehood of those prejudices; and I do not believe that a more cordial and confidential intercourse exists between any two countries than between America and France.

When I came to France in the Spring of 1787,* the Archbishop of Thoulouse* was then Minister, and at that time highly esteemed. I became much acquainted with the private Secretary of that Minister,* a man of an enlarged benevolent heart; and found, that his sentiments and my own perfectly agreed with respect to the madness of war, and the wretched impolicy of two nations, like England and France, continually worrying each other, to no other end than that of a mutual increase of burdens and taxes. That I might be assured I had not misunderstood him, nor he me, I put the substance of our opinions into writing, and sent it to him; subjoining a request, that if I should see among the people of England, any disposition to cultivate a better understanding between the two nations than had hitherto prevailed, how far I might be authorized to say that the same disposition prevailed on the part of France? He answered me by letter in the most unreserved manner, and that not for himself only, but for the Minister, with whole knowledge the letter was declared to be written.

I put this letter into the hands of Mr Burke almost three years ago,* and left it with him, where it still remains; hoping, and at the same time naturally expecting, from the opinion I had conceived of him, that he would find some opportunity of making a good use of it, for the purpose of removing those errors and prejudices, which two neighbouring nations, from the want of knowing each other, had entertained, to the injury of both.

When the French Revolution broke out, it certainly afforded to Mr Burke an opportunity of doing some good, had he been disposed to it; instead of which, no sooner did he see the old prejudices wearing away, than he immediately began sowing the seeds of a new inveteracy, as if he were afraid that England and France would cease to be enemies. That there are men in all countries who get their living by war, and by keeping up the quarrels of Nations, is as shocking as it is true; but when those who are concerned in the government of a country, make it their study to sow discord, and cultivate prejudices between Nations, it becomes the more unpardonable.

With respect to a paragraph in this Work alluding to Mr Burke's having a pension, the report has been some time in circulation, at least two months; and as a person is often the last to hear what concerns him the most to know, I have mentioned it, that Mr Burke may have an opportunity of contradicting the rumour, if he thinks proper.

THOMAS PAINE

RIGHTS OF MAN,

&c. &c.

AMONG the incivilities by which nations or individuals provoke and irritate each other, Mr Burke's pamphlet on the French Revolution is an extraordinary instance. Neither the People of France, nor the National Assembly, were troubling themselves about the affairs of England, or the English Parliament; and why Mr Burke should commence an unprovoked attack upon them, both in parliament and in public, is a conduct that cannot be pardoned on the force of manners, nor justified on that of policy.

There is scarcely an epithet of abuse to be found in the English language, with which Mr Burke has not loaded the French Nation and the National Assembly. Every thing which rancour, prejudice, ignorance, or knowledge could suggest, are poured forth in the copious fury of near four hundred pages. In the strain and on the plan Mr Burke was writing, he might have written on to as many thousands. When the tongue or the pen is let loose in a frenzy of passion, it is the man, and not the subject, that becomes exhausted.

Hitherto Mr Burke has been mistaken and disappointed in the opinions he had formed of the affairs of France; but such is the ingenuity of his hope, or the malignancy of his despair, that it furnishes him with new pretences to go on. There was a time when it was impossible to make Mr Burke beleive there would be any revolution in France.* His opinion then was, that the French had neither spirit to undertake it, nor fortitude to support it; and now that there is one, he seeks an escape, by condemning it.

Not sufficiently content with abusing the National Assembly, a great part of his work is taken up with abusing Dr Price* (one of the best-hearted men that lives), and the two societies in England known by the name of the Revolution Society, and the Society for Constitutional Information.*

Dr Price had preached a sermon on the 4th of November 1789, being the anniversary of what is called in England, the Revolution which took place 1688.* Mr Burke, speaking of this sermon, says, 'The Political Devine proceeds dogmatically to assert, that, by the principles of the Revolution, the people of England have acquired three fundamental rights:

1. To choose our own governors.
2. To cashier them for misconduct.
3. To frame a government for ourselves.'*

Dr Price does not say that the right to do these things exists in this or in that person, or in this or in that description of persons, but that it exists in the *whole*; that it is a right resident in the nation.—Mr Burke, on the contrary, denies that such a right exists in the nation, either in whole or in part, or that it exists any where; and, what is still more strange and marvellous, he says, 'that the people of England utterly disclaim such a right, and that they will resist the practical assertion of it with their lives and fortunes.'* That men should take up arms, and spend their lives and fortunes, *not* to maintain their rights, but to maintain they have *not* rights, is an entirely new species of discovery, and suited to the paradoxical genius of Mr Burke.

The method which Mr Burke takes to prove that the people of England have no such rights, and that such rights do not now exist in the nation, either in whole or in part, or any where at all, is of the same marvellous and monstrous kind with what he has already said; for his arguments are, that the persons, or the generation of persons, in whom they did exist, are dead, and with them the right is dead also. To prove this, he quotes a declaration made by parliament about a hundred years ago, to William and Mary, in these words:*

'The Lords Spiritual and Temporal, and Commons, do, in the name of the people aforesaid,—(meaning the people of England then living)—most humbly and faithfully *submit* themselves, their *heirs* and *posterities*, for EVER.' He also quotes a clause of another act of parliament made in the same reign, the terms of which, he says, 'bind us—(meaning the people of that day)—our *heirs*, and our *posterity*, to *them*, their *heirs* and *posterity*, to the end of time.'*

Mr Burke conceives his point sufficiently established by producing those clauses, which he enforces by saying that they exclude the right of the nation for *ever*: And not yet content with making such declarations, repeated over and over again, he farther says, 'that if the people of England 'possessed such a right before the Revolution, (which he acknowledges to have been the case, not only in England, but throughout Europe, at an early period), 'yet that the *English nation* did, at the time of the Revolution, most solemnly renounce and abdicate it, for themselves, and for *all their posterity, for ever.*'*

As Mr Burke occasionally applies the poison drawn from his horrid principles, not only to the English nation, but to the French Revolution and the National Assembly, and charges that august, illuminated and illuminating body of men with the epithet of *usurpers*,* I shall, *sans ceremonie*, place another system of principles in opposition to his.

The English Parliament of 1688 did a certain thing, which, for themselves and their constituents, they had a right to do, and which it appeared right should be done: But, in addition to this right, which they possessed by delegation, *they set up another right by assumption*, that of binding and controuling posterity to the end of time. The case, therefore, divides itself into two parts; the right which they possessed by delegation, and the right which they set up by assumption. The first is admitted; but, with respect to the second, I reply—

There never did, there never will, and there never can exist a parliament, or any description of men, or any genera-tion of men, in any country, possessed of the right or the power of binding and controuling posterity to the '*end of time*,' or of commanding for ever how the world shall be governed, or who shall govern it; and therefore, all such clauses, acts or declarations, by which the makers of them attempt to do what they have neither the right nor the power to do, nor the power to execute, are in themselves null and void.—Every age and generation must be as free to act for itself, *in all cases*, as the ages and generations which preceded it. The vanity and presumption of governing beyond the grave, is the most ridiculous and insolent of all tyrannies. Man has no property in man; neither has any generation a property in the generations which are to follow. The parliament or the people of 1688, or of any other period, had no more right to dispose of the people of the present day, or to bind or to controul them *in any shape whatever*, than the parliament or the people of the present day have to dispose of, bind or controul those who are to live a hundred or a thousand years hence. Every generation is, and must be, competent to all the purposes which its occasions require. It is the living, and not the dead, that are to be accommodated. When man ceases to be, his power and his wants cease with him; and having no longer any participation in the concerns of this world, he has no longer any authority in directing who shall be its governors, or how its government shall be organized, or how administered.

I am not contending for nor against any form of government, nor for nor against any party here or elsewhere. That which a whole nation chooses to do, it has a right to do. Mr Burke says, No. Where then *does* the right exist? I am contending for the rights of the *living*, and against their being willed away, and controuled and contracted for, by the manuscript assumed authority of the dead; and Mr Burke is contending for the authority of the dead over the rights and freedom of the living. There was a time when kings disposed of their crowns by will upon their deathbeds, and consigned the people, like beasts of the field, to whatever successor they appointed. This is now so exploded as scarcely to be remembered, and so monstrous as hardly to be believed: But the parliamentary clauses upon which Mr Burke builds his political church, are of the same nature.

The laws of every country must be analogous to some common principle. In England, no parent or master, nor all the authority of parliament, omnipotent as it has called itself, can bind or controul the personal freedom even of an individual beyond the age of twenty-one years:* On what ground of right, then, could the parliament of 1688, or any other parliament, bind all posterity for ever?

Those who have quitted the world, and those who are not yet arrived at it, are as remote from each other, as the utmost stretch of mortal imagination can conceive: What possible obligation, then, can exist between them; what rule or principle can be laid down, that of two non-entities, the one out of existence, and the other not in, and who never can meet in this world, the one should controul the other to the end of time?

In England, it is said that money cannot be taken out of the pockets of the people without their consent:* But who authorized, or who could authorize the parliament of 1688 to controul and take away the freedom of posterity, (who were not in existence to give or to withhold their consent,) and limit and confine their right of acting in certain cases for ever?

A greater absurdity cannot present itself to the understanding of man, than what Mr Burke offers to his readers. He tells them, and he tells the world to come, that a certain body of men, who existed a hundred years ago, made a law; and that there does not now exist in the nation, nor ever will, nor ever can, a power to alter it. Under how many subtilties, or absurdities, has the divine right to govern been imposed on the credulity of mankind! Mr Burke has discovered a new one, and he has shortened his journey to Rome,* by appealing to the power of this infallible parliament of former days; and he produces what it has done, as of divine authority: for that power must certainly be more than human, which no human power to the end of time can alter.

But Mr Burke has done some service, not to his cause, but to his country, by bringing those clauses into public view. They serve to demonstrate how necessary it is at all times to watch against the attempted encroachment of power, and to prevent its running to excess. It is somewhat extraordinary, that the offence for which James II, was expelled, that of setting up power by *assumption*, should be re-acted, under another shape and form, by the parliament that expelled him. It shews, that the rights of man were but imperfectly understood at the Revolution; for, certain it is, that the right which that parliament set up by *assumption* (for by delegation it had it not, and could not have it, because none could give it) over the perfons and freedom of posterity for ever, was of the same tyrannical unfounded kind which James attempted to set up over the parliament and the nation, and for which he was expelled. The only difference is, (for in principle they differ not), that the one was an usurper over the living, and the other over the unborn; and as the one has no better authority to stand upon than the other, both of them must be equally null and void, and of no effect.

From what, or from whence, does Mr Burke prove the right of any human power to bind posterity for ever? He has produced his clauses; but he must produce also his proofs, that such a right existed, and shew how it existed. If it ever existed, it must now exist; for whatever appertains to the nature of man, cannot be annihilated by man. It is the nature of man to die, and he will continue to die as long as he continues to be born. But Mr Burke has set up a sort of political Adam, in whom all posterity are bound for ever; he must therefore prove that his Adam possessed such a power, or such a right.

The weaker any cord, is, the less will it bear to be stretched, and the worse is the policy to stretch it, unless it is intended to break it. Had any one purposed the overthrow of Mr Burke's positions, he would have proceeded as Mr Burke has done. He would have magnified the authorities, on purpose to have called the *right* of them into question; and the instant the question of right was started, the authorities must have been given up.

It requires but a very small glance of thought to perceive, that altho' laws made in one generation often continue in force through succeeding generations, yet that they continue to derive their force from the consent of the living. A law not repealed continues in force, not because it *cannot* be repealed, but because it *is not* repealed; and the non-repealing passes for consent.

But Mr Burke's clauses have not even this qualification in their favour. They become null, by attempting to become immortal. The nature of them precludes consent. They destroy the right which they *might* have, by grounding it on a right which they *cannot* have. Immortal power is not a human right, and therefore cannot be a right of parliament. The parliament of 1688 might as well have passed an act to have authorized themselves to live for ever, as to make their authority live for ever. All therefore that can be said of those clauses is, that they are a formality of words, of as much import, as if those who used them had addressed a congratulation to themselves, and, in the oriental stile of antiquity, had said, O Parliament, live for ever!

The circumstances of the world are continually changing, and the opinions of men change also; and as government is for the living, and not for the dead, it is the living only that has any right in it. That which may be thought right and found convenient in one age, may be thought wrong and found inconvenient in another. In such cases, Who is to decide, the living, or the dead?

As almost one hundred pages of Mr Burke's book are employed upon these clauses, it will consequently follow, that if the clauses themselves, so far as they set up an *assumed, usurped* dominion over posterity for ever, are unauthoritative, and in their nature null and void; that all his voluminous inferences and declamation drawn therefrom, or founded thereon, are null and void also: and on this ground I rest the matter.

We now come more particularly to the affairs of France. Mr Burke's book has the appearance of being written as instruction to the French nation; but if I may permit myself the use of an extravagant metaphor, suited to the extravagance of the case, It is darkness attempting to illuminate light.

While I am writing this, there are accidentally before me some proposals for a declaration of rights by the Marquis de la Fayette* (I ask his pardon for using his former address, and do it only for distinction's sake) to the National Assembly, on the 11th of July 1789, three days before the taking of the Bastille;* and I cannot but remark with astonishment how opposite the sources are from which that Gentleman and Mr Burke draw their principles. Instead of referring to musty records and mouldy parchments to prove that the rights of the living are lost, 'renounced and abdicated for ever,' by those who are now no more, as Mr Burke has done, M. de la Fayette applies to the living world, and emphatically says, 'Call to mind the sentiments which Nature has engraved in the heart of every citizen, and which take a new force when they are solemnly recognized by all:—For a nation to love liberty, it is sufficient that she knows it; and to be free, it is sufficient that she wills it.'* How dry, barren, and obscure, is the source from which Mr Burke labours! and how ineffectual, though gay with flowers, are all his declamation and his arguments, compared with these clear, concise, and soul-animating sentiments! Few and short as they are, they lead on to a vast field of generous and manly thinking, and do not finish, like Mr Burke's periods, with music in the ear, and nothing in the heart.

As I have introduced M. de la Fayette, I will take the liberty of adding an anecdote respecting his farewel address to the Congress of America in 1783, and which occurred fresh to my mind when I saw Mr Burke's thundering attack on the French Revolution.—M. de la Fayette went to America at an early period of the war, and continued a volunteer in her service to the end. His conduct through the whole of that enterprise is one of the most extraordinary that is to be found in the history of a young man, scarcely then twenty years of age. Situated in a country that was like the lap of sensual pleasure, and with the means of enjoying it, how few are there to be found who would exchange such a scene for the woods and wildernesses of America, and pass the flowery years of youth in unprofitable danger and hardship! but such is the fact. When the war ended, and he was on the point of taking his final departure, he presented himself to Congress, and contemplating, in his affectionate farewel, the revolution he had seen, expressed himself in these words: *'May this great monument, raised to Liberty, serve as a lesson to the oppressor, and an example to the oppressed!'*—When this address came to the hands of Doctor Franklin,* who was then in France, he applied to Count Vergennes to have it inserted in the French Gazette,* but never could obtain his consent. The fact was, that Count

Vergennes was an aristocratical despot at home, and dreaded the example of the American revolution in France, as certain other persons now dread the example of the French revolution in England; and Mr Burke's tribute of fear (for in this light his book must be considered) runs parallel with Count Vergennes' refusal. But, to return more particularly to his work—

'We have seen (says Mr Burke) the French rebel against a mild and lawful Monarch, with more fury, outrage, and insult, than any people has been known to rise against the most illegal usurper, or the most sanguinary tyrant.'*—This is one among a thousand other instances, in which Mr Burke shews that he is ignorant of the springs and principles of the French revolution.

It was not against Louis the XVIth,* but against the despotic principles of the government, that the nation revolted. These principles had not their origin in him, but in the original establishment, many centuries back; and they were become too deeply rooted to be removed, and the augean stable* of parasites and plunderers too abominably filthy to be cleansed, by any thing short of a complete and universal revolution. When it becomes necessary to do a thing, the whole heart and soul should go into the measure, or not attempt it. That crisis was then arrived, and there remained no choice but to act with determined vigour, or not to act at all. The king was known to be the friend of the nation, and this circumstance was favourable to the enterprise. Perhaps no man bred up in the stile of an absolute King, ever possessed a heart so little disposed to the exercise of that species of power as the present King of France. But the principles of the government itself still remained the same. The Monarch and the Monarchy were distinct and separate things; and it was against the established despotism of the latter, and not against the person or principles of the former, that the revolt commenced, and the revolution has been carried.

Mr Burke does not attend to the distinction between *men* and *principles*; * and therefore, he does not see that a revolt may take place against the despotism of the latter, while there lies no charge of despotism against the former.

The natural moderation of Louis XVI. contributed nothing to alter the hereditary despotism of the monarchy. All the tyrannies of former reigns, acted under that hereditary despotism, were still liable to be revived in the hands of a successor. It was not the respite of a reign that would satisfy France, enlightened as she was then become. A casual discontinuance of the *practice* of despotism, is not a discontinuance of its *principles*; the former depends on the virtue of the individual who is in immediate possession of the power; the latter, on the virtue and fortitude of the nation. In the case of Charles I.* and James II. of England, the revolt was against the personal despotism of the men; whereas in France, it was against the hereditary despotism of the established government. But men who can consign over the rights of posterity for ever on the authority of a mouldy parchment, like Mr Burke, are not qualified to judge of this revolution. It takes in a field too vast for their views to explore, and proceeds with a mightiness of reason they cannot keep pace with.

But there are many points of view in which this revolution may be considered. When despotism has established itself for ages in a country, as in France, it is not in the person of the King only that it resides. It has the appearance of being so in show, and in nominal authority; but it is not so in practice, and in fact. It has its standard every-where. Every office and department has its despotism, founded upon custom and usage. Every place has its Bastille,* and every Bastille its despot. The original hereditary despotism resident in the person of the King, divides and subdivides itself into a thousand shapes and forms, till at last the whole of it is acted by deputation. This was the case in France; and against this species of despotism, proceeding on through an endless labyrinth of office till the source of it is scarcely perceptible, there is no mode of redress. It strengthens itself by assuming the appearance of duty, and tyrannises under the pretence of obeying.

When a man reflects on the condition which France was in from the nature of her government, he will see other causes for revolt than those which immediately connect themselves with the person or character of Louis XVI.

There were, if I may so express it, a thousand despotisms to be reformed in France, which had grown up under the hereditary despotism of the monarchy, and became so rooted as to be in a great measure independent of it. Between the monarchy, the parliament, and the church, there was a *rivalship* of despotism; besides the feudal despotism operating locally, and the ministerial despotism operating everywhere. But Mr Burke, by considering the King as the only possible object of a revolt, speaks as if France was a village, in which every thing that passed must be known to its commanding officer, and no oppression could be acted but what he could immediately controul. Mr Burke might have been in the Bastille his whole life, as well under Louis XVI. as Louis XIV.* and neither the one nor the other have known that such a man as Mr Burke existed. The despotic principles of the government were the same in both reigns, though the dispositions of the men were as remote as tyranny and benevolence.

What Mr Burke considers as a reproach to the French Revolution, (that of bringing it forward under a reign more mild* than the preceding ones), is one of its highest honours. The revolutions that have taken place in other European countries, have been excited by personal hatred. The rage was against the man, and he became the victim. But, in the instance of France, we see a revolution generated in the rational contemplation of the rights of man, and distinguishing from the beginning between persons and principles.

But Mr Burke appears to have no idea of principles, when he is contemplating governments. 'Ten years ago (says he) I could have felicitated France on her having a government, without enquiring what the nature of that government was, or how it was administered.'* Is this the language of a rational man? Is it the language of a heart feeling as it ought to feel for the rights and happiness of the human race? On this ground, Mr Burke must compliment all the governments in the world, while the victims who suffer under them, whether sold into slavery, or tortured out of existence, are wholly forgotten. It is power, and not principles, that Mr Burke venerates; and under this abominable depravity, he is disqualified to judge between them.—Thus much for his opinion as to the occasions of the French Revolution. I now proceed to other considerations.

I know a place in America called Point-no-Point; because as you proceed along the shore, gay and flowery as Mr Burke's language, it continually recedes and presents itself at a distance before you; but when you have got as far as you can go, there is no point at all. Just thus it is with Mr Burke's three hundred and fifty-six pages. It is therefore difficult to reply to him. But as the points he wishes to establish, may be inferred from what he abuses, it is in his paradoxes that we must look for his arguments.

As to the tragic paintings by which Mr Burke has outraged his own imagination, and seeks to work upon that of his readers, they are very well calculated for theatrical representation, where facts are manufactured for the sake of show, and accommodated to produce, through the weakness of sympathy, a weeping effect. But Mr Burke should recollect that he is writing History, and not *Plays*;* and that his readers will expect truth, and not the spouting rant of high-toned exclamation.

When we see a man dramatically lamenting in a publication intended to be believed, that, '*The age of chivalry is gone! that The glory of Europe is extinguished for ever! that The unbought grace of life* (if any one knows what it is), *the cheap defence of nations, the nurse of manly sentiment and heroic enterprize, is gone!*'* and all this because the Quixot* age of chivalry nonsense is gone, What opinion can we form of his judgment, or what regard can we pay to his facts? In the rhapsody of his imagination, he has discovered a world of wind-mills, and his sorrows are, that there are no Quixots to attack them. But if the age of aristocracy, like that of chivalry, should fall, (and they had originally some connection), Mr Burke, the trumpeter of the Order, may continue his parody to the end, and finish with exclaiming, '*Othello's occupation's gone!*'*

Notwithstanding Mr Burke's horrid paintings, when the French Revolution is compared with the revolutions of other countries, the astonishment will be, that it is marked with so few sacrifices; but this astonishment will cease when we reflect that *principles*, and not *persons*, were the meditated objects of destruction. The mind of the nation was acted upon by a higher stimulus than what the consideration of persons could inspire, and sought a higher conquest than could be produced by the downfal of an enemy. Among the few who fell, there do not appear to be any that were intentionally singled out. They all of them had their fate in the circumstances of the moment, and were not pursued with that long, cold-blooded, unabated revenge which pursued the unfortunate Scotch in the affair of 1745.*

Through the whole of Mr Burke's book I do not observe that the Bastille is mentioned more than once, and that with a kind of implication as if he were sorry it was pulled down, and wished it were built up again. 'We have rebuilt Newgate (says he),* and tenanted the mansion; and we have prisons almost as strong as the Bastille for those who dare to libel the Queens of France.'*[1] As to what a madman, like the person called Lord G—— G——,* might say, and to whom Newgate is rather a bedlam* than a prison, it is unworthy a rational consideration. It was a madman that libelled—and that is sufficient apology; and it afforded an opportunity for confining him, which was the thing that was wished for: But certain it is that Mr Burke, who does not call himself a madman, (whatever other people may do), has libelled, in the most unprovoked manner, and in the grossest stile of the most vulgar abuse, the whole representative authority of France; and yet Mr Burke takes his seat in the British House of Commons! From his violence and his grief, his silence on some points, and his excess on others, it is difficult not to believe that Mr Burke is sorry, extremely

---

[1] Since writing the above, two other places occur in Mr Burke's pamphlet, in which the name of the Bastille is mentioned, but in the same manner.* In the one, he introduces it in a sort of obscure question, and asks—'Will any ministers who now serve such a king, with but a decent appearance of respect, cordially obey the orders of those whom but the other day, *in his name*, they had committed to the Bastille?' In the other, the taking it is mentioned as implying criminality in the French guards who assisted in demolishing it.—'They have not (says he) forgot the taking the king's castles at Paris.'—This is Mr Burke, who pretends to write on constitutional freedom.

sorry, that arbitrary power, the power of the Pope, and the Bastille, are pulled down.

Not one glance of compassion, not one commiserating reflection, that I can find throughout his book, has he bestowed on those who lingered out the most wretched of lives, a life without hope, in the most miserable of prisons. It is painful to behold a man employing his talents to corrupt himself. Nature has been kinder to Mr Burke than he is to her. He is not affected by the reality of distress touching his heart, but by the showy resemblance of it striking his imagination. He pities the plumage, but forgets the dying bird.* Accustomed to kiss the aristocratical hand that hath purloined him from himself,* he degenerates into a composition of art, and the genuine soul of nature forsakes him. His hero or his heroine must be a tragedy-victim expiring in show, and not the real prisoner of misery, sliding into death in the silence of a dungeon.

As Mr Burke has passed over the whole transaction of the Bastille (and his silence is nothing in his favour), and has entertained his readers with reflections on supposed facts distorted into real falsehoods, I will give, since he has not, some account of the circumstances which preceded that transaction. They will serve to shew, that less mischief could scarcely have accompanied such an event, when considered with the treacherous and hostile aggravations of the enemies of the Revolution.

The mind can hardly picture to itself a more tremendous scene than what the city of Paris exhibited at the time of taking the Bastille, and for two days before and after,* nor conceive the possibility of its quieting so soon. At a distance, this transaction has appeared only as an act of heroism, standing on itself; and the close political connection it had with the Revolution is lost in the brilliancy of the achievement. But we are to consider it as the strength of the parties, brought man to man, and contending for the issue. The Bastille was to be either the prize or the prison of the assailants. The downfal of it included the idea of the downfal of Despotism; and this compounded image was become as figuratively united as Bunyan's Doubting Castle and Giant Despair.*

The National Assembly, before and at the time of taking the Bastille, was sitting at Versailles,* twelve miles distant from Paris. About a week before the rising of the Parisians, and their taking the Bastille, it was discovered that a plot was forming, at the head of which was the Count d'Artois,* the King's youngest brother, for demolishing the National Assembly, seizing its members, and thereby crushing, by a *coup de main*, all hopes and prospects of forming a free government. For the sake of humanity, as well as of freedom, it is well this plan did not succeed. Examples are not wanting to shew how dreadfully vindictive and cruel are all old governments, when they are successful against what they call a revolt.

This plan must have been some time in contemplation; because, in order to carry it into execution, it was necessary to collect a large military force round Paris; and to cut off the communication between that city and the National Assembly at Versailles. The troops destined for this service were chiefly the foreign troops in the pay of France,* and who, for this particular purpose, were drawn from the distant provinces where they were then stationed. When they were collected, to the amount of between twenty-five and thirty thousand, it was judged time to put the plan in execution. The ministry who were then in office,* and who were friendly to the Revolution, were instantly dismissed, and a new ministry formed of those who had concerted the project;—among whom was Count de Broglio,* and to his share was given the command of those troops. The character of this man, as described to me in a letter which I communicated to Mr Burke before he began to write his book, and from an authority which Mr Burke well knows was good, was that of an 'high-flying aristocrat, cool, and capable of every mischief.'*

While these matters were agitating, the National Assembly stood in the most perilous and critical situation that a body of men can be supposed to act in. They were the devoted victims,* and they knew it. They had the hearts and wishes of their country on their side, but military authority they had none. The guards of Broglio surrounded the hall where

the assembly sat, ready, at the word of command, to seize
their persons, as had been done the year before to the
parliament of Paris. Had the National Assembly deserted
their trust, or had they exhibited signs of weakness or fear,
their enemies had been encouraged, and the country de-
pressed. When the situation they stood in, the cause they
were engaged in, and the crisis they ready to burst (which
was to determine their personal and political fate, and that
of their country, and probably of Europe) are taken into one
view, none but a heart callous with prejudice, or corrupted
by dependance, can avoid interesting itself in their success.

The archbishop of Vienne was at this time president of
the National Assembly;* a person too old to undergo the
scene that a few days, or a few hours, might bring forth. A
man of more activity, and greater fortitude, was necessary;
and the National Assembly chose under the form of a vice-
president, (for the presidency still resided in the archbishop)
M. de la Fayette; and this is the only instance of a vice-
president being chosen. It was at the moment that this
storm was pending (July 11.) that a declaration of rights was
brought forward by M. de la Fayette, and is the same which
is alluded to in page 95. It was hastily drawn up, and
makes only a part of a more extensive declaration of rights,
agreed upon and adopted afterwards by the National Assembly. The particular reason for bringing it forward at this
moment, (M. de la Fayette has since informed me) was, that
if the National Assembly should fall in the threatened destruction that then surrounded it, some traces of its principles might have the chance of surviving the wreck.

Every thing now was drawing to a crisis. The event was to
be freedom or slavery. On one side, an army of nearly thirty
thousand men; on the other, an unarmed body of citizens:
for the citizens of Paris, on whom the National Assembly
must then immediately depend, were as unarmed and as
undisciplined as the citizens of London are now.—The
French guards had given strong symptoms of their being
attached to the national cause; but their numbers were
small, not a tenth part of the force that Broglio commanded,
and their officers were in the interest of Broglio.

Matters being now ripe for execution, the new ministry made their appearance in office. The reader will carry in his mind, that the Bastille was taken the 14th of July: the point of time I am now speaking to, is the 12th. Immediately on the news of the change of ministry reaching Paris, in the afternoon, all the play-houses and places of entertainment, shops and houses, were shut up. The change of ministry was considered as the prelude of hostilities, and the opinion was rightly founded.

The foreign troops began to advance towards the city. The Prince de Lambesc, who commanded a body of German cavalry, approached by the Place of Lewis XV.* which connects itself with some of the streets. In his march, he insulted and struck an old man with his sword. The French are remarkable for their respect to old age, and the insolence with which it appeared to be done, uniting with the general fermentation they were in, produced a powerful effect, and a cry of *To arms! to arms!* spread itself in a moment over the city.

Arms they had none, nor scarcely any who knew the use of them: but desperate resolution, when every hope is at stake, supplies, for a while, the want of arms. Near where the Prince de Lambesc was drawn up, were large piles of stones collected for building the new bridge, and with these the people attacked the cavalry. A party of the French guards, upon hearing the firing, rushed from their quarters and joined the people; and night coming on, the cavalry retreated.

The streets of Paris, being narrow, are favourable for defence; and the loftiness of the houses, consisting of many stories, from which great annoyance might be given, secured them against nocturnal enterprises; and the night was spent in providing themselves with every sort of weapon they could make or procure: Guns, swords, blacksmiths hammers, carpenters axes, iron crows, pikes, halberts, pitchforks, spits, clubs, &c. &c. The incredible numbers in which they assembled the next morning, and the still more incredible resolution they exhibited, embarrassed and astonished their enemies. Little did the new ministry expect such a salute.

Accustomed to slavery themselves, they had no idea that Liberty was capable of such inspiration, or that a body of unarmed citizens would dare to face the military force of thirty thousand men. Every moment of this day was employed in collecting arms, concerting plans, and arranging themselves into the best order which such an instantaneous movement could afford. Broglio continued lying round the city, but made no farther advances this day, and the succeeding night passed with as much tranquillity as such a scene could possibly admit.

But defence only was not the object of the citizens. They had a cause at stake, on which depended their freedom or their slavery. They every moment expected an attack, or to hear of one made on the National Assembly; and in such a situation, the most prompt measures are sometimes the best. The object that now presented itself was the Bastille; and the eclat of carrying such a fortress in the face of such an army, could not fail to strike a terror into the new ministry, who had scarcely yet had time to meet. By some intercepted correspondence this morning, it was discovered, that the Mayor of Paris, M. Defflesselles,* who appeared to be in the interest of the citizens, was betraying them; and from this discovery, there remained no doubt that Broglio would reinforce the Bastille the ensuing evening. It was therefore necessary to attack it that day; but before this could be done, it was first necessary to procure a better supply of arms than they were then possessed of.

There was adjoining to the city a large magazine of arms deposited at the Hospital of the Invalids,* which the citizens summoned to surrender; and as the place was not defensible, nor attempted much defence, they soon succeeded. Thus supplied, they marched to attack the Bastille; a vast mixed multitude of all ages, and of all degrees, and armed with all sorts of weapons. Imagination would fail in describing to itself the appearance of such a procession, and of the anxiety for the events which a few hours or a few minutes might produce. What plans the ministry was forming, were as unknown to the people within the city, as what the citizens were doing was unknown to the ministry; and what movements Broglio might make for the support or relief of the place, were to the citizens equally as unknown. All was mystery and hazard.

That the Bastille was attacked with an enthusiasm of heroism, such only as the highest animation of liberty could inspire, and carried in the space of a few hours, is an event which the world is fully possessed of. I am not undertaking a detail of the attack; but bringing into view the conspiracy against the nation which provoked it, and which fell with the Bastille. The prison to which the new ministry were dooming the National Assembly, in addition to its being the high altar and castle of despotism, became the proper object to begin with. This enterprise broke up the new ministry, who began now to fly from the ruin they had prepared for others. The troops of Broglio dispersed, and himself fled also.

Mr Burke has spoken a great deal about plots, but he has never once spoken of this plot against the National Assembly, and the liberties of the nation; and that he might not, he has passed over all the circumstances that might throw it in his way. The exiles who have fled from France,* whose case he so much interests himself in, and from whom he has had his lesson, fled in consequence of the miscarriage of this plot. No plot was formed against them: they were plotting against others; and those who fell, met, not unjustly, the punishment they were preparing to execute. But will Mr Burke say, that if this plot, contrived with the subtilty of an ambuscade, had succeeded, the successful party would have restrained their wrath so soon? Let the history of all old governments answer the question.

Whom has the National Assembly brought to the scaffold? None. They were themselves the devoted victims of this plot, and they have not retaliated; why then are they charged with revenge they have not acted? In the tremendous breaking forth of a whole people, in which all degrees, tempers and characters are confounded, and delivering themselves, by a miracle of exertion, from the destruction meditated against them, is it to be expected that nothing will happen? When men are sore with the sense of oppressions, and menaced with the prospect of new ones, is the calmness of philosophy, or the palsy of insensibility, to be looked for? Mr Burke exclaims against outrage; yet the greatest is that which himself has committed. His book is a volume of outrage, not apologized for by the impulse of a moment, but cherished through a space of ten months; yet Mr Burke had no provocation—no life, no interest at stake.

More of the citizens fell in this struggle than of their opponents: but four or five persons were seized by the populace, and instantly put to death; the Governor of the Bastille, and the Mayor of Paris, who was detected in the act of betraying them; and afterwards Foulon, one of the new ministry, and Berthier his son-in-law, who had accepted the office of Intendant of Paris.* Their heads were stuck upon spikes, and carried about the city; and it is upon this mode of punishment that Mr Burke builds a great part of his tragic scene. Let us therefore examine how men came by the idea of punishing in this manner.

They learn it from the governments they live under, and retaliate the punishments they have been accustomed to behold. The heads stuck upon spikes, which remained for years upon Temple-bar,* differed nothing in the horror of the scene from those carried about upon spikes at Paris: yet this was done by the English government. It may perhaps be said, that it signifies nothing to a man what is done to him after he is dead; but it signifies much to the living: it either tortures their feelings, or hardens their hearts; and in either case, it instructs them how to punish when power falls into their hands.

Lay then the axe to the root, and teach governments humanity. It is their sanguinary punishments which corrupt mankind. In England, the punishment in certain cases, is by *hanging drawing*, and *quartering*; the heart of the sufferer is cut out, and held up to the view of the populace.* In France, under the former government, the punishments were not less barbarous. Who does not remember the execution of Damien,* torn to pieces by horses? The effect of those cruel spectacles exhibited to the populace, is to destroy tenderness, or excite revenge; and by the base and false idea of governing men by terror, instead of reason, they become precedents. It is over the lowest class of mankind that government by terror is intended to operate, and it is on them that it operates to the worst effect. They have sense enough to feel they are the objects aimed at; and they inflict in their turn the examples of terror they have been instructed to practise.

There is in all European countries, a large class of people of that description which in England is called the '*mob*.' Of this class were those who committed the burnings and devastations in London in 1780,* and of this class were those who carried the heads upon spikes in Paris. Foulon and Berthier were taken up in the country, and sent to Paris, to undergo their examination at the Hotel de Ville; for the National Assembly, immediately on the new ministry coming into office, passed a decree, which they communicated to the King and Cabinet, that they (the National Assembly) would hold the ministry, of which Foulon was one, responsible for the measures they were advising and pursuing; but the mob, incensed at the appearance of Foulon and Berthier, tore them from their conductors before they were carried to the Hotel de Ville,* and executed them on the spot. Why then does Mr Burke charge outrages of this kind on a whole people? As well may he charge the riots and outrages of 1780 on all the people of London, or those in Ireland on all his countrymen.

But every thing we see or hear offensive to our feelings, and derogatory to the human character, should lead to other reflections than those of reproach. Even the beings who commit them have some claim to our consideration. How then is it that such vast classes of mankind as are distinguished by the appellation of the vulgar, or the ignorant mob, are so numerous in all old countries? The instant we ask ourselves this question, reflection feels an answer. They arise, as an unavoidable consequence, out of the ill construction of all old governments in Europe, England included with the rest. It is by distortedly exalting some men, that others are distortedly debased, till the whole is out of nature. A vast mass of mankind are degradedly thrown into the back-ground of the human picture, to bring forward with greater glare, the puppet-show of state and aristocracy. In the commencement of a Revolution, those men are rather the followers of the *camp* than of the *standard* of liberty, and have yet to be instructed how to reverence it.

I give to Mr Burke all his theatrical exaggerations for facts, and I then ask him, if they do not establish the certainty of what I here lay down? Admitting them to be true, they shew the necessity of the French Revolution, as much as any one thing he could have asserted. These outrages were not the effect of the principles of the Revolution, but of the degraded mind that existed before the Revolution, and which the Revolution is calculated to reform. Place them then to their proper cause, and take the reproach of them to your own side.

It is to the honour of the National Assembly, and the city of Paris, that during such a tremendous scene of arms and confusion, beyond the controul of all authority, they have been able, by the influence of example and exhortation, to restrain so much. Never were more pains taken to instruct and enlighten mankind, and to make them see that their interest consisted in their virtue, and not in their revenge, than have been displayed in the Revolution of France. I now proceed to make some remarks on Mr Burke's account of the expedition to Versailles,* October the 5th and 6th.

I cannot consider Mr Burke's book in scarcely any other light than a dramatic performance; and he must, I think, have considered it in the same light himself, by the poetical liberties he has taken of omitting some facts, distorting others, and making the whole machinery bend to produce a stage effect. Of this kind is his account of the expedition to Versailles. He begins this account by omitting the only facts which as causes are known to be true; every thing beyond these is conjecture even in Paris: and he then works up a tale accommodated to his own passions and prejudices.

It is to be observed throughout Mr Burke's book, that he never speaks of plots *against* the Revolution; and it is from those plots that all the mischiefs have arisen. It suits his purpose to exhibit the consequences without their causes. It is one of the arts of the drama to do so. If the crimes of men were exhibited with their sufferings, stage effect would sometimes be lost, and the audience would be inclined to approve where it was intended they should commiserate.

After all the investigations that have been made into this intricate affair, (the expedition to Versailles), it still remains enveloped in all that kind of mystery which ever accompanies events produced more from a concurrence of awkward circumstances, than from fixed design. While the characters of men are forming, as is always the case in revolutions, there is a reciprocal suspicion, and a disposition to misinterpret each other; and even parties directly opposite in principle, will sometimes concur in pushing forward the same movement with very different views, and with the hopes of its producing very different consequences. A great deal of this may be discovered in this embarrassed affair, and yet the issue of the whole was what nobody had in view.

The only things certainly known, are, that considerable uneasiness was at this time excited at Paris, by the delay of the King in not sanctioning and forwarding the decrees of the National Assembly, particularly that of the *Declaration of the Rights of Man*, and the decrees of the *fourth of August*,* which contained the foundation principles on which the constitution was to be erected. The kindest, and perhaps the fairest conjecture upon this matter is, that some of the ministers intended to make remarks and observations upon certain parts of them, before they were finally sanctioned and sent to the provinces; but be this as it may, the enemies of the revolution derived hope from the delay, and the friends of the revolution, uneasiness.

During this state of suspense, the *Garde du Corps*,* which was composed, as such regiments generally are, of persons much connected with the Court, gave an entertainment at Versailles (Oct. I,) to some foreign regiments then arrived; and when the entertainment was at the height, on a signal given, the *Garde du Corps* tore the national cockade from their hats, trampled it under foot, and replaced it with a counter cockade prepared for the purpose. An indignity of this kind amounted to defiance. It was like declaring war;

and if men will give challenges, they must expect consequences. But all this Mr Burke has carefully kept out of sight. He begins his account by saying, 'History will record, that on the morning of the 6th of October 1789, the King and Queen of France, after a day of confusion, alarm, dismay, and slaughter, lay down under the pledged security of public faith, to indulge nature in a few hours of respite, and troubled melancholy repose.'* This is neither the sober stile of history, nor the intention of it. It leaves every thing to be guessed at, and mistaken. One would at least think there had been a battle; and a battle there probably would have been, had it not been for the moderating prudence of those whom Mr Burke involves in his censures. By his keeping the *Garde du Corps* out of sight, Mr Burke has afforded himself the dramatic licence of putting the King and Queen in their places, as if the object of the expedition was against them.—But, to return to my account—

This conduct of the *Garde du Corps*, as might well be expected, alarmed and enraged the Parisians. The colours of the cause, and the cause itself, were become too united to mistake the intention of the insult, and the Parisians were determined to call the *Garde du Corps* to an account. There was certainly nothing of the cowardice of assassination in marching in the face of day to demand satisfaction, if such a phrase may be used, of a body of armed men who had voluntarily given defiance. But the circumstance which serves to throw this affair into embarrassment is, that the enemies of the revolution appear to have encouraged it, as well as its friends. The one hoped to prevent a civil war by checking it in time, and the other to make one. The hopes of those opposed to the revolution, rested in making the King of their party, and getting him from Versailles to Metz,* where they expected to collect a force, and set up a standard. We have therefore two different objects presenting themselves at the same time, and to be accomplished by the same means: the one, to chastise the *Garde du Corps*, which was the object of the Parisians; the other, to render the confusion of such a scene an inducement to the King to set off for Metz.

On the 5th of October, a very numerous body of women, and men in the disguise of women, collected round the Hotel de Ville or town-hall at Paris, and set off for Versailles. Their professed object was the *Garde du Corps*; but prudent men readily recollect that mischief is more easily begun than ended; and this impressed itself with the more force, from the suspicions already stated, and the irregularity of such a cavalcade. As soon therefore as a sufficient force could be collected, M. de la Fayette, by orders from the civil authority of Paris, set off after them at the head of twenty thousand of the Paris militia. The revolution could derive no benefit from confusion, and its opposers might. By an amiable and spirited manner of address, he had hitherto been fortunate in calming disquietudes, and in this he was extraordinarily successful; to frustrate, therefore, the hopes of those who might seek to improve this scene into a sort of justifiable necessity for the King's quitting Versailles' and withdrawing to Metz, and to prevent at the same time the consequences that might ensue between the *Garde du Corps* and this phalanx of men and women, he forwarded expresses to the King, that he was on his march to Versailles, by the orders of the civil authority of Paris, for the purpose of peace and protection, expressing at the same time the necessity of restraining the *Garde du Corps* from firing upon the people.[1]

He arrived at Versailles between ten and eleven at night. The *Garde du Corps* was drawn up, and the people had arrived some time before, but every thing had remained suspended. Wisdom and policy now consisted in changing a scene of danger into a happy event. M. de la Fayette became the mediator between the enraged parties; and the King, to remove the uneasiness which had arisen from the delay already stated, sent for the President of the National Assembly,* and signed the *Declaration of the Rights of Man*, and such other parts of the constitution as were in readiness.

It was now about one in the morning. Every thing appeared to be composed, and a general congratulation took place. By the beat of drum a proclamation was made, that

---

[1] I am warranted in asserting this, as I had it personally from M. de la Fayette, with whom I have lived in habits of friendship for fourteen years.

the citizens of Versailles would give the hospitality of their houses to their fellow-citizens of Paris. Those who could not be accommodated in this manner, remained in the streets, or took up their quarters in the churches; and at two o'clock the King and Queen retired.

In this state matters passed till the break of day, when a fresh disturbance arose from the censurable conduct of some of both parties, for such characters there will be in all such scenes. One of the *Garde du Corps* appeared at one of the windows of the palace, and the people who had remained during the night in the streets accosted him with reviling and provocative language. Instead of retiring, as in such a case prudence would have dictated, he presented his musket, fired, and killed one of the Paris militia. The peace being thus broken, the people rushed into the palace in quest of the offender. They attacked the quarters of the *Garde du Corps* within the palace, and pursued them throughout the avenues of it, and to the apartments of the King. On this tumult, not the Queen only, as Mr Burke has represented it, but every person in the palace, was awakened and alarmed; and M. de la Fayette had a second time to interpose between the parties, the event of which was, that the *Garde du Corps* put on the national cockade, and the matter ended as by oblivion, after the loss of two or three lives.

During the latter part of the time in which this confusion was acting, the King and Queen were in public at the balcony, and neither of them concealed for safety's sake, as Mr Burke insinuates. Matters being thus appeased, and tranquillity restored, a general acclamation broke forth, of *Le Roi à Paris—Le Roi à Paris*—The King to Paris. It was the shout of peace, and immediately accepted on the part of the King. By this measure, all future projects of trapanning the King* to Metz, and setting up the standard of opposition to the constitution, were prevented, and the suspicions extinguished. The King and his family reached Paris in the evening, and were congratulated on their arrival by Mr Bailley* the Mayor of Paris, in the name of the citizens. Mr Burke, who throughout his book confounds things, persons, and principles, has in his remarks on M. Bailley's address, confounded time also. He censures M. Bailley for calling it, '*un bon jour*,' a good day. Mr Burke should have informed himself, that this scene took up the space of two days, the day on which it began with every appearance of danger and mischief, and the day on which it terminated without the mischiefs that threatened; and that it is to this peaceful termination that M. Bailley alludes, and to the arrival of the King at Paris. Not less than three hundred thousand persons arranged themselves in the procession from Versailles to Paris, and not an act of molestation was committed during the whole march.

Mr Burke, on the authority of M. Lally Tollendal,* a deserter from the National Assembly, says, that on entering Paris, the people shouted, '*Tous les eveques à la lanterne.*'* All Bishops to be hanged at the lanthorn or lamp-posts. —It is surprising that nobody could hear this but Lally Tollendal, and that nobody should believe it but Mr Burke. It has not the least connection with any part of the transaction, and is totally foreign to every circumstance of it. The bishops had never been introduced before into any scene of Mr Burke's drama; Why then are they, all at once, and altogether, *tout à coup et tous ensemble,*★ introduced now? Mr Burke brings forward his bishops and his lanthorn like figures in a magic lanthorn,* and raises his scenes by contrast instead of connection. But it serves to shew, with the rest of his book, what little credit ought to be given, where even probability is set at defiance, for the purpose of defaming; and with this reflection, instead of a soliloquy in praise of chivalry, as Mr Burke has done, I close the account of the expedition to Versailles.[1]

I have now to follow Mr Burke through a pathless wilderness of rhapsodies, and a sort of descant upon governments, in which he asserts whatever he pleases, on the presumption of its being believed, without offering either evidence or reasons for so doing.

Before any thing can be reasoned upon to a conclusion,

[1] An account of the expedition to Versailles may be seen in No. 13. of the *Revolution de Paris,*★ containing the events from the 3d to the 10th of October 1789.

certain facts, principles, or data, to reason from, must be established, admitted, or denied. Mr Burke, with his usual outrage, abuses the *Declaration of the Rights of Man*, published by the National Assembly of France as the basis on which the constitution of France is built. This he calls 'paltry and blurred sheets of paper about the rights of man.'*—Does Mr Burke mean to deny that *man* has any rights? If he does, then he must mean that there are no such things as rights any where, and that he has none himself; for who is there in the world but man? But if Mr Burke means to admit that man has rights, the question then will be, What are those rights, and how came man by them originally?

The error of those who reason by precedents drawn from antiquity, respecting the rights of man, is, that they do not go far enough into antiquity. They do not go the whole way. They stop in some of the intermediate stages of an hundred or a thousand years, and produce what was then done, as a rule for the present day. This is no authority at all. If we travel still farther into antiquity, we shall find a direct contrary opinion and practice prevailing; and if antiquity is to be authority, a thousand such authorities may be produced, successively contradicting each other: But if we proceed on, we shall at last come out right; we shall come to the time when man came from the hand of his Maker. What was he then? Man. Man was his high and only title, and a higher cannot be given him.—But of titles I shall speak hereafter.

We are now got at the origin of man, and at the origin of his rights. As to the manner in which the world has been governed from that day to this, it is no farther any concern of ours than to make a proper use of the errors or the improvements which the history of it presents. Those who lived a hundred or a thousand years ago, were then moderns, as we are now. They had *their* ancients, and those ancients had others, and we also shall be ancients in our turn. If the mere name of antiquity is to govern in the affairs of life, the people who are to live an hundred or a thousand years hence, may as well take us for a precedent, as we make a precedent of those who lived an hundred or a thousand years ago. The fact is, that portions of antiquity, by proving every thing, establish nothing. It is authority against authority all the way, till we come to the divine origin of the rights of man at the creation. Here our enquiries find a resting-place, and our reason finds a home. If a dispute about the rights of man had arisen at the distance of an hundred years from the creation, it is to this source of authority they must have referred, and it is to the same source of authority that we must now refer.

Though I mean not to touch upon any sectarian principle of religion, yet it may be worth observing, that the genealogy of Christ is traced to Adam.* Why then not trace the rights of man to the creation of man? I will answer the question. Because there have been upstart governments, thrusting themselves between, and presumptuously working to *unmake* man.

If any generation of men ever possessed the right of dictating the mode by which the world should be governed for ever, it was the first generation that existed; and if that generation did it not, no succeeding generation can shew any authority for doing it, nor can set any up. The illuminating and divine principle of the equal rights of man, (for it has its origin from the Maker of man) relates, not only to the living individuals, but to generations of men succeeding each other. Every generation is equal in rights to the generations which preceded it, by the same rule that every individual is born equal in rights with his contemporary.

Every history of the creation, and every traditionary account, whether from the lettered or unlettered world, however they may vary in their opinion or belief of certain particulars, all agree in establishing one point, *the unity of man*; by which I mean, that men are all of *one degree*, and consequently that all men are born equal, and with equal natural right, in the same manner as if posterity had been continued by *creation* instead of *generation*; the latter being only the mode by which the former is carried forward; and consequently, every child born into the world must be considered as deriving its existence from God. The world is as new to him as it was to the first man that existed, and his natural right in it is of the same kind.

The Mosaic* account of the creation, whether taken as divine authority, or merely historical, is full to this point, *the unity or equality of man*. The expressions admit of no controversy. 'And God said, Let us make man in our own image. In the image of God created he him; male and female created he them.'* The distinction of sexes is pointed out, but no other distinction is even implied. If this be not divine authority, it is at least historical authority, and shews that the equality of man, so far from being a modern doctrine, is the oldest upon record.

It is also to be observed, that all the religions known in the world are founded, so far as they relate to man, on the *unity of man*, as being all of one degree. Whether in heaven or in hell, or in whatever state man be supposed to exist hereafter, the good and the bad are the only distinctions. Nay, even the laws of governments are obliged to slide into this principle, by making degrees to consist in crimes, and not in persons.

It is one of the greatest of all truths, and of the highest advantage to cultivate. By considering man in this light, and by instructing him to consider himself in this light, it places him in a close connection with all his duties, whether to his Creator, or to the creation, of which he is a part; and it is only when he forgets his origin, or, to use a more fashionable phrase, his *birth and family*, that he becomes dissolute. It is not among the least of the evils of the present existing governments in all parts of Europe, that man, considered as man, is thrown back to a vast distance from his Maker, and the artificial chasm filled up by a succession of barriers, or sort of turnpike gates, through which he has to pass. I will quote Mr Burke's catalogue of barriers that he has set up between man and his Maker. Putting himself in the character of a herald, he says—. 'We fear God—we look with *awe* to kings—with affection to parliaments—with duty to magistrates—with reverence to priests, and with respect to nobility.'* Mr Burke has forgotten to put in '*chivalry*.' He has also forgotten to put in Peter.*

The duty of man is not a wilderness of turnpike gates, through which he is to pass by tickets from one to the other.

It is plain and simple, and consists but of two points. His duty to God, which every man must feel; and with respect to his neighbour, to do as he would be done by. If those to whom power is delegated do well, they will be respected; if not, they will be despised: and with regard to those to whom no power is delegated, but who assume it, the rational world can know nothing of them.

Hitherto we have spoken only (and that but in part) of the natural rights of man. We have now to consider the civil rights of man, and to shew how the one originates from the other. Man did not enter into society to become *worse* than he was before, nor to have fewer rights than he had before, but to have those rights better secured. His natural rights are the foundation of all his civil rights. But in order to pursue this distinction with more precision, it will be necessary to mark the different qualities of natural and civil rights.

A few words will explain this. Natural rights are those which appertain to man in right of his existence. Of this kind are all the intellectual rights, or rights of the mind, and also all those rights of acting as an individual for his own comfort and happiness, which are not injurious to the natural rights of others.—Civil rights are those which appertain to man in right of his being a member of society. Every civil right has for its foundation, some natural right pre-existing in the individual, but to the enjoyment of which his individual power is not, in all cases, sufficiently competent. Of this kind are all those which relate to security and protection.

From this short review, it will be easy to distinguish between that class of natural rights which man retains after entering into society, and those which he throws into the common stock as a member of society.

The natural rights which he retains, are all those in which the *power* to execute is as perfect in the individual as the right itself. Among this class, as is before mentioned, are all the intellectual rights, or rights of the mind: consequently, religion is one of those rights. The natural rights which are not retained, are all those in which, though the right is perfect in the individual, the power to execute them is defective. They answer not his purpose. A man, by natural right, has a right to judge in his own cause; and so far as the right of the mind is concerned, he never surrenders it: But what availeth it him to judge, if he has not power to redress? He therefore deposits this right in the common stock of society, and takes the arm of society, of which he is a part, in preference and in addition to his own. Society *grants* him nothing. Every man is a proprietor in society, and draws on the capital as a matter of right.

From these premises, two or three certain conclusions will follow.

First, That every civil right grows out of a natural right; or, in other words, is a natural right exchanged.

Secondly, That civil power, properly considered as such, is made up of the aggregate of that class of the natural rights of man, which becomes defective in the individual in point of power, and answers not his purpose; but when collected to a focus, becomes competent to the purpose of every one.

Thirdly, That the power produced from the aggregate of natural rights, imperfect in power in the individual, cannot be applied to invade the natural rights which are retained in the individual, and in which the power to execute is as perfect as the right itself.

We have now, in a few words, traced man from a natural individual to a member of society, and shewn, or endeavoured to shew, the quality of the natural rights retained, and of those which are exchanged for civil rights. Let us now apply these principles to governments.

In casting our eyes over the world, it is extremely easy to distinguish the governments which have arisen out of society, or out of the social compact, from those which have not: but to place this in a clearer light than what a single glance may afford, it will be proper to take a review of the several sources from which governments have arisen, and on which they have been founded.

They may be all comprehended under three heads. First, Superstition. Secondly, Power. Thirdly, The common interest of society, and the common rights of man.

The first was a government of priestcraft, the second of conquerors, and the third of reason.

When a set of artful men pretended, through the medium of oracles, to hold intercourse with the Deity, as familiarly as they now march up the backstairs in European courts,* the world was completely under the government of superstition. The oracles were consulted, and whatever they were made to say, became the law; and this sort of government lasted as long as this sort of superstition lasted.

After these a race of conquerors arose, whose government, like that of William the Conqueror,* was founded in power, and the sword assumed the name of a scepter. Governments thus established, last as long as the power to support them lasts; but that they might avail themselves of every engine in their favour, they united fraud to force, and set up an idol which they called *Divine Right*, and which, in imitation of the Pope, who affects to be spiritual and temporal, and in contradiction to the Founder of the Christian religion, twisted itself afterwards into an idol of another shape, called *Church and State*. The key of St Peter, and the key of the Treasury,* became quartered on one another, and the wondering cheated multitude worshipped the invention.

When I contemplate the natural dignity of man; when I feel (for Nature has not been kind enough to me to blunt my feelings) for the honour and happiness of its character, I become irritated at the attempt to govern mankind by force and fraud, as if they were all knaves and fools, and can scarcely avoid disgust at those who are thus imposed upon.

We have now to review the governments which arise out of society, in contradistinction to those which arose out of superstition and conquest.

It has been thought a considerable advance towards establishing the principles of Freedom, to say, that government is a compact between those who govern and those who are governed: but this cannot be true, because it is putting the effect before the cause; for as man must have existed before governments existed, there necessarily was a time when governments did not exist, and consequently there could originally exist no governors to form such a compact with.

The fact therefore must be, that the *individuals themselves*, each in his own personal and sovereign right, *entered into a compact with each other* to produce a government: and this is the only mode in which governments have a right to arise, and the only principle on which they have a right to exist.

To possess ourselves of a clear idea of what government is, or ought to be, we must trace it to its origin. In doing this, we shall easily discover that governments must have arisen, either *out* of the people, or *over* the people. Mr Burke has made no distinction. He investigates nothing to its source, and therefore he confounds every thing: but he has signified his intention of undertaking at some future opportunity,* a comparison between the constitutions of England and France. As he thus renders it a subject of controversy by throwing the gauntlet, I take him up on his own ground. It is in high challenges that high truths have the right of appearing; and I accept it with the more readiness, because it affords me, at the same time, an opportunity of pursuing the subject with respect to governments arising out of society.

But it will be first necessary to define what is meant by constitution. It is not sufficient that we adopt the word; we must fix also a standard signification to it.

A constitution is not a thing in name only, but in fact. It has not an ideal, but a real existence; and wherever it cannot be produced in a visible form, there is none. A constitution is a thing *antecedent* to a government, and a government is only the creature of a constitution. The constitution of a country is not the act of its government, but of the people constituting a government. It is the body of elements, to which you can refer, and quote article by article; and which contains the principles on which the government shall be established, the manner in which it shall be organized, the powers it shall have, the mode of elections, the duration of parliaments, or by what other name such bodies may be called; the powers which the executive part of the government shall have; and, in fine, every thing that relates to the compleat organization of a civil government, and the principles on which it shall act, and by which it shall be bound. A constitution, therefore, is to a government, what the laws made afterwards by that government are to a court of judicature. The court of judicature does not make the laws, neither can it alter them; it only acts in conformity to the laws made: and the government is in like manner governed by the constitution.

Can then Mr Burke produce the English Constitution? If he cannot, we may fairly conclude, that though it has been so much talked about, no such thing as a constitution exists, or ever did exist, and consequently that the people have yet a constitution to form.

Mr Burke will not, I presume, deny the position I have already advanced; namely, that governments arise, either *out* of the people, or *over* the people. The English governement is one of those which arose out of a conquest, and not out of society, and consequently it arose over the people; and though it has been much modified from the opportunity of circumstances since the time of William the Conqueror, the country has never yet regenerated itself, and is therefore without a constitution.

I readily perceive the reason why Mr Burke declined going into the comparison between the English and French constitutions, because he could not but perceive, when he sat down to the task, that no such thing as a constitution existed on his side of the question. His book is certainly bulky enough to have contained all he could say on this subject, and it would have been the best manner in which people could have judged of their separate merits. Why then has he declined the only thing that was worth while to write upon? It was the strongest ground he could take, if the advantages were on his side; but the weakest, if they were not: and his declining to take it, is either a sign that he could not possess it, or could not maintain it.

Mr Burke said in a speech last winter in parliament,* That when the National Assembly first met in three Orders, (the Tiers Etats, the Clergy, and the Noblesse), France had then a good constitution. This shews, among numerous other instances, that Mr Burke does not understand what a constitution is. The persons so met, were not a *constitution*, but a *convention*, to make a constitution.

The present National Assembly of France is, strictly speaking, the personal social compact.—The members of it are the delegates of the nation in its *original* character; future assemblies will be the delegates of the nation in its *organized* character. The authority of the present Assembly is different to what the authority of future Assemblies will be. The authority of the present one is to form a constitution: the authority of future Assemblies will be to legislate according to the principles and forms prescribed in that constitution; and if experience should hereafter shew that alterations, amendments, or additions, are necessary, the constitution will point out the mode by which such things shall be done, and not leave it to the discretionary power of the future government.

A government on the principles on which constitutional governments arising out of society are established, cannot have the right of altering itself. If it had, it would be arbitrary. It might make itself what it pleased; and wherever such a right is set up, it shews there is no constitution. The act by which the English Parliament empowered itself to sit seven years,* shews there is no constitution in England. It might, by the same self-authority, have sat any greater number of years, or for life. The Bill which the present Mr Pitt brought into parliament some years ago,* to reform parliament, was on the same erroneous principle. The right of reform is in the nation in its original character, and the constitutional method would be by a general convention elected for the purpose. There is, moreover, a paradox in the idea of vitiated bodies reforming themselves.

From these preliminaries I proceed to draw some comparisons. I have already spoken of the declaration of rights; and as I mean to be as concise as possible, I shall proceed to other parts of the French constitution.

The constitution of France says,* That every man who pays a tax of sixty sous *per annum*,* (2s. and 6d. English), is an elector.—What article will Mr Burke place against this? Can any thing be more limited, and at the same time more capricious, than the qualifications of electors are in England? Limited—because not one man in an hundred (I speak much within compass) is admitted to vote: Capricious—because the lowest character that can be supposed to exist, and who has not so much as the visible means of an honest livelihood, is an elector in some places; while, in other places, the man who pays very large taxes, and has a known fair character, and the farmer who rents to the amount of three or four hundred pounds a year, with a property on that farm to three or four times that amount, is not admitted to be an elector. Every thing is out of nature, as Mr Burke says on another occasion, in this strange chaos, and all sorts of follies are blended with all sorts of crimes. William the Conqueror and his descendants parcelled out the country in this manner, and bribed some parts of it by what they called Charters, to hold the other parts of it the better subjected to their will. This is the reason why so many of those charters abound in Cornwall; the people were averse to the government established at the Conquest, and the towns were garrisoned and bribed to enslave the country. All the old charters are the badges of this conquest, and it is from this source that the capriciousness of elections arises.

The French constitution says, That the number of representatives for any place shall be in a ratio to the number of taxable inhabitants or electors.* What article will Mr Burke place against this? The county of Yorkshire, which contains near a million of souls, sends two county members; and so does the county of Rutland, which contains not an hundredth part of that number. The town of old Sarum, which contains not three houses, sends two members; and the town of Manchester, which contains upwards of sixty thousand souls, is not admitted to send any. Is there any principle in these things? Is there any thing by which you can trace the marks of freedom, or discover those of wisdom? No wonder, then, Mr Burke has declined the comparison, and endeavoured to lead his readers from the point by a wild unsystematical display of paradoxical rhapsodies.

The French constitution says, That the National Assembly shall be elected every two years.—What article will Mr Burke place against this? Why, that the nation has no right at all in the case: that the government is perfectly arbitrary with respect to this point; and he can quote for his authority, the precedent of a former parliament.

The French constitution says, There shall be no game laws,* that the farmer on whose lands wild game shall be found (for it is by the produce of his lands they are fed) shall have a right to what he can take: That there shall be no monopolies of any kind—that all trade shall be free,* and every man free to follow any occupation by which he can procure an honest livelihood, and in any place, town or city throughout the nation.—What will Mr Burke say to this? In England, game is made the property of those at whose expence it is not fed; and with respect to monopolies, the country is cut up into monopolies. Every chartered town is an aristocratical monopoly in itself, and the qualification of electors proceeds out of those chartered monopolies. Is this freedom? Is this what Mr Burke means by a constitution?

In these chartered monopolies, a man coming from another part of the country, is hunted from them as if he were a foreign enemy. An Englishman is not free of his own country: every one of those places presents a barrier in his way, and tells him he is not a freeman—that he has no rights. Within these monopolies, are other monopolies. In a city, such for instance as Bath, which contains between twenty and thirty thousand inhabitants, the right of electing representatives to parliament is monopolised by about thirty-one persons. And within these monopolies are still others. A man even of the same town, whose parents were not in circumstances to give him an occupation, is debarred, in many cases, from the natural right of acquiring one, be his genius or industry what it may.

Are these things examples to hold out to a country regenerating itself from slavery, like France?—Certainly they are not; and certain am I, that when the people of England come to reflect upon them, they will, like France, annihilate those badges of ancient oppression, those traces of a conquered nation.—Had Mr Burke possessed talents similar to the author 'On the Wealth of Nations,'* he would have comprehended all the parts which enter into, and, by assemblage, form a constitution. He would have reasoned from minutiæ to magnitude. It is not from his prejudices only, but from the disorderly cast of his genius, that he is unfitted for the subject he writes upon. Even his genius is without a constitution. It is a genius at random, and not a genius constituted. But he must say something—He has therefore mounted in the air like a balloon, to draw the eyes of the multitude from the ground they stand upon.

Much is to be learned from the French constitution. Conquest and tyranny transplanted themselves with William the Conqueror from Normandy into England, and the country is yet disfigured with the marks. May then the example of all France contribute to regenerate the freedom which a province of it destroyed!

The French constitution says, That to preserve the national representation from being corrupt, no member of the National Assembly shall be an officer of the government, a place-man, or a pensioner.*— What will Mr Burke place against this? I will whisper his answer: *Loaves and fishes.** Ah! this government of loaves and fishes has more mischief in it than people have yet reflected on. The National Assembly has made the discovery, and it holds out the example to the world. Had governments agreed to quarrel on purpose to fleece their countries by taxes, they could not have succeeded better than they have done.

Many things in the English government appear to me the reverse of what they ought to be, and of what they are said to be. The Parliament, imperfectly and capriciously elected as it is, is nevertheless *supposed* to hold the national purse in *trust* for the nation: but in the manner in which an English parliament is constructed, it is like a man being both mortgager and mortgagee; and in the case of misapplication of trust, it is the criminal fitting in judgment upon himself. If those who vote the supplies are the same persons who receive the supplies when voted, and are to account for the expenditure of those supplies to those who voted them, it is *themselves accountable to themselves*, and the Comedy of Errors concludes with the Pantomine of HUSH.* Neither the ministerial party, nor the opposition, will touch upon this case. The national purse is the common hack which each mounts upon. It is like what the country people call, 'Ride and tie—You ride a little way, and then I.'[1]—They order these things better in France.

The French constitution says, That the right of war and peace is in the nation. Where else should it reside, but in those who are to pay the expence?

In England, this right is said to reside in a *metaphor*, shewn at the Tower for sixpence or a shilling a-piece: So are the lions;* and it would be a step nearer to reason to say it resided in them, for any inanimate metaphor is no more than a hat or a cap. We can all see the absurdity of worshipping Aaron's molten calf,* or Nebuchadnezzar's golden image;* but why do men continue to practice themselves the absurdities they despise in others?

It may with reason be said, that in the manner the English nation is represented, it signifies not where this right resides, whether in the Crown, or in the Parliament. War is the common harvest of all those who participate in the division and expenditure of public money, in all countries. It is the art of *conquering at home*;* the object of it is an increase of revenue; and as revenue cannot be increased without taxes, a pretence must be made for expenditures. In reviewing the history of the English Government, its wars and its taxes, a by-stander, not blinded by prejudice, nor warped by interest, would declare, that taxes were not raised to carry on wars, but that wars were raised to carry on taxes.

Mr Burke, as a Member of the House of Commons, is a part of the English Government; and though he professes himself an enemy to war, he abuses the French Constitution, which seeks to explode it. He holds up the English Government as a model in all its parts, to France; but he should first know the remarks which the French make upon it. They contend, in favour of their own, that the portion of liberty enjoyed in England, is just enough to enslave a country by, more productively than by despotism; and that

---

[1] It is a practice in some parts of the country, when two travellers have but one horse, which like the national purse will not carry double, that the one mounts and rides two or three miles a-head, and then ties the horse to a gate, and walks on. When the second traveller arrives, he takes the horse, rides on, and passes his companion a mile or two, and ties again; and so on—*Ride and tie*.

as the real object of all despotism is revenue, a Government so formed obtains more than it could do either by direct despotism, or in a full state of freedom, and is therefore, on the ground of interest, opposed to both. They account also for the readiness which always appears in such governments for engaging in wars, by remarking on the different motives which produce them. In despotic governments, wars are the effect of pride; but in those governments in which they become the means of taxation, they acquire thereby a more permanent promptitude.

The French Constitution, therefore, to provide against both these evils, has taken away the power of declaring war from kings and ministers, and placed the right where the expence must fall.

When the question on the right of war and peace was agitating in the National Assembly, the people of England appeared to be much interested in the event, and highly to applaud the decision.—As a principle, it applies as much to one country as to another. William the Conquerer, *as a conqueror*, held this power of war and peace in himself, and his descendants have ever since claimed it under him as a right.

Although Mr Burke has asserted the right of the parliament at the Revolution to bind and controul the nation and posterity for *ever*, he denies, at the same time, that the parliament or the nation had any right to alter what he calls the succession of the crown, in any thing but in part, or by a sort of modification. By his taking this ground, he throws the case back to the *Norman Conquest*; and by thus running a line of succession springing from William the Conqueror to the present day, he makes it necessary to enquire who and what William the Conqueror was, and where he came from; and into the origin, history, and nature of what are called perogatives. Every thing must have had a beginning, and the fog of time and antiquity should be penetrated to discover it. Let then Mr Burke bring forward his William of Normandy, for it is to this origin that his argument goes. It also unfortunately happens, in running this line of succession, that another line, parallel thereto, presents itself, which is, that if the succession runs in the line of the conquest, the nation runs in the line of being conquered, and it ought to rescue itself from this reproach.

But it will perhaps be said, that tho' the power of declaring war descends in the heritage of the conquest, it is held in check by the right of the parliament to with-hold the supplies. It will always happen, when a thing is originally wrong, that amendments do not make it right; and it often happens, that they do as much mischief one way, as good the other: and such is the case here; for if the one rashly declares war as a matter of right, and the other peremptorily with-holds the supplies as a matter of right, the remedy becomes as bad, or worse than the disease. The one forces the nation to a combat, and the other ties its hands: but the more probable issue is, that the contest will end in a collusion between the parties, and be made a screen to both.

On this question of war, three things are to be considered. First, the right of declaring it: Secondly, the expence of supporting it: Thirdly, the mode of conducting it after it is declared. The French constitution places the *right* where the *expence* must fall, and this union can be only in the nation. The mode of conducting it after it is declared, it consigns to the executive department.—Were this the case in all countries, we should hear but little more of wars.

Before I proceed to consider other parts of the French constitution, and by way of relieving the fatigue of argument, I will introduce an anecdote which I had from Dr Franklin.—

While the Doctor resided in France as minister from America during the war, he had numerous proposals made to him by projectors of every country and of every kind, who wished to go to the land that floweth with milk and honey,* America; and among the rest, there was one who offered himself to be the King. He introduced his proposal to the Doctor by letter, which is now in the hands of M. Beaumarchais,* of Paris—stating, first, that as the Americans had dismissed or sent away¹ their King, that they would want another. Secondly, that himself was a Norman. Thirdly, that he was of a more ancient family than the

¹ The word he used was *renvoyé*, dismissed or sent away.

Dukes of Normandy, and of a more honourable descent, his line having never been bastardized. Fourthly, that there was already a precedent in England, of Kings coming out of Normandy: and on these grounds he rested his offer, *enjoining* that the Doctor would forward it to America. But as the Doctor neither did this, not yet sent him an answer, the projector wrote a second letter; in which he did not, it is true, threaten to go over and conquer America, but only with great dignity proposed, that if his offer was not accepted, an acknowledgment of about £30,000 might be made to him for his generosity!—Now, as all arguments respecting succession must necessarily connect that succession with some beginning, Mr Burke's arguments on this subject go to shew, that there is no English origin of kings, and that they are descendants of the Norman line in right of the Conquest. It may, therefore, be of service to his doctrine to make this story known, and to inform him, that in case of that natural extinction to which all mortality is subject, Kings may again be had from Normandy, on more reasonable terms than William the Conqueror; and consequently, that the good people of England, at the Revolution of 1688, *might have done much better*, had such a generous Norman as *this* known *their* wants, and they had known *his*. The chivalry character which Mr Burke so much admires, is certainly much earlier to make a bargain with, than a *hard-dealing Dutchman*.*— But, to return to the matters of the constitution—

The French constitution says, *There shall be no titles*,* and of consequence, all that class of equivocal generation, which in some countries is called '*aristocracy*,' and in others '*nobility*,' is done away, and the *peer* is exalted into MAN.

Titles are but nick-names, and every nick-name is a title. The thing is perfectly harmless in itself; but it marks a sort of foppery in the human character, which degrades it. It reduces man into the diminutive of man in things which are great, and the counterfeit of woman in things which are little. It talks about its fine *blue ribbon* like a girl, and shews its new *garter** like a child. A certain writer of some antiquity, says, 'When I was a child, I thought as a child; but when I became a man, I put away childish things.'*

It is, properly, from the elevated mind of France, that the folly of titles has fallen. It has outgrown the baby-cloaths of *Count* and *Duke*, and breeched itself in manhood. France has not levelled; it has exalted. It has put down the dwarf, to set up the man. The punyism of a senseless word like *Duke*, or *Count*, or *Earl*, has ceased to please. Even those who possessed them have disowned the gibberish, and as they outgrew the rickets,* have despised the rattle. The genuine mind of man, thirsting for its native home, society, contemns the gewgaws* that separate him from it. Titles are like circles drawn by the magician's wand, to contract the sphere of man's felicity. He lives immured within the Bastille of a word, and surveys at a distance the envied life of man.

Is it then any wonder that titles should fall in France? Is it not a greater wonder they should be kept up any-where? What are they? What is their worth, and 'what is their amount?' When we think or speak of a *Judge* or a *General*, we associate with it the ideas of office and character; we think of gravity in the one, and bravery in the other: but when we use a word *merely as a title*, no ideas associate with it. Through all the vocabulary of Adam, there is not such an animal as a Duke or a Count; neither can we connect any certain idea with the words. Whether they mean strength or weakness, wisdom or folly, a child or a man, or the rider or the horse, is all equivocal. What respect then can be paid to that which describes nothing, and which means nothing? Imagination has given figure and character to centaurs, satyrs, and down to all the fairy tribe; but titles baffle even the powers of fancy, and are a chimerical non-descript.

But this is not all.—If a whole country is disposed to hold them in contempt, all their value is gone, and none will own them. It is common opinion only that makes them any thing, or nothing, or worse than nothing. There is no occasion to take titles away, for they take themselves away when society concurs to ridicule them. This species of imaginary consequence has visibly declined in every part of Europe, and it hastens to its exit as the world of reason continues to rise. There was a time when the lowest class of what are called nobility was more thought of than the highest is now, and when a man in armour riding throughout Christendom in quest of adventures was more stared at than a modern Duke. The world has seen this folly fall, and it has fallen by being laughed at, and the farce of titles will follow its fate.— The patriots of France have discovered in good time, that rank and dignity in society must take a new ground. The old one has fallen through.—It must now take the substantial ground of character, instead of the chimerical ground of titles; and they have brought their titles to the altar, and made of them a burnt-offering to Reason.

If no mischief had annexed itself to the folly of titles, they would not have been worth a serious and formal destruction, such as the National Assembly have decreed them: and this makes it necessary to enquire farther into the nature and character of aristocracy.

That, then, which is called aristocracy in some countries, and nobility in others, arose out of the governments founded upon conquest. It was originally a military order, for the purpose of supporting military government, (for such were all governments founded in conquest); and to keep up a succession of this order for the purpose for which it was established, all the younger branches of those families were disinherited, and the law of *primogenitureship* set up.*

The nature and character of aristocracy shews itself to us in this law. It is a law against every law of nature, and Nature herself calls for its destruction. Establish family justice, and aristocracy falls. By the aristocratical law of primogenitureship, in a family of six children, five are exposed. Aristocracy has never more than *one* child. The rest are begotten to be devoured. They are thrown to the cannibal for prey, and the natural parent prepares the unnatural repast.

As every thing which is out of nature in man, affects, more or less, the interest of society, so does this. All the children which the aristocracy disowns (which are all, except the eldest) are, in general, cast like orphans on a parish, to be provided for by the public, but at a greater charge.— Unnecessary offices and places in governments and courts are created at the expence of the public, to maintain them.

With what kind of parental reflections can the father or

mother contemplate their younger offspring. By nature they are children, and by marriage they are heirs; but by aristocracy they are bastards and orphans. They are the flesh and blood of their parents in one line, and nothing akin to them in the other. To restore, therefore, parents to their children, and children to their parents—relations to each other, and man to society—and to exterminate the monster Aristocracy, root and branch—the French constitution has destroyed the law of PRIMOGENITURESHIP. Here then lies the monster; and Mr Burke, if he pleases, may write its epitaph.

Hitherto we have considered aristocracy chiefly in one point of view. We have now to consider it in another. But whether we view it before or behind, or side-ways, or any way else, domestically or publicly, it is still a monster.

In France, aristocracy had one feature less in its countenance, than what it has in some other countries. It did not compose a body of hereditary legislators. It was not '*a corporation of aristocracy*,'* for such I have heard M. de la Fayette describe an English House of Peers. Let us then examine the grounds upon which the French constitution has resolved against having such a House in France.

Because, in the first place, as is already mentioned, aristocracy is kept up by family tyranny and injustice.

Secondly, Because there is an unnatural unfitness in an aristocracy to be legislators for a nation. Their ideas of *distributive justice* are corrupted at the very source. They begin life by trampling on all their younger brothers and sisters, and relations of every kind, and are taught and educated so to do. With what ideas of justice or honour can that man enter a house of legislation, who absorbs in his own person the inheritance of a whole family of children, or doles out to them some pitiful portion with the insolence of a gift?

Thirdly, Because the idea of hereditary legislators is as inconsistent as that of hereditary judges, or hereditary juries; and as absurd as an hereditary mathematician, or an hereditary wise man; and as ridiculous as an hereditary poet-laureat.

Fourthly, Because a body of men holding themselves accountable to nobody, ought not to be trusted by any body.

Fifthly, Because it is continuing the uncivilized principle of governments founded in conquest, and the base idea of man having property in man, and governing him by personal right.

Sixthly, Because aristocracy has a tendency to degenerate the human species.—By the universal œconomy of nature it is known, and by the instance of the Jews it is proved, that the human species has a tendency to degenerate, in any small number of persons, when separated from the general stock of society, and intermarrying constantly with each other. It defeats even its pretended end, and becomes in time the opposite of what is noble in man. Mr Burke talks of nobility; let him shew what it is. The greatest characters the world have known, have risen on the democratic floor. Aristocracy has not been able to keep a proportionate pace with democracy. The artificial NOBLE shrinks into a dwarf before the NOBLE of Nature; and in the few instances of those (for there are some in all countries) in whom nature, as by a miracle, has survived in aristocracy, THOSE MEN DESPISE IT.—But it is time to proceed to a new subject.

The French constitution has reformed the condition of the clergy.* It has raised the income of the lower and middle classes, and taken from the higher. None is now less than twelve hundred livres (fifty pounds sterling), nor any higher than about two or three thousand pounds. What will Mr Burke place against this? Hear what he says.

He says, 'That the people of England can see without pain or grudging, an archbishop precede a duke; they can see a bishop of Durham, or a bishop of Winchester, in possession of £10,000 a-year; and cannot see why it is in worse hands than estates to the like amount in the hands of this earl or that 'squire.'* And Mr Burke offers this as an example to France.

As to the first part, whether the archbishop precedes the duke, or the duke the bishop, it is, I beleive, to the people in general, somewhat like *Sternhold* and *Hopkins*, or *Hopkins* and *Sternhold*;* you may put which you please first; and as I confess that I do not understand the merits of this case, I will not contend it with Mr Burke.

But with respect to the latter, I have something to say.—
Mr Burke has not put the case right.—The comparison is
out of order, by being put between the bishop and the earl
or the 'squire. It ought to be put between the bishop and the
curate, and then it will stand thus:—*The people of England
can see without pain or grudging, a bishop of Durham, or a
bishop of Winchester, in possession of ten thousand pounds a-
year, and a curate on thirty or forty pounds a-year, or less.*—
No, Sir, they certainly do not see those things without great
pain or grudging. It is a case that applies itself to every
man's sense of justice, and is one among many that calls
aloud for a constitution.

In France, the cry of '*the church! the church!*' was repeated
as often as in Mr Burke's book, and as loudly as when the
dissenters' bill was before the English parliament;* but the
generality of the French clergy were not to be deceived by
this cry any longer. They knew, that whatever the pretence
might be, it was themselves who were one of the principal
objects of it. It was the cry of the high beneficed clergy, to
prevent any regulation of income taking place between those
of ten thousand pounds a-year and the parish priest. They,
therefore, joined their case to those of every other oppressed
class of men, and by this union obtained redress.

The French constitution has abolished tythes,* that source
of perpetual discontent between the tythe-holder and the
parishioner. When land is held on tythe, it is in the condition
of an estate held between two parties; the one receiving one-
tenth, and the other nine-tenths of the produce: and, consequently, on principles of equity, if the estate can be
improved, and made to produce by that improvement double
or treble what it did before, or in any other ratio, the
expence of such improvement ought to be borne in like
proportion between the parties who are to share the produce.
But this is not the case in tythes; the farmer bears the whole
expence, and the tythe-holder takes a tenth of the improvement, in addition to the original tenth, and by this means
gets the value of two-tenths instead of one. This is another
case that calls for a constitution.

The French constitution hath abolished or renounced

Toleration, and *Intolerance* also, and hath established UNI-
VERSAL RIGHT OF CONSCIENCE.*

Toleration is not the *opposite* of Intolerance, but is the
counterfeit of it. Both are despotisms. The one assumes to
itself the right of with-holding Liberty of Conscience, and
the other of granting it. The one is the pope armed with fire
and faggot, and the other is the pope selling or granting
indulgencies. The former is church and state, and the latter
is church and traffic.*

But Toleration may be viewed in a much stronger light.
Man worships not himself, but his Maker; and the liberty of
conscience which he claims, is not for the service of himself,
but of his God. In this case, therefore, we must necessarily
have the associated idea of two beings; the *mortal* who
renders the worship, and the IMMORTAL BEING who is
worshipped. Toleration, therefore, places itself, not between
man and man, nor between church and church, nor between
one denomination of religion and another, but between God
and man; between the being who worships, and the BEING
who is worshipped; and by the same act of assumed authority
by which it tolerates man to pay his worship, it presumptuously and blasphemously sets itself up to tolerate the Almighty to receive it.

Were a Bill brought into any parliament, intitled 'AN ACT
to tolerate or grant liberty to the Almighty to receive the
worship of a Jew or a Turk,' or 'to prohibit the Almighty
from receiving it,' all men would startle, and call it blas-
phemy. There would be an uproar. The presumption of
toleration in religious matters would then present itself un-
masked: but the presumption is not the less because the name
of 'Man' only appears to those laws, for the associated idea of
the *worshipper* and the *worshipped* cannot be separated.—
Who, then, art thou, vain dust and ashes!* by whatever name
thou art called, whether a King, a Bishop, a Church or a
State, a Parliament, or any thing else, that obtrudest thine
insignificance between the soul of man and its Maker? Mind
thine own concerns. If he believes not as thou believest, it is a
proof that thou believest not as he believeth, and there is no
earthly power can determine between you.

With respect to what are called denominations of religion, if every one is left to judge of its own religion, there is no such thing as a religion that is wrong; but if they are to judge of each others religion, there is no such thing as a religion that is right; and therefore, all the world is right, or all the world is wrong. But with respect to religion itself, without regard to names, and as directing itself from the universal family of mankind to the Divine object of all adoration, *it is man bringing to his Maker the fruits of his heart*; and though those fruits may differ from each other like the fruits of the earth, the grateful tribute of every one is accepted.

A Bishop of Durham, or a Bishop of Winchester, or the Archbishop who heads the Dukes, will not refuse a tythe-sheaf of wheat, because it is not a cock of hay;* nor a cock of hay, because it is not a sheaf of wheat; nor a pig, because it is neither one nor the other: but these same persons, under the figure of an established church, will not permit their Maker to receive the varied tythes of man's devotion.

One of the continual choruses of Mr Burke's book is, 'Church and State.' He does not mean some one particular church, or some one particular state, but any church and state; and he uses the term as a general figure to hold forth the political doctrine of always uniting the church with the state in every country, and he censures the National Assembly for not having done this in France.—Let us bestow a few thoughts on this subject.

All religions are in their nature kind and benign, and united with principles of morality. They could not have made proselites at first, by professing any thing that was vicious, cruel, persecuting, or immoral. Like every thing else, they had their beginning; and they proceeded by persuasion, exhortation, and example. How then is it that they lose their native mildness, and become morose and intolerant?

It proceeds from the connection which Mr Burke recommends. By engendering the church with the state, a sort of mule-animal, capable only of destroying, and not of breeding up, is produced, called *The Church established by Law*. It is a stranger, even from its birth, to any parent mother on which it is begotten, and whom in time it kicks out and destroys.

The inquisition in Spain* does not proceed from the religion originally professed, but from this mule-animal, engendered between the church and the state. The burnings in Smithfield* proceeded from the same heterogeneous production; and it was the regeneration of this strange animal in England afterwards, that renewed rancour and irreligion among the inhabitants, and that drove the people called Quakers* and Dissenters to America. Persecution is not an original feature in *any* religion; but it is always the strongly-marked feature of all law-religions, or religions established by law. Take away the law-establishment, and every religion reassumes its original benignity. In America, a Catholic Priest is a good citizen, a good character, and a good neighbour; an Episcopalian* Minister is of the same description: and this proceeds, independently of the men, from there being no law-establishment in America.

If also we view this matter in a temporal sense, we shall see the ill effects it has had on the prosperity of nations. The union of church and state has impoverished Spain. The revoking the edict of Nantes* drove the silk manufacture from France into England; and church and state are now driving the cotton manufacture from England to America and France. Let then Mr Burke continue to preach his antipolitical doctrine of Church and State. It will do some good. The National Assembly will not follow his advice, but will benefit by his folly. It was by observing the ill effects of it in England, that America has been warned against it; and it is by experiencing them in France, that the National Assembly have abolished it, and, like America, have established UNIVERSAL RIGHT OF CONSCIENCE, AND UNIVERSAL RIGHT OF CITIZENSHIP.[1]

I will here cease the comparison with respect to the principles of the French constitution, and conclude this part of the subject with a few observations on the organization of the formal parts of the French and English governments.

[1] When in any country we see extraordinary circumstances taking place, they naturally lead any man who has a talent for observation and investigation, to enquire into the causes. The manufactures of Manchester, Birmingham, and Sheffield, are the principal manufactures in England. From whence did this arise? A little observation will explain the case. The principal, and the generality of the inhabitants of those places, are not of what is called in England, *the church*

The executive power in each country is in the hands of a person stiled the King; but the French constitution distinguishes between the King and the Sovereign: It considers the station of King as official, and places Sovereignty in the nation.*

The representatives of the nation, who compose the National Assembly, and who are the legislative power, originate in and from the people by election, as an inherent right in the people.—In England it is otherwise; and this arises from the original establishment of what is called its monarchy; for, as by the conquest all the rights of the people or the nation were absorbed into the hands of the Conqueror, and who added the title of King to that of Conqueror, those same matters which in France are now held as rights in the people, or in the nation, are held in England as grants from what is called the Crown. The Parliament in England, in both its branches, was erected by patents* from the descendants of the Conqueror. The House of Commons did not originate as a matter of right in the people to delegate or elect, but as a grant or boon.

established by law; and they, or their fathers, (for it is within but a few years), withdrew from the persecution of the chartered towns, where test-laws more particularly operate, and established a sort of asylum for themselves in those places. It was the only asylum that then offered, for the rest of Europe was worse.—But the case is now changing. France and America bid all comers welcome, and initiate them into all the rights of citizenship. Policy and interest, therefore, will, but perhaps too late, dictate in England, what reason and justice could not. Those manufactures are withdrawing, and are arising in other places. There is now erecting at Passey, three miles from Paris, a large cotton-mill, and several are already erected in America. Soon after the rejecting the Bill for repealing the test-law, one of the richest manufactures in England said in my hearing, 'England, Sir, is not a country for a dissenter to live in—we must go to France.' These are truths, and it is doing justice to both parties to tell them. It is chiefly the dissenters who have carried English manufacturers to the height they are now at, and the same men have it in their power to carry them away; and though those manufactures will afterwards continue to be made in those places, the foreign market will be lost. There are frequently appearing in the London Gazette, extracts from certain acts to prevent machines and persons, as far as they can extend to persons, from going out of the country. It appears from these, that the ill effects of the test-laws and church-establishment begin to be much suspected; but the remedy of force can never supply the remedy of reason. In the progress of less than a century, all the unrepresented part of England, of all denominations, which is at least a hundred times the most numerous, may begin to feel the necessity of a constitution, and then all those matters will come regularly before them.

By the French constitution, the Nation is always named before the King. The third article of the Declaration of rights says, '*The nation is essentially the source* (or fountain) *of all sovereignty.*' Mr Burke argues, that, in England, a King is the fountain—that he is the fountain of all honour.* But as this idea is evidently descended from the Conquest, I shall make no other remark upon it, than that it is the nature of conquest to turn every thing upside down; and as Mr Burke will not be refused the privilege of speaking twice,* and as there are but two parts in the figure, the *fountain* and the *spout*, he will be right the second time.

The French constitution puts the legislative before the executive; the Law before the King; *La Loi, Le Roi*. This also is in the natural order of things; because laws must have existence, before they can have execution.

A King in France does not, in addressing himself to the National Assembly, say, 'My assembly,' similar to the phrase used in England of *my* 'Parliament;' neither can he use it consistently with the constitution, nor could it be admitted. There may be propriety in the use of it in England, because, as is before mentioned, both Houses of Parliament originated from what is called the Crown by patent or boon—and not from the inherent rights of the people, as the National Assembly does in France, and whose name designates its origin.

The President of the National Assembly does not ask the King *to grant to the Assembly liberty of speech*,* as is the case with the English House of Commons. The constitutional dignity of the National Assembly cannot debase itself. Speech is, in the first place, one of the natural rights of man always retained; and with respect to the National Assembly, the use of it is their *duty*, and the nation is their *authority*. They were elected by the greatest body of men exercising the right of election the European world ever saw. They sprung not from the filth of rotten boroughs, nor are they the vassal representatives of aristocratical ones. Feeling the proper dignity of their character, they support it. Their parliamentary language, whether for or against a question, is free, bold, and manly, and extends to all the parts and circumstances of the case. If any matter or subject respecting the executive department, or the person who presides in it, (the King), comes before them, it is debated on with the spirit of men, and the language of gentlemen; and their answer, or their address, is returned in the same stile. They stand not aloof with the gaping vacuity of vulgar ignorance, nor bend with the cringe of sycophantic insignificance. The graceful pride of truth knows no extremes, and preserves, in every latitude of life, the right-angled character of man.

Let us now look to the other side of the question.—In the addresses of the English Parliaments to their Kings, we see neither the intrepid spirit of the old Parliaments of France, nor the serene dignity of the present National Assembly; neither do we see in them any thing of the stile of English manners, which border somewhat on bluntness. Since then they are neither of foreign extraction, nor naturally of English production, their origin must be fought for elsewhere, and that origin is the Norman Conquest. They are evidently of the vassalage class of manners, and emphatically mark the prostrate distance that exists in no other condition of men than between the conqueror and the conquered. That this vassalage idea and stile of speaking was not got rid of even at the Revolution of 1688, is evident from the declaration of Parliament to William and Mary, in these words: 'We do most humbly and faithfully *submit* ourselves, our heirs and posterities, for ever.' Submission is wholly a vassalage term, requgnant to the dignity of Freedom, and an echo of the language used at the Conquest.

As the estimation of all things is by comparison, the Revolution of 1688, however from circumstances it may have been exalted beyond its value, will find its level. It is already on the wane, eclipsed by the enlarging orb of reason, and the luminous revolutions of America and France. In less than another century, it will go, as well as Mr Burke's labours, 'to the family vault of all the Capulets'.* Mankind will then scarcely believe that a country calling itself free, would send to Holland for a man, and clothe him with power, on purpose to put themselves in fear of him, and give him almost a million sterling a-year for leave to *submit* themselves and their posterity, like bondmen and bond-women, for ever.

But there is a truth that ought to be made known: I have had the opportunity of seeing it; which is, *that, notwithstanding appearances, there is not any description of men that despise monarchy so much as courtiers.** But they well know, that if it were seen by others, as it is seen by them, the juggle could not be kept up. They are in the condition of men who get their living by a show, and to whom the folly of that show is so familiar that they ridicule it; but were the audience to be made as wise in this respect as themselves, there would be an end to the show and the profits with it. The difference between a republican and a courtier with respect to monar-chy, is, that the one opposes monarchy, believing it to be something; and the other laughs at it, knowing it to be nothing.

As I used sometimes to correspond with Mr Burke, believ-ing him then to be a man of sounder principles than his book shews him to be, I wrote to him last winter from Paris,* and gave him an account how prosperously matters were going on. Among other subjects in that letter, I referred to the happy situation the National Assembly were placed in; that they had taken a ground on which their moral duty and their political interest were united. They have not to hold out a language which they do not themselves believe, for the fraudulent purpose of making others believe it. Their station requires no artifice to support it, and can only be maintained by enlightening mankind. It is not their interest to cherish ignorance, but to dispel it. They are not in the case of a ministerial or an opposition party in England, who, though they are opposed, are still united to keep up the common mystery. The National Assembly must throw open a magazine of light. It must shew man the proper character of man; and the nearer it can bring him to that standard, the stronger the National Assembly becomes.

In contemplating the French constitution, we see in it a rational order of things. The principles harmonise with the forms, and both with their origin. It may perhaps be said as an excuse for bad forms, that they are nothing more than forms; but this is a mistake. Forms grow out of principles, and operate to continue the principles they grow from. It is impossible to practise a bad form on any thing but a bad principle. It cannot be ingrafted on a good one; and wherever the forms in any government are bad, it is a certain indication that the principles are bad also.

I will here finally close this subject. I began it by remarking that Mr Burke had *voluntarily* declined going into a comparison of the English and French constitutions. He apologises (in page 241)* for not doing it, by saying that he had not time. Mr Burke's book was upwards of eight months in hand, and is extended to a volume of three hundred and sixty-six pages. As his omission does injury to his cause, his apology makes it worse; and men on the English side the water will begin to consider, whether there is not some radical defect in what is called the English constitution, that made it necessary for Mr Burke to suppress the comparison, to avoid bringing it into view.

As Mr Burke has not written on constitutions, so neither has he written on the French revolution. He gives no account of its commencement or its progress. He only expresses his wonder. 'It looks,' says he, 'to me, as if I were in a great crisis, not of the affairs of France alone, but of all Europe, perhaps of more than Europe. All circumstances taken together, the French revolution is the most astonishing that has hitherto happened in the world.'*

As wise men are astonished at foolish things, and other people at wise ones, I know not on which ground to account for Mr Burke's astonishement; but certain it is, that he does not understand the French revolution. It has apparently burst forth like a creation from a chaos, but it is no more than the consequence of a mental revolution priorily existing in France. The mind of the nation had changed before hand, and the new order of things has naturally followed the new order of thoughts.—I will here, as concisely as I can, trace out the growth of the French revolution, and mark the circumstances that have contributed to produce it.

The despotism of Louis XIV, united with the gaiety of his Court, and the gaudy ostentation of his character, had so humbled, and at the same time so fascinated the mind of France, that the people appeared to have lost all sense of their own dignity, in contemplating that of their Grand Monarch: and the whole reign of Louis XV.* remarkable only for weakness and effeminacy, made no other alteration than that of spreading a sort of lethargy over the nation, from which it shewed no disposition to rise.

The only signs which appeared of the spirit of Liberty during those periods, are to be found in the writings of the French philosophers. Montesquieu, president of the Parliament of Bordeaux,* went as far as a writer under a despotic government could well proceed; and being obliged to divide himself between principle and prudence, his mind often appears under a veil, and we ought to give him credit for more than he has expressed.

Voltaire,* who was both the flatterer and the satirist of despotism, took another line. His forte lay in exposing and ridiculing the superstitions which priest-craft united with state-craft had interwoven with governments. It was not from the purity of his principles, or his love of mankind, (for satire and philanthropy are not naturally concordant), but from his strong capacity of seeing folly in its true shape, and his irresistible propensity to expose it, that he made those attacks. They were however as formidable as if the motives had been virtuous; and he merits the thanks, rather than the esteem of mankind.

On the contrary, we find in the writings of Rousseau, and the Abbé Raynal,* a loveliness of sentiment in favour of Liberty, that excites respect, and elevates the human faculties; but having raised this animation they do not direct its operations, and leave the mind in love with an object, without describing the means of possessing it.

The writings of Quesnay, Turgot, and the friends of those authors,* are of the serious kind; but they laboured under the same disadvantage with Montesquieu: their writings abound with moral maxims of government, but are rather directed to œconomise and reform the administration of the government, than the government itself.

But all those writings and many others had their weight;

and by the different manner in which they treated the subject of government, Montesquieu by his judgment and knowledge of laws, Voltaire by his wit, Rousseau and Raynal by their animation, and Quesnay and Turgot by their moral maxims and systems of œconomy, readers of every class met with something to their taste, and a spirit of political enquiry began to diffuse itself through the nation at the time the dispute between England and the then colonies of America broke out.

In the war which France afterwards engaged in, it is very well known that the nation appeared to be before hand with the French ministry. Each of them had its view: but those views were directed to different objects; the one sought liberty, and the other retaliation on England. The French officers and soldiers who after this went to America,* were eventually placed in the school of Freedom, and learned the practice as well as the principles of it by heart.

As it was impossible to separate the military events which took place in America from the principles of the American revolution, the publication of those events in France necessarily connected themselves with the principles which produced them. Many of the facts were in themselves principles; such as the declaration of American independence, and the treaty of alliance between France and America, which recognised the natural right of man, and justified resistance to oppression.

The then Minister of France, Count Vergennes,* was not the friend of America; and it is both justice and gratitude to say, that it was the Queen of France who gave the cause of America a fashion at the French Court. Court Vergennes was the personal and social friend of Dr Franklin; and the Doctor had obtained, by his sensible gracefulness, a sort of influence over him; but with respect to principles, Count Vergennes was a despot.

The situation of Dr Franklin as Minister from America to France, should be taken into the chain of circumstances. The diplomatic character is of itself the narrowest sphere of society that man can act in. It forbids intercourse by a reciprocity of suspicion; and a diplomatic is a sort of unconnected atom, continually repelling and repelled. But this was not the case with Dr Franklin. He was not the diplomatic of a Court, but of MAN. His character as a philosopher had been long established, and his circle of society in France was universal.

Count Vergennes resisted for a considerable time the publication in France of the American constitutions, translated into the French language; but even in this he was obliged to give away to public opinion, and a sort of propriety in admitting to appear what he had undertaken to defend. The American constitutions were to liberty, what a grammar is to language: they define its parts of speech, and practically construct them into syntax.

The peculiar situation of the then Marquis de la Fayette is another link in the great chain. He served in America as an American officer under a commission of Congress, and by the universality of his acquaintance, was in close friendship with the civil government of America, as well as with the military line. He spoke the language of the country, entered into the discussions on the principles of government, and was always a welcome friend at any election.

When the war closed, a vast reinforcement to the cause of Liberty spread itself over France, by the return of the French officers and soldiers. A knowledge of the practice was then joined to the theory; and all that was wanting to give it real existence, was opportunity. Man cannot, properly speaking, make circumstances for his purpose, but he always has it in his power to improve them when they occur; and this was the case in France.

M. Neckar was displaced in May 1781;* and by the ill management of the finances afterwards, and particularly during the extravagant administration of M. Calonne, the revenue of France, which was nearly twenty-four millions sterling *per* year, was become unequal to the expenditure, not because the revenue had decreased, but because the expences had increased; and this was the circumstance which the nation laid hold of to bring forward a revolution. The English Minister, Mr Pitt,* has frequently alluded to the state of the French finances in his budgets, without understanding the subject. Had the French Parliaments been as ready to register edicts for new taxes, as an English Parliament is to grant them, there had been no derangement in the finances, nor yet any revolution; but this will better explain itself as I proceed.

It will be necessary here to shew how taxes were formerly raised in France. The King, or rather the Court or Ministry acting under the use of that name, framed the edicts for taxes at their own discretion, and sent them to the Parliaments to be registered; for until they were registered by the Parliaments, they were not operative. Disputes had long existed between the Court and the Parliaments with respect to the extent of the Parliament's authority on this head. The Court insisted that the authority of Parliaments were no farther than to remonstrate or shew reasons against the tax, reserving to itself the right of determining whether the reasons were well or ill-founded; and in consequence thereof, either to withdraw the edict as a matter of choice, or to *order* it to be enregistered as a matter of authority. The Parliaments on their part insisted, that they had not only a right to remonstrate, but to reject; and on this ground they were always supported by the Nation.

But, to return to the order of my narrative—M. Calonne wanted money; and as he knew the sturdy disposition of the Parliaments with respect to new taxes, he ingeniously sought either to approach them by a more gentle means than that of direct authority, or to get over their heads by a manœuvre: and, for this purpose, he revived the project of assembling a body of men from the several provinces, under the stile of an 'Assembly of the Notables,' or Men of Note, who met in 1787, and who were either to recommend taxes to the Parliaments, or to act as a Parliament themselves. An Assembly under this name had been called in 1617.*

As we are to view this as the first practical step towards the revolution, it will be proper to enter into some particulars respecting it. The Assembly of the Notables has in some places been mistaken for the States-General, but was wholly a different body; the States-General being always by election. The persons who composed the Assembly of the Notables were all nominated by the King, and consisted of one hundred and forty members. But as M. Calonne could not depend upon a majority of this Assembly in his favour, he very ingeniously arranged them in such a manner as to make forty-four a majority of one hundred and forty: to effect this, he disposed of them into seven separate committees,* of twenty members each. Every general question was to be decided, not by a majority of persons, but by a majority of committees; and as eleven votes would make a majority in a committee, and four committees a majority of seven, M. Calonne had good reason to conclude, that as forty-four would determine any general question, he could not be out-voted. But all his plans deceived him, and in the event became his overthrow.

The then Marquis de la Fayette was placed in the second committee, of which Count D'Artois was president: and as money-matters was the object, it naturally brought into view every circumstance connected with it. M. de la Fayette made a verbal charge against Calonne, for selling crown-lands to the amount of two millions of livres, in a manner that appeared to be unknown to the King. The Count D'Artois (as if to intimidate, for the Bastille, was then in being) asked the Marquis, if he would render the charge in writing? He replied, that he would.—The Count D'Artois did not demand it, but brought a message from the King to that purport. M. de la Fayette then delivered in his charge in writing, to be given to the King, undertaking to support it. No farther proceedings were had upon this affair; but M. Calonne was soon after dismissed by the King, and set off to England.

As M. de la Fayette, from the experience of what he had seen in America, was better acquainted with the science of civil government than the generality of the members who composed the Assembly of the Notables could then be, the brunt of the business fell considerably to his share. The plan of those who had a constitution in view, was to contend with the Court on the ground of taxes, and some of them openly professed their object. Disputes frequently arose between Count D'Artois and M. de la Fayette, upon various subjects.

With respect to the arrears already incurred, the latter proposed to remedy them, by accommodating the expences to the revenue, instead of the revenue to the expences; and as objects of reform, he proposed to abolish the Bastille, and all the State-prisons throughout the nation, (the keeping of which was attended with great expence), and to suppress *Lettres de Cachet*:* But those matters were not then much attended to; and with respect to *Lettres de Cachet, a majority of the Nobles appeared to be in favour of them*.

On the subject of supplying the Treasury by new taxes, the Assembly declined taking the matter on themselves, concurring in the opinion that they had not authority. In a debate on this subject, M. de la Fayette said, that raising money by taxes could only be done by a National Assembly, freely elected by the people, and acting as their representatives. Do you mean, said the Count D'Artois, the *States General*? M. de la Fayette replied, that he did. Will you, said the Count D'Artois, sign what you say, to be given to the King? The other replied, that he not only would do this, but that he would go farther, and say, that the effectual mode would be, for the King to agree to the establishment of a Constitution.

As one of the plans had thus failed, that of getting the Assembly to act as a Parliament, the other came into view, that of recommending. On this subject, the Assembly agreed to recommend two new taxes* to be enregistered by the Parliament: The one a stamp-tax, and the other a territorial tax, or sort of land-tax. The two have been estimated at about five millions sterl. *per ann*. We have now to turn our attention to the Parliaments, on whom the business was again devolving.

The Archbishop of Thoulouse* (since Archbishop of Sens, and now a Cardinal) was appointed to the administration of the finances, soon after the dismission of Calonne. He was also made Prime Minister, an office that did not always exist in France. When this office did not exist, the Chief of each of the principal departments transacted business immediately with the King; but when a Prime Minister was appointed, they did business only with him. The Archbishop arrived to more State-authority than any Minister since the Duke de Choiseul,* and the nation was strongly disposed in his favour; but by a line of conduct scarcely to be accounted for, he perverted every opportunity, turned out a despot, and sunk into disgrace, and a Cardinal.

The Assembly of the Notables having broken up, the new Minister sent the edicts for the two new taxes recommended by the Assembly to the Parliaments, to be enregistered. They of course came first before the parliament of Paris, who returned for answer, *That with such a revenue as the Nation then supported, the name of taxes ought not to be mentioned, but for the purpose of reducing them; and threw both the edicts out.*[1]

On this refusal, the Parliament was ordered to Versailles, where, in the usual form, the King held, what under the old government was called, a Bed of Justice;* and the two edicts were enregistered in presence of the Parliament, by an order of State, in the manner mentioned in page 148. On this, the Parliament immediately returned to Paris, renewed their session in form, and ordered the enregistering to be struck out, declaring that every thing done at Versailles was illegal.* All the members of the Parliament were then served with Lettres de Cachet, and exiled to Trois;* but as they continued as inflexible in exile as before, and as vengeance did not supply the place of taxes, they were after, a short time recalled to Paris.*

The edicts were again tendered to them, and the Count D'Artois undertook to act as representative of the King. For this purpose, he came from Versailles to Paris, in a train of procession; and the Parliament were assembled to receive him. But show and parade had lost their influence in France; and whatever ideas of importance he might set off with, he had to return with those of mortification and disappointment. On alighting from his carriage to ascend the steps of the Parliament House, the crowd (which was numerously collected) threw out trite expressions, saying 'This is Monsieur D'Artois, who wants more of our money to spend.'

[1] When the English Minister, Mr Pitt, mentions the French finances again in the English Parliament, it would be well that he noticed this as an example.

The marked disapprobation which he saw, impressed him with apprehensions; and the word *Aux armes*! (*To arms*!) was given out by the officer of the guard who attended him. It was so loudly vociferated, that it echoed through the avenues of the House, and produced a temporary confusion: I was then standing in one of the apartments through which he had to pass, and could not avoid reflecting how wretched was the condition of a disrespected man.

He endeavoured to impress the Parliament by great words, and opened his authority by saying, 'The King, our Lord and Master.' The Parliament received him very coolly, and with their usual determination not to register the taxes: and in this manner the interview ended.

After this a new subject took place: In the various debates and contests which arose between the Court and the Parliaments on the subject of taxes, the Parliament of Paris at last declared, that although it had been customary for Parliaments to enregister edicts for taxes as a matter of convenience, the right belonged only to the *States-General*; and that, therefore, the Parliament could no longer with propriety continue to debate on what it had not authority to act. The King after this came to Paris, and held a meeting with the Parliament, in which he continued from ten in the morning till about six in the evening; and, in a manner that appeared to proceed from him, as if unconsulted upon with the cabinet or the ministry, gave his word to the Parliament, that the States-General should be convened.*

But after this another scene arose, on a ground different from all the former. The minister and the cabinet were averse to calling the States-General: They well knew, that if the States-General were assembled, themselves must fall; and as the King had not mentioned *any time*, they hit on a project calculated to elude, without appearing to oppose.

For this purpose, the Court set about making a sort of constitution itself: It was principally the work of M. Lamoignon,* Keeper of the Seals, who afterwards shot himself. This new arrangement consisted in establishing a body under the name of a *Cour plénière*, or full Court, in which were invested all the powers that the government might have occasion to make use of. The persons composing this Court were to be nominated by the King; the contended right of taxation was given up on the part of the King, and a new criminal code of laws, and law proceedings, was substituted in the room of the former. The thing, in many points, contained better principles than those upon which the government had hitherto been administered: but with respect to the *Cour pléniere*, it was no other than a medium through which despotism was to pass, without appearing to act directly from itself.

The Cabinet had high expectations from their new contrivance. The persons who were to compose the *Cour pléniere*, were already nominated; and as it was necessary to carry a fair appearance, many of the best characters in the the nation were appointed among the number. It was to commence on the 8th of May 1788: But an opposition arose to it, on two grounds—the one as to principle, the other as to form.

On the ground of Principle it was contended, That government had not a right to alter itself; and that if the practice was once admitted, it would grow into a principle, and be made a precedent for any future alterations the government might wish to establish: That the right of altering the government was a national right, and not a right of government.— And on the ground of Form, it was contented, That the *Cour pléniere**　was nothing more than a larger Cabinet.

The then Duke de la Rochefoucault, Luxembourg, De Noailles,* and many others, refused to accept the nomination, and strenuously opposed the whole plan. When the edict for establishing this new Court was sent to the Parliaments to be enregistered, and put into execution, they resisted also. The Parliament of Paris not only refused, but denied the authority; and the contest renewed itself between the Parliament and the Cabinet more strongly than ever. While the Parliament were sitting in debate on this subject, the Ministry ordered a regiment of soldiers to surround the House, and form a blockade. The Members sent out for beds and provision, and lived as in a besieged citadel: and as this had no effect, the commanding officer was ordered to enter the Parliament house and seize them; which he did, and some of the principal members were shut up in different prisons. About the same time a deputation of persons arrived from the province of Brittany, to remonstrate against the establishment of the *Cour pléniere*; and those the Archbishop sent to the Bastille. But the spirit of the Nation was not to be overcome; and it was so fully sensible of the strong ground it had taken, that of withholding taxes, that it contented itself with keeping up a sort of quiet resistance, which effectually overthrew all the plans at that time formed against it. The project of the *Cour pléniere* was at last obliged to be given up, and the Prime Minister not long afterwards followed its fate; and M. Neckar was recalled into office.

The attempt to establish the *Cour pléniere* had an effect upon the Nation which itself did not perceive. It was a sort of new form of government, that insensibly served to put the old one out of sight, and to unhinge it from the superstitious authority of antiquity. It was government dethroning government; and the old one, by attempting to make a new one, made a chasm.

The failure of this scheme renewed the subject of convening the States-General;* and this gave rise to a new series of politics. There was no settled form for convening the States-General: all that it positively meant, was a deputation from what was then called the Clergy, the Noblesse, and the Commons; but their numbers, or their proportions, had not been always the same. They had been convened only on extraordinary occasions, the last of which was in 1614;* their numbers were then in equal proportions, and they voted by orders.

It could not well escape the sagacity of M. Neckar, that the mode of 1614* would answer neither the purpose of the then government, nor of the nation. As matters were at that time circumstanced, it would have been too contentious to agree upon any thing. The debates would have been endless upon privileges and exemptions, in which neither the wants of the government, nor the wishes of the nation for a constitution, would have been attended to. But as he did not chuse to take the decision upon himself, he summoned again the *Assembly of the Notables*,* and referred it to them. This body was in general interested in the decision, being chiefly of the aristocracy and the high-paid clergy; and they decided in favour of the mode of 1614. This decision was against the sense of the Nation, and also against the wishes of the Court; for the aristocracy opposed itself to both, and contended for privileges independent of either. The subject was then taken up by the Parliament, who recommended, that the number of the Commons should be equal to the other two; and that they should all sit in one house, and vote in one body. The number finally determined on was twelve hundred: six hundred to be chosen by the Commons, (and this was less than their proportion ought to have been when their worth and consequence is considered on a national scale), three hundred by the Clergy, and three hundred by the Aristocracy; but with respect to the mode of assembling themselves, whether together or apart, or the manner in which they should vote, those matters were referred.[1]

The election that followed, was not a contested election,* but an animated one. The candidates were not men, but principles. Societies were formed in Paris, and committees

[1] Mr Burke, (and I must take the liberty of telling him he is very unacquainted with French affairs), speaking upon this subject, says, 'The first thing that struck me in the calling the States-General, was a great departure from the ancient course;'—and he soon after says, 'From the moment I read the list, I saw distinctly, and very nearly as it has happened, all that was to follow.'—Mr Burke certainly did not see all that was to follow. I endeavoured to impress him, as well before as after the States-General met, that there would be a *revolution*; but was not able to make him see it, neither would he believe it. How then he could distinctly see all the parts, when the whole was out of sight, is beyond my comprehension. And with respect to the 'departure from the ancient course,' besides the natural weakness of the remark, it shews that he is unacquainted with circumstances. The departure was necessary, from the experience had upon it, that the ancient course was a bad one. The States-General of 1614 were called at the commencement of the civil war in the minority of Louis XIII; but by the clash of arranging them by orders, they increased the confusion they were called to compose. The Author of *L'Intrigue du Cabinet* (Intrigue of the Cabinet), who wrote before any revolution was thought of in France, speaking of the States-General of 1614, says, 'They held the public in suspense five months; and by the questions agitated therein, and the heat with which they were put, it appears that the Great (*les grands*) thought more to satisfy their *particularly* passions, than to procure the good of the nation; and the whole time passed away in altercations, ceremonies, and parade.' L'Intrigue du Cabinet, vol. i, p. 329.*

of correspondence and communication established throughout the nation, for the purpose of enlightening the people,
and explaining to them the principles of civil government;
and so orderly was the election conducted, that it did not
give rise even to the rumour of tumult.

The States-General were to meet at Versailles in April
1789, but did not assemble till May. They situated themselves in three separate chambers, or rather the Clergy and
the Aristocracy withdrew each into a separate chamber. The
majority of the aristocracy claimed what they called the
priviledge of voting as a separate body, and of giving their
consent or their negative in that manner; and many of the
bishops and the high-beneficed clergy claimed the same
privilege on the part of their Order.

The *Tiers État* (as they were then called) disowned any
knowledge of artificial Orders and artificial privileges; and
they were not only resolute on this point, but somewhat
disdainful. They began to consider aristocracy as a kind of
fungus growing out of the corruption of society, that could
not be admitted even as a branch of it; and from the
disposition the aristocracy had shewn by upholding Lettres
de Cachet, and in sundry other instances, it was manifest
that no constitution could be formed by admitting men in
any other character than as National Men.

After various altercations on this head, the Tiers Etat or
Commons (as they were then called) declared themselves*
(on a motion made for that purpose by the Abbé Sieyes)
'THE REPRESENTATIVES OF THE NATION; *and that the
two Orders could be considered but as deputies of corporations,
and could only have a deliberative voice when they assembled in
a national character with the national representatives.'* This
proceeding extinguished the stile of *Etats Généraux*, or
States-General, and erected it into the stile it now bears,
that of L'Assemble Nationale, or National Assembly.

This motion was not made in a precipitate manner: It was
the result of cool deliberation, and concerted between the
national representatives and the patriotic members of the
two chambers, who saw into the folly, mischief, and injustice
of artificial privileged distinctions. It was become evident,

that no constitution, worthy of being called by that name, could be established on any thing less than a national ground. The aristocracy had hitherto opposed the despotism of the Court, and affected the language of patriotism; but it opposed it as its rival (as the English Barons opposed King John),* and it now opposed the nation from the same motives.

On carrying this motion, the national representatives, as had been concerted, sent an invitation to the two chambers, to unite with them in a national character, and proceed to business. A majority of the clergy,* chiefly of the parish priests, withdrew from the clerical chamber, and joined the nation; and forty-five from the other chamber joined in like manner. There is a sort of secret history belonging to this last circumstance, which is necessary to its explanation: It was not judged prudent that all the patriotic members of the chamber stiling itself the Nobles, should quit it at once; and in consequence of this arrangement, they drew off by degrees, always leaving some, as well to reason the case, as to watch the suspected. In a little time, the numbers increased from forty-five to eighty, and soon after to a greater number; which, with a majority of the clergy, and the whole of the national representatives, put the mal-contents in a very diminutive condition.

The King, who, very different from the general class called by that name, is a man of a good heart, shewed himself disposed to recommend an union of the three chambers, on the ground the National Assembly had taken; but the mal-contents exerted themselves to prevent it, and began now to have another project in view. Their numbers consisted of a majority of the aristocratical chamber, and a minority of the clerical chamber, chiefly of bishops and high-beneficed clergy; and these men were determined to put every thing to issue, as well by strength as by stratagem. They had no objection to a constitution; but it must be such a one as themselves should dictate, and suited to their own views and particular situations. On the other hand, the Nation disowned knowing any thing of them but as citizens, and was determined to shut out all such up-start pretensions.

The more aristocracy appeared, the more it was despised; there was a visible imbecillity and want of intellects in the majority, a sort of *je ne sais quoi*, that while it affected to be more than citizen, was less than man. It lost ground from contempt more than from hatred; and was rather jeered at as an ass, than dreaded as a lion. This is the general character or aristocracy, or what are called Nobles or Nobility, or rather No-ability, in all countries.

The plan of the mal-contents consisted now of two things; either to deliberate and vote by chambers, (or orders), more especially on all questions respecting a constitution, (by which the aristocratical chamber would have had a negative on any article of the constitution); or, in case they could not accomplish this object, to overthrow the National Assembly entirely.

To effect one or other of these objects, they began now to cultivate a friendship with the despotism they had hitherto attempted to rival, and the Count D'Artois became their chief. The King (who has since declared himself deceived into their measures) held, according to the old form, *a Bed of Justice*,* in which he accorded to the deliberation and vote *par tete* (by head) upon several subjects; but reserved the deliberation and vote upon all questions respecting a constitution, to the three chambers separately. This declaration of the King was made against the advice of M. Neckar, who now began to perceive that he was growing out of fashion at Court, and that another minister was in contemplation.

As the form of sitting in separate chambers was yet apparently kept up, though essentially destroyed, the national representatives, immediately after this declaration of the King, resorted to their own chambers to consult on a protest against it; and the minority of the chamber (calling itself the Nobles), who had joined the national cause, retired to a private house to consult in like manner. The mal-contents had by this time concerted their measures with the Court, which Count D'Artois* undertook to conduct; and as they saw from the discontent which the declaration excited, and the opposition making against it, that they could not obtain a controul over the intended constitution by a separate vote, they prepared themselves for their final object—that of conspiring against the National Assembly, and overthrowing it.

The next morning, the door of the chamber of the National Assembly was shut against them, and guarded by troops; and the Members were refused admittance. On this, they withdrew to a tennis-ground in the neighbourhood of Versailles, as the most convenient place they could find, and, after renewing their session, took an oath never to separate from each other, under any circumstance whatever, death excepted, until they had established a constitution. As the experiment of shutting up the house had no other effect than that of producing a closer connection in the Members, it was opened again the next day, and the public business recommenced in the usual place.

We now are to have in view the forming of the new Ministry, which was to accomplish the overthrow of the National Assembly. But as force would be necessary, orders were issued to assemble thirty thousand troops, the command of which was given to Broglio, one of the new-intended Ministry, who was recalled from the country for this purpose. But as some management was necessary to keep this plan concealed till the moment it should be ready for execution, it is to this policy that a declaration made by Count D'Artois must be attributed, and which is here proper to be introduced.

It could not but occur, that while the mal-contents continued to resort to their chambers separate from the National Assembly, that more jealously would be excited than if they were mixed with it, and that the plot might be suspected. But as they had taken their ground, and now wanted a pretence for quitting it, it was necessary that one should be devised. This was effectually accomplished by a declaration made by Count D'Artois, '*That if they took not a part in the National Assembly, the life of the King would be endangered*': on which they quitted their chambers, and mixed with the Assembly in one body.

At the time this declaration was made, it was generally treated as a piece of absurdity in Count D'Artois, and calculated merely to relieve the outstanding Members of the two chambers from the diminutive situation they were put in; and if nothing more had followed, this conclusion would have been good. But as things best explain themselves by their events, this apparent union was only a cover to the machinations which were secretly going on; and the declaration accommodated itself to answer that purpose. In a little time the National Assembly found itself surrounded by troops, and thousands more were daily arriving. On this a very strong declaration was made by the National Assembly to the King, remonstrating on the impropriety of the measure, and demanding the reason. The King, who was not in the secret of this business, as himself afterwards declared, gave substantially for answer, that he had no other object in view than to preserve the public tranquillity, which appeared to be much disturbed.

But in a few days from this time, the plot unravelled itself. M. Neckar and the Ministry were displaced, and a new one formed, of the enemies of the Revolution; and Broglio, with between twenty-five and thirty thousand foreign troops, was arrived to support them. The mask was now thrown off, and matters were come to a crisis. The event was, that in the space of three days, the new Ministry and their abettors found it prudent to fly the nation; the Bastille was taken, and Broglio and his foreign troops dispersed; as is already related in the former part of this work.

There are some curious circumstances in the history of this short-lived ministry, and this short-lived attempt at a counter-revolution. The palace of Versailles, where the Court was sitting, was not more than four hundred yards distant from the hall where the National Assembly was sitting. The two places were at this moment like the separate head-quarters of two combatant armies; yet the Court was as perfectly ignorant of the information which had arrived from Paris to the National Assembly, as if it had resided at an hundred miles distance. The then Marquis de la Fayette, who (as has been already mentioned) was chosen to preside in the National Assembly on this particular occasion, named, by order of the Assembly, three successive deputations to the King, on the day, and up to the evening on which the Bastille was taken, to inform and confer with him on the state of affairs: but the ministry, who knew not so much as that it was attacked, precluded all communication, and were solacing themselves how dextrously they had succeeded; but in a few hours the accounts arrived so thick and fast, that they had to start from their desks and run. Some set off in one disguise, and some in another, and none in their own character. Their anxiety now was to outride the news lest they should be stopt, which, though it flew fast, flew not so fast as themselves.

It is worth remarking, that the National Assembly neither pursued those fugitive conspirators, nor took any notice of them, nor sought to retaliate in any shape whatever. Occupied with establishing a constitution founded on the Rights of Man and the Authority of the People, the only authority on which Government has a right to exist in any country, the National Assembly felt none of those mean passions which mark the character of impertinent governments, founding themselves on their own authority, or on the absurdity of hereditary succession. It is the faculty of the human mind to become what it contemplates, and to act in unison with its object.

The conspiracy being thus dispersed, one of the first works of the National Assembly, instead of vindictive proclamations, as has been the case with other governments, published a Declaration of the Rights of Man, as the basis on which the new constitution was to be built, and which is here subjoined:

DECLARATION OF THE
RIGHTS OF MAN AND OF CITIZENS,
By the National Assembly of France.

' THE Representatives of the people of FRANCE, formed into a NATIONAL ASSEMBLY, considering that ignorance, neglect, or contempt of human rights, are the sole causes of public misfortunes and corruptions of Government, have resolved to set forth, in a solemn declaration, these natural, imprescriptible, and unalienable rights: that this declaration being constantly present to the minds of the members of the body social, they may be ever kept attentive to their rights and their duties: that the acts of the legislative and executive powers of Government, being capable of being every moment compared with the end of political institutions, may be more respected: and also, that the future claims of the citizens, being directed by simple and incontestible principles, may always tend to the maintenance of the Constitution, and the general happiness.

'For these reasons, the NATIONAL ASSEMBLY doth recognize and declare, in the presence of the Supreme Being, and with the hope of his blessing and favour, the following *sacred* rights of men and of citizens:

I. *Men are born, and always continue, free, and equal in respect of their rights. Civil distinctions, therefore, can be founded only on public utility.*

II. *The end of all political associations, is, the preservation of the natural and imprescriptible rights of man; and these rights are liberty, property, security, and resistance of oppression.*

III. The nation is essentially the source of all sovereignty; nor can any INDIVIDUAL, *or* ANY BODY OF MEN, *be entitled to any authority which is not expressly derived from it.*

IV. Political Liberty consists in the power of doing whatever does not injure another. The exercise of the natural rights of every man, has no other limits than those which are necessary to secure to every *other* man the free exercise of the same rights; and these limits are determinable only by the law.

V. The law ought to prohibit only actions hurtful to society. What is not prohibited by the law, should not be hindered; nor should any one be compelled to that which the law does not require.

VI. The law is an expression of the will of the community. All citizens have a right to concur, either personally, or by their representatives, in its formation. It should be the same to all, whether it protects or punishes; and *all being equal in its sight, are equally eligible to all honours, places, and employments, according to their different abilities, without any other distinction than that created by their virtues and talents.*

VII. No man should be accused, arrested, or held in confinement, except in cases determined by the law, and according to the forms which it has prescribed. All who promote, solicit, execute, or cause to be executed, arbitrary orders, ought to be punished; and every citizen called upon, or apprehended by virtue of the law, ought immediately to obey, and renders himself culpable by resistance.

VIII. The law ought to impose no other penalties but such as are absolutely and evidently necessary: and no one ought to be punished, but in virtue of a law promulgated before the offence, and legally applied.

IX. Every man being presumed innocent till he has been convicted, whenever his detention becomes indispensible, all rigour to him, more than is necessary to secure his person, ought to be provided against by the law.

X. No man ought to be molested on account of his opinions, not even on account of his *religious* opinions, provided his avowal of them does not disturb the public order established by the law.

XI. The unrestrained communication of thoughts and opinions being one of the most precious rights of man, every citizen may speak, write, and publish freely, provided he is responsible for the abuse of this liberty in cases determined by the law.

XII. A public force being necessary to give security to the rights of men and of citizens, that force is instituted for the benefit of the community, and not for the particular benefit of the persons with whom it is entrusted.

XIII. A common contribution being necessary for the support of the public force, and for defraying the other expences of government, it ought to be divided equally among the members of the community, according to their abilities.

XIV. Every citizen has a right, either by himself or his representative, to a free voice in determining the necessity of public contributions, the appropriation of them, and their amount, mode of assessment, and duration.

XV. Every community has a right to demand of all its agents, an account of their conduct.

XVI. Every community in which a separation of powers and a security of rights is not provided for, wants a constitution.

XVII. The right to property being inviolable and sacred, no one ought to be deprived of it, except in cases of evident public necessity, legally ascertained, and on condition of a previous just indemnity.'

OBSERVATIONS ON THE DECLARATION OF RIGHTS.

THE three first articles comprehend in general terms, the whole of a Declaration of Rights: All the succeeding articles either originate from them, or follow as elucidations. The 4th, 5th, and 6th, define more particularly what is only generally expressed in the 1st, 2d, and 3d.

The 7th, 8th, 9th, 10th, and 11th articles, are declaratory of *principles* upon which laws shall be constructed, conformable to *rights* already declared. But it is questioned by some very good people in France, as well as in other countries, whether the 10th article sufficiently guarantees the right it is intended to accord with: besides which, it takes off from the divine dignity of religion, and weakens its operative force upon the mind, to make it a subject of human laws. It then presents itself to Man, like light intercepted by a cloudy medium, in which the source of it is obscured from his sight, and he sees nothing to reverence in the dusky ray.'

' There is a single idea, which, if it strikes rightly upon the mind either in a legal or a religious sense, will prevent any man, or any body of men, or any government, from going wrong on the subject of Religion; which is, that before any human institutions of government was known in the world, there existed, if I may to express it, a compact between God and Man, from the beginning of time; and that as the relation and condition which man in his *individual person* stands in towards his Maker, cannot be changed, or any-ways altered by any human laws or human authority, that religious devotion, which is a part of this compact, cannot so much as be made a subject of human laws; and that all laws must conform themselves to this prior existing compact, and not assume to make the compact conform to the laws, which, besides being human, are subsequent thereto. The first act of man, when he looked around and saw himself a creature which he did not make, and a world furnished for his reception, must have been devotion, and devotion must ever continue sacred to every individual man, *as it appears right to him*; and governments do mischief by interfering.

The remaining articles, beginning with the twelfth, are substantially contained in the principles of the preceding articles; but, in the particular situation which France then was, having to undo what was wrong, as well as to set up what was right, it was proper to be more particular than what in another condition of things would be necessary.

While the Declaration of Rights was before the National Assembly, some of its members remarked, that if a Declaration of Rights was published, it should be accompanied by a Declaration of Duties. The observation discovered a mind that reflected, and it only erred by not reflecting far enough. A Declaration of Rights is, by reciprocity, a Declaration of Duties also. Whatever is my right as a man, is also the right of another; and it becomes my duty to guarantee, as well as to possess.

The three first articles are the basis of Liberty, as well individual as national; nor can any country be called free, whose government does not take its beginning from the principles they contain, and continue to preserve them pure; and the whole of the Declaration of Rights is of more value to the world, and will do more good, than all the laws and statutes that have yet been promulgated.

In the declaration exordium which prefaces the Declaration of Rights, we see the solemn and majestic spectacle of a Nation opening its commission, under the auspices of its Creator, to establish a Government; a scene so new, and so transcendantly unequalled by any-thing in the European world, that the name of a Revolution is diminutive of its character, and it rises into a Regeneration of man. What are the present Governments of Europe, but a scene of iniquity and oppression? What is that of England? Do not its own inhabitants say, It is a market where every man has his price, and where corruption is common traffic, at the expence of a deluded people? No wonder, then, that the French Revolution is traduced. Had it confined itself merely to the destruction of flagrant despotism, perhaps Mr Burke and some others had been silent. Their cry now is, 'It is gone too far:' that is, it has gone too far for them. It stares corruption in the face, and the venal tribe are all alarmed.

Their fear discovers itself in their outrage, and they are but publishing the groans of a wounded vice. But from such opposition, the French Revolution, instead of suffering, receives an homage. The more it is struck, the more sparks it will emit; and the fear is, it will not be struck enough. It has nothing to dread from attacks: Truth has given it an establishment; and Time will record it with a name as lasting as his own.

Having now traced the progress of the French Revolution through most of its principal stages, from its commencement, to the taking of the Bastille, and its establishment by the Declaration of Rights, I will close the subject with the energetic apostrophe of M. de la Fayette—*May this great monument raised to Liberty, serve as a lesson to the oppressor, and an example to the oppressed!*[1]

MISCELLANEOUS CHAPTER

To prevent interrupting the argument in the preceding part of this work, or the narrative that follows it, I reserved some observations to be thrown together into a Miscellaneous Chapter; by which variety might not be censured for confusion. Mr Burke's Book is *all* Miscellany. His intention was to make an attack on the French Revolution; but instead of proceeding with an orderly arrangement, he has stormed it with a mob of ideas tumbling over and destroying one another.

But this confusion and contradiction in Mr Burke's Book is easily accounted for.—When a man in a long cause attempts to steer his course by any thing else than some polar truth or principle, he is sure to be lost. It is beyond the compass of his capacity to keep all the parts of an argument together, and make them unite in one issue, by any other means than having this guide always in view. Neither

---

[1] See page 96 of this work.—N.B. Since the taking of the Bastille, the occurrences have been published: but the matters recorded in this narrative, are prior to that period; and some of them, as may be easily seen, can be but very little known.

memory nor invention will supply the want of it. The former fails him, and the latter betrays him.

Notwithstanding the nonsense, for it deserves no better name, that Mr Burke has asserted about hereditary rights, and hereditary succession, and that a Nation has not a right to form a Government for itself; it happened to fall in his way to give some account of what Government is. '*Government*, says he, *is a contrivance of human wisdom.*'*

Admitting that Government is a contrivance of human *wisdom*, it must necessarily follow, that hereditary succession, and hereditary rights, (as they are called), can make no part of it, because it is impossible to make wisdom hereditary; and on the other hand, *that* cannot be a wise contrivance, which in its operation may commit the government of a nation to the wisdom of an ideot. The ground which Mr Burke now takes, is fatal to every part of his cause. The argument changes from hereditary rights to hereditary wisdom; and the question is, Who is the wisest man? He must now shew that every one in the line of hereditary succession was a Solomon, or his title is not good to be a king.—What a stroke has Mr Burke now made! To use a sailors phrase, he has *swabbed the deck*, and scarcely left a name legible in the list of Kings; and he has mowed down and thinned the House of Peers, with a scythe as formidable as Death and Time.

But Mr Burke appears to have been aware of this retort; and he has taken care to guard against it, by making government to be not only a *contrivance* of human wisdom, but a *monopoly* of wisdom. He puts the nation as fools on one side, and places his government of wisdom, all wise men of Gotham, on the other side; and he then proclaims, and says, that '*Men have a* RIGHT *that their* WANTS *should be provided for by this wisdom.*'* Having thus made proclamation, he next proceeds to explain to them what their *wants* are, and also what their *rights* are. In this he has succeeded dextrously, for he makes their wants to be a *want* of wisdom; but as this is but cold comfort, he then informs them, that they have a *right* (not to any of the wisdom) but to be governed by it: and in order to impress them with a solemn reverence for this monopoly-government of wisdom, and of its vast capacity for all purposes, possible or impossible, right or wrong, he proceeds with astrological mysterious importance, to tell to them its powers, in these words—'The Rights of men in government are their advantages; and these are often in balances between differences of good; and in compromises sometimes between *good* and *evil*, and sometimes between *evil* and *evil*. Political reason is a *computing principle*; adding—subtracting—multiplying—and dividing, morally, and not metaphysically or mathematically, true moral demonstrations.'*

As the wondering audience, whom Mr Burke supposes himself talking to, may not understand all this learned jargon, I will undertake to be its interpreter. The meaning then, good people, of all this, is, *That government is governed by no principle whatever; that it can make evil good, or good evil, just as it pleases. In short, that government is arbitrary power.*

But there are some things which Mr Burke has forgotten. *First,* He has not shewn where the wisdom originally came from: and *secondly,* he has not shewn by what authority it first began to act. In the manner he introduces the matter, it is either government stealing wisdom, or wisdom stealing government. It is without an origin, and its powers without authority. In short, it is usurpation.

Whether it be from a sense of shame, or from a consciousness of some radical defect in a government necessary to be kept out of sight, or from both, or from any other cause, I undertake not to determine; but so it is, that a monarchical reasoner never traces government to its source, or from its source. It is one of the *shibboleths** by which he may be known. A thousand years hence, those who shall live in America or in France, will look back with contemplative pride on the origin of their governments, and say, *This was the work of our glorious ancestors!* But what can a monarchical talker say? What has he to exult in? Alas! he has nothing. A certain something forbids him to look back to a beginning, lest some robber or some Robin Hood* should rise from the long obscurity of time, and say, *I am the origin!* Hard as Mr

Burke laboured the Regency Bill and Hereditary Succession*
two years ago, and much as he dived for precedents, he still
had not boldness enough to bring up William of Normandy,
and say, *There is the head of the list! there is the fountain of
honour!* the son of a prostitute, and the plunderer of the
English nation.

The opinions of men with respect to government, are
changing fast in all countries. The revolutions of America
and France have thrown a beam of light over the world,
which reaches into man. The enormous expence of governments have provoked people to think, by making them feel:
and when once the veil begins to rend, it admits not of
repair. Ignorance is of a peculiar nature: once dispelled, and
it is impossible to re-establish it. It is not originally a thing
of itself, but is only the absence of knowledge; and though
man may be *kept* ignorant, he cannot be *made* ignorant. The
mind, in discovering truth, acts in the same manner as it
acts through the eye in discovering objects; when once any
object has been seen, it is impossible to put the mind back to
the same condition it was in before it saw it. Those who talk
of a counter revolution in France, shew how little they
understand of man. There does not exist in the compass of
language, an arrangement of words to express so much as
the means of effecting a counter revolution. The means
must be an obliteration of knowledge; and it has never yet
been discovered, how to make man *unknow* his knowledge,
or *unthink* his thoughts.

Mr Burke is labouring in vain to stop the progress of
knowledge; and it comes with the worse grace from him, as
there is a certain transaction known in the city, which
renders him suspected of being a pensioner in a fictitious
name. This may account for some strange doctrine he has
advanced in his book, which, though he points it at the
Revolution Society, is effectually directed against the whole
Nation.

'The King of England,' says he, 'holds *his* Crown (for it
does not belong to the Nation, according to Mr Burke) in
contempt of the choice of the Revolution Society, who have
not a single vote for a King among them either *individually*

or *collectively*; and his Majesty's heirs, each in their time and order, will come to the Crown *with the same contempt* of their choice, with which his Majesty has succeeded to that which he now wears.'*

As to who is King in England or elsewhere, or whether there is any King at all, or whether the people chuse a Cherokee Chief, or a Hessian Hussar* for a King, it is not a matter that I trouble myself about—be that to themselves; but with respect to the doctrine, so far as it relates to the Rights of Men and Nations, it is as abominable as any thing ever uttered in the most enslaved country under heaven. Whether it sounds worse to my ear, by not being accustomed to hear such despotism, than what it does to the ear of another person, I am not so well a judge of; but of its abominable principle I am at no loss to judge.

It is not the Revolution Society that Mr Burke means; it is the Nation, as well in its *original*, as in its *representative* character; and he has taken care to make himself understood, by saying that they have not a vote either *collectively* or *individually*. The Revolution Society is composed of citizens of all denominations, and of members of both the Houses of Parliament; and consequently, if there is not a right to a vote in any of the characters, there can be no right to any, either in the nation, or in its parliament. This ought to be a caution to every country, how it imports foreign families to be kings. It is somewhat curious to observe, that although the people of England have been in the habit of talking about kings, it is always a Foreign House of kings; hating Foreigners, yet governed by them.—It is now the House of Brunswick,* one of the petty tribes of Germany.

It has hitherto been the practice of the English Parliaments, to regulate what was called the succession, (taking it for granted, that the Nation then continued to accord to the form of annexing a monarchical branch to its government; for without this, the Parliament could not have had authority to have sent either to Holland or to Hanover, or to impose a King upon the Nation against its will.) And this must be the utmost limit to which Parliament can go upon the case; but the right of the Nation goes to the *whole* case, because it has the right of changing its *whole* form of government. The right of a Parliament is only a right in trust, a right by delegation, and that but from a very small part of the Nation; and one of its Houses has not even this. But the right of the Nation is an original right, as universal as taxation. The Nation is the paymaster of every thing, and every thing must conform to its general will.

I remember taking notice of a speech in what is called the English House of Peers, by the then Earl of Shelburne,* and I think it was at the time he was Minister, which is applicable to this case. I do not directly charge my memory with every particular; but the words and the purport, as nearly as I remember, were these: *That the form of a Government was a matter wholly at the will of a Nation, at all times: that if it chose a monarchical form, it had a right to have it so; and if it afterwards chose to be a Republic, it had a right to be a Republic, and to say to a King, 'We have no longer any occasion for you.'*

When Mr Burke says that 'His Majesty's heirs and successors, each in their time and order, will come to the crown with the *same contempt* of their choice with which His Majesty has succeeded to that he wears,'* it is saying too much even to the humblest individual in the country; part of whose daily labour goes towards making up the million sterling a year, which the country gives the person it stiles a King. Government with insolence, is despotism; but when contempt is added, it becomes worse; and to pay for contempt, is the excess of slavery. This species of Government comes from Germany; and reminds me of what one of the Brunswick soldiers told me, who was taken prisoner by the Americans in the late war: 'Ah!' said he, 'America is a fine free country, it is worth the people's fighting for; I know the difference by knowing my own: in my country, if the prince says, Eat straw, we eat straw.' God help that country, thought I, be it England or elsewhere, whose liberties are to be protected by German principles of government, and Princes of Brunswick!

As Mr Burke sometimes speaks of England, sometimes of France, and sometimes of the world, and of government in general, it is difficult to answer his book without apparently meeting him on the same ground. Although principles of Government are general subjects, it is next to impossible in many cases to separate them from the idea of place and circumstance; and the more so when circumstances are put for arguments, which is frequently the case with Mr Burke.

In the former part of his book, addressing himself to the people of France, he says, 'No experience has taught us, (meaning the English), 'that in any other course or method than that of an *hereditary crown*, can our liberties be regularly perpetuated and preserved sacred as our *hereditary right*,'* I ask Mr Burke, who is to take them away?—M. de la Fayette, in speaking to France, says, '*For a Nation to be free, it is sufficient that she wills it.*' But Mr Burke represents England as wanting capacity to take care of itself, and that its liberties must be taken care of by a King holding it in 'contempt.' If England is sunk to this, it is preparing itself to eat straw, as in Hanover or in Brunswick. But besides the folly of the declaration, it happens that the facts are all against Mr Burke. It was by the Government *being hereditary*, that the liberties of the people were endangered. Charles I. and James II. are instances of this truth; yet neither of them went so far as to hold the Nation in contempt.

As it is sometimes of advantage to the people of one country, to hear what those of other countries have to say respecting it, it is possible that the people of France may learn something from Mr Burke's book, and that the people of England may also learn something from the answers it will occasion. When Nations fall out about freedom, a wide field of debate is opened. The argument commences with the rights of war, without its evils; and as knowledge is the object contended for, the party that sustains the defeat obtains the prize.

Mr Burke talks about what he calls an hereditary crown, as if it were some production of Nature; or as if, like Time, it had a power to operate, not only independently, but in spite of man; or as if it were a thing or a subject universally consented to. Alas! it has none of those properties, but is the reverse of them all. It is a thing in imagination, the propriety of which is more than doubted, and the legality of which in a few years will be denied.

But, to arrange this matter in a clearer view than what general expressions can convey, it will be necessary to state the distinct heads under which (what is called) an hereditary crown, or, more properly speaking, an hereditary succession to the Government of a Nation, can be considered; which are,

First, The right of a particular Family to establish itself.

Secondly, The right of a Nation to establish a particular Family.

With respect to the *first* of these heads, that of a Family establishing itself with hereditary powers on its own authority, and independent of the consent of a Nation, all men will concur in calling it despotism; and it would be trespassing on their understanding to attempt to prove it.

But the *second* head, that of a Nation establishing a particular Family with *hereditary powers*, does not present itself as despotism on the first reflection; but if men will permit a second reflection to take place, and carry that reflection forward but one remove out of their own persons to that of their offspring, they will then see that hereditary succession becomes in its consequences the same despotism to others, which they reprobated for themselves. It operates to preclude the consent of the succeeding generation; and the preclusion of consent is despotism. When the person who at any time shall be in possession of a Government, or those who stand in succession to him, shall say to a Nation, I hold this power in 'contempt' of you, it signifies not on what authority he pretends to say it. It is no relief, but an aggravation to a person in slavery, to reflect that he was sold by his parent; and as that which heightens the criminality of an act cannot be produced to prove the legality of it, hereditary succession cannot be established as a legal thing.

In order to arrive at a more perfect decision on this head, it will be proper to consider the generation which undertakes to establish a Family with *hereditary powers*, a-part and separate from the generations which are to follow; and also to consider the character in which the *first* generation acts with respect to succeeding generations.

The generation which first selects a person, and puts him at the head of its Government, either with the title of King, or any other distinction, acts its *own choice*, be it wise or foolish, as a free agent for itself. The person so set up is not hereditary, but selected and appointed; and the generation who sets him up, does not live under an hereditary government, but under a government of its own choice and establishment. Were the generation who sets him up, and the person so let up, to live for ever, it never could become hereditary succession; and of consequence, hereditary succession can only follow on the death of the first parties.

As therefore hereditary succession is out of the question with respect to the *first* generation, we have now to consider the character in which *that* generation acts with respect to the commencing generation, and to all succeeding ones.

It assumes a character, to which it has neither right nor title. It changes itself from a *Legislator* to a *Testator*, and affects to make its Will, which is to have operation after the demise of the makers, to bequeath the Government; and it not only attempts to bequeath, but to establish on the succeeding generation, a new and different form of government under which itself lived. Itself, as is already observed, lived not under an hereditary Government, but under a Government of its own choice and establishment; and it now attempts, by virtue of a will and testament, (and which it has not authority to make), to take from the commencing generation, and all future ones, the rights and free agency by which itself acted.

But, exclusive of the right which any generation has to act collectively as a testator, the objects to which it applies itself in this case, are not within the compass of any law, or of any will or testament.

The rights of men in society, are neither deviseable, nor transferable, nor annihilable, but are descendable only; and it is not in the power of any generation to intercept finally, and cut off the descent. If the present generation, or any other, are disposed to be slaves, it does not lessen the right

of the succeeding generation to be free: wrongs cannot have
a legal descent. When Mr Burke attempts to maintain, that
the *English Nation did at the Revolution of* 1688, *most solemnly
renounce and abdicate their rights for themselves, and for all
their posterity for ever;** he speaks a language that merits not
reply, and which can only excite contempt for his prostitute
principles, or pity for his ignorance.

In whatever light hereditary succession, as growing out of
the will and testament of some former generation, presents
itself, it is an absurdity. A cannot make a will to take from B
the property of B, and give it to C; yet this is the manner in
which (what is called) hereditary succession by law operates.
A certain former generation made a will, to take away the
rights of the commencing generation, and all future ones,
and convey those rights to a third person, who afterwards
comes forward, and tells them, in Mr Burke's language, that
they have *no rights*, that their rights are already bequeathed
to him, and that he will govern in *contempt* of them. From
such principles, and such ignorance, Good Lord deliver the
world!

But, after all, what is this metaphor called a crown, or
rather what is monarchy? Is it a thing, or is it a name, or is it
a fraud? Is it 'a contrivance of human wisdom,' or of human
craft to obtain money from a nation under specious pretences? Is it a thing necessary to a nation? If it is, in what
does that necessity consist, what services does it perform,
what is its business, and what are its merits? Doth the virtue
consist in the metaphor, or in the man? Doth the goldsmith
that makes the crown, make the virtue also? Doth it operate
like Fortunatus's wishing-cap, or Harlequin's wooden
sword?* Doth it make a man a conjuror? In fine, what is it?
It appears to be a something going much out of fashion,
falling into ridicule, and rejected in some countries both as
unnecessary and expensive. In America it is considered as
an absurdity; and in France it has so far declined, that the
goodness of the man, and the respect for his personal character, are the only things that preserve the appearance of its
existence.

If Government be what Mr Burke describes it, 'a contrivance of human wisdom,' I might ask him, if wisdom was at such a low ebb in England, that it was become necessary to import it from Holland and from Hanover? But I will do the country the justice to say, that was not the case; and even if it was, it mistook the cargo. The wisdom of every country, when properly exerted, is sufficient for all its purposes; and there could exist no more real occasion in England to have sent for a Dutch Stadtholder, or a German Elector,* than there was in America to have done a similar thing. If a country does not understand its own affairs, how is a foreigner to understand them, who knows neither its laws, its manners, nor its language? If there existed a man so transcendantly wise above all others, that his wisdom was necessary to instruct a nation, some reason might be offered for monarchy; but when we cast our eyes about a country, and observe how every part understands its own affairs; and when we look around the world, and see that of all men in it, the race of kings are the most insignificant in capacity, our reason cannot fail to ask us—What are those men kept for?

If there is any thing in monarchy which we people of America do not understand, I wish Mr Burke would be so kind as to inform us. I see in America, a government extending over a country ten times as large as England, and conducted with regularity, for a fortieth part of the expence which government costs in England. If I ask a man in America, if he wants a King? he retorts, and asks me if I take him for an ideot? How is it that this difference happens? are we more or less wise than others? I see in America, the generality of people living in a stile of plenty unknown in monarchical countries; and I see that the principle of its government, which is that of the *equal Rights of Man*, is making a rapid progress in the world.

If monarchy is a useless thing, why is it kept up anywhere? and if a necessary thing, how can it be dispensed with? That *civil government* is necessary, all civilized nations will agree; but civil government is republican government.* All that part of the government of England which begins with the office of constable, and proceeds through the department of magistrate, quarter-session, and general assize, including trial by jury, is republican government. Nothing of monarchy appears in any part of it, except the name which William the Conqueror imposed upon the English, that of obliging them to call him 'Their Sovereign Lord the King.'

It is easy to conceive, that a band of interested men, such as Placemen, Pensioners, Lords of the bed-chamber, Lords of the kitchen, Lords of the necessary-house, and the Lord knows what besides, can find as many reasons for monarchy as their salaries, paid at the expence of the country, amount to; but if I ask the farmer, the manufacturer, the merchant, the tradesman and down through all the occupations of life to the common labourer, what service monarchy is to him? he can give me no answer. If I ask him what monarchy is, he believes it is something like a sinecure.

Notwithstanding the taxes of England amount to almost seventeen millions a-year, said to be for the expences of Government, it is still evident that the sense of the Nation is left to govern itself, and does govern itself by magistrates and juries, almost at its own charge, on republican principles, exclusive of the expence of taxes. The salaries of the Judges are almost the only charge that is paid out of the revenue. Considering that all the internal Government is executed by the people, the taxes of England ought to be the lightest of any nation in Europe; instead of which, they are the contrary. As this cannot be accounted for on the score of civil government, the subject necessarily extends itself to the monarchical part.

When the people of England sent for George the First, (and it would puzzle a wiser man than Mr Burke to discover for what he could be wanted, or what service he could render), they ought at least to have conditioned for the abandonment of Hanover.* Besides the endless German intrigues that must follow from a German Elector being King of England, there is a natural impossibility of uniting in the same person the principles of Freedom and the principles of Despotism, or, as it is usually called in England, Arbitrary Power. A German Elector is in his electorate a despot: How then could it be expected that he should be attached to principles of liberty in one country, while his interest in another was to be supported by despotism? The union cannot exist; and it might easily have been foreseen, that German Electors would make German Kings, or, in Mr Burke's words, would assume government with 'contempt'. The English have been in the habit of considering a King of England only in the character in which he appears to them: whereas the same person, while the connection lasts, has a home-seat in another country, the interest of which is different to their own, and the principles of the governments in opposition to each other—To such a person England will appear as a town-residence, and the Electorate as the estate. The English may wish, as I believe they do, success to the principles of Liberty in France, or in Germany; but a German Elector trembles for the fate of despotism in his electorate: and the Dutchy of Mecklenburgh,* where the present Queen's family governs, is under the same wretched state of arbitrary power, and the people in slavish vassalage.

There never was a time when it became the English to watch continental intrigues more circumspectly than at the present moment, and to distinguish the politics of the Electorate from the politics of the Nation. The revolution of France has entirely changed the ground with respect to England and France, as nations: but the German despots, with Prussia at their head, are combining against Liberty; and the fondness of Mr Pitt for office, and the interest which all his family-connections have obtained, do not give sufficient security against this intrigue.

As every thing which passes in the world becomes matter for history, I will now quit this subject, and take a concise review of the state of parties and politics in England, as Mr Burke has done in France.

Whether the present reign commenced with contempt, I leave to Mr Burke: certain however it is, that it had strongly that appearance. The animosity of the English Nation, it is very well remembered, ran high;* and, had the true principles of Liberty been as well understood then as they now promise to be, it is probable the Nation would not have patiently submitted to so much. George the First and Second were sensible of a rival in the remains of the Stuarts; and as they could not but consider themselves as standing on their good behaviour, they had prudence to keep their German principles of Government to themselves; but as the Stuart family wore away, the prudence became less necessary.

The contest between rights, and what were called prerogatives, continued to heat the Nation till some time after the conclusion of the American War, when all at once it fell a calm—Execration exchanged itself for applause, and Court popularity sprung up like a mushroom in a night.

To account for this sudden transition, it is proper to observe, that there are two distinct species of popularity; the one excited by merit, the other by resentment. As the Nation had formed itself into two parties, and each was extolling the merits of its parliamentary champions for and against prerogative, nothing could operate to give a more general shock than an immediate coalition of the champions themselves.* The partisans of each being thus suddenly left in the lurch, and mutually heated with disgust at the measure, felt no other relief than uniting in a common execration against both. A higher stimulus of resentment being thus excited, than what the contest on prerogatives had occasioned, the Nation quitted all former objects of rights and wrongs, and sought only that of gratification. The indignation at the Coalition, so effectually superseded the indignation against the Court, as to extinguish it; and without any change of principles on the part of the Court, the same people who had reprobated its despotism, united with it, to revenge themselves on the Coalition Parliament. The case was not, which they liked best,—but, which they hated most; and the least hated passed for love. The dissolution of the Coalition Parliament, as it afforded the means of gratifying the resentment of the Nation, could not fail to be popular; and from hence arose the popularity of the Court.

Transitions of this kind exhibit a Nation under the government of temper, instead of a fixed and steady principle; and having once committed itself, however rashly, it feels itself urged along to justify by continuance its first proceeding.— Measures which at other times it would censure, it now approves, and acts persuasion upon itself to suffocate its judgment.

On the return of a new Parliament,* the new Minister, Mr Pitt, found himself in a secure majority: and the nation gave him credit, not out of regard to himself, but because it had resolved to do it out of resentment to another.—He introduced himself to public notice by a proposed Reform of Parliament, which in its operation would have amounted to a public justification of corruption.* The Nation was to be at the expence of buying up the rotten boroughs, whereas it ought to punish the persons who deal in the traffic.

Passing over the two bubbles, of the Dutch business, and the million a-year to sink the national debt,* the matter which most presents itself, is the affair of the Regency. Never, in the course of my observation, was delusion more successfully acted, nor a nation more completely deceived.— But, to make this appear, it will be necessary to go over the circumstances.

Mr Fox had stated in the House of Commons, that the Prince of Wales, as heir in succession, had a right in himself to assume the government.* This was opposed by Mr Pitt; and, so far as the opposition was confined to the doctrine, it was just. But the principles which Mr Pitt maintained on the contrary side, were as bad, or worse in their extent, than those of Mr Fox; because they went to establish an aristocracy over the Nation, and over the small representation it has in the House of Commons.

Whether the English form of Government be good or bad, is not in this case the question; but, taking it as it stands, without regard to its merits or demerits, Mr Pitt was farther from the point than Mr Fox.

It is supposed to consist of three parts:—while therefore the Nation is disposed to continue this form, the parts have a *national standing*, independent of each other, and are not the creatures of each other. Had Mr Fox passed through Parliament, and said, that the person alluded to claimed on the ground of the Nation, Mr Pitt must then have contended (what he called) the right of the Parliament, against the right of the Nation.

By the appearance which the contest made, Mr Fox took the hereditary ground, and Mr Pitt the parliamentary ground; but the fact is, they both took hereditary ground, and Mr Pitt took the worst of the two.

What is called the Parliament, is made up of two Houses; one of which is more hereditary, and more beyond the controul of the Nation, than what the Crown (as it is called) is supposed to be. It is an hereditary aristocracy, assuming and asserting indefeasible, irrevokable rights and authority, wholly independent of the Nation. Where then was the merited popularity of exalting this hereditary power over another hereditary power less independent of the Nation than what itself assumed to be, and of absorbing the rights of the Nation into a House over which it has neither election nor controul?

The general impulse of the Nation was right; but it acted without reflection. It approved the opposition made to the right set up by Mr Fox, without perceiving that Mr Pitt was supporting another indefeasible right, more remote from the Nation, in opposition to it.

With respect to the House of Commons, it is elected but by a small part of the Nation; but were the election as universal as taxation, which it ought to be, it would still be only the organ of the Nation, and cannot possess inherent rights.—When the National Assembly of France resolves a matter, the resolve is made in right of the Nation; but Mr Pitt, on all national questions, so far as they refer to the House of Commons, absorbs the rights of the Nation into the organ, and makes the organ into a Nation, and the Nation itself into a cypher.

In a few words, the question on the Regency was a question on a million a-year, which is appropriated to the executive department: and Mr Pitt could not possess himself of any management of this sum, without setting up the supremacy of Parliament; and when this was accomplished, it was indifferent who should be Regent, as he must be Regent at his own cost. Among the curiosities which this contentious debate afforded, was that of making the Great Seal into a King;* the affixing of which to an act, was to be royal authority. If, therefore, Royal Authority is a Great Seal, it consequently is in itself nothing; and a good Constitution would be of infinitely more value to the Nation, than what the three Nominal Powers, as they now stand, are worth.

The continual use of the word *Constitution* in the English Parliament, shews there is none; and that the whole is merely a form of Government without a Constitution, and constituting itself with what powers it pleases. If there were a Constitution, it certainly could be referred to; and the debate on any constitutional point, would terminate by producing the Constitution. One member says, This is Constitution; and another says, That is Constitution—To-day it is one thing; and to-morrow, it is something else—while the maintaining the debate proves there is none. Constitution is now the cant word of Parliament, tuning itself to the ear of the Nation. Formerly it was the *universal Supremacy of Parliament*—the *omnipotence of Parliament*. But since the progress of Liberty in France, those phrases have a despotic harshness in their note; and the English Parliament have catched the fashion from the National Assembly, but without the substance, of speaking of *Constitution*.

As the present generation of people in England did not make the Government, they are not accountable for any of its defects; but that sooner or later it must come into their hands to undergo a constitutional reformation, is as certain as that the same thing has happened in France. If France, with a revenue of nearly twenty-four millions sterling, with an extent of rich and fertile country above four times larger than England, with a population of twenty-four millions of inhabitants to support taxation, with upwards of ninety millions sterling of gold and silver circulating in the nation, and with a debt less than the present debt of England*—still found it necessary, from whatever cause, to come to a settlement of its affairs, it solves the problem of funding for both countries.

It is out of the question to say how long what is called the English constitution has lasted, and to argue from thence how long it is to last; the question is, how long can the funding system last? It is a thing but of modern invention, and has not yet continued beyond the life of a man; yet in that short space it has so far accumulated, that, together with the current expences, it requires an amount of taxes at least equal to the whole landed rental of the nation in acres to defray the annual expenditure. That a government could not always have gone on by the same system which has been followed for the last seventy years, must be evident to every man; and for the same reason it cannot always go on.

The funding system is not money; neither is it, properly speaking, credit. It in effect creates upon paper the sum which it appears to borrow, and lays on a tax to keep the imaginary capital alive by the payment of interest, and sends the annuity to market, to be sold for paper already in circulation. If any credit is given, it is to the disposition of the people to pay the tax, and not to the government which lays it on. When this disposition expires, what is supposed to be the credit of Government expires with it. The instance of France under the former Government, shews that it is impossible to compel the payment of taxes by force, when a whole nation is determined to take its stand upon that ground.

Mr Burke, in his review of the finances of France,* states the quantity of gold and silver in France, at about eighty-eight millions sterling. In doing this, he has, I presume, divided by the difference of exchange, instead of the standard of twenty-four livres to a pound sterling; for M. Neckar's statement, from which Mr Burke's is taken, is *two thousand two hundred millions of livres*, which is upwards of ninety-one millions and an half sterling.

M. Neckar in France, and Mr George Chalmers of the Office of Trade and Plantation in England, of which Lord Hawkesbury* is president, published nearly about the same time (1786) an account of the quantity of money in each nation, from the returns of the Mint of each nation. Mr Chalmers, from the returns of the English Mint at the Tower of London, states the quantity of money in England, including Scotland and Ireland, to be twenty millions sterling.[1]

---

[1] See *Estimate of the Comparative Strength of Great Britain*, by G. Chalmers.

M. Neckar[1] says, that the amount of money in France, recoined from the old coin which was called in, was two thousand five hundred millions of livres, (upwards of one hundred and four millions sterling); and, after deducting for waste, and what may be in the West Indies, and other possible circumstances, states the circulation quantity at home, to be ninety-one millions and an half sterling; but, taking it as Mr Burke has put it, it is sixty-eight millions more than the national quantity in England.

That the quantity of money in France cannot be under this sum, may at once be seen from the state of the French Revenue, without referring to the records of the French Mint for proofs. The revenue of France prior to the Revolution, was nearly twenty-four millions sterling; and as paper had then no existence in France, the whole revenue was collected upon gold and silver; and it would have been impossible to have collected such a quantity of revenue upon a less national quantity than M. Neckar has stated. Before the establishment of paper in England, the revenue was about a fourth part of the national amount of gold and silver, as may be known by referring to the revenue prior to King William, and the quantity of money stated to be in the nation at that time, which was nearly as much as it is now.

It can be of no real service to a Nation, to impose upon itself, or to permit itself to be imposed upon; but the prejudices of some, and the imposition of others, have always represented France as a nation possessing but little money—whereas the quantity is not only more than four times what the quantity is in England, but is considerably greater on a proportion of numbers. To account for this deficiency on the part of England, some reference should be had to the English system of funding. It operates to multiply paper, and to substitute it in the room of money, in various shapes; and the more paper is multiplied, the more opportunities are afforded to export the specie; and it admits of a possibility (by extending it to small notes) of increasing paper till there is no money left.*

[1] See *Administration of the Finances of France, Vol. III.* by M. Neckar.*

I know this is not a pleasant subject to English readers; but the matters I am going to mention, are so important in themselves, as to require the attention of men interested in money-transactions of a public nature.—There is a circumstance stated by M. Neckar, in his treatise on the administration of the finances, which has never been attended to in England, but which forms the only basis whereon to estimate the quantity of money (gold and silver) which ought to be in every nation in Europe, to preserve a relative proportion with other nations.

Lisbon and Cadiz are the two ports into which (money) gold and silver from South America are imported, and which afterwards divides and spreads itself over Europe by means of commerce, and increases the quantity of money in all parts of Europe. If, therefore, the amount of the annual importation into Europe can be known, and the relative proportion of the foreign commerce of the several nations by which it is distributed can be ascertained, they give a rule, sufficiently true, to ascertain the quantity of money which ought to be found in any nation, at any given time.

M. Neckar shews from the registers of Lisbon and Cadiz, that the importation of gold and silver into Europe, is five millions sterling annually. He has not taken it on a single year, but on an average of fifteen succeeding years, from 1763 to 1777, both inclusive; in which time, the amount was one thousand eight hundred million livres, which is seventy-five millions sterling.[1]

From the commencement of the Hanover succession in 1714, to the time Mr Chalmers published, is seventy-two years; and the quantity imported into Europe, in that time, would be three hundred and sixty millions sterling.

If the foreign commerce of Great Britain be stated at a sixth part of what the whole foreign commerce of Europe amounts to, (which is probably an inferior estimation to what the gentlemen at the Exchange would allow) the proportion which Britain should draw by commerce of this sum, to keep herself on a proportion with the rest of Europe, would

[1] *Administration of the Finances of France, Vol. III.*

be also a sixth part, which is sixty millions sterling; and if the same allowance for waste and accident be made for England which M. Neckar makes for France, the quantity remaining after these deductions would be fifty-two millions; and this sum ought to have been in the nation (at the time Mr Chalmers published) in addition to the sum which was in the nation at the commencement of the Hanover succession, and to have made in the whole at least sixty-six millions sterling; instead of which, there were but twenty millions, which is forty-six millions below its proportionate quantity.

As the quantity of gold and silver imported into Lisbon and Cadiz, is more exactly ascertained than that of any commodity imported into England; and as the quantity of money coined at the Tower of London, is still more positively known; the leading facts do not admit of controversy. Either, therefore, the commerce of England is unproductive of profit, or the gold and silver which it brings in, leak continually away by unseen means, at the average rate of about three quarters of a million a-year, which, in the course of seventy-two years, accounts for the deficiency; and its absence is supplied by paper.[1]

[1] Whether the English commerce does not bring in money, or whether the Government sends it out after it is brought in, is a matter which the parties concerned can best explain; but that the deficiency exists, is not in the power of either to disprove. While Dr Price, Mr Eden (now Auckland),* Mr Chalmers, and others, were debating whether the quantity of money in England was greater or less than at the Revolution, the circumstance was not adverted to, that since the Revolution, there cannot have been less than four hundred millions sterling imported into Europe; and therefore, the quantity in England ought at least to have been four times greater than it was at the Revolution, to be on a proportion with Europe. What England is now doing by paper, is what she would have been able to have done by solid money, if gold and silver had come into the nation in the proportion it ought, or had not been sent out; and she is endeavouring to restore by paper, the balance she has lost by money. It is certain, that the gold and silver which arrive annually in the register-ships to Spain and Portugal, do not remain in those countries. Taking the value half in gold and half in silver, it is about four hundred tons annually; and from the number of ships and galloons employed in the trade of bringing those metals from South America to Portugal and Spain, the quantity sufficiently proves itself, without referring to the registers.

In the situation England now is, it is impossible she can increase in money. High taxes not only lessen the property of the individuals, but they lessen also the money-capital of a nation, by inducing smuggling, which can only be carried on by gold and silver. By the politics which the British Government have carried on with the Inland Powers of Germany and the Continent, it has made an enemy of all the Maritime Powers, and is therefore obliged to keep up a large navy; but though the navy is built in England, the naval stores must be purchased from

The Revolution of France is attended with many novel circumstances, not only in the political sphere, but in the circle of money transactions. Among other, it shews that a Government may be in a state of insolvency, and a Nation rich. So far as the fact is confined to the late Government of France, it was insolvent; because the Nation would no longer support its extravagance, and therefore it could no longer support itself—but with respect to the Nation, all the means existed. A Government may be said to be insolvent, every time it applies to a Nation to discharge its arrears. The insolvency of the late Government of France, and the present Government of England, differed in no other respect than as the disposition of the people differ. The people of France refused their aid to the old Government; and the people of England submit to taxation without enquiry. What is called the Crown in England, has been insolvent several times; the last of which, publicly known, was in May 1777, when it applied to the Nation to discharge upwards of £600,000, private debts,* which otherwise it could not pay.

It was the error of Mr Pitt, Mr Burke, and all those who were unacquainted with the affairs of France, to confound the French Nation with the French Government. The French Nation, in effect, endeavoured to render the late Government insolvent, for the purpose of taking Government into its own hands; and it reserved its means for the

abroad, and that from countries where the greater part must be paid for in gold and silver. Some fallacious rumours have been set afloat in England to induce a belief of money, and, among others, that of the French refugees bringing great quantities. The idea is ridiculous. The general part of the money in France is silver; and it would take upwards of twenty of the largest broad wheel waggons, with ten horses each, to remove one million sterling of silver. Is it then to be supposed, that a few people fleeing on horse-back, or in post-chaises, in a secret manner, and having the French Custom-House to pass, and the sea to cross, could bring even a sufficiency for their own expences?

When millions of money are spoken of, it should be recollected, that such sums can only accumulate in a country by slow degrees, and a long procession of time. The most frugal system that England could now adopt, would not recover, in a century, the balance she has lost in money since the commencement of the Hanover succession. She is seventy millions behind France, and she must be in some considerable proportion behind every country in Europe, because the returns of the English Mint do not shew an increase of money, while the registers of Lisbon and Cadiz shew an European increase of between three and four hundred millions sterling.

support of the new Government. In a country of such vast extent and population as France, the natural means cannot be wanting; and the political means appear the instant the Nation is disposed to permit them. When Mr Burke, in a speech last Winter in the British Parliament, *cast his eyes over the map of Europe, and saw a chasm that once was France,** he talked like a dreamer of dreams. The same natural France existed as before, and all the natural means existed with it. The only chasm was that which the extinction of despotism had left, and which was to be filled up with a constitution more formidable in resources than the power which had expired.

Although the French Nation rendered the late Government insolvent, it did not permit the insolvency to act towards the creditors; and the creditors considering the Nation as the real paymaster, and the Government only as the agent, rested themselves on the Nation, in preference to the Government. This appears greatly to disturb Mr Burke, as the precedent is fatal to the policy by which Governments have supposed themselves secure. They have contracted debts, with a view of attaching what is called the monied interest of a Nation to their support; but the example in France shews, that the permanent security of the creditor is in the Nation, and not in the Government; and that in all possible revolutions that may happen in Governments, the means are always with the Nation, and the Nation always in existence. Mr Burke argues, that the creditors ought to have abided the fate of the Government which they trusted; but the National Assembly considered them as the creditors of the Nation, and not of the Government—of the master, and not of the steward.

Notwithstanding the late Government could not discharge the current expences, the present Government has paid off a great part of the capital. This has been accomplished by two means; the one by lessening the expences of Government, and the other by the sale of the monastic and ecclesiastical landed estates.* The devotees and penitent debauchees, extortioners and misers of former days, to ensure themselves a better world than that which they were about to leave, had bequeathed immense property in trust to the priesthood, for *pious uses*; and the priesthood kept it for themselves. The National Assembly has ordered it to be sold for the good of the whole Nation, and the priesthood to be decently provided for.

In consequence of the Revolution, the annual interest of the debt of France will be reduced at least six millions sterling, by paying off upwards of one hundred millions of the capital; which, with lessening the former expences of Government at least three millions, will place France in a situation worthy the imitation of Europe.

Upon a whole review of the subject, how vast is the contrast! While Mr Burke has been talking of a general bankruptcy in France, the National Assembly has been paying off the capital of its debt; and while taxes have increased near a million a-year in England, they have lowered several millions a-year in France. Not a word has either Mr Burke or Mr Pitt said about French affairs, or the state of the French finances, in the present Session of Parliament. The subject begins to be too well understood, and imposition serves no longer.

There is a general enigma running through the whole of Mr Burke's Book. He writes in a rage against the National Assembly; but what is he enraged about? If his assertions were as true as they are groundless, and that France, by her Revolution, had annihilated her power, and become what he calls a *chasm*, it might excite the grief of a Frenchman, (considering himself as a national man), and provoke his rage against the National Assembly; but why should it excite the rage of Mr Burke?—Alas! it is not the Nation of France that Mr Burke means, but the COURT; and every Court in Europe, dreading the same fate, is in mourning. He writes neither in the character of a Frenchman nor an Englishman, but in the fawning character of that creature known in all countries, and a friend to none, a COURTIER. Whether it be the Court of Versailles, or the Court of St James or Carlton-House,* or the Court in expectation, signifies not; for the caterpillar principle of all Courts and Courtiers are alike. They form a common policy throughout Europe, detached and separate from the interest of Nations: and while they appear to quarrel, they agree to plunder. Nothing can be more terrible to a Court or a Courtier, than the Revolution of France. That which is a blessing to Nations, is bitterness to them; and as their existence depends on the duplicity of a country, they tremble at the approach of principles, and dread the precedent that threatens their overthrow.

CONCLUSION

REASON and Ignorance, the opposites of each other, influence the great bulk of mankind. If either of these can be rendered sufficiently extensive in a country, the machinery of Government goes easily on. Reason obeys itself; and Ignorance submits to whatever is dictated to it.

The two modes of Government which prevail in the world, are, *first*, Government by election and representation: *Secondly*, Government by hereditary succession. The former is generally known by the name of republic; the latter by that of monarchy and aristocracy.

Those two distinct and opposite forms, erect themselves on the two distinct and opposite bases of Reason and Ignorance.—As the exercise of Government requires talents and abilities, and as talents and abilities cannot have hereditary descent, it is evident that hereditary succession requires a belief from man, to which his reason cannot subscribe, and which can only be established upon his ignorance; and the more ignorant any country is, the better it is fitted for this species of Government.

On the contrary, Government in a well-constituted republic, requires no belief from man beyond what his reason can give. He sees the *rationale* of the whole system, its origin and its operation; and as it is best supported when best understood, the human faculties act with boldness, and acquire, under this form of Government, a gigantic manliness.

As, therefore, each of those forms acts on a different base, the one moving freely by the aid of reason, the other by ignorance; we have next to consider, what it is that gives motion to that species of Government which is called mixed Government,* or, as it is sometimes ludicrously stiled, a Government of *this*, *that*, and *t'other*.

The moving power in this species of Government, is of necessity, Corruption. However imperfect election and representation may be in mixed Governments, they still give exercise to a greater portion of reason than is convenient to the hereditary Part; and therefore it becomes necessary to buy the reason up. A mixed Government is an imperfect every-thing, cementing and soldering the discordant parts together by corruption, to act as a whole. Mr Burke appears highly disgusted, that France, since she had resolved on a revolution, did not adopt what he calls '*A British Constitution*;' and the regretful manner in which he expresses himself on this occasion, implies a suspicion, that the British Constitution needed something to keep its defects in countenance.

In mixed Governments there is no responsibility: the parts cover each other till responsibility is lost; and the corruption which moves the machine, contrives at the same time its own escape. When it is laid down as a maxim, that *a King can do no wrong*, it places him in a state of similar security with that of ideots and persons insane, and responsibility is out of the question with respect to himself. It then descends upon the Minister, who shelters himself under a majority in Parliament, which, by places, pensions, and corruption, he can always command; and that majority justifies itself by the same authority with which it protects the Minister. In this rotatory motion, responsibility is thrown off from the parts, and from the whole.

When there is a Part in a Government which can do no wrong, it implies that it does nothing; and is only the machine of another power, by whose advice and direction it acts. What is supposed to be the King in mixed Governments, is the Cabinet; and as the Cabinet is always a part of the Parliament, and the members justifying in one character what they advise and act in another, a mixed Government becomes a continual enigma; entailing upon a country, by the quantity of corruption necessary to solder the parts, the expence of supporting all the forms of Government at once, and finally resolving itself into a Government by Committee; in which the advisers, the actors, the approvers, the justifiers, the persons responsible, and the persons not responsible, are the same persons.

By this pantomimical contrivance, and change of scene and character, the parts help each other out in matters which neither of them singly would assume to act. When money is to be obtained, the mass of variety apparently dissolves, and a profusion of parliamentary praises passes between the parts. Each admires with astonishment, the wisdom, the liberality, the disinterestedness of the other; and all of them breathe a pitying sigh at the burthens of the Nation.

But in a well-constituted republic, nothing of this soldering, praising, and pitying, can take place; the representation being equal throughout the country, and compleat in itself, however it may be arranged into legislative and executive, they have all one and the same natural source. The parts are not foreigners to each other, like democracy, aristocracy, and monarchy. As there are no discordant distinctions, there is nothing to corrupt by compromise, nor confound by contrivance. Public measures appeal of themselves to the understanding of the Nation, and, resting on their own merits, disown any flattering application to vanity. The continual whine of lamenting the burden of taxes, however successfully it may be practised in mixed Governments, is inconsistent with the sense and spirit of a republic. If taxes are necessary, they are of course advantageous; but if they require an apology, the apology itself implies an impeachment. Why then is man thus imposed upon, or why does he impose upon himself?

When men are spoken of as kings and subjects, or when Government is mentioned under the distinct or combined heads of monarchy, aristocracy, and democracy, what is it that *reasoning* man is to understand by the terms? If there really existed in the world two or more distinct and separate *elements* of human power, we should then see the several origins to which those terms would descriptively apply: but as there is but one species of man, there can be but one

element of human power; and that element is man himself.
Monarchy, aristocracy, and democracy, are but creatures of
imagination; and a thousand such may be contrived, as well
as three.

From the Revolutions of America and France, and the
symptoms that have appeared in other countries, it is evident
that the opinion of the world is changed with respect to
systems of Government, and that revolutions are not within
the compass of political calculations. The progress of time
and circumstances, which men assign to the accomplishment
of great changes, is too mechanical to measure the force of
the mind, and the rapidity of reflection, by which revolutions
are generated: All the old governments have received a
shock from those that already appear, and which were once
more improbable, and are a greater subject of wonder, than
a general revolution in Europe would be now.

When we survey the wretched condition of man under the
monarchical and hereditary systems of Government, dragged
from his home by one power, or driven by another, and
impoverished by taxes more than by enemies, it becomes
evident that those systems are bad, and that a general revolution in the principle and construction of Governments is
necessary.

What is government more than the management of the
affairs of a Nation? It is not, and from its nature cannot be,
the property of any particular man or family, but of the
whole community, at whose expence it is supported; and
though by force or contrivance it has been usurped into an
inheritance, the usurpation cannot alter the right of things.
Sovereignty, as a matter of right, appertains to the Nation
only, and not to any individual; and a Nation has at all times
an inherent indefeasible right to abolish any form of Government it finds inconvenient, and establish such as accords
with its interest, disposition, and happiness. The romantic
and barbarous distinction of men into Kings and subjects,
though it may suit the condition of courtiers, cannot that of
citizens; and is exploded by the principle upon which Governments are now founded. Every citizen is a member of the

Sovereignty, and, as such, can acknowledge no personal subjection; and his obedience can be only to the laws.

When men think of what Government is, they must necessarily suppose it to possess a knowledge of all the objects and matters upon which its authority is to be exercised. In this view of Government, the republican system, as established by America and France, operates to embrace the whole of a Nation; and the knowledge necessary to the interest of all the parts, is to be found in the center, which the parts by representation form: But the old Governments are on a construction that excludes knowledge as well as happiness; Government by Monks, who know nothing of the world beyond the walls of a Convent, is as consistent as government by Kings.

What were formerly called Revolutions, were little more than a change of persons, or an alteration of local circumstances. They rose and fell like things of course, and had nothing in their existence or their fate that could influence beyond the spot that produced them. But what we now see in the world, from the Revolutions of America and France, are a renovation of the natural order of things, a system of principles as universal as truth and the existence of man, and combining moral with political happiness and national prosperity.

'I. *Men are born and always continue free, and equal in respect of their rights. Civil distinctions, therefore, can be founded only on public utility.*

II. *The end of all political associations is the preservation of the natural and imprescriptible rights of man; and these rights are liberty, property, security, and resistance of oppression.*

III. *The Nation is essentially the source of all Sovereignty;* nor can any INDIVIDUAL, or ANY BODY OF MEN, be entitled to any authority which is not expressly derived from it.'

In these principles, there is nothing to throw a Nation into confusion by inflaming ambition. They are calculated to call forth wisdom and abilities, and to exercise them for the public good, and not for the emolument or aggrandizement of particular descriptions of men or families. Monarchical sovereignty, the enemy of mankind, and the source of misery, is abolished; and sovereignty itself is restored to its natural and original place, the Nation. Were this the case throughout Europe, the cause of wars would be taken away.

It is attributed to Henry the Fourth of France, a man of an enlarged and benevolent heart, that he proposed, about the year 1610, a plan for abolishing war in Europe.* The plan consisted in constituting an European Congress, or as the French Authors stile it, a Pacific Republic; by appointing delegates from the several Nations, who were to act as a Court of arbitration in any disputes that might arise between nation and nation.

Had such a plan been adopted at the time it was proposed, the taxes of England and France, as two of the parties, would have been at least ten millions sterling annually to each Nation less than they were at the commencement of the French Revolution.

To conceive a cause why such a plan has not been adopted, (and that instead of a Congress for the purpose of *preventing* war, it has been called only to *terminate* a war, after a fruitless expence of several years), it will be necessary to consider the interest of Governments as a distinct interest to that of Nations.

Whatever is the cause of taxes to a Nation, becomes also the means of revenue to a Government. Every war terminates with an addition of taxes, and consequently with an addition of revenue; and in any event of war, in the manner they are now commenced and concluded, the power and interest of Governments are increased. War, therefore, from its productiveness, as it easily furnishes the pretence of necessity for taxes and appointments to places and offices, becomes a principal part of the system of old Governments; and to establish any mode to abolish war, however advantageous it might be to Nations, would be to take from such Government the most lucrative of its branches. The frivolous matters upon which war is made, shew the disposition and avidity of Governments to uphold the system of war, and betray the motives upon which they act.

Why are not Republics plunged into war, but because the

nature of their Government does not admit of an interest distinct from that of the Nation? Even Holland, though an ill-constructed Republic,* and with a commerce extending over the world, existed nearly a century without war: and the instant the form of Government was changed in France, the republican principles of peace and domestic prosperity and œconomy arose with the new Government; and the same consequences would follow the same causes in other Nations.

As war is the system of Government on the old construction, the animosity which Nations reciprocally entertain, is nothing more than what the policy of their Governments excites, to keep up the spirit of the system. Each Government accuses the other of perfidy, intrigue, and ambition, as a means of heating the imagination of their respective Nations, and incensing them to hostilities. Man is not the enemy of man, but through the medium of a false system of Government. Instead, therefore, of exclaiming against the ambition of Kings, the exclamation should be directed against the principle of such Governments; and instead of seeking to reform the individual, the wisdom of a Nation should apply itself to reform the system.

Whether the forms and maxims of Governments which are still in practice, were adapted to the condition of the world at the period they were established, is not in this case the question. The older they are, the less correspondence can they have with the present state of things. Time, and change of circumstances and opinions, have the same progressive effect in rendering modes of Government obsolete, as they have upon customs and manners.—Agriculture, commerce, manufactures, and the tranquil arts, by which the prosperity of Nations is best promoted, require a different system of Government, and a different species of knowledge to direct its operations, than what might have been required in the former condition of the world.

As it is not difficult to perceive, from the enlightened state of mankind, that hereditary Governments are verging to their decline, and that Revolutions on the broad basis of national sovereignty, and Government by representation, are making their way in Europe, it would be an act of wisdom to anticipate their approach, and produce Revolutions by reason and accommodation, rather than commit them to the issue of convulsions.

From what we now see, nothing of reform in the political world ought to be held improbable. It is an age of Revolutions, in which every thing may be looked for. The intrigue of Courts, by which the system of war is kept up, may provoke a confederation of Nations to abolish it: and an European Congress, to patronize the progress of free Government, and promote the civilization of Nations with each other, is an event nearer in probability, than once were the revolutions and alliance of France and America.

RIGHTS OF MAN

PART THE SECOND

COMBINING

PRINCIPLE AND PRACTICE.

TO M. DE LA FAYETTE

AFTER an acquaintance of nearly fifteen years, in difficult situations in America, and various consultations in Europe, I feel a pleasure in presenting to you this small treatise, in gratitude for your services to my beloved America, and as a testimony of my esteem for the virtues, public and private, which I know you to possess.

The only point upon which I could ever discover that we differed, was not as to principles of government, but as to time. For my own part, I think it equally as injurious to good principles to permit them to linger, as to push them on too fast. That which you suppose accomplishable in fourteen or fifteen years, I may believe practicable in a much shorter period. Mankind, as it appears to me, are always ripe enough to understand their true interest, provided it be presented clearly to their understanding, and that in a manner not to create suspicion by any thing like self-design, nor offend by assuming too much. Where we would with to reform we must not reproach.

When the American revolution was established, I felt a disposition to sit serenely down and enjoy the calm. It did not appear to me that any object could afterwards arise great enough to make me quit tranquillity, and feel as I had felt before. But when principle, and not place, is the energetic cause of action, a man, I find, is every where the same.

I am now once more in the public world; and as I have not a right to contemplate on so many years of remaining life as you have, I am resolved to labour as fast as I can; and as I am anxious for your aid and your company, I wish you to hasten your principles, and overtake me.

If you make a campaign the ensuing spring,* which it is most probable there will be no occasion for, I will come and join you. Should the campaign commence, I hope it will terminate in the extinction of German despotism, and in establishing the freedom of all Germany. When France shall be surrounded with revolutions, she will be in peace and safety, and her taxes, as well as those of Germany, will consequently become less.

Your sincere,
Affectionate Friend,
THOMAS PAINE.

London, Feb. 9, 1792

PREFACE

WHEN I began the chapter entitled the '*Conclusion*' in the former part of the RIGHTS OF MAN, published last year, it was my intention to have extended it to a greater length; but in casting the whole matter in my mind which I wished to add, I found that I must either make the work too bulky, or contract my plan too much. I therefore brought it to a close as soon as the subject would admit, and reserved what I had further to say to another opportunity.

Several other reasons contributed to produce this determination. I wished to know the manner in which a work, written in a style of thinking and expression different to what had been customary in England, would be received before I proceeded farther. A great field was opening to the view of mankind by means of the French Revolution. Mr Burke's outrageous opposition thereto brought the controversy into England. He attacked principles which he knew (from information) I would contest with him, because they are principles I believe to be good, and which I have contributed to establish, and conceive myself bound to defend. Had he not urged the controversy, I had most probably been a silent man.

Another reason for deferring the remainder of the work was, that Mr Burke promised in his first publication to renew the subject at another opportunity, and to make a comparison of what he called the English and French Constitutions. I therefore held myself in reserve for him. He has published two works since, without doing this; which he certainly would not have omitted, had the comparison been in his favour.

In his last work, '*His appeal from the new to the old Whigs*,'* he has quoted about ten pages from the *Rights of Man*, and having given himself the trouble of doing this, says, 'he shall not attempt in the smallest degree to refute them,' meaning the principles therein contained. I am enough acquainted with Mr Burke to know, that he would if he could. But instead of contesting them, he immediately after consoles himself with saying, that 'he has done his part.'—He has not done his part. He has not performed his promise of a comparison of constitutions. He started the controversy, he gave the challenge, and has fled from it; and he is now *a case in point* with his own opinion, that, '*the age of chivalry is gone!*'

The title, as well as the substance of his last work, his '*Appeal*,' is his condemnation. Principles must stand on their own merits, and if they are good they certainly will. To put them under the shelter of other men's authority, as Mr Burke has done, serves to bring them into suspicion. Mr Burke is not very fond of dividing his honours, but in this case he is artfully dividing the disgrace.

But who are those to whom Mr Burke has made his appeal? A set of childish thinkers and half-way politicians born in the last century; men who went no farther with any principle than as it suited their purpose as a party; the nation was always left out of the question; and this has been the character of every party from that day to this. The nation sees nothing in such works, or such politics worthy its attention. A little matter will move a party, but it must be something great that moves a nation.

Though I see nothing in Mr Burke's Appeal worth taking much notice of, there is, however, one expression upon which I shall offer a few remarks.—After quoting largely from the *Rights of Man*, and declining to contest the principles contained in that work, he says, 'This will most probably be done (*if such writings shall be thought to deserve any other refutation than that of criminal justice*) by others, who may think with Mr Burke and with the same zeal.'*

In the first place, it has not yet been done by any body. Not less, I believe, than eight or ten pamphlets intended as answers to the former part of the 'Rights of Man' have been published by different persons, and not one of them, to my knowledge, has extended to a second edition, nor are even the titles of them so much as generally remembered. As I am averse to unnecessarily multiplying publications, I have answered none of them. And as I believe that a man may write himself out of reputation when nobody else can do it, I am careful to avoid that rock.

But as I would decline unnecessary publications on the one hand, so would I avoid every thing that might appear like sullen pride on the other. If Mr Burke, or any person on his side the question, will produce an answer to the 'Rights of Man,' that shall extend to an half, or even to a fourth part of the number of copies to which the Rights of Man extended, I will reply to his work. But until this be done, I shall so far take the sense of the public for my guide (and the world knows I am not a flatterer) that what they do not think worth while to read, is not worth mine to answer. I suppose the number of copies to which the first part of the *Rights of Man* extended, taking England, Scotland, and Ireland, is not less than between forty and fifty thousand.

I now come to remark on the remaining part of the quotation I have made from Mr Burke.

'If,' says he, 'such writings shall be thought to deserve any other refutation than that of *criminal* justice.'

Pardoning the pun, it must be *criminal* justice indeed that should condemn a work as a substitute for not being able to refute it. The greatest condemnation that could be passed upon it would be a refutation. But in proceeding by the method Mr Burke alludes to, the condemnation would, in the final event, pass upon the criminality of the process and not upon the work, and in this case, I had rather be the author, than be either the judge, or the jury, that should condemn it.

But to come at once to the point. I have differed from some professional gentlemen on the subject of prosecutions, and I since find they are falling into my opinion, which I will here state as fully, but as concisely as I can.

I will first put a case with respect to any law, and then compare it with a government, or with what in England is, or has been, called a constitution.

It would be an act of despotism, or what in England is called arbitrary power, to make a law to prohibit investigating the principles, good or bad, on which such a law, or any other is founded.

If a law be bad, it is one thing to oppose the practice of it, but it is quite a different thing to expose its errors, to reason on its defects, and to shew cause why it should be repealed, or why another ought to be substituted in its place. I have always held it an opinion (making it also my practice) that it is better to obey a bad law, making use at the same time of every argument to shew its errors and procure its repeal, than forcibly to violate it; because the precedent of breaking a bad law might weaken the force, and lead to a discretionary violation, of those which are good.

The case is the same with respect to principles and forms of government, or to what are called constitutions and the parts of which they are composed.

It is for the good of nations, and not for the emolument or aggrandizement of particular individuals, that government ought to be established, and that mankind are at the expence of supporting it. The defects of every government and constitution, both as to principle and form must, on a parity of reasoning, be as open to discussion as the defects of a law, and it is a duty which every man owes to society to point them out. When those defects, and the means of remedying them are generally seen by a nation, that nation will reform its government or its constitution in the one case, as the government repealed or reformed the law in the other. The operation of government is restricted to the making and the administering of laws; but it is to a nation that the right of forming or reforming, generating or regenerating constitutions and governments belong; and consequently those subjects, as subjects of investigation, are always before a country *as a matter of right*, and cannot, without invading the general rights of that country, be made subjects for prosecution. On this ground I will meet Mr Burke whenever he please. It is better that the whole argument should come out, than to seek to stifle it. It was himself that opened the controversy, and he ought not to desert it.

I do not believe that monarchy and aristocracy will continue seven years longer in any of the enlightened countries in Europe. If better reasons can be shewn for them than against them, they will stand; if the contrary, they will not.

Mankind are not now to be told they shall not think, or they shall not read; and publications that go no farther than to investigate principles of government, to invite men to reason and to reflect, and to shew the errors and excellences of different systems, have a right to appear. If they do not excite attention, they are not worth the trouble of a prosecution; and if they do, the prosecution will amount to nothing, since it cannot amount to a prohibition of reading. This would be a sentence on the public, instead of the author, and would also be the most effectual mode of making or hastening revolutions.

On all cases that apply universally to a nation, with respect to systems of government, a jury of *twelve* men is not competent to decide. Where there are no witnesses to be examined, no facts to be proved, and where the whole matter is before the whole public, and the merits or demerits of it resting on their opinion; and where there is nothing to be known in a court, but what every body knows out of it, every twelve men is equally as good a jury as the other, and would most probably reverse each other's verdict; or from the variety of their opinions, not be able to form one. It is one case, whether a nation approve a work, or a plan; but it is quite another case, whether it will commit to any such jury the power of determining whether that nation have a right to, or shall reform its government, or not. I mention those cases, that Mr Burke may see I have not written on Government without reflecting on what is Law, as well as on what are Rights.—The only effectual jury in such cases would be, a convention of the whole nation fairly elected; for in all such cases the whole nation is the vicinage.* If Mr Burke will propose such a jury, I will wave all privileges of being the citizen of another country, and, defending its principles, abide the issue, provided he will do the same; for my opinion is, that his work and his principles would be condemned instead of mine.

As to the prejudices which men have from education and habit, in favour of any particular form or system of government, those prejudices have yet to stand the test of reason and reflection. In fact, such prejudices are nothing. No man is prejudiced in favour of a thing, knowing it to be wrong. He is attached to it on the belief of its being right; and when he see it is not so, the prejudice will be gone. We have but a defective idea of what prejudice is. It might be said, that until men think for themselves the whole is prejudice, and *not opinion*; for that only is opinion which is the result of reason and reflection. I offer this remark, that Mr Burke may not confide too much in what has been the customary prejudices of the country.

I do not believe that the people of England have ever been fairly and candidly dealt by. They have been imposed upon by parties, and by men assuming the character of leaders. It is time that the nation should rise above those trifles. It is time to dismiss that inattention which has so long been the encouraging cause of stretching taxation to excess. It is time to dismiss all those songs and toasts which are calculated to enslave, and operate to suffocate reflection.* On all such subjects men have but to think, and they will neither act wrong nor be misled. To say that any people are not fit for freedom, is to make poverty their choice, and to say they had rather be loaded with taxes than not. If such a case could be proved, it would equally prove, that those who govern are not fit to govern them, for they are a part of the same national mass.

But admitting governments to be changed all over Europe; it certainly may be done without convulsion or revenge. It is not worth making changes or revolutions, unless it be for some great national benefit; and when this shall appear to a nation, the danger will be, as in America and France, to those who oppose; and with this reflection I close my Preface.

THOMAS PAINE

London, Feb. 9, 1792

CONTENTS

RIGHTS OF MAN

INTRODUCTION

WHAT Archimedes said of the mechanical powers, may be applied to Reason and Liberty: '*Had we,*' said he, '*a place to stand upon, we might raise the world.*'*

The revolution of America presented in politics what was only theory in mechanics. So deeply rooted were all the governments of the old world, and so effectually had the tyranny and the antiquity of habit established itself over the mind, that no beginning could be made in Asia, Africa, or Europe, to reform the political condition of man. Freedom had been hunted round the globe; reason was considered as rebellion; and the slavery of fear had made men afraid to think.

But such is the irresistible nature of truth, that all it asks, and all it wants, is the liberty of appearing. The sun needs no inscription to distinguish him from darkness; and no sooner did the American governments display themselves to the world, than despotism felt a shock, and man began to contemplate redress.

The independence of America, considered merely as a separation from England, would have been a matter but of little importance, had it not been accompanied by a revolution in the principles and practice of governments. She made a stand, not for herself only, but for the world, and looked beyond the advantages herself could receive. Even the Hessian, though hired to fight against her, may live to bless his defeat; and England, condemning the viciousness of its government, rejoice in its miscarriage.

As America was the only spot in the political world, where the principles of universal reformation could begin, so also was it the best in the natural world. An assemblage of circumstances conspired, not only to give birth, but to add gigantic maturity to its principles. The scene which that country presents to the eye of a spectator, has something in it which generates and encourages great ideas. Nature appears to him in magnitude. The mighty objects he beholds, act upon his mind by enlarging it, and he partakes of the greatness he contemplates.—Its first settlers were emigrants from different European nations, and of diversified professions of religion, retiring from the governmental persecutions of the old world, and meeting in the new, not as enemies, but as brothers. The wants which necessarily accompany the cultivation of a wilderness produced among them a state of society, which countries, long harassed by the quarrels and intrigues of governments, had neglected to cherish. In such a situation man becomes what he ought. He sees his species, not with the inhuman idea of a natural enemy, but as kindred; and the example shews to the artificial world, that man must go back to Nature for information.

From the rapid progress which America makes in every species of improvement, it is rational to conclude, that if the governments of Asia, Africa, and Europe, had begun on a principle similar to that of America, or had not been very early corrupted therefrom, that those countries must by this time have been in a far superior condition to what they are. Age after age has passed away, for no other purpose than to behold their wretchedness.—Could we suppose a spectator who knew nothing of the world, and who was put into it merely to make his observations, he would take a great part of the old world to be new, just struggling with the difficulties and hardships of an infant settlement. He could not suppose that the hordes of miserable poor, with which old countries abound, could be any other than those who had not yet had time to provide for themselves. Little would he think they were the consequence of what in such countries is called government.

If, from the more wretched parts of the old world, we look at those which are in an advanced stage of improvement, we still find the greedy hand of government thrusting itself into every corner and crevice of industry, and grasping the spoil of the multitude. Invention is continually exercised, to furnish new pretences for revenue and taxation. It watches prosperity as its prey, and permits none to escape without a tribute.

As revolutions have begun, (and as the probability is always greater against a thing beginning, than of proceeding after it has begun), it is natural to expect that other revolutions will follow. The amazing and still increasing expences with which old governments are conducted, the numerous wars they engage in or provoke, the embarrassments they throw in the way of universal civilization and commerce, and the oppression and usurpation they act at home, have wearied out the patience, and exhausted the property of the world. In such a situation, and with the examples already existing, revolutions are to be looked for. They are become subjects of universal conversation, and may be considered as the *Order of the day*.

If systems of government can be introduced, less expensive, and more productive of general happiness, than those which have existed, all attempts to oppose their progress will in the end be fruitless. Reason, like time, will make its own way, and prejudice will fall in a combat with interest. If universal peace, civilization, and commerce, are ever to be the happy lot of man, it cannot be accomplished but by a revolution in the system of governments. All the monarchical governments are military. War is their trade, plunder and revenue their objects. While such governments continue, peace has not the absolute security of a day. What is the history of all monarchical governments, but a disgustful picture of human wretchedness, and the accidental respite of a few years repose? Wearied with war, and tired with human butchery, they sat down to rest and called it peace. This certainly is not the condition that Heaven intended for man; and if *this be monarchy*, well might monarchy be reckoned among the sins of the Jews.*

The revolutions which formerly took place in the world, had nothing in them that interested the bulk of mankind. They extended only to a change of persons and measures but not of principles, and rose or fell among the common transactions of the moment. What we now behold, may not improperly be called a '*counter revolution*.'* Conquest and tyranny, at some early period, dispossessed man of his rights, and he is now recovering them. And as the tide of all human affairs has its ebb and flow in directions contrary to each other, so also is it in this. Government founded on a *moral theory, on a system of universal peace, on the indefeasible hereditary Rights of Man*, is now revolving from west to east, by a stronger impulse than the government of the sword revolved from east to west. It interests not particular individuals, but nations, in its progress, and promises a new æra to the human race.

The danger to which the success of revolutions is most exposed, is that of attempting them before the principles on which they proceed, and the advantages to result from them, are sufficiently seen and understood. Almost every thing appertaining to the circumstances of a nation, has been absorbed and confounded under the general and mysterious word *government*. Though it avoids taking to its account the errors it commits, and the mischiefs it occasions, it fails not to arrogate to itself whatever has the appearance of prosperity. It robs industry of its honours, by pedanticly making itself the cause of its effects; and purloins from the general character of man, the merits that appertain to him as a social being.

It may therefore be of use, in this day of revolutions, to discriminate between those things which are the effect of government, and those which are not. This will best be done by taking a review of society and civilization, and the consequences resulting therefrom, as things distinct from what are called governments. By beginning with this investigation, we shall be able to assign effects to their proper cause, and analize the mass of common errors.

CHAPTER I

OF SOCIETY AND CIVILIZATION

GREAT part of that order which reigns among mankind is not the effect of government. It has its origin in the principles of society and the natural constitution of man. It existed prior to government, and would exist if the formality of government was abolished. The mutual dependance and reciprocal interest which man has upon man, and all the parts of a civilized community upon each other, create that great chain of connection which holds it together. The landholder, the farmer, the manufacturer, the merchant, the tradesman, and every occupation, prospers by the aid which each receives from the other, and from the whole. Common interest regulates their concerns, and forms their law; and the laws which common usage ordains, have a greater influence than the laws of government. In fine, society performs for itself almost every thing which is ascribed to government.

To understand the nature and quantity of government proper for man, it is necessary to attend to his character. As Nature created him for social life, she fitted him for the station she intended. In all cases she made his natural wants greater than his individual powers. No one man is capable, without the aid of society, of supplying his own wants; and those wants, acting upon every individual, impel the whole of them into society, as naturally as gravitation acts to a center.

But she has gone further. She has not only forced man into society, by a diversity of wants, which the reciprocal aid of each other can supply, but she has implanted in him a system of social affections, which, though not necessary to his existence, are essential to his happiness. There is no period in life when this love for society ceases to act.* It begins and ends with our being.

If we examine, with attention, into the composition and

constitution of man, the diversity of his wants, and the diversity of talents in different men for reciprocally accommodating the wants of each other, his propensity to society, and consequently to preserve the advantages resulting from it, we shall easily discover, that a great part of what is called government is mere imposition.

Government is no farther necessary than to supply the few cases to which society and civilization are not conveniently competent; and instances are not wanting to shew, that every thing which government can usefully add thereto, has been performed by the common consent of society, without government.

For upwards of two years from the commencement of the American war, and to a longer period in several of the American States, there were no established forms of government. The old governments had been abolished, and the country was too much occupied in defence, to employ its attention in establishing new governments; yet during this interval, order and harmony were preserved as inviolate as in any country in Europe. There is a natural aptness in man, and more so in society, because it embraces a greater variety of abilities and resource, to accommodate itself to whatever situation it is in. The instant formal government is abolished, society begins to act. A general association takes place, and common interest produces common security.

So far is it from being true, as has been pretended, that the abolition of any formal government is the dissolution of society, that it acts by a contrary impulse, and brings the latter the closer together. All that part of its organization which it had committed to its government, devolves again upon itself, and acts through its medium. When men, as well from natural instinct, as from reciprocal benefits, have habituated themselves to social and civilized life, there is always enough of its principles in practice to carry them through any changes they may find necessary or convenient to make in their government. In short, man is so naturally a creature of society, that it is almost impossible to put him out of it.

Formal government makes but a small part of civilized

life; and when even the best that human wisdom can devise is established, it is a thing more in name and idea, than in fact. It is to the great and fundamental principles of society and civilization—to the common usage universally consented to, and mutually and reciprocally maintained—to the unceasing circulation of interest, which, passing through its million channels, invigorates the whole mass of civilized man—it is to these things, infinitely more than to any thing which even the best instituted government can perform, that the safety and prosperity of the individual and of the whole depends.

The more perfect civilization is, the less occasion has it for government, because the more does it regulate its own affairs, and govern itself; but so contrary is the practice of old governments to the reason of the case, that the expences of them increase in the proportion they ought to diminish. It is but few general laws that civilized life requires, and those of such common usefulness, that whether they are enforced by the forms of government or not, the effect will be nearly the same. If we consider what the principles are that first condense men into society, and what the motives that regulate their mutual intercourse afterwards, we shall find, by the time we arrive at what is called government, that nearly the whole of the business is performed by the natural operation of the parts upon each other.

Man, with respect to all those matters, is more a creature of consistency than he is aware, or that governments would wish him to believe. All the great laws of society are laws of nature. Those of trade and commerce, whether with respect to the intercourse of individuals, or of nations, are laws of mutual and reciprocal interest. They are followed and obeyed, because it is the interest of the parties so to do, and not on account of any formal laws their governments may impose or interpose.

But how often is the natural propensity to society disturbed or destroyed by the operations of government! When the latter, instead of being ingrafted on the principles of the former, assumes to exist for itself, and acts by partialities of favour and oppression, it becomes the cause of the mischiefs it ought to prevent.

If we look back to the riots and tumults, which at various times have happened in England, we shall find, that they did not proceed from the want of a government, but that government was itself the generating cause; instead of consolidating society it divided it; it deprived it of its natural cohesion, and engendered discontents and disorders, which otherwise would not have existed. In those associations which men promiscuously form for the purpose of trade, or of any concern, in which government is totally out of the question, and in which they act merely on the principles of society, we see how naturally the various parties unite; and this shews, by comparison, that governments, so far from being always the cause or means of order, are often the destruction of it. The riots of 1780* had no other source than the remains of those prejudices, which the government itself had encouraged. But with respect to England there are also other causes.

Excess and inequality of taxation, however disguised in the means, never fail to appear in their effects. As a great mass of the community are thrown thereby into poverty and discontent, they are constantly on the brink of commotion; and, deprived, as they unfortunately are, of the means of information, are easily heated to outrage. Whatever the apparent cause of any riots may be, the real one is always want of happiness. It shews that something is wrong in the system of government, that injures the felicity by which society is to be preserved.

But as fact is superior to reasoning, the instance of America presents itself to confirm these observations.—If there is a country in the world, where concord, according to common calculation, would be least expected, it is America. Made up, as it is, of people from different nations,[1] accus-

---

[1] That part of America which is generally called New-England, including New-Hampshire, Massachusetts, Rhode-Island, and Connecticut, is peopled chiefly by English descendants. In the state of New-York, about half are Dutch, the rest English, Scotch, and Irish. In New-Jersey, a mixture of English and Dutch, with some Scotch and Irish. In Pennsylvania, about one third are English, another Germans, and the remainder Scotch and Irish, with some Swedes. The States to the southward have a greater proportion of English than the middle States, but in all of them there is a mixture; and besides those enumerated, there

tomed to different forms and habits of government, speaking different languages, and more different in their modes of worship, it would appear that the union of such a people was impracticable; but by the simple operation of constructing government on the principles of society and the rights of man, every difficulty retires, and all the parts are brought into cordial unison. There, the poor are not oppressed, the rich are not privileged. Industry is not mortified by the splendid extravagance of a court rioting at its expence. Their taxes are few, because their government is just; and as there is nothing to render them wretched, there is nothing to engender riots and tumults.

A metaphysical man,* like Mr Burke, would have tortured his invention to discover how such a people could be governed. He would have supposed that some must be managed by fraud, others by force, and all by some contrivance; that genius must be hired to impose upon ignorance, and shew and parade to fascinate the vulgar. Lost in the abundance of his researches, he would have resolved and re-resolved, and finally overlooked the plain and easy road that lay directly before him.

One of the great advantages of the American revolution has been, that it led to a discovery of the principles, and laid open the imposition of governments. All the revolutions till then had been worked within the atmosphere of a court, and never on the great floor of a nation. The parties were always of the class of courtiers; and whatever was their rage for reformation, they carefully preserved the fraud of the profession.

In all cases they took care to represent government as a thing made up of mysteries, which only themselves understood; and they hid from the understanding of the nation, the only thing that was beneficial to know, namely, *That government is nothing more than a national association acting on the principles of society.*

HAVING thus endeavoured to shew, that the social and

---

are a considerable number of French, and some few of all the European nations lying on the coast. The most numerous religious denomination are the Presbyterians; but no one sect is established above another, and all men are equally citizens.

civilized state of man is capable of performing within itself, almost every thing necessary to its protection and government, it will be proper, on the other hand, to take a review of the present old governments, and examine whether their principles and practice are correspondent thereto.

CHAPTER II

OF THE ORIGIN OF THE PRESENT
OLD GOVERNMENTS

IT is impossible that such governments as have hitherto
existed in the world, could have commenced by any other
means than a total violation of every principle sacred and
moral. The obscurity in which the origin of all the present
old governments is buried, implies the iniquity and disgrace
with which they began. The origin of the present government of America and France will ever be remembered,
because it is honourable to record it; but with respect to the
rest, even Flattery has consigned them to the tomb of time,
without an inscription.

It could have been no difficult thing in the early and
solitary ages of the world, while the chief employment of
men was that of attending flocks and herds, for a banditti of
ruffians* to overrun a country, and lay it under contributions. Their power being thus established, the chief of the
band contrived to lose the name of Robber in that of Monarch; and hence the origin of Monarchy and Kings.

The origin of the government of England, so far as relates
to what is called its line of monarchy, being one of the latest,
is perhaps the best recorded. The hatred which the Norman
invasion and tyranny begat, must have been deeply rooted
in the nation, to have outlived the contrivance to obliterate
it. Though not a courtier will talk of the curfeu-bell,* not a
village in England has forgotten it.

Those bands of robbers having parcelled out the world,
and divided it into dominions, began, as is naturally the
case, to quarrel with each other. What at first was obtained
by violence, was considered by others as lawful to be taken,
and a second plunderer succeeded the first. They alternately
invaded the dominions which each had assigned to himself,
and the brutality with which they treated each other explains
the original character of monarchy. It was ruffian torturing

ruffian. The conqueror considered the conquered, not as his prisoner, but his property. He led him in triumph rattling in chains, and doomed him, at pleasure, to slavery or death. As time obliterated the history of their beginning, their successors assumed new appearances, to cut off the entail of their disgrace, but their principles and objects remained the same. What at first was plunder, assumed the softer name of revenue; and the power originally usurped, they affected to inherit.

From such beginning of governments, what could be expected, but a continual system of war and extortion? It has established itself into a trade. The vice is not peculiar to one more than to another, but is the common principle of all. There does not exist within such governments, a stamina whereon to ingraft reformation; and the shortest and most effectual remedy is to begin anew.

What scenes of horror, what perfection of iniquity, present themselves in contemplating the character, and reviewing the history of such governments! If we would delineate human nature with a baseness of heart, and hypocrisy of countenance, that reflection would shudder at and humanity disown, it is kings, courts, and cabinets, that must sit for the portrait. Man, naturally as he is, with all his faults about him, is not up to the character.

Can we possibly suppose that if governments had originated in a right principle, and had not an interest in pursuing a wrong one, that the world could have been in the wretched and quarrelsome condition we have seen it? What inducement has the farmer, while following the plough, to lay aside his peaceful pursuits, and go to war with the farmer of another country? or what inducement has the manufacturer? What is dominion to them, or to any class of men in a nation? Does it add an acre to any man's estate, or raise its value? Are not conquest and defeat each of the same price, and taxes the never-failing consequence?—Though this reasoning may be good to a nation, it is not so to a government. War is the Pharo table of governments,* and nations the dupes of the game.

If there is any thing to wonder at in this miserable scene

of governments, more than might be expected, it is the progress which the peaceful arts of agriculture, manufacture and commerce have made, beneath such a long accumulating load of discouragement and oppression. It serves to shew, that instinct in animals does not act with stronger impulse, than the principles of society and civilization operate in man. Under all discouragements, he pursues his object, and yields to nothing but impossibilities.

CHAPTER III

OF THE OLD AND NEW SYSTEMS
OF GOVERNMENT

NOTHING can appear more contradictory than the principles on which the old governments began, and the condition to which society, civilization, and commerce, are capable of carrying mankind. Government on the old system, is an assumption of power, for the aggrandisement of itself; on the new, a delegation of power, for the common benefit of society. The former supports itself by keeping up a system of war; the latter promotes a system of peace, as the true means of enriching a nation. The one encourages national prejudices; the other promotes universal society, as the means of universal commerce. The one measures its prosperity, by the quantity of revenue it extorts; the other proves its excellence, by the small quantity of taxes it requires.

Mr Burke has talked of old and new whigs. If he can amuse himself with childish names and distinctions, I shall not interrupt his pleasure. It is not to him, but to the Abbé Sieyes,* that I address this chapter. I am already engaged to the latter gentleman, to discuss the subject of monarchical government; and as it naturally occurs in comparing the old and new systems, I make this the opportunity of presenting to him my observations. I shall occasionally take Mr Burke in my way.

Though it might be proved that the system of government now called the NEW, is the most ancient in principle of all that have existed, being founded on the original inherent Rights of Man: yet, as tyranny and the sword have suspended the exercise of those rights for many centuries past, it serves better the purpose of distinction to call it the *new*, than to claim the right of calling it the old.

The first general distinction between those two systems, is, that the one now called the old is *hereditary*, either in whole or in part; and the new is entirely *representative*. It rejects all hereditary government:

First, As being an imposition on mankind.

Secondly, As inadequate to the purposes for which government is necessary.

With respect to the first of these heads—It cannot be proved by what right hereditary government could begin: neither does there exist within the compass of mortal power, a right to establish it. Man has no authority over posterity in matters of personal right; and therefore, no man, or body of men, had, or can have, a right to set up hereditary government. Were even ourselves to come again into existence, instead of being succeeded by posterity, we have not now the right of taking from ourselves the rights which would then be ours. On what ground, then, do we pretend to take them from others?

All hereditary government is in its nature tyranny. An heritable crown, or an heritable throne, or by what other fanciful name such things may be called, have no other significant explanation than that mankind are heritable property. To inherit a government, is to inherit the people, as if they were flocks and herds.

With respect to the second head, that of being inadequate to the purposes for which government is necessary, we have only to consider what government essentially is, and compare it with the circumstances to which hereditary succession is subject.

Government ought to be a thing always in full maturity. It ought to be so constructed as to be superior to all the accidents to which individual man is subject; and therefore, hereditary succession, by being *subject to them all*, is the most irregular and imperfect of all the systems of government.

We have heard the *Rights of Man* called a *levelling* system;* but the only system to which the word *levelling* is truly applicable, is the hereditary monarchical system. It is a system of *mental levelling*. It indiscriminately admits every species of character to the same authority. Vice and virtue, ignorance and wisdom, in short, every quality, good or bad, is put on the same level. Kings succeed each other, not as rationals, but as animals. It signifies not what their mental or moral characters are. Can we then be surprised at the abject state of the human mind in monarchical countries, when the government itself is formed on such an abject levelling system?—It has no fixed character. To day it is one thing; to-morrow it is something else. It changes with the temper of every succeeding individual, and is subject to all the varieties of each. It is government through the medium of passions and accidents. It appears under all the various characters of childhood, decrepitude, dotage, a thing at nurse, in leading-strings, or in crutches. It reverses the wholesome order of nature. It occasionally puts children over men, and the conceits of hon-age over wisdom and experience. In short, we cannot conceive a more ridiculous figure of government, than hereditary succession, in all its cases, presents.

Could it be made a decree in nature, or an edict registered in heaven, and man could know it, that virtue and wisdom should invariably appertain to hereditary succession, the objections to it would be removed; but when we see that nature acts as if she disowned and sported with the hereditary system; that the mental characters of successors, in all countries, are below the average of human understanding; that one is a tyrant, another an ideot, a third insane, and some all three together, it is impossible to attach confidence to it, when reason in man has power to act.

It is not to the Abbé Sieyes that I need apply this reasoning; he has already saved me that trouble, by giving his own opinion upon the case. 'If it be asked,' says he, 'what is my opinion with respect to hereditary right, I answer, without hesitation, That, in good theory, an hereditary transmission of any power or office, can never accord with the laws of a true representation. Hereditaryship is, in this sense, as much an attaint upon principle, as an outrage upon society. But let us,' continues he, 'refer to the history of all elective monarchies and principalities: Is there one in which the elective mode is not worse than the hereditary succession?'*

As to debating on which is the worst of the two, is admitting both to be bad; and herein we are agreed. The preference which the Abbé has given, is a condemnation of the thing that he prefers. Such a mode of reasoning on such a subject is inadmissible, because it finally amounts to an accusation upon Providence, as if she had left to man no other choice with respect to government than between two evils, the best of which he admits to be '*an attaint upon principle, and an outrage upon society.*'

Passing over, for the present, all the evils and mischiefs which monarchy has occasioned in the world, nothing can more effectually prove its uselessness in a state of *civil government*, than making it hereditary. Would we make any office hereditary that required wisdom and abilities to fill it? and where wisdom and abilities are not necessary, such an office, whatever it may be, is superfluous or insignificant.

Hereditary succession is a burlesque upon monarchy. It puts it in the most ridiculous light, by presenting it as an office which any child or ideot may fill. It requires some talents to be a common mechanic; but, to be a king, requires only the animal figure of man—a sort of breathing automation. This sort of superstition may last a few years more, but it cannot long resist the awakened reason and interest of man.

As to Mr Burke, he is a stickler for monarchy, not altogether as a pensioner,* if he is one, which I believe, but as a political man. He has taken up a contemptible opinion of mankind, who, in their turn, are taking up the same of him. He considers them as a herd of beings that must be governed by fraud, effigy and shew; and an idol would be as good a figure of monarchy with him, as a man. I will, however, do him the justice to say, that, with respect to America, he has been very complimentary. He always contended, at least in my hearing, that the people of America were more enlightened than those of England, or of any country in Europe; and that therefore the imposition of shew was not necessary in their governments.

Though the comparison between hereditary and elective monarchy, which the Abbé has made, is unnecessary to the case, because the representative system rejects both; yet, were I to make the comparison, I should decide contrary to what he has done.

The civil wars which have originated from contested hereditary claims, are more numerous, and have been more dreadful, and of longer continuance, than those which have been occasioned by election. All the civil wars in France arose from the hereditary system; they were either produced by hereditary claims, or by the imperfection of the hereditary form, which admits of regencies, or monarchy at nurse. With respect to England, its history is full of the same misfortunes. The contests for succession between the Houses of York and Lancaster,* lasted a whole century; and others of a similar nature, have renewed themselves since that period. Those of 1715 and 1745,* were of the same kind. The succession war for the crown of Spain,* embroiled almost half Europe. The disturbances in Holland* are generated from the hereditaryship of the Stadtholder. A government calling itself free, with an hereditary office, is like a thorn in the flesh, that produces a fermentation which endeavours to discharge it.

But I might go further, and place also foreign wars, of whatever kind, to the same cause. It is by adding the evil of hereditary succession to that of monarchy, that a permanent family-interest is created, whose constant objects are dominion and revenue. Poland, though an elective monarchy, has had fewer wars than those which are hereditary; and it is the only government that has made a voluntary essay, though but a small one, to reform* the condition of the country.

Having thus glanced at a few of the defects of the old, or hereditary systems of government, let us compare it with the new, or representative system.

The representative system takes society and civilization for its basis; nature, reason, and experience, for its guide.

Experience, in all ages, and in all countries, has demonstrated, that it is impossible to controul Nature in her distribution of mental powers. She gives them as she pleases. Whatever is the rule by which she, apparently to us, scatters them among mankind, that rule remains a secret to man. It would be as ridiculous to attempt to fix the hereditaryship of human beauty, as of wisdom. Whatever wisdom constituently is, it is like a seedless plant; it may be reared when it appears, but it cannot be voluntarily produced. There is always a sufficiency somewhere in the general mass of society for all purposes; but with respect to the parts of society, it is continually changing its place. It rises in one to-day, in another tomorrow, and has most probably visited in rotation every family of the earth, and again withdrawn.

As this is the order of nature, the order of government must necessarily follow it, or government will, as we see it does, degenerate into ignorance. The hereditary system, therefore, is as repugnant to human wisdom, as to human rights; and is as absurd, as it unjust.

As the republic of letters brings forward the best literary productions, by giving to genius a fair and universal chance; so the representative system of government is calculated to produce the wisest laws, by collecting wisdom from where it can be found. I smile to myself when I contemplate the ridiculous insignificance into which literature and all the sciences would sink, were they made hereditary; and I carry the same idea into governments. An hereditary governor is as inconsistent as an hereditary author. I know not whether Homer or Euclid had sons:* but I will venture an opinion, that if they had, and had left their works unfinished, those sons could not have completed them.

Do we need a stronger evidence of the absurdity of hereditary government, than is seen in the descendants of those men, in any line of life, who once were famous? Is there scarcely an instance, in which there is not a total reverse of the character? It appears as if the tide of mental faculties flowed as far as it could in certain channels, and then forsook its course, and arose in others. How irrational then is the hereditary system which establishes channels of power, in company with which wisdom refuses to flow! By continuing this absurdity, man is perpetually in contradiction with himself; he accepts, for a king, or a chief magistrate, or a legislator, a person whom he would not elect for a constable.

It appears to general observation, that revolutions create genius and talents; but those events do no more than bring them forward. There is existing in man, a mass of sense lying in a dormant state, and which, unless something excites it to action, will descend with him, in that condition, to the grave. As it is to the advantage of society that the whole of its faculties should be employed, the construction of government ought to be such as to bring forward, by a quiet and regular operation, all that extent of capacity which never fails to appear in revolutions.

This cannot take place in the insipid state of hereditary government, not only because it prevents, but because it operates to benumb. When the mind of a nation is bowed down by any political superstition in its government, such as hereditary succession is, it loses a considerable portion of its powers on all other subjects and objects. Hereditary succession requires the same obedience to ignorance, as to wisdom; and when once the mind can bring itself to pay this indiscriminate reverence, it descends below the stature of mental manhood. It is fit to be great only in little things. It acts a treachery upon itself, and suffocates the sensations that urge to detection.

Though the ancient governments present to us a miserable picture of the condition of man, there is one which above all others exempts itself from the general description. I mean the democracy of the Athenians.* We see more to admire, and less to condemn, in that great, extraordinary people, than in any thing which history affords.

Mr Burke is so little acquainted with constituent principles of government, that he confounds democracy and representation together. Representation was a thing unknown in the ancient democracies. In those the mass of the people met and enacted laws (grammatically speaking) in the first person. Simple democracy was no other than the common-hall of the ancients. It signifies the *form*, as well as the public principle of the government. As these democracies increased in population, and the territory extended, the simple democratical form became unwieldy and impracticable; and as the system of representation was not known, the consequence was, they either degenerated convulsively into monarchies, or became absorbed into such as then existed. Had the system of representation been then understood, as it now is, there is no reason to believe that those forms of government, now called monarchical or aristocratical, would ever have taken place. It was the want of some method to consolidate the parts of society, after it became too populous, and too extensive for the simple democratical form, and also the lax and solitary condition of shepherds and herdsmen in other parts of the world, that afforded opportunities to those unnatural modes of government to begin.

As it is necessary to clear away the rubbish of errors, into which the subject of government has been thrown, I shall proceed to remark on some others.

It has always been the political craft of courtiers and court-governments, to abuse something which they called republicanism; but what republicanism was, or is, they never attempt to explain. Let us examine a little into this case.

The only forms of government are, the democratical, the aristocratical, the monarchical, and what is now called the representative.

What is called a *republic*,* is not any *particular form* of government. It is wholly characteristical of the purport, matter, or object for which government ought to be instituted, and on which it is to be employed, RES-PUBLICA, the public affairs, or the public good; or, literally translated, the *public thing*. It is a word of a good original, referring to what ought to be the character and business of government; and in this sense it is naturally opposed to the word *monarchy*, which has a base original signification. It means arbitrary power in an individual person; in the exercise of which, *himself*, and not the *res-publica*, is the object.

Every government that does not act on the principle of a *Republic*, or in other words, that does not make the *res-publica* its whole and sole object, is not a good government. Republican government is no other than government established and conducted for the interest of the public, as well individually as collectively. It is not necessarily connected with any particular form, but it most naturally associates with the representative form, as being best calculated to secure the end for which a nation is at the expence of supporting it.

Various forms of government have affected to style themselves a republic. Poland calls itself a republic, which is an hereditary aristocracy, with what is called an elective monarchy. Holland calls itself a republic, which is chiefly aristocratical, with an hereditary stadtholdership. But the government of America, which is wholly on the system of representation, is the only real republic in character and in practice, that now exists. Its government has no other object than the public business of the nation, and therefore it is properly a republic; and the Americans have taken care that THIS, and no other, shall always be the object of their government, by their rejecting every thing hereditary, and establishing government on the system of representation only.

Those who have said that a republic is not a *form* of government calculated for countries of great extent,* mistook, in the first place, the *business* of a government, for a *form* of government; for the *res-publica* equally appertains to every extent of territory and population. And, in the second place, if they meant any thing with respect to *form*, it was the simple democratical form, such as was the mode of government in the ancient democracies, in which there was no representation. The case, therefore, is not, that a republic cannot be extensive, but that it cannot be extensive on the simple democratical form; and the question naturally presents itself, *What is the best form of government for conducting the* RES-PUBLICA, *or the* PUBLIC BUSINESS *of a nation, after it becomes too extensive and populous for the simple democratical form?*

It cannot be monarchy, because monarchy is subject to an objection of the same amount to which the simple democratical form was subject.

It is possible that an individual may lay down a system of principles, on which government shall be constitutionally established to any extent of territory. This is no more than an operation of the mind, acting by its own powers. But the practice upon those principles, as applying to the various and numerous circumstances of a nation, its agriculture, manufacture, trade, commerce, &c. &c. requires a knowledge of a different kind, and which can be had only from the various parts of society. It is an assemblage of practical knowledge, which no one individual can possess; and therefore the monarchical form is as much limited, in useful practice, from the incompetency of knowledge, as was the democratical form, from the multiplicity of population. The one degenerates, by extension, into confusion; the other, into ignorance and incapacity, of which all the great monarchies are an evidence. The monarchical form, therefore, could not be a substitute for the democratical, because it has equal inconveniences.

Much less could it when made hereditary. This is the most effectual of all forms to preclude knowledge. Neither could the high democratical mind have voluntarily yielded itself to be governed by children and idiots, and all the motley insignificance of character, which attends such a mere animal-system, the disgrace and the reproach of reason and of man.

As to the aristocratical form, it has the same vices and defects with the monarchical, except that the chance of abilities is better from the proportion of numbers, but there is still no security for the right use and application of them.[1]

Referring, then, to the original simple democracy, it affords the true data from which government on a large scale can begin. It is incapable of extension, not from its principle, but from the inconvenience of its form; and monarchy and aristocracy, from their incapacity. Retaining, then, democracy as the ground, and rejecting the corrupt systems of monarchy and aristocracy, the representative system naturally presents itself; remedying at once the defects of the simple democracy as to form, and the incapacity of the other two with respect to knowledge.

Simple democracy was society governing itself without the aid of secondary means. By ingrafting representation upon democracy, we arrive at a system of government capable of embracing and confederating all the various interests and every extent of territory and population; and that also with advantages as much superior to hereditary government, as the republic of letters is to hereditary literature.

It is on this system that the American government is

[1] For a character of aristocracy, the reader is referred to *Rights of Man*, Part I, page 131.

founded. It is representation ingrafted upon democracy. It has fixed the form by a scale parallel in all cases to the extent of the principle. What Athens was in miniature, America will be in magnitude. The one was the wonder of the ancient world; the other is becoming the admiration and model of the present. It is the easiest of all the forms of government to be understood, and the most eligible in practice; and excludes at once the ignorance and insecurity of the hereditary mode, and the inconvenience of the simple democracy.

It is impossible to conceive a system of government capable of acting over such an extent of territory, and such a circle of interests, as is immediately produced by the operation of representation. France, great and populous as it is, is but a spot in the capaciousness of the system. It adapts itself to all possible cases. It is preferable to simple democracy even in small territories. Athens, by representation, would have outrivalled her own democracy.

That which is called government, or rather that which we ought to conceive government to be, is no more than some common center, in which all the parts of society unite. This cannot be accomplished by any method so conducive to the various interests of the community, as by the representative system. It concentrates the knowledge necessary to the interest of the parts, and of the whole. It places government in a state of constant maturity. It is, as has been already observed, never young, never old. It is subject neither to nonage, nor dotage. It is never in the cradle, nor on crutches. It admits not of a separation between knowledge and power, and is superior, as government always ought to be, to all the accidents of individual man, and is therefore superior to what is called monarchy.

A nation is not a body, the figure of which is to be represented by the human body; but is like a body contained within a circle, having a common center, in which every radius meets; and that center is formed by representation. To connect representation with what is called monarchy, is eccentric government. Representation is of itself the delegated monarchy of a nation, and cannot debate itself by dividing it with another.

Mr Burke has two or three times, in his parliamentary speeches, and in his publications, made use of a jingle of words that convey no ideas. Speaking of government, he says, 'It is better to have monarchy for its basis, and republicanism for its corrective, than republicanism for its basis, and monarchy for its corrective.'*—If he means that it is better to correct folly with wisdom, than wisdom with folly, I will no otherwise contend with him, than that it would be much better to reject the folly entirely.

But what is this thing which Mr Burke calls monarchy? Will he explain it? All men can understand what representation is; and that it must necessarily include a variety of knowledge and talents. But, what security is there for the same qualities on the part of monarchy? or, when this monarchy is a child, where then is the wisdom? What does it know about government? Who then is the monarch, or where is the monarchy? If it is to be performed by regency, it proves it to be a farce. A regency is a mock species of republic, and the whole of monarchy deserves no better description. It is a thing as various as imagination can paint. It has none of the stable character that government ought to possess. Every succession is a revolution, and every regency a counter-revolution. The whole of it is a scene of perpetual court cabal and intrigue, of which Mr Burke is himself an instance. To render monarchy consistent with government, the next in succession should not be born a child, but a man at once, and that man a Solomon. It is ridiculous that nations are to wait, and government be interrupted, till boys grow to be men.

Whether I have too little sense to see, or too much to be imposed upon; whether I have too much or too little pride, or of any thing else, I leave out of the question; but certain it is, that what is called monarchy, always appears to me a silly, contemptible thing. I compare it to something kept behind a curtain, about which there is a great deal of bustle and fuss, and a wonderful air of seeming solemnity; but when, by any accident, the curtain happens to be open, and the company see what it is, they burst into laughter.

In the representative system of government, nothing of

this can happen. Like the nation itself, it possesses a perpetual stamina, as well of body as of mind, and presents itself on the open theatre of the world in a fair and manly manner. Whatever are its excellences or its defects, they are visible to all. It exists not by fraud and mystery; it deals not in cant and sophistry; but inspires a language, that, passing from heart to heart, is felt and understood.

We must shut our eyes against reason, we must basely degrade our understanding, not to see the folly of what is called monarchy. Nature is orderly in all her works; but this is a mode of government that counteracts nature. It turns the progress of the human faculties upside down. It subjects age to be governed by children, and wisdom by folly.

On the contrary, the representative system is always parallel with the order and immutable laws of nature, and meets the reason of man in every part. For example:

In the American federal government, more power is delegated to the President of the United States, than to any other individual member of congress.* He cannot, therefore, be elected to this office under the age of thirty-five years. By this time the judgment of man becomes matured, and he has lived long enough to be acquainted with men and things, and the country with him.—But on the monarchical plan, (exclusive of the numerous chances there are against every man born into the world, of drawing a prize in the lottery of human faculties), the next in succession, whatever he may be, is put at the head of a nation, and of a government, at the age of eighteen years. Does this appear like an act of wisdom? Is it consistent with the proper dignity and the manly character of a nation? Where is the propriety of calling such a lad the father of the people?—In all other cases, a person is a minor until the age of twenty-one years. Before this period, he is not trusted with the management of an acre of land, or with the heritable property of a flock of sheep, or an herd of swine; but, wonderful to tell! he may, at the age of eighteen years, be trusted with a nation.

That monarchy is all a bubble, a mere court artifice to procure money, is evident, (at least to me), in every character in which it can be viewed. It would be impossible, on the rational system of representative government, to make out a bill of expences to such an enormous amount as this deception admits. Government is not of itself a very chargeable institution. The whole expence of the federal government of America, founded, as I have already said, on the system of representation, and extending over a country nearly ten times as large as England, is but six hundred thousand dollars, or one hundred and thirty-five thousand pounds sterling.

I presume, that no man in his sober senses, will compare the character of any of the kings of Europe with that of General Washington. Yet, in France, and also in England, the expence of the civil list only, for the support of one man, is eight times greater than the whole expence of the federal government in America. To assign a reason for this, appears almost impossible. The generality of people in America, especially the poor, are more able to pay taxes, than the generality of people either in France or England.

But the case is, that the representative system diffuses such a body of knowledge throughout a nation, on the subject of government, as to explode ignorance and preclude imposition. The craft of courts cannot be acted on that ground. There is no place for mystery; no where for it to begin. Those who are not in the representation, know as much of the nature of business as those who are. An affectation of mysterious importance would there be scouted. Nations can have no secrets; and the secrets of courts, like those of individuals, are always their defects.

In the representative system, the reason for every thing must publicly appear. Every man is a proprietor in government, and considers it a necessary part of his business to understand. It concerns his interest, because it affects his property. He examines the cost, and compares it with the advantages; and above all, he does not adopt the slavish custom of following what in other governments are called LEADERS.

It can only be by blinding the understanding of man, and making him believe that government is some wonderful mysterious thing, that exessive revenues are obtained. Monarchy is well calculated to ensure this end. It is the property of government; a thing kept up to amuse the ignorant, and quiet them into taxes.

The government of a free country, properly speaking, is not in the persons, but in the laws. The enacting of those requires no great expence; and when they are administered, the whole of civil government is performed—the rest is all court contrivance.

CHAPTER IV

OF CONSTITUTIONS

THAT men mean distinct and separate things when they speak of constitutions and of governments, is evident; or, why are those terms distinctly and separately used? A constitution is not the act of a government, but of a people constituting a government; and government without a constitution, is power without a right.

All power exercised over a nation, must have some beginning. It must be either delegated, or assumed. There are no other sources. All delegated power is trust, and all assumed power is usurpation. Time does not alter the nature and quality of either.

In viewing this subject, the case and circumstances of America present themselves as in the beginning of a world; and our enquiry into the origin of government is shortened, by referring to the facts that have arisen in our own day. We have no occasion to roam for information into the obscure field of antiquity, nor hazard ourselves upon conjecture. We are brought at once to the point of seeing government begin, as if we had lived in the beginning of time. The real volume, not of history, but of facts, is directly before us, unmutilated by contrivance, or the errors of tradition.

I will here concisely state the commencement of the American constitutions; by which the difference between constitutions and governments will sufficiently appear.

It may not be improper to remind the reader, that the United States of America consist of thirteen separate states, each of which established a government for itself, after the declaration of independence, done the fourth of July 1776. Each state acted independently of the rest, in forming its government; but the same general principle pervades the whole. When the several state governments were formed, they proceeded to form the federal government, that acts over the whole in all matters which concern the interest of the whole, or which relate to the intercourse of the several states with each other, or with foreign nations. I will begin with giving an instance from one of the state governments, (that of Pennsylvania), and then proceed to the federal government.

The state of Pennsylvania,* though nearly of the same extent of territory as England, was then divided into only twelve counties. Each of those counties had elected a committee at the commencement of the dispute with the English government; and as the city of Philadelphia, which also had its committee, was the most central for intelligence, it became the center of communication to the several county committees. When it became necessary to proceed to the formation of a government, the committee of Philadelphia proposed a conference of all the county committees, to be held in that city, and which met the latter end of July 1776.

Though these committees had been elected by the people, they were not elected expressly for the purpose, nor invested with the authority, of forming a constitution; and as they could not, consistently with the American idea of rights, assume such a power, they could only confer upon the matter, and put it into a train of operation. The conferrees, therefore, did no more than state the case, and recommend to the several counties to elect six representatives for each county, to meet in convention at Philadelphia, with powers to form a constitution, and propose it for public consideration.

This convention, of which Benjamin Franklin was president, having met and deliberated, and agreed upon a constitution, they next ordered it to be published, not as a thing established, but for the consideration of the whole people, their approbation or rejection, and then adjourned to a stated time. When the time of adjournment was expired, the convention re-assembled; and as the general opinion of the people in approbation of it was then known, the constitution was signed, sealed, and proclaimed on the *authority of the people* and the original instrument deposited as a public record. The convention then appointed a day for the general election of the representatives who were to compose the government, and the time it should commence; and having done this, they dissolved, and returned to their several homes and occupations.

In this constitution were laid down, first, a declaration of rights. Then followed the form which the government should have, and the powers it should possess—the authority of the courts of judicature, and of juries—the manner in which elections should be conducted, and the proportion of representatives to the number of electors—the time which each succeeding assembly should continue, which was one year—the mode of levying, and of accounting for the expenditure, of public money—of appointing public officers, &c. &c. &c.

No article of this constitution could be altered or infringed at the discretion of the government that was to ensue. It was to that government a law. But as it would have been unwise to preclude the benefit of experience, and in order also to prevent the accumulation of errors, if any should be found, and to preserve an unison of government with the circumstances of the state at all times, the constitution provided, that, at the expiration of every seven years, a convention should be elected, for the express purpose of revising the constitution, and making alterations, additions, or abolitions therein, if any such should be found necessary.

Here we see a regular process—a government issuing out of a constitution, formed by the people in their original character; and that constitution serving, not only as an authority, but as a law of controul to the government. It was the political bible of the state. Scarcely a family was without it. Every member of the government had a copy; and nothing was more common, when any debate arose on the principle of a bill, or on the extent of any species of authority, than for the members to take the printed constitution out of their pocket, and read the chapter with which such matter in debate was connected.

Having thus given an instance from one of the states, I will shew the proceedings by which the federal constitution of the United States arose and was formed.

Congress, at its two first meetings,* in September 1774,

and May 1775, was nothing more than a deputation from the legislatures of the several provinces, afterwards states; and had no other authority than what arose from common consent, and the necessity of its acting as a public body. In every thing which related to the internal affairs of America, congress went no further than to issue recommendations to the several provincial assemblies, who at discretion adopted them or not. Nothing on the part of congress was compulsive; yet, in this situation, it was more faithfully and affectionately obeyed, than was any government in Europe. This instance, like that of the national assembly in France, sufficiently shews, that the strength of government does not consist in any thing *within* itself, but in the attachment of a nation, and the interest which the people feel in supporting it. When this is lost, government is but a child in power; and though, like the old government of France, it may harrass individuals for a while, it but facilitates its own fall.

After the declaration of independence, it became consistent with the principle on which representative government is founded, that the authority of congress should be defined and established. Whether that authority should be more or less than congress then discretionarily exercised, was not the question. It was merely the rectitude of the measure.

For this purpose, the act, called the act of confederation, (which was a sort of imperfect federal constitution), was proposed, and, after long deliberation, was concluded in the year 1781. It was not the act of congress, because it is repugnant to the principles of representative government that a body should give power to itself. Congress first informed the several states, of the powers which it conceived were necessary to be invested in the union, to enable it to perform the duties and services required from it; and the states severally agreed with each other, and concenterated in congress those powers.

It may not be improper to observe, that in both those instances, (the one of Pennsylvania, and the other of the United States), there is no such thing as the idea of a compact between the people on one side, and the government on the other. The compact was that of the people with each other, to produce and constitute a government. To suppose that any government can be a party in a compact with the whole people, is to suppose it to have existence before it can have a right to exist. The only instance in which a compact can take place between the people and those who exercise the government, is, that the people shall pay them, while they chuse to employ them.

Government is not a trade which any man or body of men has a right to set up and exercise for his own emolument, but is altogether a trust, in right of those by whom that trust is delegated, and by whom it is always resumeable. It has of itself no rights; they are altogether duties.

Having thus given two instances of the original formation of a constitution, I will shew the manner in which both have been changed since their first establishment.

The powers vested in the governments of the several states, by the state constitutions, were found, upon experience, to be too great; and those vested in the federal government, by the act of confederation, too little. The defect was not in the principle, but in the distribution of power.

Numerous publications, in pamphlets and in the newspapers, appeared, on the propriety and necessity of new modelling the federal government. After some time of public discussion, carried on through the channel of the press, and in conversations, the state of Virginia,* experiencing some inconvenience with respect to commerce, proposed holding a continental conference; in consequence of which, a deputation from five or six of the state assemblies met at Anapolis in Maryland, in 1786. This meeting, not conceiving itself sufficiently authorised to go into the business of a reform, did no more than state their general opinions of the propriety of the measure, and recommend that a convention of all the states should be held the year following.

This convention met at Philadelphia in May 1787, of which General Washington was elected president. He was not at that time connected with any of the state governments, or with congress. He delivered up his commission when the war ended, and since then had lived a private citizen.

The convention went deeply into all the subjects; and

having, after a variety of debate and investigation, agreed among themselves upon the several parts of a federal constitution, the next question was, the manner of giving it authority and practice.

For this purpose, they did not, like a cabal of courtiers, send for a Dutch Stadtholder, or a German Elector; but they referred the whole matter to the sense and interest of the country.

They first directed, that the proposed constitution should be published. Secondly, that each state should elect a convention, expressly for the purpose of taking it into consideration, and of ratifying or rejecting it; and that as soon as the approbation and ratification of any nine states should be given, that those states should proceed to the election of their proportion of members to the new federal government; and that the operation of it should then begin, and the former federal government cease.

The several states proceeded accordingly to elect their conventions. Some of those conventions ratified the constitution by very large majorities, and two or three unanimously. In others there were much debate and division of opinion. In the Massachusetts convention, which met at Boston, the majority was not above nineteen or twenty, in about three hundred members; but such is the nature of representative government, that it quietly decides all matters by majority. After the debate in the Massachusetts convention was closed, and the vote taken, the objecting members rose, and declared, *'That though they had argued and voted against it, because certain parts appeared to them in a different light to what they appeared to other members; yet, as the vote had decided in favour of the constitution as proposed, they should give it the same practical support as if they had voted for it.'**

As soon as nine states had concurred, (and the rest followed in the order their conventions were elected), the old fabric of the federal government was taken down, and the new one erected, of which General Washington is president.—In this place I cannot help remarking, that the character and services of this gentleman are sufficient to put all those men called kings to shame. While they are receiving from the sweat and labours of mankind, a prodigality of pay, to which neither their abilities nor their services can entitle them, he is rendering every service in his power, and refusing every pecuniary reward. He accepted no pay as commander in chief; he accepts none as president of the United States.*

After the new federal constitution was established, the state of Pennsylvania, conceiving that some parts of its own constitution required to be altered, elected a convention for that purpose. The proposed alterations were published, and the people concurring therein, they were established.

In forming those constitutions, or in altering them, little or no inconvenience took place. The ordinary course of things was not interrupted, and the advantages have been much. It is always the interest of a far greater number of people in a nation to have things right, than to let them remain wrong; and when public matters are open to debate, and the public judgment free, it will not decide wrong, unless it decides too hastily.

In the two instances of changing the constitutions, the governments then in being were not actors either way. Government has no right to make itself a party in any debate respecting the principles or modes of forming, or of changing, constitutions. It is not for the benefit of those who exercise the powers of government, that constitutions, and the governments issuing from them, are established. In all those matters, the right of judging and acting are in those who pay, and not in those who receive.

A constitution is the property of a nation, and not of those who exercise the government. All the constitutions of America are declared to be established on the authority of the people. In France, the word nation is used instead of the people; but in both cases, a constitution is a thing antecedent to the government, and always distinct therefrom.

In England, it is not difficult to perceive that every thing has a constitution, except the nation. Every society and association that is established, first agreed upon a number of original articles, digested into form, which are its constitution. It then appointed its officers, whose powers and authorities are described in that constitution, and the government of that society then commenced. Those officers, by whatever name they are called, have no authority to add to, alter, or abridge the original articles. It is only to the constituting power that this right belongs.

From the want of understanding the difference between a constitution and a government, Dr Johnson, and all writers of his description, have always bewildered themselves. They could not but perceive, that there must necessarily be a *controuling* power* existing somewhere, and they placed this power in the discretion of the persons exercising the government, instead of placing it in a constitution formed by the nation. When it is in a constitution, it has the nation for its support, and the natural and the political controuling powers are together. The laws which are enacted by governments, controul men only as individuals, but the nation, through its constitution, controuls the whole government, and has a natural ability so to do. The final controuling power, therefore, and the original constituting power, are one and the same power.

Dr Johnson could not have advanced such a position in any country where there was a constitution; and he is himself an evidence, that no such thing as a constitution exists in England.—But it may be put as a question, not improper to be investigated, That if a constitution does not exist, how came the idea of its existence so generally established?

In order to decide this question, it is necessary to consider a constitution in both its cases:—First, as creating a government and giving it powers. Secondly, as regulating and restraining the powers so given.

If we begin with William of Normandy, we find that the government of England was originally a tyranny, founded on an invasion and conquest of the country. This being admitted, it will then appear, that the exertion of the nation, at different periods, to abate that tyranny, and render it less intolerable, has been credited for a constitution.

Magna Charta,* as it was called, (it is now like an almanack of the same date,) was no more than compelling the government to renounce a part of its assumptions. It did not create and give powers to government in the manner a constitution does; but was, as far as it went, of the nature of a re-conquest, and not of a constitution; for could the nation have totally expelled the usurpation, as France has done its despotism, it would then have had a constitution to form.

The history of the Edwards and the Henries, and up to the commencement of the Stuarts,* exhibits as many instances of tyranny as could be acted within the limits to which the nation had restricted it. The Stuarts endeavoured to pass those limits, and their fate is well known. In all those instances we see nothing of a constitution, but only of restrictions on assumed power.

After this, another William, descended from the same stock, and claiming from the same origin, gained possession; and of the two evils, *James* and *William*, the nation preferred what it thought the least; since, from circumstances, it must take one. The act, called the Bill of Rights,* comes here into view. What is it, but a bargain, which the parts of the government made with each other to divide powers, profits, and privileges? You shall have so much, and I will have the rest; and with respect to the nation, it said, for *your share, you shall have the right of petitioning*. This being the case, the bill of rights is more properly a bill of wrongs, and of insult. As to what is called the convention parliament,* it was a thing that made itself, and then made the authority by which it acted. A few persons got together, and called themselves by that name. Several of them had never been elected, and none of them for the purpose.

From the time of William, a species of government arose, issuing out of this coalition bill of rights; and more so, since the corruption introduced at the Hanover succession,* by the agency of Walpole; that can be described by no other name than a despotic legislation. Though the parts may embarrass each other, the whole has no bounds; and the only right it acknowledges out of itself, is the right of petitioning. Where then is the constitution either that gives or that restrains power?

It is not because a part of the government is elective, that makes it less, a despotism, if the persons so elected, possess afterwards, as a parliament, unlimited powers. Election, in this case, becomes separated from representation, and the candidates are candidates for despotism.

I cannot believe that any nation, reasoning on its own rights, would have thought of calling those things *a constitution*, if the cry of constitution had not been set up by the government. It has got into circulation like the words *bore* and *quoz*,* by being chalked up in the speeches of parliament, as those words were on window shutters and door posts; but whatever the constitution may be in other respects, it has undoubtedly been *the most productive machine of taxation that was ever invented.* The taxes in France, under the new constitution, are not quite thirteen shillings per head,[1] and the taxes in England, under what is called its present constitution, are forty-eight shillings and sixpence per head, men, women, and children, amounting to nearly seventeen millions sterling, besides the expence of collection, which is upwards of a million more.

In a country like England, where the whole of the civil government is executed by the people of every town and country, by means of parish officers, magistrates, quarterly sessions, juries, and assize; without any trouble to what is called the government, or any other expence to the revenue than the salary of the judges, it is astonishing how such a mass of taxes can be employed. Not even the internal defence of the country is paid out of the revenue. On all occassions, whether real or contrived, recourse is continually had to new loans and new taxes. No wonder, then, that a machine of government so advantageous to the advocates of a court, should be so triumphantly extolled! No wonder, that St James's or St Stephen's* should echo with the continual cry of constitution! No wonder, that the French revolution

---

[1] The whole amount of the assessed taxes of France, for the present year, is three hundred millions of livres, which is twelve millions and a half sterling; and the incidental taxes are estimated at three millions, making in the whole fifteen millions and a half; which, among twenty-four millions of people, is not quite thirteen shillings per head. France has lessened her taxes since the revolution, nearly nine millions sterling annually. Before the revolution, the city of Paris paid a duty* of upwards of thirty per cent. on all articles brought into the city. This tax was collected at the city gates. It was taken off on the first of last May, and the gates taken down.

should be reprobated, and the *res-publica* treated with reproach! The *red book* of England, like the red book of France, will explain the reason.[1]

I will now, by way of relaxation, turn a thought or two to Mr Burke. I ask his pardon for neglecting him so long.

'America,' says he, (in his speech on the Canada constitution bill)* 'never dreamed of such absurd doctrine as the *Rights of Man*.'

Mr Burke is such a bold presumer, and advances his assertions and his premises with such a deficiency of judgment, that, without troubling ourselves about principles of philosophy or politics, the mere logical conclusions they produce, are ridiculous. For instance,

If governments, as Mr Burke asserts, are not founded on the Rights of MAN, and are founded on *any rights* at all, they consequently must be founded, on the rights of *something* that is *not man*. What then is that something?

Generally speaking, we know of no other creatures that inhabit the earth than man and beast; and in all cases, where only two things offer themselves, and one must be admitted, a negation proved on any one, amounts to an affirmative on the other; and therefore, Mr Burke, by proving against the Rights of *Man*, proves in behalf of the *beast*; and consequently, proves that government is a beast: and as difficult things sometimes explain each other, we now see the origin of keeping wild beasts in the Tower;* for they certainly can be of no other use than to shew the origin of the government. They are in the place of a constitution. O John Bull,* what honours thou hast lost by not being a wild beast. Thou mightest, on Mr Burke's system, have been in the Tower for life.

If Mr Burke's arguments have not weight enough to keep one serious, the fault is less mine than his; and as I am willing to make an apology to the reader for the liberty I have taken, I hope Mr Burke will also make his for giving the cause.

[1] What was called the *livre rouge*, or the red book, in France, was not exactly similar to the court calendar* in England; but it sufficiently shewed how a great part of the taxes was lavished.

Having thus paid Mr Burke the compliment of remembering him, I return to the subject.

From the want of a constitution in England to restrain and regulate the wild impulse of power, many of the laws are irrational and tyrannical, and the administration of them vague and problematical.

The attention of the government of England, (for I rather chuse to call it by this name, than the English government) appears, since its political connection with Germany, to have been so completely engrossed and absorbed by foreign affairs, and the means of raising taxes, that it seems to exist for no other purposes. Domestic concerns are neglected; and, with respect to regular law, there is scarcely such a thing.

Almost every case now must be determined by some precedent, be that precedent good or bad, or whether it properly applies or not; and the practice is become so general, as to suggest a suspicion, that it proceeds from a deeper policy than at first sight appears.

Since the revolution of America, and more so since that of France, this preaching up the doctrine of precedents, drawn from times and circumstances antecedent to those events, has been the studied practice of the English government. The generality of those precedents are founded on principles and opinions, the reverse of what they ought; and the greater distance of time they are drawn from, the more they are to be suspected. But by associating those precedents with a superstitious reverence for ancient things, as monks shew relics and call them holy, the generality of mankind are deceived into the design. Governments now act as if they were afraid to awaken a single reflection in man. They are softly leading him to the sepulchre of precedents, to deaden his faculties and call his attention from the scene of revolutions. They feel that he is arriving at knowledge faster than they wish, and their policy of precedents is the barometer of their fears. This political popery, like the ecclesiastical popery of old, has had its day, and is hastening to its exit. The ragged relic and the antiquated precedent, the monk and the monarch, will moulder together.

Government by precedent, without any regard to the principle of the precedent, is one of the vilest systems that can be set up. In numerous instances, the precedent ought to operate as a warning, and not as an example, and requires to be shunned instead of imitated; but instead of this, precedents are taken in the lump, and put at once for constitution and for law.

Either the doctrine of precedents is policy to keep man in a state of ignorance, or it is a practical consession that wisdom degenerates in governments as governments increase in age, and can only hobble along by the stilts and crutches of precedents. How is it that the same persons who would proudly be thought wiser than their predecessors, appear at the same time only as the ghosts of departed wisdom? How strangely is antiquity treated! To answer some purposes it is spoken of as the times of darkness and ignorance, and to answer others, it is put for the light of the world.

If the doctrine of precedents, is to be followed, the expences of government need not continue the same. Why pay men extravagantly, who have but little to do? If every thing that can happen is already in precedent, legislation is at an end, and precedent, like a dictionary, determines every case. Either, therefore, government has arrived at its dotage, and requires to be renovated, or all the occasions for exercising its wisdom have occured.

We now see all over Europe, and particularly in England, the curious phænomenon of a nation looking one way, and a government the other—the one forward and the other backward. If governments are to go on by precedent, while nations go on by improvement, they must at last come to a final separation; and the sooner, and the more civilly, they determine this point, the better.[1]

Having thus spoken of constitutions generally, as things distinct from actual governments, let us proceed to consider the parts of which a constitution is composed.

[1] In England, the improvements in agriculture, useful arts, manufactures, and commerce, have been made in opposition to the genius of its government, which is that of following precedents. It is from the enterprize and industry of the

Opinions differ more on this subject, than with respect to the whole. That a nation ought to have a constitution, as a rule for the conduct of its government, is a simple question in which all men, not directly courtiers, will agree. It is only on the component parts that questions and opinions multiply.

But this difficulty, like every other, will diminish when put into a train of being rightly understood.

The first thing is, that a nation has a right to establish a constitution.

Whether it exercises this right in the most judicious manner at first, is quite another case. It exercises it agreeably to the judgment it possesses; and by continuing to do so, all errors will at last be exploded.

When this right is established in a nation, there is no fear that it will be employed to its own injury. A nation can have no interest in being wrong.

Though all the constitutions of America are on one general principle, yet no two of them are exactly alike in their component parts, or in the distribution of the powers which they give to the actual governments. Some are more, and others less complex.

In forming a constitution, it is first necessary to consider what are the ends for which government is necessary? Secondly, what are the best means, and the least expensive, for accomplishing those ends?

Government is nothing more than a national association; and the object of this association is the good of all, as well individually as collectively. Every man wishes to pursue his occupation, and to enjoy the fruits of his labours, and the produce of his property in peace and safety, and with the least possible expence. When these things are accomplished, all the objects for which government ought to be established are answered.

individuals, and their numerous associations, in which, tritely speaking, government is neither pillow nor bolster, that these improvements have proceeded. No man thought about the government, or who was *in*, or who was *out*, when he was planning or executing those things; and all he had to hope, with respect to government, was, *that it would let him alone*. Three or four very silly ministerial news-papers* are continually offending against the spirit of national improvement, by ascribing it to a minister. They may with as much truth ascribe this book to a minister.

It has been customary to consider government under three distinct general heads. The legislative, the executive, and the judicial.

But if we permit our judgment to act unincumbered by the habit of multiplied terms, we can perceive no more than two divisions of power, of which civil government is composed, namely, that of legislating or enacting laws, and that of executing or administering them. Every thing, therefore, appertaining to civil government, classes itself under one or other of these two divisions.

So far as regards the execution of the laws, that which is called the judicial power, is strictly and properly the executive power of every country. It is that power to which every individual has appeal, and which causes the laws to be executed; neither have we any other clear idea with respect to the official execution of the laws. In England, and also in America and France, this power begins with the magistrate, and proceeds up through all the courts of judicature.

I leave to courtiers to explain what is meant by calling monarchy the executive power. It is merely a name in which acts of government are done; and any other, or none at all, would answer the same purpose. Laws have neither more nor less authority on this account. It must be from the justness of their principles, and the interest which a nation feels therein, that they derive support; if they require any other than this, it is a sign that something in the system of government is imperfect. Laws difficult to be executed cannot be generally good.

With respect to the organization of the *legislative power*, different modes have been adopted in different countries. In America it is generally composed of two houses.* In France it consists but of one, but in both countries it is wholly by representation.

The case is, that mankind (from the long tyranny of assumed power) have had so few opportunities of making the necessary trials on modes and principles of government, in order to discover the best, *that government is but now beginning to be known*, and experience is yet wanting to determine many particulars.

The objections against two houses are, first, that there is an inconsistency in any part of a whole legislature, coming to a final determination by vote on any matter, whilst *that matter*, with respect to *that whole*, is yet only in a train of deliberation, and consequently open to new illustrations.

Secondly, That by taking the vote on each, as a separate body, it always admits of the possibility, and is often the case in practice, that the minority governs the majority, and that, in some instances, to a degree of great inconsistency.

Thirdly, That two houses arbitrarily checking or controuling each other is inconsistent; because it cannot be proved, on the principles of just representation, that either should be wiser or better than the other. They may check in the wrong as well as in the right,—and therefore, to give the power where we cannot give the wisdom to use it, nor be assured of its being rightly used, renders the hazard at least equal to the precaution.[1]

The objection against a single house is, that it is always in a condition of committing itself too soon.—But it should at the same time be remembered, that when there is a constitution which defines the power, and establishes the principles within which a legislature shall act, there is already a more effectual check provided, and more powerfully operating,

---

[1] With respect to the two houses, of which the English Parliament is composed, they appear to be effectually influenced into one, and, as a legislature, to have no temper of its own. The minister, whoever he at any time may be, touches it as with an opium wand, and it sleeps obedience.

But if we look at the distinct abilities of the two houses, the difference will appear so great, as to shew the inconsistency of placing power where there can be no certainty of the judgment to use it. Wretched as the state of representation is in England, it is manhood compared with what is called the house of Lords; and so little is this nick-named house regarded, that the people scarcely inquire at any time what it is doing. It appears also to be most under influence, and the furthest removed from the general interest of the nation. In the debate on engaging in the Russian and Turkish war,* the majority in the house of peers in favour of it was upwards of ninety, when in the other house, which is more than double its numbers, the majority was sixty-three.

The proceedings on Mr Fox's bill, respecting the rights of juries,* merits also to be noticed. The persons called the peers were not the objects of that bill. They are already in possession of more privileges than that bill gave to others. They are their own jury, and if any of that house were prosecuted for a libel, he would not suffer, even upon conviction, for the first offence. Such inequality in laws ought not to exist in any country. The French constitution says, That *the law is the same to every individual, whether to protect or to punish. All are equal in its sight.*

than any other check can be. For example,

Were a bill to be brought into any of the American legislatures, similar to that which was passed into an act by the English parliament, at the commencement of George the First, to extend the duration of the assemblies to a longer period than they now sit,* the check is in the constitution, which in effect says, *Thus far shalt thou go and no further*.

But in order to remove the objection against a single house, (that of acting with too quick an impulse,) and at the same time to avoid the inconsistencies, in some cases absurdities, arising from two houses, the following method has been proposed as an improvement upon both.

First, To have but one representation.

Secondly, To divide that representation, by lot, into two or three parts.

Thirdly, That every proposed bill, shall be first debated in those parts by succession, that they may become the hearers of each other, but without taking any vote. After which the whole representation to assemble for a general debate and determination by vote.

To this proposed improvement has been added another, for the purpose of keeping the representation in a state of constant renovation; which is, that one-third of the representation of each county, shall go out at the expiration of one year, and the number be replaced by new elections.—Another third at the expiration of the second year replaced in like manner, and every third year to be a general election.[1]

But in whatever manner the separate parts of a constitution may be arranged, there is *one* general principle that distinguishes freedom from slavery, which is, that all *hereditary government over a people is to them a species of slavery, and representative government is freedom*.

Considering government in the only light in which it should be considered, that of a NATIONAL ASSOCIATION; it ought to be so constructed as not to be disordered by any

---

[1] As to the state of representation in England, it is too absurd to be reasoned upon. Almost all the represented parts are decreasing in population, and the unrepresented parts are increasing. A general convention of the nation is necessary to take the whole state of its government into consideration.*

accident happening among the parts; and, therefore, no extraordinary power, capable of producing such an effect, should be lodged in the hands of any individual. The death, sickness, absence, or defection, of any one individual in a government, ought to be a matter of no more consequence, with respect to the nation, than if the same circumstance had taken place in a member of the English Parliament, or the French National Assembly.

Scarcely any thing presents a more degrading character of national greatness, than its being thrown into confusion by any thing happening to, or acted by, an individual; and the ridiculousness of the scene is often increased by the natural insignificance of the person by whom it is occasioned. Were a government so constructed, that it could not go on unless a goose or a gander were present in the senate, the difficulties would be just as great and as real on the flight or sickness of the goose, or the gander, as if it were called a King. We laugh at individuals for the silly difficulties they make to themselves, without perceiving, that the greatest of all ridiculous things are acted in governments.[1]

All the constitutions of America are on a plan that excludes the childish embarrassments which occur in monarchical countries. No suspension of government can there take place for a moment, from any circumstance whatever. The system of representation provides for every thing, and is the only system in which nations and governments can always appear in their proper character.

[1] It is related, that in the canton of Berne, in Swisserland, it had been customary, from time immemorial, to keep a bear at the public expence, and the people had been taught to believe, that if they had not a bear they should all be undone. It happened some years ago, that the bear, then in being, was taken sick and died too suddenly to have his place immediately supplied with another. During this interregnum the people discovered, that the corn grew, and the vintage flourished, and the sun and moon continued to rise and set, and every thing went on the same as before, and, taking courage from these circumstances, they resolved not to keep any more bears; for, said they, 'a bear is a very voracious, expensive animal, and we were obliged to pull out his claws, lest he should hurt the citizens.'

The story of the bear of Berne was related in some of the French news-papers, at the time of the flight of Louis XVI. and the application of it to monarchy could not be mistaken in France; but it seems, that the aristocracy of Berne applied it to themselves, and have since prohibited the reading of French news-papers.

As extraordinary power, ought not to be lodged in the hands of any individual, so ought there to be no appropriations of public money to any person, beyond what his services in a state may be worth. It signifies not whether a man be called a president, a king, an emperor, a senator, or by any other name, which propriety or folly may devise, or arrogance assume, it is only a certain service he can perform in the state; and the service of any such individual in the rotine of office, whether such office be called monarchical, presidential, senatorial, or by any other name or title, can never exceed the value of ten thousand pounds a year. All the great services that are done in the world are performed by volunteer characters, who accept nothing for them; but the rotine of office is always regulated to such a general standard of abilities as to be within the compass of numbers in every country to perform, and therefore cannot merit very extraordinary recompence. *Government*, says Swift, *is a plain thing, and fitted to the capacity of many heads.**

It is inhuman to talk of a million sterling a year, paid out of the public taxes of any country, for the support of any individual, whilst thousands who are forced to contribute thereto, are pining with want, and struggling with misery. Government does not consist in a contrast between prisons and palaces, between poverty and pomp; it is not instituted to rob the needy of his mite, and increase the wretchedness of the wretched.—But of this part of the subject I shall speak hereafter, and confine myself at present to political observations.

When extraordinary power and extraordinary pay are allotted to any individual in a government, he becomes the center, round which every kind of corruption generates and forms. Give to any man a million a year, and add thereto the power of creating and disposing of places, at the expence of a country, and the liberties of that country are no longer secure. What is called the splendor of a throne is no other than the corruption of the state. It is made up of a band of parasites, living in luxurious indolence, out of the public taxes.

When once such a vicious system is established it becomes

the guard and protection of all inferior abuses. The man who is in the receipt of a million a year is the last person to promote a spirit of reform, lest, in the event, it should reach to himself. It is always his interest to defend inferior abuses, as so many out-works to protect the citadel; and in this species of political fortification, all the parts have such a common dependence that it is never to be expected they will attack each other.[1]

Monarchy would not have continued so many ages in the world, had it not been for the abuses it protects. It is the master-fraud, which shelters all others. By admitting a participation of the spoil, it makes itself friends; and when it ceases to do this, it will cease to be the idol of courtiers.

As the principle on which constitutions are now formed rejects all hereditary pretentions to government, it also rejects all that catalogue of assumptions known by the name of prerogatives.

If there is any government where prerogatives might with apparent safety be entrusted to any individual, it is in the fœderal government of America. The President of the United States of America is elected only for four years. He is not only responsible in the general sense of the word, but a particular mode is laid down in the constitution for trying

---

[1] It is scarcely possible to touch on any subject, that will not suggest an allusion to some corruption in governments. The simile of '*fortifications*,' unfortunately involves with it a circumstance, which is directly in point with the matter above alluded to.

Among the numerous instances of abuse which have been acted or protected by governments, ancient or modern, there is not a greater than that of quartering a man and his heirs upon the public, to be maintained at its expence.

Humanity dictates a provision for the poor; but by what right, moral or political, does any government assume to say, that the person called the Duke of Richmond,* shall be maintained by the public? Yet, if common report is true, not a beggar in London can purchase his wretched pittance of coal, without paying towards the civil list of the Duke of Richmond. Were the whole produce of this imposition but a shilling a year, the iniquitous principle would be still the same; but when it amounts, as it is said to do, to not less than twenty thousand pounds *per ann.* the enormity is too serious to be permitted to remain—This is one of the effects of monarchy and aristocracy.

In stating this case, I am led by no personal dislike. Though I think it mean in any man to live upon the public, the vice originates in the government; and so general is it become, that whether the parties are in the ministry or in the opposition, it makes no difference: they are sure of the guarantee of each other.

him. He cannot be elected under thirty-five years of age; and he must be a native of the country.

In a comparison of these cases with the government of England, the difference when applied to the latter amounts to an absurdity. In England the person who exercises prerogative is often a foreigner; always half a foreigner, and always married to a foreigner. He is never in full natural or political connection with the country, is not responsible for any thing, and becomes of age at eighteen years, yet such a person is permitted to form foreign alliances, without even the knowledge of the nation, and to make war and peace without its consent.

But this is not all. Though such a person cannot dispose of the government, in the manner of a testator, he dictates the marriage connections, which, in effect, accomplishes a great part of the same end. He cannot directly bequeath half the government to Prussia, but he can form a marriage partnership that will produce almost the same thing. Under such circumstances, it is happy for England that she is not situated on the continent, or she might, like Holland, fall under the dictatorship of Prussia. Holland, by marriage,* is as effectually governed by Prussia, as if the old tyranny of bequeathing the government had been the means.

The presidency in America, (or, as it is sometimes called, the executive,) is the only office from which a foreigner is excluded, and in England it is the only one to which he is admitted. A foreigner cannot be a member of parliament, but he may be what is called a king. If there is any reason for excluding foreigners, it ought to be from those offices where mischief can most be acted, and where, by uniting every bias of interest and attachment, the trust is best secured.

But as nations proceed in the great business of forming constitutions, they will examine with more precision into the nature and business of that department which is called the executive. What the legislative and judicial departments are, every one can see; but with respect to what, in Europe, is called the executive, as distinct from those two, it is either a political superfluity or a chaos of unknown things.

Some kind of official department, to which reports shall be made from the different parts of a nation, or from abroad, to be laid before the national representatives, is all that is necessary; but there is no consistency in calling this the executive; neither can it be considered in any other light than as inferior to the legislative. The sovereign authority in any country is the power of making laws, and every thing else is an official department.

Next to the arrangement of the principles and the organization of the several parts of a constitution, is the provision to be made for the support of the persons to whom the nation shall confide the administration of the constitutional powers.

A nation can have no right to the time and services of any person at his own expence, whom it may chuse to employ or entrust in any department whatever; neither can any reason be given for making provision for the support of any one part of a government and not for the other.

But, admitting that the honour of being entrusted with any part of a government is to be considered a sufficient reward, it ought to be so to every person alike. If the members of the legislature of any country are to serve at their own expence, that which is called the executive, whether monarchical, or by any other name, ought to serve in like manner. It is inconsistent to pay the one, and accept the service of the other gratis.

In America, every department in the government is decently provided for; but no one is extravagantly paid. Every member of Congress, and of the assemblies, is allowed a sufficiency for his expences. Whereas in England, a most prodigal provision is made for the support of one part of the government, and none for the other, the consequence of which is, that the one is furnished with the means of corruption, and the other is put into the condition of being corrupted. Less than a fourth part of such expence, applied as it is in America, would remedy a great part of the corruption.

Another reform in the American constitutions, is the exploding all oaths of personality. The oath of allegiance in

America is to the nation only. The putting any individual as a figure for a nation is improper. The happiness of a nation is the superior object, and therefore the intention of an oath of allegiance ought not to be obscured by being figuratively taken,* to, or in the name of, any person. The oath, called the civic oath,* in France, viz. the *'nation, the law, and the king,'* is improper. If taken at all, it ought to be as in America, to the nation only. The law may or may not be good; but, in this place, it can have no other meaning, than as being conducive to the happiness of the nation, and therefore is included in it. The remainder of the oath is improper, on the ground, that all personal oaths ought to be abolished. They are the remains of tyranny on one part, and slavery on the other; and the name of the CREATOR ought not to be introduced to witness the degradation of his creation; or if taken, as is already mentioned, as figurative of the nation, it is in this place redundant. But whatever apology may be made for oaths at the first establishment of a government, they ought not to be permitted afterwards. If a government requires the support of oaths, it is a sign that it is not worth supporting, and ought not to be supported. Make government what it ought to be, and it will support itself.

To conclude this part of the subject:—One of the greatest improvements that has been made for the perpetual security and progress of constitutional liberty, is the provision which the new constitutions make for occasionally revising, altering, and amending them.

The principle upon which Mr Burke formed his political creed, that *'of binding and controuling posterity to the end of time, and of renouncing and abdicating the rights of all posterity for ever,'* is now become too detestable to be made a subject of debate; and, therefore, I pass it over with no other notice than exposing it.

Government is but now beginning to be known. Hitherto it has been the mere exercise of power, which forbad all effectual enquiry into rights, and grounded itself wholly on possession. While the enemy of liberty was its judge, the progress of its principles must have been small indeed.

The constitutions of America, and also that of France,

have either affixed a period for their revision, or laid down the mode by which improvements shall be made. It is perhaps impossible to establish any thing that combines principles with opinions and practice, which the progress of circumstances, through a length of years, will not in some measure derange, or render inconsistent; and, therefore, to prevent inconveniences accumulating, till they discourage reformations or provoke revolutions, it is best to provide the means of regulating them as they occur. The Rights of Man are the rights of all generations of men, and cannot be monopolized by any. That which is worth following, will be followed for the sake of its worth; and it is in this that its security lies, and not in any conditions with which it may be encumbered. When a man leaves property to his heirs, he does not connect it with an obligation that they shall accept it. Why then should we do otherwise with respect to constitutions?

The best constitution that could now be devised, consistent with the condition of the present moment, may be far short of that excellence which a few years may afford. There is a morning of reason rising upon man on the subject of government, that has not appeared before. As the barbarism of the present old governments expires, the moral condition of nations with respect to each other will be changed. Man will not be brought up with the savage idea of considering his species as his enemy, because the accident of birth gave the individuals existence in countries distinguished by different names; and as constitutions have always some relation to external as well as to domestic circumstances, the means of benefiting by every change, foreign or domestic, should be a part of every constitution.

We already see an alteration in the national disposition of England and France towards each other, which, when we look back to only a few years, is itself a revolution. Who could have foreseen, or who would have believed, that a French National Assembly would ever have been a popular toast in England, or that a friendly alliance of the two nations should become the wish of either. It shews, that man, were he not corrupted by governments, is naturally the friend of man, and that human nature is not of itself vicious. That spirit, of jealously and ferocity, which the governments of the two countries inspired, and which they rendered subservient to the purpose of taxation, is now yielding to the dictates of reason, interest, and humanity. The trade of courts is beginning to be understood, and the affectation of mystery, with all the artificial sorcery by which they imposed upon mankind, is on the decline. It has received its death-wound; and though it may linger, it will expire.

Government ought to be as much open to improvement as any thing which appertains to man, instead of which it has been monopolized from age to age, by the most ignorant and vicious of the human race. Need we any other proof of their wretched management, than the excess of debts and taxes with which every nation groans, and the quarrels into which they have precipitated the world?

Just emerging from such a barbarous condition, it is too soon to determine to what extent of improvement govern-ment may yet be carried. For what we can foresee, all Europe may form but one great republic, and man be free of the whole.

CHAPTER V

WAYS AND MEANS OF IMPROVING THE CONDITION OF EUROPE, INTERSPERSED WITH MISCELLANEOUS OBSERVATIONS

IN contemplating a subject that embraces with equatorial magnitude the whole region of humanity, it is impossible to confine the pursuit in one single direction. It takes ground on every character and condition that appertains to man, and blends the individual, the nation, and the world.

From a small spark, kindled in America, a flame has arisen, not to be extinguished. Without consuming, like the *Ultima Ratio Regum*,* it winds its progress from nation to nation, and conquers by a silent operation. Man finds himself changed, he scarcely perceives how. He acquires a knowledge of his rights by attending justly to his interest, and discovers in the event that the strength and powers of despotism consist wholly in the fear of resisting it, and that, in order '*to be free, it is sufficient that he wills it.*'

Having in all the preceding parts of this work endeavoured to establish a system of principles as a basis, on which governments ought to be erected; I shall proceed in this, to the ways and means of rendering them into practice. But in order to introduce this part of the subject with more propriety, and stronger effect, some preliminary observations, deducible from, or connected with, those principles, are necessary.

Whatever the form or constitution of government may be, it ought to have no other object than the *general* happiness. When, instead of this, it operates to create and encrease wretchedness in any of the parts of society, it is on a wrong system, and reformation is necessary.

Customary language has classed the condition of man under the two descriptions of civilized and uncivilized life. To the one it has ascribed felicity and affluence; to the other hardship and want. But, however, our imagination may be impressed by painting and comparison, it is nevertheless true, that a great portion of mankind, in what are called civilized countries, are in a state of poverty and wretchedness, far below the condition of an Indian. I speak not of one country, but of all. It is so in England, it is so all over Europe. Let us enquire into the cause.

It lies not in any natural defect in the principles of civilization, but in preventing those principles having an universal operation; the consequence of which is, a perpetual system of war and expence, that drains the country, and defeats the general felicity of which civilization is capable.

All the European governments (France now excepted) are constructed not on the principle of universal civilization, but on the reverse of it. So far as those governments relate to each other, they are in the same condition as we conceive of savage uncivilized life; they put themselves beyond the law as well of GOD as of man, and are, with respect to principle and reciprocal conduct, like so many individuals in a state of nature.

The inhabitants of every country, under the civilization of laws, easily civilize together, but governments being yet in an uncivilized state, and almost continually at war, they pervert the abundance which civilized life produces to carry on the uncivilized part to a greater extent. By thus engrafting the barbarism of government upon the internal civilization of a country, it draws from the latter and more especially from the poor, a great portion of those earnings, which should be applied to their own subsistence and comfort.— Apart from all reflections of morality and philosophy, it is a melancholy fact, that more than one-fourth of the labour of mankind is annually consumed by this barbarous system.

What has served to continue this evil, is the pecuniary advantage, which all the governments of Europe have found in keeping up this state of uncivilization. It affords to them pretences for power, and revenue, for which there would be neither occasion nor apology, if the circle of civilization were rendered compleat. Civil government alone, or the government of laws, is not productive of pretences for many taxes; it operates at home, directly under the eye of the country, and precludes the possibility of much imposition. But when the scene is laid in the uncivilized contention of governments, the field of pretences is enlarged, and the country, being no longer a judge, is open to every imposition, which governments please to act.

Not a thirtieth, scarcely a fortieth, part of the taxes which are raised in England are either occasioned by, or applied to, the purposes of civil government. It is not difficult to see, that the whole which the actual government does in this respect, is to enact laws, and that the country administers and executes them, at its own expence, by means of magistrates, juries, sessions, and assize, over and above the taxes which it pays.

In this view of the case, we have two distinct characters of government; the one the civil government, or the government of laws, which operates at home, the other the court or cabinet government, which operates abroad, on the rude plan of uncivilized life; the one attended with little charge, the other with boundless extravagance; and so distinct are the two, that if the latter were to sink, as it were by a sudden opening of the earth, and totally disappear, the former would not be deranged. It would still proceed, because it is the common interest of the nation that it should, and all the means are in practice.

Revolutions, then, have for their object, a change in the moral condition of governments, and with this change the burthen of public taxes will lessen, and civilization will be left to the enjoyment of that abundance, of which it is now deprived.

In contemplating the whole of this subject, I extend my views into the department of commerce. In all my publications, where the matter would admit, I have been an advocate for commerce,* because I am a friend to its effects. It is a pacific system, operating to cordialize mankind, by rendering nations, as well as individuals, useful to each other. As to mere theoretical reformation, I have never preached it up. The most effectual process is that of improving the condition of man by means of his interest; and it is on this ground that I take my stand.

If commerce were permitted to act to the universal extent it is capable, it would extirpate the system of war, and produce a revolution in the uncivilized state of governments. The invention of commerce has arisen since those governments began, and is the greatest approach towards universal civilization, that has yet been made by any means not immediately flowing from moral principles.

Whatever has a tendency to promote the civil intercourse of nations, by an exchange of benefits, is a subject as worthy of philosophy as of politics. Commerce is no other than the traffic of two individuals, multiplied on a scale of numbers; and by the same rule that nature intended the intercourse of two, she intended that of all. For this purpose she has distributed the materials of manufactures and commerce, in various and distant parts of a nation and of the world; and as they cannot be procured by war so cheaply or so commodiously as by commerce, she has rendered the latter the means of extirpating the former.

As the two are nearly the opposites of each other, consequently, the uncivilized state of European governments is injurious to commerce. Every kind of destruction or embarrassment serves to lessen the quantity, and it matters but little in what part of the commercial world the reduction begins. Like blood, it cannot be taken from any of the parts, without being taken from the whole mass in circulation, and all partake of the loss. When the ability in any nation to buy is destroyed, it equally involves the seller. Could the government of England destroy the commerce of all other nations, she would most effectually ruin her own.

It is possible that a nation may be the carrier for the world, but she cannot be the merchant. She cannot be the seller and the buyer of her own merchandize. The ability to buy must reside out of herself; and, therefore, the prosperity of any commercial nation is regulated by the prosperity of the rest. If they are poor she cannot be rich, and her condition, be it what it may, is an index of the height of the commercial tide in other nations.

That the principles of commerce, and its universal operation may be understood, without understanding the practice, is a position that reason will not deny; and it is on this ground only that I argue the subject. It is one thing in the counting-house, in the world it is another. With respect to its operation it must necessarily be contemplated as a reciprocal thing; that only one half its powers resides within the nation, and that the whole is as effectually destroyed by destroying the half that resides without, as if the destruction had been committed on that which is within; for neither can act without the other.

When in the last, as well as in former wars, the commerce of England sunk, it was because the general quantity was lessened every where; and it now rises, because commerce is in a rising state in every nation. If England, at this day, imports and exports more than at any former period, the nations with which she trades must necessarily do the same; her imports are their exports, and *vice versa*.

There can be no such thing as a nation flourishing alone in commerce; she can only participate; and the destruction of it in any part must necessarily affect all. When, therefore, governments are at war, the attack is made upon the common stock of commerce, and the consequence is the same as if each had attacked his own.

The present increase of commerce is not to be attributed to ministers, or to any political contrivances, but to its own natural operations in consequence of peace. The regular markets had been destroyed, the channels of trade broken up, the high road of the seas infested with robbers of every nation, and the attention of the world called to other objects. Those interruptions have ceased, and peace has restored the deranged condition of things to their proper order.[1]

It is worth remarking, that every nation reckons the balance of trade in its own favour; and therefore something must be irregular in the common ideas upon this subject.

---

[1] In America, the increase of commerce is greater in proportion than in England. It is, at this time, at least one half more than at any period prior to the revolution. The greatest number of vessels cleared out of the port of Philadelphia, before the commencement of the war, was between eight and nine hundred. In the year 1788, the number was upwards of twelve hundred. As the state of Pennsylvania is estimated as an eighth part of the United States in population, the whole number of vessels must now be nearly ten thousand.

The fact, however, is true, according to what is called a balance; and it is from this cause that commerce is universally supported. Every nation feels the advantage, or it would abandon the practice: but the deception lies in the mode of making up the accounts, and in attributing what are called profits to a wrong cause.

Mr Pitt has sometimes amused himself, by shewing what he called a balance of trade from the custom-house books.* This mode of calculation, not only affords no rule that is true, but one that is false.

In the first place, Every cargo that departs from the custom-house, appears on the books as an export; and, according to the custom-house balance, the losses at sea, and by foreign failures, are all reckoned on the side of profit, because they appear as exports.

Secondly, Because the importation by the smuggling trade does not appear on the custom-house books, to arrange against the exports.

No balance, therefore, as applying to superior advantages, can be drawn from those documents; and if we examine the natural operation of commerce, the idea is fallacious; and if true, would soon be injurious. The great support of commerce consists in the balance being a level of benefits among all nations.

Two merchants of different nations trading together, will both become rich, and each makes the balance in his own favour; consequently, they do not get rich out of each other; and it is the same with respect to the nations in which they reside. The case must be, that each nation must get rich out of its own means, and increases that riches by something which it procures from another in exchange.

If a merchant in England sends an article of English manufacture abroad, which costs him a shilling at home, and imports something which sells for two, he makes a balance of one shilling in his own favour: but this is not gained out of the foreign nation or the foreign merchant, for he also does the same by the article he receives, and neither has a balance of advantage upon the other. The original value of the two articles in their proper countries were but two shillings; but by changing their places, they acquire a new idea of value, equal to double what they had at first, and that increased value is equally divided.

There is no otherwise a balance on foreign than on domestic commerce. The merchants of London and Newcastle trade on the same principles, as if they resided in different nations, and make their balances in the same manner: yet London does not get rich out of Newcastle, any more than Newcastle out of London: but coals, the merchandize of Newcastle, have an additional value at London, and London merchandize has the same at Newcastle.

Though the principle of all commerce is the same, the domestic, in a national view, is the part the most beneficial; because the whole of the advantages, on both sides, rests within the nation; whereas, in foreign commerce, it is only a participation of one half.

The most unprofitable of all commerce is that connected with foreign dominion. To a few individuals it may be beneficial, merely because it is commerce; but to the nation it is a loss. The expence of maintaining dominion more than absorbs the profits of any trade. It does not increase the general quantity in the world, but operates to lessen it; and as a greater mass would be afloat by relinquishing dominion, the participation without the expence would be more valuable than a greater quantity with it.

But it is impossible to engross commerce by dominion; and therefore it is still more fallacious. It cannot exist in confined channels, and necessarily breaks out by regular or irregular means, that defeat the attempt; and to succeed would be still worse. France, since the revolution, has been more than indifferent as to foreign possessions; and other nations will become the same, when they investigate the subject with respect to commerce.

To the expence of dominion is to be added that of navies, and when the amount of the two are subtracted from the profits of commerce, it will appear, that what is called the balance of trade, even admitting it to exist, is not enjoyed by the nation, but absorbed by the government.

The idea of having navies for the protection of commerce

is delusive. It is putting the means of destruction for the means of protection. Commerce needs no other protection than the reciprocal interest which every nation feels in supporting it—it is common stock—it exists by a balance of advantages to all; and the only interuption it meets, is from the present uncivilized state of governments, and which it is its common interest to reform.[1]

Quitting this subject, I now proceed to other matters.— As it is necessary to include England in the prospect of a general reformation, it is proper to enquire into the defects of its government. It is only by each nation reforming its own, that the whole can be improved, and the full benefit of reformation enjoyed. Only partial advantages can flow from partial reforms.

France and England are the only two countries in Europe where a reformation in government could have successfully begun. The one secure by the ocean, and the other by the immensity of its internal strength, could defy the malignancy of foreign despotism. But it is with revolutions as with commerce, the advantages increase by their becoming general, and double to either what each would receive alone.

As a new system is now opening to the view of the world, the European courts are plotting to counteract it.* Alliances, contrary to all former systems, are agitating, and a common interest of courts is forming against the common interest of man. This combination draws a line that runs throughout Europe, and presents a cause so entirely new, as to exclude all calculations from former circumstances. While despotism warred with despotism, man had no interest in the contest; but in a cause that unites the soldier with the citizen, and nation with nation, the despotism of courts, though it feels the danger, and meditates revenge, is afraid to strike.

No question has arisen within the records of history that pressed with the importance of the present. It is not whether

---

[1] When I saw Mr Pitt's mode of estimating the balance of trade, in one of his parliamentary speeches, he appeared to me to know nothing of the nature and interest of commerce; and no man has more wantonly tortured it than himself. During a period of peace, it has been havocked with the calamities of war. Three times has it been thrown into stagnation, and the vessels unmaned by impressing, within less than four years of peace.*

this or that party shall be in or out, or whig or tory, or high or low* shall prevail; but whether man shall inherit his rights, and universal civilization take place? Whether the fruits of his labours shall be enjoyed by himself, or consumed by the profligacy of governments? Whether robbery shall be banished from courts, and wretchedness from countries?

When, in countries that are called civilized, we see age going to the workhouse and youth to the gallows, something must be wrong in the system of government. It would seem, by the exterior appearance of such countries, that all was happiness; but there lies hidden from the eye of common observation, a mass of wretchedness that has scarcely any other chance, than to expire in poverty or infamy. Its entrance into life is marked with the presage of its fate; and until this is remedied, it is in vain to punish.

Civil government does not consist in executions; but in making that provision for the instruction of youth, and the support of age, as to exclude, as much as possible, profligacy from the one, and despair from the other. Instead of this, the resources of a country are lavished upon kings, upon courts, upon hirelings, imposters, and prostitutes; and even the poor themselves, with all their wants upon them, are compelled to support the fraud that oppresses them.

Why is it, that scarcely any are executed but the poor? The fact is a proof, among other things, of a wretchedness in their condition. Bred up without morals, and cast upon the world without a prospect, they are the exposed sacrifice of vice and legal barbarity. The millions that are superfluously wasted upon governments, are more than sufficient to reform those evils, and to benefit the condition of every man in a nation, not included within the purlieus of a court. This I hope to make appear in the progress of this work.

It is the nature of compassion to associate with misfortune. In taking up this subject I seek no recompence—I fear no consequence. Fortified with that proud integrity, that disdains to triumph or to yield, I will advocate the Rights of Man.

It is to my advantage that I have served an apprenticeship to life. I know the value of moral instruction, and I have seen the danger of the contrary.

At an early period, little more than sixteen years of age, raw and adventurous, and heated with the false heroism of a master[1] who had served in a man of war, I began the carver of my own fortune, and entered on board the Terrible, Privateer, Capt. Death.* From this adventure I was happily prevented by the affectionate and moral remonstrance of a good father, who, from his own habits of life, being of the Quaker profession, must begin to look upon me as lost. But the impression, much as it effected at the time, began to wear away, and I entered afterwards in the King of Prussia Privateer, Capt. Mendez, and went with her to sea. Yet, from such a beginning, and with all the inconvenience of early life against me, I am proud to say, that with a persever-ance undismayed by difficulties, a disinterestedness that compelled respect, I have not only contributed to raise a new empire in the world, founded on a new system of government, but I have arrived at an eminence in political literature, the most difficult of all lines to succeed and excel in, which aristocracy, with all its aids, has not been able to reach or to rival.

Knowing my own heart, and feeling myself, as I now do, superior to all the skirmish of party, the inveteracy of inter-ested or mistaken opponents, I answer not to falsehood or abuse, but proceed to the defects of the English government.[2]

---

[1] Rev. William Knowles, master of the grammar school of Thetford, in Norfolk.

[2] Politics and self-interest have been so uniformly connected, that the world, from being so often deceived, has a right to be suspicious of public characters: but with regard to myself, I am perfectly easy on this head. I did not, at my first setting out in public life, nearly seventeen years ago, turn my thoughts to subjects of government from motives of interest; and my conduct from that moment to this, proves the fact. I saw an opportunity, in which I thought I could do some good, and I followed exactly what my heart dictated. I neither read books, nor studied other people's opinions. I thought for myself. The case was this:

During the suspension of the old governments in America, both prior to, and at the breaking out of hostilities, I was struck with the order and decorum with which every thing was conducted; and impressed with the idea, that a little more than what society naturally performed, was all the government that was necessary; and that monarchy and aristocracy were frauds and impositions upon mankind. On these principles I published the pamphlet *Common Sense*. The success it met with was beyond any thing since the invention of printing. I gave the copy right up to every state in the union, and the demand ran to not less than one hundred thousand copies. I continued the subject in the same manner, under the title of the *Crisis*, till the complete establishment of the revolution.

After the declaration of independence, Congress unanimously, and unknown to me, appointed me secretary in the foreign department.* This was agreeable to me, because it gave me the opportunity of seeing into the abilities of foreign courts, and their manner of doing business. But a misunderstanding arising between congress and me, respecting one of their commissioners, then in Europe, Mr Silas Deane, I resigned the office, and declined, at the same time, the pecuniary offers made me by the ministers of France and Spain, M. Gerard and Don Juan Mirralles.*

I had by this time so completely gained the ear and confidence of America, and my own independence was become so visible as to give me a range in political writing, beyond, perhaps, what any man ever possessed in any country; and what is more extraordinary, I held it undiminished to the end of the war, and enjoy it in the same manner to the present moment. As my object was not myself, I set out with the determination, and happily with the disposition, of not being moved by praise or censure, friendship or calumny, nor of being drawn from my purpose by any personal altercation; and the man who cannot do this, is not fit for a public character.

When the war ended, I went from Philadelphia to Borden-Town, on the east bank of the Delaware, where I have a small place. Congress was at this time at Prince-Town, fifteen miles distant; and General Washington had taken his head-quarters at Rocky-Hill, within the neighbourhood of Congress, for the purpose of resigning up his commission, (the object for which he accepted it being accomplished,) and of retiring to private life. While he was on this business, he wrote me the letter which I here subjoin.

Rocky-Hill, Sept. 10, 1783.

I have learned since I have been at this place, that you are at Borden-Town. Whether for the sake of retirement or œconomy, I know not. Be it for either, for both, or whatever it may, if you will come to this place, and partake with me, I shall be exceedingly happy to see you at it.

Your presence may remind Congress of your past services to this country; and if it is in my power to impress them, command my best exertions with freedom, as they will be rendered chearfully by one, who entertains a lively sense of the importance of your works, and who, with much pleasure, subscribes himself.

Your sincere friend,
G. WASHINGTON.

During the war, in the latter end of the year 1780, I formed to myself a design of coming over to England; and communicated it to General Greene, who was then in Philadelphia, on his route to the southward, General Washington being then at too great a distance to communicate with immediately. I was strongly impressed with the idea, that if I could get over to England, without being known, and only remain in safety till I could get out a publication, that I could open the eyes of the country with respect to the madness and stupidity of its government. I saw that the parties in parliament had pitted themselves as far as they could go, and could make no new impressions on each other. General Greene entered fully into my views; but the affair of Arnold and Andre* happening just after, he changed his mind, and, under strong apprehensions for my safety, wrote very pressingly to me from Anapolis, in Maryland, to give up the design, which, with some reluctance, I did. Soon after this I accompanied Col. Lawrens,* son of Mr Lawrens, who was then in the Tower, to France, on business from Congress. We landed at L'Orient; and while I remained there, he being gone forward, a

I begin with charters and corporations.*

It is a perversion of terms to say, that a charter gives rights. It operates by a contrary effect, that of taking rights away. Rights are inherently in all the inhabitants; but charters, by annulling those rights in the majority, leave the right by exclusion in the hands of a few. If charters were constructed so as to express in direct terms, '*that every inhabitant, who is not a member of a corporation, shall not exercise the right of voting,*' such charters would, in the face, be charters, not of rights, but of exclusion. The effect is the same under the form they now stand; and the only persons on whom they operate, are the persons whom they exclude. Those whose rights are guaranteed, by not being taken away, exercise no other rights, than as members of the community they are entitled to without a charter; and, therefore, all charters have no other than an indirect negative operation. They do not give rights to A, but they make a difference in favour of A by taking away the right of B, and consequently are instruments of injustice.

But charters and corporations have a more extensive evil effect, than what relates merely to elections. They are sources of endless contentions in the places where they exist; and they lessen the common rights of national society. A native

circumstance occurred, that renewed my former design. An English packet from Falmouth to New-York, with the government dispatches on board, was brought into L'Orient. That a packet should be taken, is no extraordinary thing; but that the dispatches should be taken with it, will scarcely be credited, as they are always flung at the cabin window, in a bag loaded with cannon-ball, and ready to be sunk at a moment. The fact, however, is as I have stated it, for the dispatches came into my hands, and I read them. The capture, as I was informed, succeeded by the following stratagem:—The captain of the Madame privateer, who spoke English, on coming up with the packet, passed himself for the captain of an English frigate, and invited the captain of the packet on board, which, when done, he sent some of his own hands back, and secured the mail. But be the circumstance of the capture what it may, I speak with certainty as to the government dispatches. They were sent up to Paris, to Count Vergennes, and when Col. Lawrens and myself returned to America, we took the originals to Congress.

By these dispatches I saw into the stupidity of the English cabinet, far more than I otherwise could have done, and I renewed my former design. But Col. Lawrens was so unwilling to return alone; more especially, as among other matters, we had a charge of upwards of two hundred thousand pounds sterling in money, that I gave into his wishes, and finally gave up my plan. But I am now certain, that if I could have executed it, that it would not have been altogether unsuccessful.

of England, under the operation of these charters and corporations, cannot be said to be an Englishman in the full sense
of the word. He is not free of the nation, in the same manner
that a Frenchman is free of France, and an American of
America. His rights are circumscribed to the town, and, in
some cases, to the parish of his birth; and all other parts,
though in his native land, are to him as a foreign country.
To acquire a residence in these, he must undergo a local
naturalization by purchase, or he is forbidden or expelled
the place. This species of feudality is kept up to aggrandize
the corporations at the ruin of towns; and the effect is
visible.

The generality of corporation towns are in a state of
solitary decay, and prevented from further ruin, only by
some circumstance in their situation, such as a navigable
river, or a plentiful surrounding country. As population is
one of the chief sources of wealth, (for without it land itself
has no value,) every thing which operates to prevent it must
lessen the value of property; and as corporations have not
only this tendency, but directly this effect, they cannot but
be injurious. If any policy were to be followed, instead of
that of general freedom, to every person to settle where he
chose, (as in France or America,) it would be more consistent
to give encouragement to new comers, than to preclude their
admission by exacting premiums from them.[1]

The persons most immediately interested in the abolition
of corporations, are the inhabitants of the towns where
corporations are established. The instances of Manchester,
Birmingham, and Sheffield, shew, by contrast, the injury
which those Gothic institutions are to property and com-

[1] It is difficult to account for the origin of charter and corporation towns,
unless we suppose them to have arisen out of, or been connected with, some
species of garrison service. The times in which they began justify this idea. The
generality of those towns have been garrisons; and the corporations were charged
with the care of the gates of the towns, when no military garrison was present.
Their refusing or granting admission to strangers, which has produced the custom
of giving, selling, and buying freedom, has more of the nature of garrison
authority than civil government. Soldiers are free of all corporations throughout
the nation, by the same propriety that every soldier is free of every garrison, and
no other persons are. He can follow any employment, with the permission of his
officers, in any corporation town throughout the nation.

merce. A few examples may be found, such as that of London, whose natural and commercial advantage, owing to its situation on the Thames, is capable of bearing up against the political evils of a corporation; but in almost all other cases the fatality is too visible to be doubted or denied.

Though the whole nation is not so directly affected by the depression of property in corporation towns as the inhabitants themselves, it partakes of the consequence. By lessening the value of property, the quantity of national commerce is curtailed. Every man is a customer in proportion to his ability; and as all parts of a nation trade with each other, whatever affects any of the parts; must necessarily communicate to the whole.

As one of the houses of the English parliament is, in a great measure, made up of elections from these corporations; and as it is unnatural that a pure stream should flow from a foul fountain, its vices are but a continuation of the vices of its origin. A man of moral honour and good political principles, cannot submit to the mean drudgery and disgraceful arts, by which such elections are carried. To be a successful candidate, he must be destitute of the qualities that constitute a just legislator: and being thus disciplined to corruption by the mode of entering into parliament, it is not to be expected that the representative should be better than the man.

Mr Burke, in speaking of the English representation, has advanced as bold a challenge as ever was given in the days of chivalry. 'Our representation,' says he, 'has been found *perfectly adequate to all the purposes* for which a representation of the people can be desired or devised. I defy,' continues he, 'the enemies of our constitution to shew the contrary.'*—This declaration from a man, who has been in constant opposition to all the measures of parliament the whole of his political life, a year or two excepted, is most extraordinary; and, comparing him with himself, admits of no other alternative, than that he acted against his judgment as a member, or has declared contrary to it as an author.

But it is not in the representation only that the defects lie, and therefore I proceed in the next place to the aristocracy.

What is called the House of Peers, is constituted on a ground very similar to that, against which there is a law in other cases. It amounts to a combination of persons in one common interest. No reason can be given, why an house of legislation should be composed entirely of men whole occupation consists in letting landed property, than why it should be composed of those who hire, or of brewers, or bakers, or any other separate class of men.

Mr Burke calls this house, '*the great ground and pillar of security to the landed interest.*'* Let us examine this idea.

What pillar of security does the landed interest require more than any other interest in the state, or what right has it to a distinct and separate representation from the general interest of a nation? The only use to be made of this power, (and which it has always made,) is to ward off taxes from itself, and throw the burthen upon such articles of consumption by which itself would be least affected.

That this has been the consequence, (and will always be the consequence of constructing governments on combinations,) is evident with respect to England, from the history of its taxes.

Notwithstanding taxes have encreased and multiplied upon every article of common consumption, the land-tax, which more particularly affects this 'pillar,' has diminished. In 1788, the amount of the land-tax was 1,950,000£.* which is half a million less than it produced almost an hundred years ago,[1] notwithstanding the rentals are in many instances doubled since that period.

Before the coming of the Hanoverians, the taxes were divided in nearly equal proportions between the land and articles of consumption,* the land bearing rather the largest share: but since that æra, nearly thirteen millions annually of new taxes have been thrown upon consumption. The consequence of which has been a constant encrease in the number and wretchedness of the poor, and in the amount of the poor-rates. Yet here again the burthen does not fall in equal proportions on the aristocracy with the rest of the

---

[1] See Sir John Sinclair's History of the Revenue. The land-tax in 1646 was £2,473,499.*

community. Their residences, whether in town or country, are not mixed with the habitations of the poor. They live apart from distress, and the expence of relieving it. It is in manufacturing towns and labouring villages that those burthens press the heaviest; in many of which it is one class of poor supporting another.

Several of the most heavy and productive taxes are so contrived, as to give an exemption to this pillar, thus standing in its own defence. The tax upon beer* brewed for sale does not affect the aristocracy, who brew their own beer free of this duty. It falls only on those who have not conveniency or ability to brew, and who must purchase it in small quantities. But what will mankind think of the justice of taxation, when they know, that this tax alone, from which the aristocracy are from circumstances exempt, is nearly equal to the whole of the land-tax, being in the year 1788, and it is not less now, 1,666,152£. and with its proportion of the taxes on malt and hops, it exceeds it.—That a single article, thus partially consumed, and that chiefly by the working part, should be subject to a tax, equal to that on the whole rental of a nation, is, perhaps, a fact not to be paralleled in the histories of revenues.

This is one of the consequences resulting from an house of legislation, composed on the ground of a combination of common interest; for whatever their separate politics as to parties may be, in this they are united. Whether a combination acts to raise the price of any article for sale, or the rate of wages; or whether it acts to throw taxes from itself upon another class of the community, the principle and the effect are the same; and if the one be illegal, it will be difficult to shew that the other ought to exist.

It is to no use to say, that taxes are first proposed in the house of commons; for as the other house has always a negative, it can always defend itself; and it would be ridiculous to suppose that its acquiescence in the measures to be proposed were not understood before hand. Besides which, it has obtained so much influence by borough-traffic, and so many of its relations and connections* are distributed on both sides of the commons, as to give it, besides an absolute negative in one house, a preponderancy in the other, in all matters of common concern.

It is difficult to discover what is meant by the *landed interest*, if it does not mean a combination of aristocratical land-holders, opposing their own pecuniary interest to that of the farmer, and every branch of trade, commerce, and manufacture. In all other respects it is the only interest that needs no partial protection. It enjoys the general protection of the world. Every individual, high or low, is interested in the fruits of the earth; men, women, and children, of all ages and degrees, will turn out to assist the farmer, rather than a harvest should not be got in; and they will not act thus by any other property. It is the only one for which the common prayer of mankind is put up, and the only one that can never fail from the want of means. It is the interest, not of the policy, but of the existence of man, and when it ceases he must cease to be.

No other interest in a nation stands on the same united support. Commerce, manufactures, arts, sciences, and every thing else, compared with this, are supported but in parts. Their prosperity or their decay has not the same universal influence. When the vallies laugh and sing,* it is not the farmer only, but all creation that rejoices. It is a prosperity that excludes all envy; and this cannot be said of any thing else.

Why then does Mr Burke talk of his house of peers, as the pillar of the landed interest? Were that pillar to sink into the earth, the same landed property would continue, and the same ploughing, sowing, and reaping would go on. The aristocracy are not the farmers who work the land, and raise the produce, but are the mere consumers of the rent; and when compared with the active world, are the drones, a seraglio of males, who neither collect the honey nor form the hive, but exist only for lazy enjoyment.

Mr Burke, in his first essay, called aristocracy, '*the Corinthian capital of polished society*.'* Towards compleating the figure, he has now added the *pillar*; but still the base is wanting; and whenever a nation chuses to act a Samson, not blind, but bold, down go the temple of Dagon,* the Lords and the Philistines.

If a house of legislation is to be composed of men of one class, for the purpose of protecting a distinct interest, all the other interests should have the same. The inequality, as well as the burthen of taxation, arises from admitting it in one case, and not in all. Had there been an house of farmers, there had been no game laws; or an house of merchants and manufacturers, the taxes had neither been so unequal nor so excessive. It is from the power of taxation being in the hands of those who can throw so great a part of it from their own shoulders, that it has raged without a check.

Men of small or moderate estates, are more injured by the taxes being thrown on articles of consumption, than they are eased by warding it from landed property, for the following reasons:

First, They consume more of the productive taxable articles, in proportion to their property, than those of large estates.

Secondly, Their residence is chiefly in towns, and their property in houses; and the encrease of the poor-rates, occasioned by taxes on consumption, is in much greater proportion than the land-tax has been favoured. In Birmingham, the poor-rates are not less than seven shillings in the pound. From this, as is already observed, the aristocracy are in a great measure exempt.

There are but a part of the mischiefs flowing from the wretched scheme of an house of peers.

As a combination, it can always throw a considerable portion of taxes from itself; and as an hereditary house, accountable to nobody, it resembles a rotten borough, whose consent is to be courted by interest. There are but few of its members, who are not in some mode or other participaters, or disposers of the public money. One turns a candle-holder, or a lord in waiting; another a lord of the bed-chamber, a groom of the stole,* or any insignificant nominal office, to which a salary is annexed, paid out of the public taxes, and which avoids the direct appearance of corruption. Such situations are derogatory to the character of man; and where they can be submitted to, honour cannot reside.

To all these are to be added the numerous dependants,

the long list of younger branches and distant relations, who are to be provided for at the public expence; in short, were an estimation to be made of the charge of aristocracy to a nation, it will be found nearly equal to that of supporting the poor. The Duke of Richmond alone (and there are cases similar to his) takes away as much for himself as would maintain two thousand poor and aged persons.* Is it, then, any wonder, that under such a system of government, taxes and rates have multiplied to their present extent?

In stating these matters, I speak an open and disinterested language, dictated by no passion but that of humanity. To me, who have not only refused offers,* because I thought them improper, but have declined rewards I might with reputation have accepted, it is no wonder that meanness and imposition appear disgustful. Independence is my happiness, and I view things as they are, without regard to place or person; my country is the world, and my religion is to do good.

Mr Burke, in speaking of the aristocratical law of primogeniture, says, 'it is the standing law of our landed inheritance; and which, without question, has a tendency, and I think,' continues he, 'a happy tendency, to preserve a character of weight and consequence.'*

Mr Burke may call this law what he pleases, but humanity and impartial reflection will denounce it a law of brutal injustice. Were we not accustomed to the daily practice, and did we only hear of it as the law of some distant part of the world, we should conclude that the legislators of such countries had not yet arrived at a state of civilization.

As to its preserving a character of *weight and consequence*, the case appears to me directly the reverse. It is an attaint upon character; a sort of privateering on family property. It may have weight among dependent tenants, but it gives none on a scale of national, and, much less of universal character. Speaking for myself, my parents were not able to give me a shilling, beyond what they gave me in education; and to do this they distressed themselves: yet, I possess more of what is called consequence, in the world, than any one in Mr Burke's catalogue of aristocrats.

Having thus glanced at some of the defects of the two houses of parliament, I proceed to what is called the crown upon which I shall be very concise.

It signifies a nominal office of a million sterling a year, the business of which consists in receiving the money. Whether the person be wise or foolish, sane or insane, a native or a foreigner, matters not. Every ministry acts upon the same idea that Mr Burke writes, namely, that the people must be hood-winked, and held in superstitious ignorance by some bugbear or other; and what is called the crown answers this purpose, and therefore it answers all the purposes to be expected from it. This is more than can be said of the other two branches.

The hazard to which this office is exposed in all countries, is not from any thing that can happen to the man, but from what may happen to the nation—the danger of its coming to its senses.

It has been customary to call the crown the executive power, and the custom is continued, though the reason has ceased.

It was called the *executive*,* because the person whom it signified used, formerly, to sit in the character of a judge, in administering or executing the laws. The tribunals were then a part of the court. The power, therefore, which is now called the judicial, is what was called the executive; and, consequently, one or other of the terms is redundant, and one of the offices useless. When we speak of the crown now, it means nothing; it signifies neither a judge nor a general: besides which it is the laws that govern, and not the man. The old terms are kept up, to give an appearance of consequence to empty forms; and the only effect they have is that of increasing expences.

Before I proceed to the means of rendering governments more conductive to the general happiness of mankind, than they are at present, it will not be improper to take a review of the progress of taxation in England.

It is a general idea, that when taxes are once laid on, they are never taken off. However true this may have been of late, it was not always so. Either, therefore, the people of former times were more watchful over government than those of the present, or government was administered with less extravagance.

It is now seven hundred years since the Norman conquest, and the establishment of what is called the crown. Taking this portion of time in seven separate periods of one hundred years each, the amount of the annual taxes, at each period, will be as follows:—

Annual amount of taxes levied by William the Conqueror, beginning in the year 1066,	£400,000
Annual amount of taxes at one hundred years from the conquest, (1166)	200,000
Annual amount of taxes at two hundred years from the conquest, (1266)	150,000
Annual amount of taxes at three hundred years from the conquest, (1366)	130,000
Annual amount of taxes at four hundred years from the conquest, (1466)	100,000

These statements, and those which follow, are taken from Sir John Sinclair's History of the Revenue;* by which it appears, that taxes continued decreasing for four hundred years, at the expiration of which time they were reduced three-fourths, viz. from four hundred thousand pounds to one hundred thousand. The people of England of the present day, have a traditionary and historical idea of the bravery of their ancestors; but whatever their virtues or their vices might have been, they certainly were a people who would not be imposed upon, and who kept government in awe as to taxation, if not as to principle. Though they were not able to expel the monarchical usurpation, they restricted it to a republican œconomy of taxes.

Let us now review the remaining three hundred years.

Annual amount of taxes at five hundred years from the conquest, (1566)	£500,000
Annual amount of taxes at six hundred years from the conquest, (1666)	1,800,000
Annual amount of taxes at the present time, (1791)	17,000,000

The difference between the first four hundred years and the last three, is so astonishing, as to warrant an opinion, that the national character of the English has changed. It would have been impossible to have dragooned the former English, into the excess of taxation that now exists; and when it is considered that the pay of the army, the navy, and of all the revenue-officers, is the same now as it was above a hundred years ago, when the taxes were not above a tenth part of what they are at present, it appears impossible to account for the enormous increase and expenditure, on any other ground, than extravagance, corruption, and intrigue.[1]

[1] Several of the court newspapers have of late made frequent mention of Wat Tyler. That his memory should be traduced by court sycophants, and all those who live on the spoil of a public, is not to be wondered at. He was, however, the means of checking the rage and injustice of taxation in his time, and the nation owed much to his valour. The history is concisely this:—In the time of Richard the second, a poll-tax was levied, of one shilling per head, upon every person in the nation, of whatever estate or condition, on poor as well as rich, above the age of fifteen years. If any favour was shewn in the law, it was to the rich rather than to the poor; as no person could be charged more than twenty shillings for himself, family, and servants, though ever so numerous; while all other families, under the number of twenty, were charged per head. Poll-taxes had always been odious; but this being also oppressive and unjust, it excited, as it naturally must, universal detestation among the poor and middle classes. The person known by the name of Wat Tyler, whose proper name was Walter, and a tyler by trade, lived at Deptford. The gatherer of the poll-tax, on coming to his house, demanded tax for one of his daughters, whom Tyler declared was under the age of fifteen. The tax-gatherer insisted on satisfying himself, and began an indecent examination of the girl, which enraging the father, he struck him with a hammer, that brought him to the ground, and was the cause of his death.

This circumstance served to bring the discontents to an issue. The inhabitants of the neighbourhood espoused the cause of Tyler, who, in a few days was joined, according to some histories, by upwards of fifty thousand men, and chosen their chief. With this force he marched to London, to demand an abolition of the tax, and a redress of other grievances. The court, finding itself in a forlorn condition, and unable to make resistance, agreed, with Richard at its head, to hold a conference with Tyler in Smithfield, making many fair professions, courtier like, of its dispositions to redress the oppressions. While Richard and Tyler were in conversation on these matters, each being on horseback, Walworth, then mayor of London, and one of the creatures of the court, watched an opportunity, and like a cowardly assassin, stabbed Tyler with a dagger; and two or three others falling upon him, he was instantly sacrificed.

Tyler appears to have been an intrepid disinterested man, with respect to himself. All his proposals made to Richard, were on a more just and public ground, than those which had been made to John by the Barons; and notwithstanding the sycophancy of historians, and men like Mr Burke, who seek to gloss over a base action of the court by traducing Tyler, his fame will outlive their falsehood. If the Barons merited a monument to be erected in Runnymede,* Tyler merits one in Smithfield.

With the revolution of 1688, and more so since the Hanover succession, came the destructive system of continental intrigues, and the rage for foreign wars and foreign dominion; systems of such secure mystery that the expences admit of no accounts; a single line stands for millions. To what excess taxation might have extended, had not the French revolution contributed to break up the system, and put an end to pretences, is impossible to say. Viewed, as that revolution ought to be, as the fortunate means of lessening the load of taxes of both countries, it is of as much importance to England as to France; and, if properly improved to all the advantages of which it is capable, and to which it leads, deserve as much celebration in one country as the other.

In pursuing this subject, I shall begin with the matter that first presents itself, that of lessening the burthen of taxes; and shall then add such matters and propositions, respecting the three countries of England, France, and America, as the present prospect of things appears to justify: I mean, an alliance of the three, for the purposes that will be mentioned in their proper place.

What has happened may happen again. By the statement before shewn of the progress of taxation, it is seen, that taxes have been lessened to a fourth part of what they had formerly been. Though the present circumstances do not admit of the same reduction, yet it admits of such a beginning, as may accomplish that end in less time, than in the former case.

The amount of taxes for the year, ending at Michaelmas 1788,* was as follows:

Land-tax,	£1,950,000
Customs,	3,789,274
Excise, (including old and new malt,)	6,751,727
Stamps,	1,278,214
Miscellaneous taxes and incidents,	1,803,755
	£15,572,970

Since the year 1788, upwards of one million, new taxes, have been laid on, besides the produce from the lotteries;

and as the taxes have in general been more productive since than before, the amount may be taken, in round numbers, at £17,000,000.

N.B. The expence of collection and the drawbacks, which together amount to nearly two millions, are paid out of the gross amount;* and the above is the nett sum paid into the exchequer.

This sum of seventeen millions is applied to two different purposes; the one to pay the interest of the national debt,* the other to the current expences of each year. About nine millions are appropriated to the former; and the remainder, being nearly eight millions, to the latter. As to the million, said to be applied to the reduction of the debt, it is so much like paying with one hand and taking out with the other, as not to merit much notice.

It happened, fortunately for France, that she possessed national domains* for paying off her debt, and thereby lessening her taxes: but as this is not the case in England, her reduction of taxes can only take place by reducing the current expences, which may now be done to the amount of four or five millions annually, as will hereafter appear. When this is accomplished, it will more than counterbalance the enormous charge of the American war; and the saving will be from the same source from whence the evil arose.

As to the national debt, however heavy the interest may be in taxes; yet, as it serves to keep alive a capital, useful to commerce, it balances by its effects a considerable part of its own weight; and as the quantity of gold and silver in England is, by some means or other, short of its proper proportion,[1] (being not more than twenty millions, whereas it should be sixty,) it would, besides the injustice, be bad policy to extinguish a capital that serves to supply that defect. But with respect to the current expence, whatever is saved therefrom is gain. The excess may serve to keep corruption alive, but it has no re-action on credit and commerce, like the interest of the debt.

[1] Foreign intrigue, foreign wars, and foreign dominions, will in a great measure account for the deficiency.

It is now very probable, that the English government (I do not mean the nation) is unfriendly to the French revolution. Whatever serves to expose the intrigue and lessen the influence of courts, by lessening taxation, will be unwelcome to those who feed upon the spoil. Whilst the clamour of French intrigue, arbitrary power, popery, and wooden shoes* could be kept up, the nation was easily allured and alarmed into taxes. Those days are now past; deception, it is to be hoped, has reaped its last harvest, and better times are in prospect for both countries, and for the world.

Taking it for granted, that an alliance may be formed between England, France, and America, for the purposes hereafter to be mentioned, the national expences of France and England may consequently be lessened. The same fleets and armies will no longer be necessary to either, and the reduction can be made ship for ship on each side. But to accomplish these objects, the governments must necessarily be fitted to a common and correspondent principle. Confidence can never take place, while an hostile disposition remains in either, or where mystery and secrecy on one side, is opposed to candour and openness on the other.

These matters admitted, the national expences might be put back, *for the sake of a precedent*, to what they were at some period when France and England were not enemies. This, consequently, must be prior to the Hanover succession, and also to the revolution of 1688.[1] The first instance that presents itself, antecedent to those dates, is in the very wasteful and profligate times of Charles the Second; at

---

[1] I happened to be in England at the celebration of the centenary of the revolution of 1688. The characters of William and Mary* have always appeared to me detestable; the one seeking to destroy his uncle, and the other her father, to get possession of power themselves; yet, as the nation was disposed to think something of that event, I felt hurt at feeing it ascribe the whole reputation of it to a man who had undertaken it as a jobb, and who, besides what he otherwise got, charged six hundred thousand pounds for the expence of the little fleet that brought him from Holland. George the First acted the same close-fisted part as William had done, and bought the Duchy of Bremin* with the money he got from England, two hundred and fifty thousand pounds over and above his pay as king; and having thus purchased it at the expence of England, added it to his Hanoverian dominions for his own private profit. In fact, every nation that does not govern itself, is governed as a jobb. England has been the prey of jobbs ever since the revolution.

which time England and France acted as allies. If I have chosen a period of great extravagance, it will serve to shew modern extravagance in a still worse light; especially as the pay of the navy, the army, and the revenue officers has not encreased since that time.

The peace establishment* was then as follows:—See Sir John Sinclair's History of the Revenue.

Navy,	300,000
Army,	212,000
Ordnance,	40,000
Civil List,	462,115
	£1,014,115

The parliament, however, settled the whole annual peace establishment at 1,200,000.[1] If we go back to the time of Elizabeth, the amount of all the taxes was but half a million, yet the nation sees nothing during that period, that reproaches it with want of consequence.

All circumstances then taken together, arising from the French revolution, from the approaching harmony and reciprocal interest of the two nations, the abolition of court intrigue on both sides, and the progress of knowledge in the science of government, the annual expenditure might be put back to one million and an half, viz.

Navy,	500,000
Army,	500,000
Expences of government,	500,000
	£1,500,000

Even this sum is six times greater than the expences of government are in America, yet the civil internal government in England, (I mean that administered by means of quarter sessions, juries, and assize, and which, in fact, is nearly the

[1] Charles, like his predecessors and successors, finding that war was the harvest of governments, engaged in a war with the Dutch,* the expence of which encreased the annual expenditure to £1,800,000, as stated under the date of 1666; but the peace establishment was but £1,200,000.

whole, and performed by the nation,) is less expence upon the revenue, than the same species and portion of government is in America.

It is time that nations should be rational, and not be governed like animals, for the pleasure of their riders. To read the history of kings, a man would be almost inclined to suppose that government consisted in stag-hunting, and that every nation paid a million a year to a huntsman. Man ought to have pride, or shame enough to blush at being thus imposed upon, and when he feel his proper character, he will. Upon all subjects of this nature, there is often passing in the mind, a train of ideas he has not yet accustomed himself to encourage and communicate. Restrained by something that puts on the character of prudence, he acts the hypocrite upon himself as well as to others. It is, however, curious to observe how soon this spell can be dissolved. A single expression, boldly conceived and uttered, will sometimes put a whole company into their proper feelings; and whole nations are acted upon in the same manner.

As to the offices of which any civil government may be composed, it matters but little by what names they are described. In the rotine of business, as before observed, whether a man be stiled a president, a king, an emperor, a senator, or any thing else, it is impossible that any service he can perform, can merit from a nation more than ten thousand pounds a year; and as no man should be paid beyond his services, so every man of a proper heart will not accept more. Public money ought to be touched with the most scrupulous consciousness of honour. It is not the produce of riches only, but of the hard earnings of labour and poverty. It is drawn even from the bitterness of want and misery. Not a beggar passes, or perishes in the streets, whose mite is not in that mass.

Were it possible that the Congress of America, could be so lost to their duty, and to the interest of their constituents, as to offer General Washington, as president of America, a million a year, he would not, and he could not, accept it. His sense of honour is of another kind. It has cost England almost seventy millions sterling, to maintain a family imported from abroad, of very inferior capacity to thousands in the nation, and scarcely a year has passed that has not produced some new mercenary application. Even the physicians bills have been sent to the public to be paid.* No wonder that jails are crowded, and taxes and poor-rates encreased. Under such systems, nothing is to be looked for but what has already happened; and as to reformation, whenever it come, it must be from the nation, and not from the government.

To shew that the sum of five hundred thousand pounds is more than sufficient to defray all the expences of government, exclusive of navies and armies, the following estimate is added for any country, of the same extent as England.

In the first place, three hundred representatives, fairly elected, are sufficient for all the purposes to which legislation can apply, and preferable to a larger number. They may be divided into two or three houses, or meet in one, as in France, or in any manner a constitution shall direct.

As representation is always considered, in free countries, as the most honourable of all stations, the allowance made to it is merely to defray the expence which the representatives incur by that service, and not to it as an office.

If an allowance, at the rate of five hundred pounds *per ann.* be made to every representative, deducting for non-attendance, the expence, if the whole number attended for six months, each year, would be   £75,000

The official departments cannot reasonably exceed the following number, with the salaries annexed:

Three offices, at ten thousand pounds each*		30,000
Ten ditto,	at £5000 each	50,000
Twenty ditto,	at £2000 each	40,000
Forty ditto,	at £1000 each	40,000
Two hundred ditto,	at £500 each	100,000
Three hundred ditto,	at £200 each	60,000
Five hundred ditto,	at £100 each	50,000
Seven hundred ditto,	at £75 each	52,500
		£497,500

If a nation chuse, it can deduct four *per cent.* from all offices, and make one of twenty thousand *per ann.*

All revenue officers are paid out of the monies they collect, and therefore, are not in this estimation.

The foregoing is not offered as an exact detail of offices, but to shew the number and rate of salaries which five hundred thousand pounds will support; and it will, on experience, be found impracticable to find business sufficient to justify even this expence. As to the manner in which office business is now performed, the Chiefs, in several offices, such as the post-office, and certain offices in the exchequer, &c. do little more than sign their names three or four times a year; and the whole duty is performed by under clerks.

Taking, therefore, one million and an half as a sufficient peace establishment for all the honest purposes of government, which is three hundred thousand pounds more than the peace establishment in the profligate and prodigal times of Charles the Second, (notwithstanding, as has been already observed, the pay and salaries of the army, navy, and revenue officers, continue the same as at that period,) there will remain a surplus of upwards of six millions out of the present current expences. The question then will be, how to dispose of this surplus.

Whoever has observed the manner in which trade and taxes twist themselves together, must be sensible of the impossibility of separating them suddenly.

First. Because the articles now on hand are already charged with the duty, and the reduction cannot take place on the present stock.

Secondly. Because, on all those articles on which the duty is charged in the gross, such as *per* barrel, hogshead, hundred weight, or tun, the abolition of the duty does not admit of being divided down so as fully to relieve the consumer, who purchases by the pint, or the pound. The last duty laid on strong beer and ale, was three shillings *per* barrel, which, if taken off, would lessen the purchase only half a farthing *per* pint, and consequently, would not reach to practical relief.

This being the condition of a great part of the taxes, it

will be necessary to look for such others as are free from this embarrassment, and where the relief will be direct and visible, and capable of immediate operation.

In the first place, then, the poor-rates are a direct tax* which every house-keeper feels, and who knows also, to a farthing, the sum which he pays. The national amount of the whole of the poor rates is not positively known, but can be procured. Sir John Sinclair, in his History of the Revenue, has stated it at £2,100,587.* A considerable part of which is expended in litigations, in which the poor, instead of being relieved, are tormented. The expence, however, is the same to the parish from whatever cause it arises.

In Birmingham, the amount of the poor-rates is fourteen thousand pounds a year. This, though a large sum, is moderate, compared with the population. Birmingham is said to contain seventy thousand souls,* and on a proportion of seventy thousand to fourteen thousand pounds poor-rates, the national amount of poor-rates, taking the population of England at seven millions, would be but one million four hundred thousand pounds. It is, therefore, most probable, that the population of Birmingham is over-rated. Fourteen thousand pounds is the proportion upon fifty thousand souls, taking two millions of poor-rates as the national amount.*

Be it, however, what it may, it is no other than the consequence of the excessive burthen of taxes, for, at the time when the taxes were very low, the poor were able to maintain themselves; and there were no poor-rates.[1] In the present state of things, a labouring man, with a wife and two or three children, does not pay less than between seven and eight pounds a year in taxes. He is not sensible of this, because it is disguised to him in the articles which he buys, and he thinks only of their dearness; but as the taxes take from him, at least, a fourth part of his yearly earnings, he is consequently disabled from providing for a family, especially, if himself, or any of them, are afflicted with sickness.

The first step, therefore, of practical relief, would be to abolish the poor-rates entirely, and in lieu thereof, to make a

---

[1] Poor-rates began about the time of Henry the Eighth, when the taxes began to encrease, and they have encreased as the taxes encreased ever since.

remission of taxes to the poor of double the amount of the present poor-rates, viz. four millions annually out of the surplus taxes. By this measure, the poor would be benefited two millions, and the house-keepers two millions. This alone would be equal to a reduction of one hundred and twenty millions of the national debt,* and consequently equal to the whole expence of the American war.

It will then remain to be considered, which is the most effectual mode of distributing this remission of four millions.

It is easily seen, that the poor are generally composed of large families of children, and old people past their labour. If these two classes are provided for, the remedy will so far reach to the full extent of the case, that what remains will be incidental, and, in a great measure, fall within the compass of benefit clubs, which, though of humble invention, merit to be ranked among the best of modern institutions.

Admitting England to contain seven million of souls; if one-fifth thereof are of that class of poor which need support, the number will be one million four hundred thousand. Of this number, one hundred and forty thousand will be aged poor, as will be hereafter shewn, and for which a distinct provision will be proposed.

There will then remain one million two hundred and sixty thousand, which, at five souls to each family, amount to two hundred and fifty-two thousand families, rendered poor from the expence of children and the weight of taxes.

The number of children under fourteen years of age, in each of those families, will be found to be about five to every two families; some having two, and others three; some one, and others four; some none, and others five; but it rarely happens that more than five are under fourteen years of age, and after this age they are capable of service or of being apprenticed.

Allowing five children (under fourteen years) to every two families,

The number of children will be   630,000
The number of parents were they all living, would
   be   504,000

It is certain, that if the children are provided for, the parents are relieved of consequence, because it is from the expence of bringing up children that their poverty arises.

Having thus ascertained the greatest number that can be supposed to need support on account of young families, I proceed to the mode of relief or distribution, which is,

To pay as a remission of taxes to every poor family, out of the surplus taxes, and in room of poor-rates, four pounds a year for every child under fourteen years of age; enjoining the parents of such children to send them to school, to learn reading, writing, and common arithmetic; the ministers of every parish, of every denomination, to certify jointly to an office, for that purpose, that this duty is performed.

The amount of this expence will be,

For six hundred and thirty thousand children, at four pounds
    per ann. each,   £2,520,000

By adopting this method, not only the poverty of the parents will be relieved, but ignorance will be banished from the rising generation, and the number of poor will hereafter become less, because their abilities, by the aid of education, will be greater. Many a youth, with good natural genius, who is apprenticed to a mechanical trade, such as a carpenter, joiner, millwright, shipwright, blacksmith, &c. is prevented getting forward the whole of his life, from the want of a little common education when a boy.

I now proceed to the case of the aged.

I divide age into two classes. First, the approach of age beginning at fifty. Secondly, old age commencing at sixty.

At fifty,* though the mental faculties of man are in full vigour, and his judgment better than at any preceeding date, the bodily powers for laborious life are on the decline. He cannot bear the same quantity of fatigue as at an earlier period. He begins to earn less, and is less capable of enduring wind and weather; and in those more retired employments where much sight is required, he fails apace, and sees himself, like an old horse, beginning to be turned adrift.

At sixty his labour ought to be over, at least from direct

necessity. It is painful to see old age working itself to death, in what are called civilized countries, for daily bread.

To form some judgment of the number of those above fifty years of age, I have several times counted the persons I met in the streets of London, men, women, and children, and have generally found that the average is about one in sixteen or seventeen. If it be said that aged persons do not come much in the streets, so neither do infants; and a great proportion of grown children are in schools, and in work shops as apprentices. Taking then sixteen for a divisor, the whole number of persons, in England, of fifty years and upwards of both sexes, rich and poor, will be four hundred and twenty thousand.

The persons to be provided for out of this gross number will be, husbandmen, common labourers, journeymen of every trade and their wives, sailors, and disbanded soldiers, worn out servants of both sexes, and poor widows.

There will be also a considerable number of middling tradesmen, who having lived decently in the former part of life, begin, as age approaches, to lose their business, and at last fall to decay.

Besides these, there will be constantly thrown off from the revolutions of that wheel,* which no man can stop, nor regulate, a number from every class of life connected with commerce and adventure.

To provide for all those accidents, and whatever else may befal, I take the number of persons, who at one time or other of their lives, after fifty years of age, may feel it necessary or comfortable to be better supported, than they can support themselves, and that not as a matter of grace and favour, but of right, at one third of the whole number, which is one hundred and forty thousand, as stated in page 125, and for whom a distinct provision was proposed to be made. If there be more, society notwithstanding the shew and pomposity of government, is in a deplorable condition in England.

Of this one hundred and forty thousand, I take one half, seventy thousand, to be of the age of fifty and under sixty, and the other half to be sixty years and upwards.—Having thus ascertained the probable proportion of the number of aged persons, I proceed to the mode of rendering their condition comfortable, which is,

To pay to every such person of the age of fifty years, and until he shall arrive at the age of sixty, the sum of six pounds *per ann.* out of the surplus taxes; and ten pounds *per ann.** during life after the age of sixty. The expence of which will be,

Seventy thousand persons at £6 *per ann.*	420,000
Seventy thousand ditto at £10 *per ann.*	700,000
	£1,120,000

This support, as already remarked, is not of the nature of a charity, but of a right. Every person in England, male and female, pays on an average in taxes, two pounds eight shillings and sixpence *per ann.* from the day of his (or her) birth; and, if the expence of collection be added, he pays two pounds eleven shillings and sixpence; consequently, at the end of fifty years he has paid one hundred and twenty-eight pounds fifteen shillings; and at sixty, one hundred and fifty-four pounds ten shillings. Converting, therefore, his (or her) individual tax into a tontine,* the money he shall receive after fifty years, is but little more than the legal interest of the nett money he has paid; the rest is made up from those whole circumstances do not require them to draw such support, and the capital in both cases defrays the expences of government. It is on this ground that I have extended the probable claims to one third of the number of aged persons in the nation.—Is it then better that the lives of one hundred and forty thousand aged persons be rendered comfortable, or that a million a year of public money be expended on any one individual, and him often of the most worthless or insignificant character? Let reason and justice, let honour and humanity, let even hypocrisy, sycophancy and Mr Burke, let George, let Louis, Leopold, Frederic, Catharine, Cornwallis, or Tippoo Saib,* answer the question.[1]

---

[1] Reckoning the taxes by families, five to a family, each family pays on an average, 12*l.* 17*s.* 6*d. per ann.* to this sum are to be added the poor-rates. Though

The sum thus remitted to the poor will be,

To two hundred and fifty-two thousand poor families, containing six hundred and thirty thousand children,	2,520,000
To one hundred and forty thousand aged persons,	1,120,000
	£3,640,000

There will then remain three hundred and sixty thousand pounds out of the four millions, part of which may be applied as follows:

After all the above cases are provided for, there will still be a number of families who, though not properly of the class of poor, yet find it difficult to give education to their children; and such children, under such a case, would be in a worse condition than if their parents were actually poor. A nation under a well regulated government, should permit none to remain uninstructed. It is monarchical and aristocratical government only that requires ignorance for its support.

Suppose then four hundred thousand children to be in this condition, which is a greater number than ought to be supposed, after the provisions already made, the method will be,

To allow for each of those children ten shillings a year for the expence of schooling, for six years each, which will give them six months schooling each year, and half a crown a year for paper and spelling books.

all pay taxes in the articles they consume, all do not pay poor-rates. About two millions are exempted, some as not being house-keepers, others as not being able, and the poor themselves who receive the relief. The average, therefore, of poor-rates on the remaining number, is forty shillings for every family of five persons, which makes the whole average amount of taxes and rates, 14*l*. 17*s*. 6*d*. For six persons, 17*l*. 17*s*. For seven persons, 20*l*. 16*s*. 6*d*.

The average of taxes in America, under the new or representative system of government, including the interest of the debt contracted in the war, and taking the population at four million of souls, which it now amounts to, and it is daily encreasing, is five shillings per head, men, women, and children. The difference, therefore, between the two governments, is as under,

	England.			America.		
	l.	*s.*	*d.*	*l.*	*s.*	*d.*
For a family of five persons	14	17	6	1	5	0
For a family of six persons	17	17	0	1	10	0
For a family of seven persons	20	16	6	1	15	0

The expence of this will be annually[1] £250,000

There will then remain one hundred and ten thousand pounds.

Notwithstanding the great modes of relief which the best instituted and best principled government may devise, there will still be a number of smaller cases, which it is good policy as well as beneficence in a nation to consider.

Were twenty shillings to be given to every woman immediately on the birth of a child, who should make the demand, and none will make it whose circumstances do not require it, it might relieve a great deal of instant distress.

There are about two hundred thousand births yearly in England; and if claimed, by one fourth,

The amount would be   50,000

And twenty shillings to every new-married couple who should claim in like manner. This would not exceed the sum of   £20,000

Also twenty thousand pounds to be appropriated to defray the funeral expences of persons, who, travelling for work, may die at a distance from their friends. By relieving parishes from this charge,* the sick stranger will be better treated.

I shall finish this part of the subject with a plan adapted to the particular condition of a metropolis, such as London.

Cases are continually occurring in a metropolis different to those which occur in the country, and for which a different, or rather an additional mode of relief is necessary. In the country, even in large towns, people have a knowledge of each other, and distress never rises to that extreme

---

[1] Public schools do not answer* the general purpose of the poor. They are chiefly in corporation towns, from which the country towns and villages are excluded; or if admitted, the distance occasions a great loss of time. Education, to be useful to the poor, should be on the spot; and the best method, I believe, to accomplish this, is to enable the parents to pay the expence themselves. There are always persons of both sexes to be found in every village, especially when growing into years, capable of such an undertaking. Twenty children, at ten shillings each, (and that not more than six months each year) would be as much as some livings amount to in the remote parts of England; and there are often distressed clergymen's widows to whom such an income would be acceptable. Whatever is given on this account to children answers two purposes, to them it is education, to those who educate them it is a livelihood.

height it sometimes does in a metropolis. There is no such thing in the country as persons, in the literal sense of the word, starved to death, or dying with cold from the want of a lodging. Yet such cases, and others equally as miserable, happen in London.

Many a youth comes up to London full of expectations, and with little or no money, and unless he gets immediate employment he is already half undone; and boys bred up in London without any means of a livelihood, and as it often happens of dissolute parents, are in a still worse condition; and servants long out of place are not much better off. In short, a world of little cases are continually arising, which busy or affluent life knows not of, to open the first door to distress. Hunger is not among the postponeable wants, and a day, even a few hours, in such a condition, is often the crisis of a life of ruin.

These circumstances, which are the general cause of the little thefts and pilferings that lead to greater, may be prevented. There yet remain twenty thousand pounds out of the four millions of surplus taxes, which, with another fund hereafter to be mentioned, amounting to about twenty thousand pounds more, cannot be better applied than to this purpose. The plan then will be,

First, To erect two or more buildings, or take some already erected, capable of containing at least six thousand persons, and to have in each of these places as many kinds of employment as can be contrived, so that every person who shall come may find something which he or she can do.

Secondly, To receive all who shall come, without enquiring who or what they are. The only condition to be, that for so much, or so many hours work, each person shall receive so many meals of wholesome food, and a warm lodging, at least as good as a barrack. That a certain portion of what each person's work shall be worth shall be reserved, and given to him, or her, on their going away; and that each person shall stay as long, or as short time, or come as often as he chuse, on these conditions.

If each person staid three months, it would assist by rotation twenty-four thousand persons annually, though the real number, at all times, would be but six thousand. By establishing an asylum of this kind, such persons to whom temporary distresses occur, would have an opportunity to recruit themselves, and be enabled to look out for better employment.

Allowing that their labour paid but one half the expence of supporting them, after reserving a portion of their earnings for themselves, the sum of forty thousand pounds additional would defray all other charges for even a greater number than six thousand.

The fund very properly convertible to this purpose, in addition to the twenty thousand pounds, remaining of the former fund, will be the produce of the tax upon coals, and so iniquitously and wantonly applied to the support of the Duke of Richmond. It is horrid that any man, more especially at the price coals now are, should live on the distresses of a community; and any government permitting such an abuse, deserves to be dismissed. This fund is said to be about twenty thousand pounds *per annum*.

I shall now conclude this plan with enumerating the several particulars, and then proceed to other matters.

The enumeration is as follows:

First, Abolition of two million poor-rates.

Secondly, Provision for two hundred and fifty-two thousand poor families.

Thirdly, Education for one million and thirty thousand children.

Fourthly, Comfortable provision for one hundred and forty thousand aged persons.

Fifthly, Donation of twenty shillings each for fifty thousand births.

Sixthly, Donation of twenty shillings each for twenty thousand marriages.

Seventhly, Allowance of twenty thousand pounds for the funeral expences of persons travelling for work, and dying at a distance from their friends.

Eighthly, Employment, at all times, for the casual poor in the cities of London and Westminster.

By the operation of this plan, the poor laws, those instruments of civil torture, will be superceded, and the wasteful expence of litigation prevented. The hearts of the humane will not be shocked by ragged and hungry children, and persons of seventy and eighty years of age begging for bread. The dying poor will not be dragged from place to place to breathe their last, as a reprisal of parish upon parish. Widows will have a maintenance for their children, and not be carted away, on the death of their husbands, like culprits and criminals; and children will no longer be considered as encreasing the distresses of their parents. The haunts of the wretched will be known, because it will be to their advantage, and the number of petty crimes, the offspring of distress and poverty, will be lessened. The poor, as well as the rich, will then be interested in the support of government, and the cause and apprehension of riots and tumults will cease.—Ye who sit in ease, and solace yourselves in plenty, and such there are in Turkey and Russia, as well as in England, and who say to yourselves, 'Are we not well off,' have ye thought of these things? When ye do, ye will cease to speak and feel for yourselves alone.

The plan is easy in practice. It does not embarrass trade by a sudden interruption in the order of taxes, but effects the relief by changing the application of them; and the money necessary for the purpose can be drawn from the excise collections, which are made eight times a year in every market town in England.

Having now arranged and concluded this subject, I proceed to the next.

Taking the present current expences at seven millions and an half, which is the least amount they are now at, there will remain (after the sum of one million and an half be taken for the new current expences, and four millions for the before mentioned service) the sum of two millions; part of which to be applied as follows:

Though fleets and armies, by an alliance with France, will, in a great measure, become useless, yet the persons who have devoted themselves to those services, and have thereby unfitted themselves for other lines of life, are not to be sufferers by the means that make others happy. They are a different description of men to those who form or hang about a court.

A part of the army will remain at least for some years, and also of the navy, for which a provision is already made in the former part of this plan of one million, which is almost half a million more than the peace establishment of the army and navy in the prodigal times of Charles the Second.

Suppose then fifteen thousand soldiers to be disbanded, and to allow to each of those men three shillings a week during life, clear of all deductions, to be paid in the same manner as the Chelsea College pensioners* are paid, and for them to return to their trades and their friends; and also to add fifteen thousand sixpences per week to the pay of the soldiers who shall remain; the annual expence will be,

To the pay of fifteen thousand disbanded
   soldiers, at three shillings per week,   £117,000
Additional pay to the remaining soldiers,   19,500

           Carried forward   136,500

Suppose that the pay to the officers of
   the disbanded corps be of the same
   amount as the sum allowed to the men,   117,000

                        253,500

To prevent bulky estimations, admit the
   same sum to the disbanded navy as to
   the army, and the same increase of pay,   253,500

                Total   507,000

Every year some part of this sum of half a million (I omit the odd seven thousand pounds for the purpose of keeping the account unembarrassed) will fall in, and the whole of it in time, as it is on the ground of life annuities, except the encreased pay of twenty-nine thousand pounds. As it falls in, a part of the taxes may be taken off; for instance, when thirty thousand pounds fall in the duty on hops may be wholly taken off; and as other parts fall in, the duties on candles and soap may be lessened, till at last they will totally cease.

There now remains at least one million and an half of surplus taxes.

The tax on houses and windows* is one of those direct taxes, which, like the poor-rates, is not confounded with trade; and, when taken off, the relief will be instantly felt. This tax falls heavy on the middling class of people.

The amount of this tax by the returns of 1788, was,

	l.	*s.*	*d.*
Houses and windows by the act of 1766,	385,459	11	7
Ditto by the act of 1779,	130,739	14	5½
Total	516,199	6	0½

If this tax be struck off, there will then remain about one million of surplus taxes, and as it is always proper to keep a sum in reserve, for incidental matters, it may be best not to extend reductions further, in the first instance, but to consider what may be accomplished by other modes of reform.

Among the taxes most heavily felt is the commutation tax.* I shall, therefore, offer a plan for its abolition, by substituting another in its place, which will affect three objects at once:

First, That of removing the burthen to where it can best be borne.

Secondly, Restoring justice among families by a distribution of property.

Thirdly, Extirpating the overgrown influence arising from the unnatural law of primogeniture, and which is one of the principal sources of corruption at elections.

The amount of the commutation
   tax by the returns of 1788, was,   £771,657 0 0

When taxes are proposed, the country is amused by the plausible language of taxing luxuries. One thing is called a luxury at one time, and something else at another; but the real luxury does not consist in the article, but in the means of procuring it, and this is always kept out of sight.

I know not why any plant or herb of the field should be a greater luxury in one country than another, but an overgrown estate in either is a luxury at all times, and as such is the proper object of taxation. It is, therefore, right to take those kind tax-making gentlemen up on their own word, and argue on the principle themselves have laid down, that of *taxing luxuries*. If they, or their champion Mr Burke, who, I fear, is growing out of date like the man in armour, can prove that an estate of twenty, thirty, or forty thousand pounds a year is not a luxury, I will give up the argument.

Admitting that any annual sum, say for instance, one thousand pounds, is necessary or sufficient for the support of a family, consequently the second thousand is of the nature of a luxury, the third still more so, and by proceeding on, we shall at last arrive at a sum that may not improperly be called a prohibitable luxury. It would be impolitic to set bounds to property acquired by industry, and therefore it is right to place the prohibition beyond the probable acquisition to which industry can extend; but there ought to be a limit to property, or the accumulation of it, by bequest. It should pass in some other line. The richest in every nation have poor relations, and those often very near in consanguinity.

The following table of progressive taxation is constructed on the above principles, and as a substitute for the commutation tax. It will reach the point of prohibition by a regular operation, and thereby supercede the aristocratical law of primogeniture.

TABLE I.

A tax on all estates of the clear yearly value of fifty pounds, after deducting the land tax, and up

	s.	d.	
To £500	0	3	per pound
From 500 to 1000	0	6	per pound
On the second thousand	0	9	per pound
On the third ditto	1	0	per pound
On the fourth ditto	1	6	per pound
On the fifth ditto	2	0	per pound
On the sixth ditto	3	0	per pound

	s.	d.	
On the seventh ditto	4	o	per pound
On the eighth ditto	5	o	per pound
On the ninth ditto	6	o	per pound
On the tenth ditto	7	o	per pound
On the eleventh ditto	8	o	per pound
On the twelfth ditto	9	o	per pound
On the thirteenth ditto	10	o	per pound
On the fourteenth ditto	11	o	per pound
On the fifteenth ditto	12	o	per pound
On the sixteenth ditto	13	o	per pound
On the seventeenth ditto	14	o	per pound
On the eighteenth ditto	15	o	per pound
On the nineteenth ditto	16	o	per pound
On the twentieth ditto	17	o	per pound
On the twenty-first ditto	18	o	per pound
On the twenty-second ditto	19	o	per pound
On the twenty-third ditto	20	o	per pound

The foregoing table shews the progression per pound on every progressive thousand. The following table shews the amount of the tax on every thousand separately, and in the last column, the total amount of all the separate sums collected.

TABLE II.

	d.	l.	s.	d.
An estate of £50 *per ann.* at 3 per pd. pays		o	12	6
100	3	1	5	0
200	3	2	10	0
300	3	3	15	0
400	3	5	0	0
500	3	7	5	0

After 500l.—the tax of sixpence per pound takes place on the second 500l.—consequently an estate of 1000l. *per ann.* pays 21l. 15s. and so on,

		l.	*s.*	*d.*		*l.*	*s.*	Total amount. *l.*	*s.*
For the	1st	500 at	0	3	per pound	7	5 ⎱		
	2d	500 at	0	6		14	10 ⎰	21	15
	2d	1,000 at	0	9		37	10	59	5
	3d	1,000 at	1	0		50	0	109	5
	4th	1,000 at	1	6		75	0	184	5
	5th	1,000 at	2	0		100	0	284	5
	6th	1,000 at	3	0		150	0	434	5
	7th	1,000 at	4	0		200	0	634	5
	8th	1,000 at	5	0		250	0	880	5
	9th	1,000 at	6	0		300	0	1,180	5
	10th	1,000 at	7	0		350	0	1,530	5
	11th	1,000 at	8	0		400	0	1,930	5
	12th	1,000 at	9	0		450	0	2.380	5
	13th	1,000 at	10	0		500	0	2,880	5
	14th	1,000 at	11	0		550	0	3,430	5
	15th	1,000 at	12	0		600	0	4,030	5
	16th	1,000 at	13	0		650	0	4,680	5
	17th	1,000 at	14	0		700	0	5,380	5
	18th	1,000 at	15	0		750	0	6,130	5
	19th	1,000 at	16	0		800	0	6,930	5
	20th	1,000 at	17	0		850	0	7,780	5
	21st	1,000 at	18	0		900	0	8,680	5
	22d	1,000 at	19	0		950	0	9,630	5
	23d	1,000 at	20	0		1,000	0	10,630	5

At the twenty-third thousand the tax becomes twenty shillings in the pound, and consequently every thousand beyond that sum can produce no profit but by dividing the estate. Yet formidable as this tax appears, it will not, I believe, produce so much as the commutation tax; should it produce more, it ought to be lowered to that amount upon estates under two or three thousand a year.

On small and middling estates it is lighter (as it is intended to be) than the commutation tax. It is not till after seven or eight thousand a year that it begins to be heavy. The object is not so much the produce of the tax, as the justice of the measure. The aristocracy has screened itself too much, and this serves to restore a part of the lost equilibrium.

As an instance of its screening itself, it is only necessary to look back to the first establishment of the excise laws, at what is called the Restoration, or the coming of Charles the Second. The aristocratical interest then in power, commuted the feudal services itself was under by laying a tax on beer brewed for *sale*;* that is, they compounded with Charles for an exemption from those services for themselves and their heirs, by a tax to be paid by other people. The aristocracy do not purchase beer brewed for sale, but brew their own beer free of the duty, and if any commutation at that time were necessary, it ought to have been at the expence of those for whom the exemptions from those services were intended;¹ instead of which it was thrown on an entire different class of men.

But the chief object of this progressive tax (besides the justice of rendering taxes more equal than they are) is, as already stated, to extirpate the overgrown influence arising from the unnatural law of primogeniture, and which is one of the principal sources of corruption at elections.

It would be attended with no good consequences to en-quire how such vast estates as thirty, forty, or fifty thousand a year could commence, and that at a time when commerce and manufactures were not in a state to admit of such acquisitions. Let it be sufficient to remedy the evil by putting them in a condition of descending again to the community, by the quiet means of apportioning them among, all the heirs and heiresses of those families. This will be the more necessary, because hitherto the aristocracy have quartered their younger children and connections upon the public in useless posts, places, and offices, which when abolished will leave them destitute, unless the law of primo-geniture be also abolished or superceded.

A progressive tax will, in a great measure, effect this

---

¹ The tax on beer brewed for sale, from which the aristocracy are exempt, is almost one million more than the present commutation tax, being by the returns of 1788, 1,666,152*l.* and consequently they ought to take on themselves the amount of the commutation tax, as they are already exempted from one which is almost one million greater.

object, and that as a matter of interest to the parties most immediately concerned, as will be seen by the following table; which shews the nett produce upon every estate, after subtracting the tax. By this it will appear, that after an estate exceeds thirteen or fourteen thousand a year, the remainder produces but little profit to the holder, and consequently

TABLE III.

Shewing the nett produce of every estate from one thousand to twenty-three thousand pounds a year.

No. of thousands per ann.	Total tax subtracted.	Net produce.
	£	£
1,000	21	979
2,000	59	1,941
3,000	109	2,891
4,000	184	3,816
5,000	284	4,716
6,000	434	5,566
7,000	634	6,366
8,000	880	7,120
9,000	1,180	7,820
10,000	1,530	8,470
11,000	1,930	9,070
12,000	2,380	9,620
13,000	2,880	10,120
14,000	3,430	10,570
15,000	4,030	10,970
16,000	4,680	11,320
17,000	5,380	11,620
18,000	6,130	11,870
19,000	6,930	12,170
20,000	7,780	12,220
21,000	8,680	12,320
22,000	9,630	12,370
23,000	10,630	12,370

N.B. The odd shillings are dropped in this table.

will pass either to the younger children, or to other kindred.

According to this table, an estate cannot produce more then 12,370*l.* clear of the land tax and the progressive tax, and therefore the dividing such estates will follow as a matter of family interest. An estate of 23,000*l.* a year, divided into five estates of four thousand each and one of three, will be charged only 1129*l.* which is but five *per cent.* but if held by one possessor will be charged 10,630*l.*

Although an enquiry into the origin of those estates be unnecessary, the continuation of them in their present state is another subject. It is a matter of national concern. As hereditary estates, the law has created the evil, and it ought also to provide the remedy. Primogeniture ought to be abolished, not only because it is unnatural and unjust, but because the country suffers by its operation. By cutting off (as before observed) the younger children from their proper portion of inheritance, the public is loaded with the expence of maintaining them; and the freedom of elections violated by the overbearing influence which this unjust monopoly of family property produces. Nor is this all. It occasions a waste of national property. A considerable part of the land of the country is rendered unproductive by the great extent of parks and chases which this law serves to keep up, and this at a time when the annual production of grain is not equal to the national consumption.[1]—In short, the evils of the aristocratical system are so great and numerous, so inconsistent with every thing that is just, wise, natural, and beneficent, that when they are considered, there ought not to be a doubt that many, who are now classed under that description, will wish to see such a system abolished.

What pleasure can they derive from contemplating the exposed condition, and almost certain beggary of their younger offspring? Every aristocratical family has an append-age of family beggars hanging round it, which in a few ages, or a few generations, are shook off, and console themselves with telling their tale in alms-houses, work-houses, and prisons. This is the natural consequence of aristocracy. The

[1] See the reports on the corn trade.*

peer and the beggar are often of the same family. One extreme produces the other: to make one rich many must be made poor; neither can the system be supported by other means.

There are two classes of people to whom the laws of England are particularly hostile, and those the most helpless; younger children and the poor. Of the former I have just spoken; of the latter I shall mention one instance out of the many that might be produced, and with which I shall close this subject.

Several laws are in existence for regulating and limiting workmen's wages.* Why not leave them as free to make their own bargains, as the law-makers are to let their farms and houses? Personal labour is all the property they have. Why is that little, and the little freedom they enjoy to be infringed? But the injustice will appear stronger, if we consider the operation and effect of such laws. When wages are fixed by what is called a law, the legal wages remain stationary, while every thing else is in progression; and as those who make that law, still continue to lay on new taxes by other laws, they encrease the expence of living by one law, and take away the means by another.

But if those gentlemen law-makers and tax-makers thought it right to limit the poor pittance which personal labour can produce, and on which a whole family is to be supported, they certainly must feel themselves happily indulged in a limitation on their own part, of not less than twelve thousand a year, and that of property they never acquired, (nor probably any of their ancestors) and of which they have made so ill a use.

Having now finished this subject, I shall bring the several particulars into one view, and then proceed to other matters.

The first EIGHT ARTICLES are brought forward from page 300.

1. Abolition of two million poor-rates.
2. Provision for two hundred and fifty-two thousand poor families, at the rate of four pounds per head for each child

under fourteen years of age; which, with the addition of two hundred and fifty thousand pounds, provides also education for one million and thirty thousand children.

3. Annuity of six pounds (per ann.) each for all poor persons, decayed tradesmen, or others (supposed seventy thousand) of the age of fifty years, and until sixty.

4. Annuity of ten pounds each for life for all poor persons, decayed tradesmen, and others (supposed seventy thousand) of the age of sixty years.

5. Donation of twenty shillings each for fifty thousand births.

6. Donation of twenty shillings each for twenty thousand marriages.

7. Allowance of twenty thousand pounds for the funeral expences of persons travelling for work, and dying at a distance from their friends.

8. Employment at all times for the casual poor in the cities of London and Westminster.

SECOND ENUMERATION

9. Abolition of the tax on houses and windows.

10. Allowance of three shillings per week for life to fifteen thousand disbanded soldiers, and a proportionable allowance to the officers of the disbanded corps.

11. Encrease of pay to the remaining soldiers of 19,500*l.* annually.

12. The same allowance to the disbanded navy, and the same encrease of pay, as to the army.

13. Abolition of the commutation tax.

14. Plan of a progressive tax, operating to extirpate the unjust and unnatural law of primogeniture, and the vicious influence of the aristocratical system.[1]

There yet remains, as already stated, one million of surplus taxes. Some part of this will be required for circumstances

---

[1] When enquiries are made into the condition of the poor, various degrees of distress will most probably be found, to render a different arrangement preferable to that which is already proposed. Widows with families will be in greater want than where there are husbands living. There is also a difference in the expence of living in different countries; and more so in fuel.

that do not immediately present themselves, and such part as shall not be wanted, will admit a further reduction of taxes equal to that amount.

Among the claims that justice requires to be made, the condition of the inferior revenue officers will merit attention. It is a reproach to any government to waste such an immensity of revenue in sinecures and nominal and unnecessary places and offices, and not allow even a decent livelihood to those on whom the labour falls. The salary of the inferior officers of the revenue* has stood at the petty pittance of less than fifty pounds a year for upwards of one hundred years. It ought to be seventy. About one hundred and twenty thousand pounds applied to this purpose, will put all those salaries in a decent condition.

This was proposed to be done almost twenty years ago, but the treasury-board then in being startled at it, as it might lead to similar expectations from the army and navy; and the event was, that the King, or somebody for him, applied to parliament to have his own salary raised an hundred thousand a year, which being done, every thing else was laid aside.

With respect to another class of men, the inferior clergy, I forbear to enlarge on their condition; but all partialities and prejudices for, or against, different modes and forms of

	£
Suppose then fifty thousand extraordinary cases, at the rate of 10*l.* per family per ann.	500,000
100,000 Families, at 8*l.* per family per ann.	800,000
100,000 Families, at 7*l.* per family per ann.	700,000
104,000 Families, at 5*l.* per family per ann.	520,000
And instead of ten shillings per head for the education of other children, to allow fifty shillings per family for that purpose to fifty thousand families	250,000
	2,770,000
140,000 Aged persons as before,	1,120,000
	3,890,000

This arrangement amounts to the same sum as stated in page 297, including the 250,000*l.* for education; but it provides (including the aged people) for four hundred and four thousand families, which is almost one third of the families in England.

religion aside, common justice will determine, whether there ought to be an income of twenty or thirty pounds a year to one man, and of ten thousand to another. I speak on this subject with the more freedom, because I am known not to be a Presbyterian; and therefore the cant cry of court sycophants, about church and meeting, kept up to amuse and bewilder the nation, cannot be raised against me.

Ye simple men, on both sides the question, do ye not see through this courtly craft? If ye can be kept disputing and wrangling about church and meeting, ye just answer the purpose of every courtier, who lives the while on the spoil of the taxes, and laughs at your credulity. Every religion is good that teaches man to be good; and I know of none that instructs him to be bad.

All the before-mentioned calculations, suppose only sixteen millions and an half of taxes paid into the exchequer, after the expence of collection and drawbacks at the custom-house and excise-office are deducted; whereas the sum paid into the exchequer is very nearly, if not quite, seventeen millions. The taxes raised in Scotland and Ireland are expended in those countries, and therefore their savings will come out of their own taxes; but if any part be paid into the English exchequer, it might be remitted. This will not make one hundred thousand pounds a year difference.

There now remains only the national debt to be considered. In the year 1789, the interest, exclusive of the tontine, was 9,150,138*l.* How much the capital has been reduced since that time the minister best knows. But after paying the interest, abolishing the tax on houses and windows, the commutation tax, and the poor rates; and making all the provisions for the poor, for the education of children, the support of the aged, the disbanded part of the army and navy, and encreasing the pay of the remainder, there will be a surplus of one million.

The present scheme of paying off the national debt appears to me, speaking as an indifferent person, to be an ill-concerted, if not a fallacious job. The burthen of the national debt consists not in its being so many millions, or so many hundred millions, but in the quantity of taxes collected every year to pay the interest. If this quantity continue the same, the burthen of the national debt is the same to all intents and purposes, be the capital more or less. The only knowledge which the public can have of the reduction of the debt, must be through the reduction of taxes for paying the interest. The debt, therefore, is not reduced one farthing to the public by all the millions that have been paid; and it would require more money now to purchase up the capital, than when the scheme began.

Digressing for a moment at this point, to which I shall return again, I look back to the appointment of Mr Pitt, as minister.

I was then in America. The war was over; and though resentment had ceased, memory was still alive.

When the news of the coalition arrived,* though it was a matter of no concern to me as a citizen of America, I felt it as a man. It had something in it which shocked, by publicly sporting with decency, if not with principle. It was impudence in Lord North; it was want of firmness in Mr Fox.

Mr Pitt was, at that time, what may be called a maiden character in politics. So far from being hackneyed, he appeared not to be initiated into the first mysteries of court intrigue. Every thing was in his favour. Resentment against the coalition served as friendship to him, and his ignorance of vice was credited for virtue. With the return of peace, commerce and prosperity would rise of itself; yet even this encrease was thrown to his account.

When he came to the helm the storm was over, and he had nothing to interrupt his course. It required even ingenuity to be wrong, and he succeeded. A little time shewed him the same sort of man as his predecessors had been. Instead of profiting by those errors which had accumulated a burthen of taxes unparalleled in the world, he sought, I might almost say, he advertised for enemies, and provoked means to encrease taxation. Aiming at something, he knew not what, he ransacked Europe and India for adventures,* and abandoning the fair pretensions he began with, became the knight-errant of modern times.

It is unpleasant to see character throw itself away. It is

more so to see one's-self deceived. Mr Pitt had merited nothing, but he promised much. He gave symptoms of a mind superior to the meanness and corruption of courts. His apparent candour encouraged expectations; and the public confidence, stunned, wearied, and confounded by a chaos of parties, revived and attached itself to him. But mistaking, as he has done, the disgust of the nation against the coalition, for merit in himself, he has rushed into measures, which a man less supported would not have presumed to act.

All this seems to shew that change of ministers amounts to nothing. One goes out, another comes in, and still the same measures, vices, and extravagance are pursued. It signifies not who is minister. The defect lies in the system. The foundation and the superstructure of the government is bad. Prop it as you please, it continually links into court government, and ever will.

I return, as I promised, to the subject of the national debt, that offspring of the Dutch-Anglo revolution, and its handmaid the Hanover succession.

But it is now too late to enquire how it began. Those to whom it is due have advanced the money; and whether it was well or ill spent, or pocketed, is not their crime. It is, however, easy to see, that as the nation proceeds in contemplating the nature and principles of government, and to understand taxes, and make comparisons between those of America, France, and England, it will be next to impossible to keep it in the same torpid state it has hitherto been. Some reform must, from the necessity of the case, soon begin. It is not whether these principles press with little or much force in the present moment. They are out. They are abroad in the world, and no force can stop them. Like a secret told, they are beyond recall; and he must be blind indeed that does not see that a change is already beginning.

Nine millions of dead taxes is a serious thing; and this not only for bad, but in a great measure for foreign government. By putting the power of making war into the hands of foreigners who came for what they could get, little else was to be expected than what has happened.

Reasons are already advanced in this work shewing that

whatever the reforms in the taxes may be, they ought to be made in the current expences of government, and not in the part applied to the interest of the national debt. By remitting the taxes of the poor, *they* will be totally relieved, and all discontent on their part will be taken away; and by striking off such of the taxes as are already mentioned, the nation will more than recover the whole expence of the mad American war.

There will then remain only the national debt as a subject of discontent; and in order to remove, or rather to prevent this, it would be good policy in the stock-holders themselves to consider it as property, subject like all other property, to bear some portion of the taxes. It would give to it both popularity and security, and as a great part of its present inconvenience is balanced by the capital which it keeps alive, a measure of this kind would so far add to that balance as to silence objections.

This may be done by such gradual means as to accomplish all that is necessary with the greatest ease and convenience.

Instead of taxing the capital, the best method would be to tax the interest by some progressive ratio, and to lessen the public taxes in the same proportion as the interest diminished.

Suppose the interest was taxed one halfpenny in the pound the first year, a penny more the second, and to proceed by a certain ratio to be determined upon, always less than any other tax upon property. Such a tax would be subtracted from the interest at the time of payment, without any expence of collection.

One halfpenny in the pound would lessen the interest and consequently the taxes, twenty thousand pounds. The tax on waggons amounts to this sum, and this tax might be taken off the first year. The second year the tax on female servants, or some other of the like amount might also be taken off, and by proceeding in this manner, always applying the tax raised from the property of the debt towards its extinction, and not carry it to the current services, it would liberate itself.

The stockholders, notwithstanding this tax, would pay less taxes than they do now. What they would save by the extinction of the poor-rates, and the tax on houses and windows, and the commutation tax, would be considerably greater than what this tax, slow, but certain in its operation, amounts to.

It appears to me to be prudence to look out for measures that may apply under any circumstance that may approach. There is, at this moment, a crisis in the affairs of Europe that requires it. Preparation now is wisdom. If taxation be once let loose, it will be difficult to re-instate it; neither would the relief be so effectual, as to proceed by some certain and gradual reduction.

The fraud, hypocrisy, and imposition of governments, are now beginning to be too well understood to promise them any long career. The farce of monarchy and aristocracy, in all countries, is following that of chivalry, and Mr Burke is dressing for the funeral. Let it then pass quietly to the tomb of all other follies, and the mourners be comforted.

The time is not very distant when England will laugh at itself for sending to Holland, Hanover, Zell, or Brunswick* for men, at the expence of a million a year, who understood neither her laws, her language, nor her interest, and whose capacities would scarcely have fitted them for the office of a parish constable. If government could be trusted to such hands, it must be some easy and simple thing indeed, and materials fit for all the purposes may be found in every town and village in England.

When it shall be said in any country in the world, my poor are happy; neither ignorance nor distress is to be found among them; my jails are empty of prisoners, my streets of beggars; the aged are not in want, the taxes are not oppressive; the rational world is my friend, because I am the friend of its happiness: when these things can be said, then may that country boast its constitution and its government.

Within the space of a few years we have seen two Revolutions, those of America and France. In the former, the contest was long, and the conflict severe; in the latter, the nation acted with such a consolidated impulse, that having no foreign enemy to contend with, the revolution was complete in power the moment it appeared. From both those instances it is evident, that the greatest forces that can be brought into the field of revolutions, are reason and common interest. Where these can have the opportunity of acting, opposition dies with fear, or crumbles away by conviction. It is a great standing which they have now universally obtained; and we may hereafter hope to see revolutions, or changes in governments, produced with the same quiet operation by which any measure, determinable by reason and discussion, is accomplished.

When a nation changes its opinion and habits of thinking, it is no longer to be governed as before; but it would not only be wrong, but bad policy, to attempt by force what ought to be accomplished by reason. Rebellion consists in forcibly opposing the general will of a nation, whether by a party or by a government.* There ought, therefore, to be in every nation a method of occasionally ascertaining the state of public opinion with respect to government. On this point the old government of France was superior to the present government of England, because, on extraordinary occasions, recourse could be had to what was then called the States General. But in England there are no such occasional bodies; and as to those who are now called Representatives, a great part of them are mere machines of the court, placemen, and dependants.

I presume, that though all the people of England pay taxes, not an hundredth part of them are electors, and the members of one of the houses of parliament represent nobody but themselves. There is, therefore, no power but the voluntary will of the people that has a right to act in any matter respecting a general reform; and by the same right that two persons can confer on such a subject, a thousand may. The object, in all such preliminary proceedings, is to find out what the general sense of a nation is, and to be governed by it. If it prefer a bad or defective government to a reform, or chuse to pay ten times more taxes than there is occasion for, it has a right so to do; and so long as the majority do not impose conditions on the minority, different to what they impose on themselves, though there may be much error, there is no injustice. Neither will the error continue long. Reason and discussion will soon bring things right, however wrong they may begin. By such a process no tumult is to be apprehended. The poor, in all countries, are naturally both peaceable and grateful in all reforms in which their interest and happiness is included. It is only by neglecting and rejecting them that they become tumultuous.

The objects that now press on the public attention are, the French revolution, and the prospect of a general revolution in governments. Of all nations in Europe, there is none so much interested in the French revolution as England. Enemies for ages, and that at a vast expence, and without any national object, the opportunity now presents itself of amicably closing the scene, and joining their efforts to reform the rest of Europe. By doing this, they will not only prevent the further effusion of blood, and encrease of taxes, but be in a condition of getting rid of a considerable part of their present burthens, as has been already stated. Long experience however has shewn, that reforms of this kind are not those which old governments wish to promote; and therefore it is to nations, and not to such governments, that these matters present themselves.

In the preceding part of this work, I have spoken of an alliance between England, France, and America, for purposes that were to be afterwards mentioned. Though I have no direct authority on the part of America, I have good reason to conclude, that she is disposed to enter into a consideration of such a measure, provided, that the governments with which she might ally, acted as national governments, and not as courts enveloped in intrigue and mystery. That France as a nation, and a national government, would prefer an alliance with England, is a matter of certainty. Nations, like individuals, who have long been enemies, without knowing each other, or knowing why, become the better friends when they discover the errors and impositions under which they had acted.

Admitting, therefore, the probability of such a connection, I will state some matters by which such an alliance, together with that of Holland, might render service, not only to the parties immediately concerned, but to all Europe.

It is, I think, certain, that if the fleets of England, France, and Holland were confederated, they could propose, with effect, a limitation to, and a general dismantling of all the navies in Europe, to a certain proportion to be agreed upon.

First, That no new ship of war shall be built by any power in Europe, themselves included.

Secondly, That all the navies now in existence shall be put back, suppose to one-tenth of their present force. This will save to France and England at least two millions sterling annually to each, and their relative force to be in the same proportion as it is now. If men will permit themselves to think, as rational beings ought to think, nothing can appear more ridiculous and absurd, exclusive of all moral reflections, than to be at the expence of building navies, filling them with men, and then hauling them into the ocean, to try which can sink each other fastest. Peace, which costs nothing, is attended with infinitely more advantage, than any victory with all its expence. But this, though it best answers the purpose of nations, does not that of court governments, whose habited policy is pretence for taxation, places, and offices.

It is, I think, also certain, that the above confederated powers, together with that of the United States of America, can propose with effect, to Spain, the independance of South America, and the opening those countries of immense extent and wealth to the general commerce of the world, as North America now is.

With how much more glory, and advantage to itself, does a nation act, when it exerts its powers to rescue the world from bondage, and to create itself friends, than when it employs those powers to encrease ruin, desolation, and misery. The horrid scene that is now acting by the English government in the East-Indies,* is fit only to be told of Goths and Vandals, who, destitute of principle, robbed and tortured the world they were incapable of enjoying.

The opening of South America would produce an immense field of commerce, and a ready money market for manufactures, which the eastern world does not. The East is already a country full of manufactures, the importation of which is not only an injury to the manufactures of England, but a drain upon its specie. The balance against England by this trade is regularly upwards of half a million annually sent out in the East-India ships in silver; and this is the reason, together with German intrigue, and German subsidies, there is so little silver in England.

But any war is harvest to such governments, however ruinous it may be to a nation. It serves to keep up deceitful expectations which prevent a people looking into the defects and abuses of government. It is the *lo here!* and the *lo there!* that amuses and cheats the multitude.

Never did so great an opportunity offer itself to England, and to all Europe, as is produced by the two Revolutions of America and France. By the former, freedom has a national champion in the Western world; and by the latter, in Europe. When another nation shall join France, despotism and bad government will scarcely dare to appear. To use a trite expression, the iron is becoming hot all over Europe. The insulted German and the enslaved Spaniard, the Russ and the Pole, are beginning to think. The present age will hereafter merit to be called the Age of reason,* and the present generation will appear to the future as the Adam of a new world.

When all the governments of Europe shall be established on the representative system, nations will become acquainted, and the animosities and prejudices fomented by the intrigue and artifice of courts, will cease. The oppressed soldier will become a freeman; and the tortured sailor,* no longer dragged along the streets like a felon, will pursue his mercantile voyage in safety. It would be better that nations should continue the pay of their soldiers during their lives, and give them their discharge and restore them to freedom and their friends, and cease recruiting, than retain such multitudes at the same expence, in a condition useless to society and themselves. As soldiers have hitherto been treated in most countries, they might be said to be without a friend. Shunned by the citizen on an apprehension of being enemies to liberty, and too often insulted by those who commanded them, their condition was a double oppression. But where genuine principles of liberty pervade a people, every thing is restored to order; and the soldier civily treated, returns the civility.

In contemplating revolutions, it is easy to perceive that they may arise from two distinct causes; the one, to avoid or get rid of some great calamity; the other, to obtain some great and positive good; and the two may be distinguished by the names of active and passive revolutions. In those which proceed from the former cause, the temper becomes incensed and sowered;* and the redress, obtained by danger, is too often sullied by revenge. But in those which proceed from the latter, the heart, rather animated than agitated, enters serenely upon the subject. Reason and discussion, persuasion and conviction, become the weapons in the contest, and it is only when those are attempted to be suppressed that recource is had to violence. When men unite in agreeing that a *thing is good*, could it be obtained, such as relief from a burden of taxes and the extinction of corruption, the object is more than half accomplished. What they approve as the end, they will promote in the means.

Will any man say, in the present excess of taxation, falling so heavily on the poor, that a remission of five pounds annually of taxes to one hundred and four thousand poor families is not a *good thing*? Will he say, that a remission of seven pounds annually to one hundred thousand other poor families—of eight pounds annually to another hundred thousand poor families, and of ten pounds annually to fifty thousand poor and widowed families, are not *good things*? And to proceed a step farther in this climax, will he say, that to provide against the misfortunes to which all human life is subject, by securing six pounds annually for all poor, distressed, and reduced persons of the age of fifty and until sixty, and of ten pounds annually after sixty is not a *good thing*?

Will he say, that an abolition of two million of poor-rates to the house-keepers, and of the whole of the house and window-light tax and of the commutation tax is not a *good thing*? Or will he say, that to abolish corruption is a *bad thing*?

If, therefore, the good to be obtained be worthy of a

passive, rational, and costless revolution, it would be bad policy to prefer waiting for a calamity that should force a violent one. I have no idea, considering the reforms which are now passing and spreading throughout Europe, that England will permit herself to be the last; and where the occasion and the opportunity quietly offer, it is better than to wait for a turbulent necessity. It may be considered as an honour to the animal faculties of man to obtain redress by courage and danger, but it is far greater honour to the rational faculties to accomplish the same object by reason, accommodation, and general consent.[1]

As reforms, or revolutions, call them which you please, extend themselves among nations, those nations will form connections and conventions, and when a few are thus confederated, the progress will be rapid, till despotism and corrupt government be totally expelled, at least out of two quarters of the world, Europe and America. The Algerine piracy may then be commanded to cease,* for it is only by the malicious policy of old governments, against each other, that it exists.

Throughout this work, various and numerous as the subjects are, which I have taken up and investigated, there is only a single paragraph upon religion, viz. '*that every religion is good, that teaches man to be good.*'

I have carefully avoided to enlarge upon the subject, because I am inclined to believe, that what is called the

---

[1] I know it is the opinion of many of the most enlightened characters in France (there always will be those who see farther into events than others) not only among the general mass of citizens, but of many of the principal members of the former National Assembly,* that the monarchical plan will not continue many years in that country. They have found out, that as wisdom cannot be made hereditary, power ought not; and that, for a man to merit a million stirling a year from a nation, he ought to have a mind capable of comprehending from an atom to a universe; which, if he had, he would be above receiving the pay. But they wished not to appear to lead the nation faster than its own reason and interest dictated. In all the conversations where I have been present upon this subject, the idea always was, that when such a time, from the general opinion of the nation, shall arrive, that the honourable and liberal method would be, to make a handsome present in fee simple to the person whoever he may be, that shall then be in the monarchical office, and for him to retire to the enjoyment of private life, possessing his share of general rights and privileges, and to be no more accountable to the public for his time and his conduct than any other citizen.

present ministry wish to see contentions about religion kept up, to prevent the nation turning its attention to subjects of government. It is, as if they were to say, 'Look that way, or any way, but this.'

But as religion is very improperly made a political machine, and the reality of it is thereby destroyed, I will conclude this work with stating in what light religion appears to me.

If we suppose a large family of children, who, on any particular day, or particular circumstance, made it a custom to present to their parent some token of their affection and gratitude, each of them would make a different offering, and most probably in a different manner. Some would pay their congratulations in themes of verse or prose, by some little devices, as their genius dictated, or according to what they thought would please; and, perhaps, the least of all, not able to do any of those things, would ramble into the garden, or the field, and gather what it thought the prettiest flower it could find, though, perhaps, it might be but a simple weed. The parent would be more gratified by such variety, than if the whole of them had acted on a concerted plan, and each had made exactly the same offering. This would have the cold appearance of contrivance, or the harsh one of controul. But of all unwelcome things, nothing could more afflict the parent than to know, that the whole of them had afterwards gotten together by the ears, boys and girls, fighting, scratching, reviling, and abusing each other about which was the best or the worst present.

Why may we not suppose, that the great Father of all is pleased with variety of devotion; and that the greatest offence we can act, is that by which we seek to torment and render each other miserable. For my own part, I am fully satisfied that what I am now doing, with an endeavour to conciliate mankind, to render their condition happy, to unite nations that have hitherto been enemies, and to extirpate the horrid practice of war, and break the chains of slavery and oppression, is acceptable in his sight, and being the best service I can perform, I act it chearfully.

I do not believe that any two men, on what are called

doctrinal points, think alike who think at all. It is only those who have not thought that appear to agree. It is in this case as with what is called the British constitution. It has been taken for granted to be good, and encomiums have supplied the place of proof. But when the nation come to examine into its principles and the abuses it admits, it will be found to have more defects than I have pointed out in this work and the former.

As to what are called national religions, we may, with as much propriety, talk of national Gods. It is either political craft or the remains of the Pagan system, when every nation had its separate and particular deity. Among all the writers of the English church clergy, who have treated on the general subject of religion, the present Bishop of Landaff* has not been excelled, and it is with much pleasure that I take the opportunity of expressing this token of respect.

I have now gone through the whole of the subject, at least, as far as it appears to me at present. It has been my intention for the five years I have been in Europe, to offer an address to the people of England on the subject of government, if the opportunity presented itself before I returned to America. Mr Burke has thrown it in my way, and I thank him. On a certain occasion three years ago,* I pressed him to propose a national convention to be fairly elected for the purpose of taking the state of the nation into consideration; but I found, that however strongly the parliamentary current was then setting against the party he acted with, their policy was to keep every thing within that field of corruption, and trust to accidents. Long experience had shewn that, parliaments would follow any change of ministers, and on this they rested their hopes and their expectations.

Formerly, when divisions arose, respecting governments, recourse was had to the sword, and a civil war ensued. That savage custom is exploded by the new system, and reference is had to national conventions. Discussion and the general will arbitrates the question, and to this, private opinion yields with a good grace, and order is preserved uninterrupted.

Some gentlemen have affected to call the principles upon which this work and the former part of *Rights of Man* are founded, 'a new fangled doctrine.' The question is not whether those principles are new or old, but whether they are right or wrong. Suppose the former, I will shew their effect by a figure easily understood.

It is now towards the middle of February. Were I to take a turn into the country, the trees would present a leafless winterly appearance. As people are apt to pluck twigs as they walk along, I perhaps might do the same, and by chance might observe, that a *single bud* on that twig had begun to swell. I should reason very unnaturally, or rather not reason at all, to suppose *this* was the *only* bud in England which had this appearance. Instead of deciding thus, I should instantly conclude, that the same appearance was beginning, or about to begin, every where; and though the vegetable sleep will continue longer on some trees and plants than on others, and though some of them may not *blossom* for two or three years, all will be in leaf in the summer, except those which are *rotten*. What pace the political summer may keep with the natural, no human foresight can determine. It is, however, not difficult to perceive that the spring is begun.—Thus wishing, as I sincerely do, freedom and happiness to all nations, I close the

SECOND PART.

APPENDIX

As the publication of this work has been delayed beyond the time intended, I think it not improper, all circumstances considered, to state the causes that have occasioned the delay.

The reader will probably observe, that some parts in the plan contained in this work for reducing the taxes, and certain parts in Mr Pitt's speech at the opening of the present session, Tuesday, January 31,* are so much alike, as to induce a belief, that either the Author had taken the hint from Mr Pitt, or Mr Pitt from the Author.—I will first point out the parts that are similar, and then state such circumstances as I am acquainted with, leaving the reader to make his own conclusion.

Considering it almost an unprecedented case, that taxes should be proposed to be taken off, it is equally as extraordinary that such a measure should occur to two persons at the same time; and still more so, (considering the vast variety and multiplicity of taxes) that they should hit on the same specific taxes. Mr Pitt has mentioned, in his speech, the tax on *Carts and Waggons*—that on *Female Servants*—the lowering the tax on *Candles*, and the taking off the tax of three shillings on *Houses* having under seven windows.

Every one of those specific taxes are a part of the plan contained in this work, and proposed also to be taken off. Mr Pitt's plan, it is true, goes no farther than to a reduction of three hundred and twenty thousand pounds; and the reduction proposed in this work to nearly six millions. I have made my calculations on only sixteen millions and an half of revenue, still asserting that it was 'very nearly, if not quite, seventeen millions.' Mr Pitt states it at 16,690,000. I know enough of the matter to say, that he has not *over*stated it. Having thus given the particulars, which correspond in this work and his speech, I will state a chain of circumstances that may lead to some explanation.

The first hint for lessening the taxes, and that as a consequence flowing from the French revolution, is to be found
in the ADDRESS and DECLARATION of the Gentlemen who
met at the Thatched-House Tavern,* August 20, 1791.
Among many other particulars stated in that Address, is the
following, put as an interrogation to the government opposers of the French Revolution. '*Are they sorry that the pretence
for new oppressive taxes, and the occasion for continuing many
old taxes will be at an end*?

It is well known, that the persons who chiefly frequent
the Thatched House Tavern, are men of court connections,
and so much did they take this Address and Declaration
respecting the French revolution and the reduction of taxes
in disgust, that the Landlord was under the necessity of
informing the Gentlemen, who composed the meeting of the
twentieth of August, and who proposed holding another
meeting, that he could not receive them.[1]

What was only hinted at in the Address and Declaration,
respecting taxes and principles of government, will be found
reduced to a regular system in this work. But as Mr Pitt's
speech contains some of the same things respecting taxes, I
now come to give the circumstances before alluded to.

The case is: This work was intended to be published just
before the meeting of Parliament,* and for that purpose a
considerable part of the copy was put into the printer's
hands* in September, and all the remaining copy, as far as

---

[1] The gentleman who signed the address and declaration as chairman of the
meeting, M. Horne Tooke, being generally supposed to be the person who drew it
up, and having spoken much in commendation of it, has been jocularly accused of
praising his own work. To free him from this embarassment, and to save him the
repeated trouble of mentioning the author, as he has not failed to do, I make no
hesitation in saying, that as the opportunity of benefiting by the French Revolution
easily occurred to me, I drew up the publication in question, and shewed it to him
and some other gentlemen; who, fully approving it, held a meeting for the
purpose of making it public, and subscribed to the amount of fifty guineas to
defray the expence of advertising. I believe there are at this time, in England, a
greater number of men acting on disinterested principles, and determined to look
into the nature and practices of government themselves, and not blindly trust, as
has hitherto been the case, either to government generally, or to parliaments, or
to parliamentary opposition, than at any former period. Had this been done
a century ago, corruption and taxation had not arrived to the height they are
now at.

pages 316–17, which contains the parts to which Mr Pitt's speech is similar, was given to him full six weeks before the meeting of parliament, and he was informed of the time at which it was to appear. He had composed nearly the whole about a fortnight before the time of Parliament meeting, and had printed as far as page 284, and had given me a proof of the next sheet, up to page 295. It was then in sufficient forwardness to be out at the time proposed, as two other sheets were ready for striking off. I had before told him, that if he thought he should be straightened for time, I would get part of the work done at another press, which he desired me not to do. In this manner the work stood on the Tuesday fortnight preceding the meeting of Parliament, when all at once, without any previous intimation, though I had been with him the evening before, he sent me, by one of his workmen, all the remaining copy, from page 284, declining to go on with the work *on any consideration*.

To account for this extraordinary conduct I was totally at a loss, as he stopped at the part where the arguments on systems and principles of government closed, and where the plan for the reduction of taxes, the education of children, and the support of the poor and the aged begins; and still more especially, as he had, at the time of his beginning to print, and before he had seen the whole copy, offered a thousand pounds for the copy-right, together with the future copy-right of the former part of the Rights of Man. I told the person who brought me this offer that I should not accept it, and wished it not to be renewed, giving him as my reason, that though I believed the printer to be an honest man, I would never put it in the power of any printer or publisher to suppress or alter a work of mine, by making him master of the copy, or give to him the right of selling it to any minister, or to any other person, or to treat as a mere matter of traffic, that which I intended should operate as a principle.

His refusal to complete the work (which he could not purchase) obliged me to seek for another printer, and this of consequence would throw the publication back till after the meeting of Parliament, otherways it would have appeared that Mr Pitt had only taken up a part of the plan which I had more fully stated.

Whether that gentleman, or any other, had seen the work, or any part of it, is more than I have authority to say. But the manner in which the work was returned, and the particular time at which this was done, and that after the offers he had made, are suspicious circumstances. I know what the opinion of booksellers and publishers is upon such a case, but as to my own opinion, I chuse to make no declaration. There are many ways by which proof sheets may be procured by other persons before a work publicly appear; to which I shall add a certain circumstance, which is,

'A ministerial bookseller in Piccadilly* who has been employed, as common report says, by a clerk of one of the boards closely connected with the ministry (the board of trade and plantation of which Hawksbury is president) to publish what he calls my Life (I wish his own life and that those of the cabinet were as good) used to have his books printed at the same printing-office that I employed; but when the former part of *Rights of Man* came out, he took his work away in dudgeon; and about a week or ten days before the printer returned my copy, he came to make him an offer of his work again, which was accepted. This would consequently give him admission into the printing-office where the sheets of this work were then lying; and as booksellers and printers are free with each other, he would have the opportunity of seeing what was going on.—Be the case however as it may, Mr Pitt's plan, little and diminutive as it is, would have had a very awkward appearance, had this work appeared at the time the printer had engaged to finish it.

I have now stated the particulars which occasioned the delay, from the proposal to purchase, to the refusal to print. If all the Gentlemen are innocent, it is very unfortunate for them that such a variety of suspicious circumstances should, without any design, arrange themselves together.

Having now finished this part, I will conclude with stating another circumstance.

About a fortnight or three weeks before the meeting of

Parliament, a small addition, amounting to about twelve shillings and six pence a year, was made to the pay of the soldiers, or rather, their pay was docked so much less. Some Gentlemen who knew, in part, that this work would contain a plan of reforms respecting the oppressed condition of soldiers, wished me to add a note to the work, signifying, that the part upon that subject had been in the printer's hands some weeks before that addition of pay was proposed. I declined doing this, lest it should be interpreted into an air of vanity, or an endeavour to excite suspicion (for which, perhaps, there might be no grounds) that some of the government gentlemen, had, by some means or other, made out what this work would contain: and had not the printing been interrupted so as to occasion a delay beyond the time fixed for publication, nothing contained in this appendix would have appeared.

THOMAS PAINE

LETTER

ADDRESSED TO THE

ADDRESSERS, ON THE
LATE PROCLAMATION.

COULD I have commanded circumstances with a wish, I know not of any that would have more generally promoted the progress of knowledge, than the late Proclamation, and the numerous rotten Borough and Corporation Addresses thereon.* They have not only served as advertisements, but they have excited a spirit of enquiry into principles of government, and a desire to read the RIGHTS OF MAN, in places, where that spirit and that work were before unknown.

The people of England, wearied and stunned with parties, and alternately deceived by each, had almost resigned the prerogative of thinking. Even curiosity had expired, and a universal langour had spread itself over the land. The opposition was visibly no other that a contest for power, whilst the mass of the nation stood torpidly by as the prize.

In this hopeless state of things, the First Part of RIGHTS OF MAN made its appearance. It had to combat with a strange mixture of prejudice and indifference; it stood exposed to every species of newspaper abuse; and besides this, it had to remove the obstructions which Mr Burke's rude and outrageous attack on the French Revolution had artfully raised.

But how easily does even the most illiterate reader distinguish the spontaneous sensations of the heart, from the laboured productions of the brain. Truth, whenever it can fully appear, is a thing so naturally familiar to the mind, that an acquaintance commences at first sight. No artificial light, yet discovered, can display all the properties of day-light; so neither can the best invented fiction fill the mind with every conviction which truth begets.

To overthrow Mr Burke's fallacious work was scarcely the operation of a day. Even the phalanx of Placemen and Pensioners who had given the tone to the multitude, by clamouring forth his political fame, became suddenly silent; and the final event to himself has been, that as he rose like a rocket, he fell like the stick.

It seldom happens, that the mind rests satisfied with the simple detection of error or imposition.—Once put into motion, *that* motion soon becomes accelerated: where it had intended to stop, it discovers new reasons to proceed, and renews and continues the pursuit far beyond the limits it first prescribed to itself.—Thus it has happened to the people of England. From a detection of Mr Burke's incoherent rhapsodies, and distorted facts, they began an enquiry into first principles of Government, whilst himself, like an object left far behind, became invisible and forgotten.

Much as the First Part of RIGHTS OF MAN impressed at its first appearance, the progressive mind soon discovered that it did not go far enough. It detected errors; it exposed absurdities; it shook the fabric of political superstition; it generated new ideas; but it did not produce a regular system of principles in the room of those which it displaced. And, if I may guess at the mind of the Government-party, they beheld it as an unexpected gale that would soon blow over, and they forbore, like sailors in threatening weather, to whistle, lest they should encrease the wind.* Every thing, on their part, was profound silence.

When the Second Part of 'RIGHTS OF MAN, *combining Principle and Practice*,' was preparing to appear, they affected, for a while, to act with the same policy as before; but finding their silence had no more influence in stilling the progress of the work, than it would have in stopping the progress of time, they changed their plan, and affected to treat it with clamorous contempt. The Speech-making Placemen and Pensioners, and Place-expectants, in both Houses of Parliament, the *Outs* as well as the *Ins*,* represented it as a silly, insignificant performance; as a work incapable of producing any effect; as something, which they were sure the good sense of the people would either despite or indignantly spurn; but such was the overstrained awkwardness with which they harangued and encouraged each other, that in the very act of declaring their confidence they betrayed their fears.

As most of the rotten Borough Addressers are obscured in holes and corners throughout the country, and to whom a newspaper arrives as rarely as an almanac, they most probably have not had the opportunity of knowing how this part of the farce (the original prelude to all the Addresses) has been acted. For *their* information, I will suspend a while the more serious purpose of my Letter, and entertain them with two or three Speeches in the last Session of Parliament, which will serve them for politics till Parliament meets again.

You must know, Gentlemen, that the Second Part of RIGHTS OF MAN, (the book against which you have been presenting Addresses, though, it is most probable, that many of you did not know it) was to have come out precisely at the time that Parliament last met. It happened not to be published till a few days after. But as it was very well known that the book would shortly appear, the parliamentary Orators entered into a very cordial coalition to cry the book down, and they began their attack by crying up the *blessings* of the Constitution.

Had it been your fate to have been there, you could not but have been moved at the heart-and-pockets-felt congratulations that passed between all the parties on this subject of *blessings*; for the *Outs* enjoy places and pensions and sinecures as well as *Ins*, and are as devoutly attached to the firm of the house.

One of the most conspicuous of this motley groupe is the Clerk of the Court of King's Bench, who calls himself Lord Stormont.* He is also called Justice General of Scotland, and Keeper of Scoon (an opposition man) and he draws from the public for these nominal offices, not less, as I am informed, than six thousand pounds a year, and he is, most probably, at the trouble of counting the money, and signing a receipt, to shew, perhaps, that he is qualified to be Clerk as well as Justice. He spoke as follows:[1]

'THAT *we* shall *all* be unanimous, in expressing *our* attachment to the constitution of these realms *I am confident*. It is a subject upon which there can be *no* divided opinion in *this house*. I do not pretend to be deep read in the knowledge of

---

[1] See his Speech in the Morning Chronicle of Feb. 1.

the Constitution, but *I take upon me* to say, that from the extent of *my* knowledge (*for I have so many thousands a year for nothing*) it appears to *me*, that from the period of the Revolution, for it was by no means created then, it has been, both in *theory* and *practice*, the *wisest* system that ever was formed. I never was (*he means he never was* till now) a dealer in *political cant*. My life has not been occupied in *that way*, but the speculations of late years *seem to have taken a turn, for which I cannot account.* When I came into public life, the political pamphlets of the time, however they might be charged with the heat and violence of parties, were agreed in extolling the radical beauties of the Constitution itself. I remember (*he means he has forgotten*) a most captivating eulogium on its *charms* by Lord Bolingbroke,* where he recommends his readers to contemplate it in all its aspects, with the assurance that it would be found more estimable the more it was *seen*. I do *not recollect* his precise words, but I wish that men who write upon these subjects would take *this for their model*, instead of the political pamphlets, which I am told, are now in circulation, (such, I suppose, as *Rights of Man*)—pamphlets which I have *not read*, and whose purport I know only by *report*, (he means, perhaps, by the *noise* they make.) This, however, I am sure, that pamphlets tending to unsettle the public reverence for the *constitution*, will have very little influence. They can do very little harm—for (*by the bye, he is no dealer in political cant*) *the English are a sober-thinking people, and are more intelligent, more solid, more steady in their opinions, than any people I ever had the fortune to see.* (This is pretty well laid on, though, for a new beginner.) But if there should ever come a time when the propagation of those doctrines should agitate the public mind, I am *sure*, for *every one* of your Lordships, that no attack will be made on the constitution, from which it is *truly said* that *we* derive *all our* prosperity, without raising *every one* of your Lordships to its support. It will then be found that there is no difference among *us*, but that *we* are *all* determined to *stand* or *fall* together, in defence of the 'inestimable system'—of places and pensions.

After Stormont, on the opposition side, sat down, up rose

another noble Lord! on the ministerial side, *Grenville*.* This man ought to be as strong in the back as a mule, or the *sire* of a mule, or it would crack with the weight of places and offices. He rose, however, without feeling any incumbrance, full master of his weight; and thus said *this* noble Lord to *t'other* noble Lord!

'The *patriotic* and *manly* manner in which the noble Lord has declared *his* sentiments on the subject of the constitution, demands *my cordial* approbation. The noble Viscount has *proved*, that however we may differ on *particular measures*, amidst all the jars and dissonance of *parties*, we are unanimous in *principle*. There is a *perfect* and *entire consent* (between *us*) in the love and maintenance of the constitution as *happily subsisting*. It must *undoubtedly* give your Lordships *concern*, to find, that the *time is come*! (heigh ho!) when there is *propriety* in these expressions of regard TO (o! o! o!) THE CONSTITUTION. And that there are men (confound—their—po—li—tics) who disseminate doctrines *hostile* to the *genuine spirit* of our *well balanced system*, (it is certainly well balanced when both sides hold places and pensions at once.) I agree with the noble Viscount that they have not (I hope) *much success*. I am convinced that there is no danger to be apprehended from their attempts: but it is *truly* important and *consolatary* (to us place-men, I suppose) to know, that if there should ever arise a serious alarm, there is but one *spirit, one sense*, (and that sense I presume is not *common sense*) and *one* determination in *this* house.'—which undoubtedly is to hold all their places and pensions as long as they can.

Both those speeches (excepting the parts enclosed in parentheses, which are added for the purpose of *illustration*) are copied *verbatim* from the Morning Chronicle of the 1st of February last; and when the situation of the speakers is considered, the one in the opposition, and the other in the ministry, and both of them living at the public expence, by sinecure, or nominal places and offices, it required a very unblushing front to be able to deliver them. Can those men seriously suppose any nation to be so completely blind as not to see through them? Can Stormont imagine that the *political cant*, with which he has larded his harangue, will conceal the craft? Does he not know that there never was a cover large enough to hide *itself*? Or can Grenville believe, that his credit with the public encreases with his avarice for places?

But, if these orators will accept a service from me, in return for the allusions they have made to the *Rights of Man*, I will make a speech for either of them to deliver on the excellence of the constitution, that shall be as much to the purpose as what they have spoken, or as *Bolingbroke's captivating encomium*. Here it is.

'THAT we shall all be unanimous in expressing our attachment to the constitution, I am confident. It is, my Lords, incomprehensibly good: but the great wonder of all is the wisdom; for it is, my Lords, *the wisest system that ever was formed*.

'With respect to us noble Lords, though the world does not know it, it is very well known to us, that we have more wisdom than we know what to do with; and what is still better, my Lords, we have it all in stock. I defy your Lordships to prove, that a tittle of it has been used yet; and if we do but go on, my Lords, with the frugality we have hitherto done, we shall leave to our heirs and successors, when we go out of the world, the whole stock of wisdom, *untouched*, that we brought in; and there is no doubt but they will follow our example. This, my Lords, is one of the blessed effects of the hereditary system; for we can never be without wisdom so long as we keep it by us, and do not use it.

'But, my Lords, as all this wisdom is hereditary property, for the sole benefit of us and our heirs, and as it is necessary that the people should know where to get a supply for their own use, the excellence of our constitution has provided a King for this very purpose, and for *no other*. But, my Lords, I perceive a defect to which the constitution is subject, and which I propose to remedy by bringing a bill into Parliament for that purpose.

'The constitution, my Lords, out of delicacy, I presume, has left it as a matter of *choice* to a King whether he will be wise or not. It has not, I mean, my Lords, insisted upon it as a constitutional point, which, I conceive, it ought to have done; for I pledge myself to your Lordships to prove, and that with *true patriotic boldness*, that he has *no choice in the matter*. The bill, my Lords, that I shall bring in will be to declare, that the constitution, according to the true intent and meaning thereof, does not invest the King with this choice; our ancestors were too wise to do that; and, in order to prevent any doubts that might otherwise arise, I shall prepare, my Lords, an enacting clause, to fix the wisdom of Kings, by act of Parliament; and then, my Lords, our Constitution will be the wonder of the world!

'Wisdom, my Lords, is the one thing needful; but that there may be no mistake in this matter, and that we may proceed consistently with the true wisdom of the constitution, I shall propose a *certain criterion*, whereby the *exact quantity of wisdom* necessary for a King may be known. [Here should be a cry of Hear him! Hear him!]

'It is recorded, my Lords, in the Statutes at Large of the Jews,* "a book, my Lords, which I have not read, and whose purport I know only by report," *but perhaps the bench of Bishops can recollect something about it*, that Saul gave the most convincing proofs of royal wisdom before he was made a King, *for he was sent to seek his father's asses, and he could not find them.**

'Here, my Lords, we have, most happily for us, a case in point: This precedent ought to be established by act of Parliament; and every King, before he be crowned, should be sent to seek his father's asses, and if he cannot find them, he shall be declared wise enough to be King, according to the true meaning of our excellent constitution. All, therefore, my Lords, that will be necessary to be done, by the enacting clause that I shall bring in, will be to invest the King before hand with the quantity of wisdom necessary for this purpose, lest he should happen not to possess it; and this, my Lords, we can do without making use of any of our own.

'We further read, my Lords, in the said Statutes at Large of the Jews, that Samuel, who certainly was as mad as any Man-of-Rights-Man now a-days, (hear him! hear him!) was highly displeased, and even exasperated, at the proposal of the Jews to have a King,* and he warned them against it with all that assurance and impudence of which he was master. I have been, my Lords, at the trouble of going all the way to *Paternoster-row*,* to procure an extract from the printed copy. I was told that I should meet with it there, or in *Amen-corner*,* for I was then going, my Lords, to rummage for it among the curiosities of the *Antiquarian Society*.*—I will read the extract to your Lordships, to shew how little Samuel knew of the matter.

'The extract, my Lords, is from 1 *Samuel*, chap. 8.*

"And Samuel told all the words of the Lord unto the people, that asked of him a King.

"And he said, this will be the manner of the King that shall reign over you: he will take your sons, and appoint them for himself, for his chariots, and to be his horsemen; and some shall run before his chariots.

"And he will appoint him captains over thousands, and captains over fifties, and will set them to ear his ground, and to reap his harvest, and to make his instruments of war, and instruments of his chariots.

"And he will take your daughters to be confectionaries, and to be cooks, and to be bakers.

"And he will take your fields, and your vineyards, and your olive-yards, even the best of them, and give them to his servants.

"And he will take the tenth of your feed, and of your vineyards, and give to his officers, and to his servants.

"And he will take your men-servants, and your maid-servants, and your goodliest young men, and your asses, and put them to his work.

"And he will take the tenth of your sheep, and ye shall be his servants.

"And ye shall cry out in that day, because of your King, which ye shall have chosen you; and the Lord will not hear you on that day."

'Now, my Lords, what can we think of this man Samuel? Is there a word of truth, or any thing like truth, in all that he has said? He pretended to be a prophet, or a wise man, but has not the event proved him to be a fool, or an incendiary? Look around, my Lords, and see if any thing has happened that he pretended to foretell? Has not the most profound peace reigned throughout the world ever since Kings were in fashion? Are not, for example, the present Kings of Europe the most peaceable of mankind, and the Empress of Russia the very milk of human kindness? It would not be worth having Kings, my Lords, if it were not that they never go to war.

'If we look at home, my Lords, do we not see the same things here as are seen every where else? Are our young men taken to be horsemen, or foot soldiers, any more than in Germany or in Prussia, or in Hanover or in Hesse? Are not our sailors as safe at land as at sea?* Are they ever dragged from their homes, like oxen to the slaughter-house, to serve on board ships of war? When they return from the perils of a long voyage with the merchandize of distant countries, does not every man sit down under his own vine and his own fig-tree,* in perfect security? Is the tenth of our seed taken by tax gatherers,* or is any part of it given to the King's servants? In short, *is not every thing as free from taxes as the light from Heaven*!

'Ah! my Lords, do we not see the blessed effect of having Kings in every thing we look at? Is not the G. R. or the broad R. stampt upon every thing?* Even the shoes, the gloves, and the hats that we wear, are enriched with the impression, and all our candles blaze a burnt-offering.

'Besides these blessings, my Lords, that cover us from the sole of the foot to the crown of the head, do we not see a race of youths growing up to be Kings, who are the very paragons of virtue? There is not one of them, my Lords, but might be trusted with untold gold, as safely as the other. Are they not "*more sober, more intelligent, more solid, more steady*," and withall, more learned, more wise, more every thing, than any youths *we* "*ever had the fortune to see*." Ah! my Lords, they are *a hopeful family*.

'The blessed prospect of succession, which the nation has at this moment before its eyes, is a most undeniable proof of the excellence of our constitution, and of the blessed hereditary system; for nothing, my Lords, but a constitution founded on the truest and purest wisdom, could admit such heaven-born and heaven-taught characters into the government.—Permit me now, my Lords, to recal your attention to the libellous chapter I have just read about Kings. I mention this, my Lords, because it is my intention to move for a bill to be brought into Parliament to expunge that chapter from the Bible, and that the Lord Chancellor,* with the assistance of the Prince of Wales, the Duke of York, and the Duke of Clarence, be requested to write a chapter in the room of it; and that Mr Burke do see that it be truly canonical, and faithfully inserted.'—FINIS.

If the Clerk of the Court of King's Bench should chuse to be the orator of this luminous encomium on the constitution, I hope he will get it well by heart before he attempt to deliver it, and not to have to apologize to Parliament, as he did in the case of Bolingbroke's encomium, for forgetting his lesson; and, with this admonition, I leave him.

Having thus informed the Addressers of what passed at the meeting of Parliament, I return to take up the subject at the part where I broke off in order to introduce the preceding speeches.

I was then stating, that the first policy of the Government party was silence, and the next, clamorous contempt; but as people generally choose to read and judge for themselves, the work still went on, and the affectation of contempt, like the silence that preceded it, passed for nothing.

Thus foiled in their second scheme, their evil genius, like a will-with-a-wisp, led them to a third; when all at once, as if it had been unfolded to them by a fortune-teller, or Mr Dundas* had discovered it by second sight, this once harmless, insignificant book, without undergoing the alteration of a single letter, became a most wicked and dangerous Libel. The whole Cabinet, like a ship's crew, became alarmed; all hands were piped upon deck, as if a conspiracy of elements was forming around them, and out came the Proclamation and the Prosecution; and Addresses supplied the place of prayers.

Ye silly swains, thought I to myself, why do you torment

yourselves thus? The RIGHTS OF MAN is a book calmly and rationally written; why then are you so disturbed? Did you see how little or how suspicious such conduct makes you appear, even cunning alone, had you no other faculty, would hush you into prudence. The plans, principles, and arguments, contained in that work, are placed before the eyes of the nation, and of the world, in a fair, open, and manly manner, and nothing more is necessary than to refute them. Do this, and the whole is done; but if ye cannot, so neither can ye suppress the reading, nor convict the Author; for that Law, in the opinion of all good men, would convict itself, that should condemn what cannot be refuted.

Having now shewn the Addressers the several stages of the business, prior to their being called upon, like Cæsar in the Tyber, crying to Cassius, '*help, Cassius, or I sink!*'* I next come to remark on the policy of the Government, in promoting Addresses; on the consequences naturally resulting therefrom; and on the conduct of the persons concerned.

With respect to the policy, it evidently carries with it every mark and feature of disguised fear. And it will hereafter be placed in the history of extraordinary things, that a pamphlet should be produced by an individual, unconnected with any sect or party, and not seeking to make any, and almost a stranger in the land, that should compleatly frighten a whole Government, and that in the midst of its most triumphant security. Such a circumstance cannot fail to prove, that either the pamphlet has irresistible powers, or the Government very extraordinary defects, or both. The Nation exhibits no signs of fear at the Rights of Man; why then should the Government, unless the interest of the two are really opposite to each other, and the secret is beginning to be known? That there are two distinct classes of men in the nation, those who pay taxes, and those who receive and live upon the taxes, is evident at first sight; and when taxation is carried to excess, it cannot fail to disunite those two, and something of this kind is now beginning to appear.

It is also curious to observe, amidst all the fume and bustle about Proclamations and Addresses, kept up by a few noisy and interested men, how little the mass of the nation seem to care about either. They appear to me, by the indifference they shew, not to believe a word the Proclamation contains; and as to the Addresses, they travel to London with the silence of a funeral, and having announced their arrival in the Gazette,* are deposited with the ashes of their predecessors, and Mr Dundas writes their *hic jacet.**

One of the best effects which the Proclamation, and its echo the Addresses have had, has been that of exciting and spreading curiosity; and it requires only a single reflection to discover, that the object of all curiosity is knowledge. When the mass of the nation saw that Placemen, Pensioners, and Borough-mongers, were the persons that stood forward to promote Addresses, it could not fail to create suspicions that the public good was not their object; that the character of the books, or writings, to which such persons obscurely alluded, not daring to mention them, was directly contrary to what they described them to be, and that it was necessary that every man, for his own satisfaction, should exercise his proper right, and read and judge for himself.

But how will the persons who have been induced to read the *Rights of Man*, by the clamour that has been raised against it, be surprized to find, that, instead of a wicked, inflamatory work, instead of a licencious and profligate performance, it abounds with principles of government that are uncontrovertible—with arguments which every reader will feel, are unanswerable—with plans for the increase of commerce and manufactures—for the extinction of war—for the education of the children of the poor—for the comfortable support of the aged and decayed persons of both sexes—for the relief of the army and navy, and, in short, for the promotion of every thing that can benefit the moral, civil and political condition of Man.

Why, then, some calm observer will ask, why is the work prosecuted, is these be the goodly matters it contains? I will tell thee, friend; it contains also a plan for the reduction of Taxes, for lessening the immense expences of Government, for abolishing sinecure Places and Pensions; and it proposes applying the redundant taxes, that shall be saved by these reforms, to the purposes mentioned in the former paragraph, instead of applying them to the support of idle and profligate Placemen and Pensioners.

Is it, then, any wonder that Placemen and Pensioners, and the whole train of Court expectants, should become the promoters of Addresses, Proclamations, and Prosecutions? or, is it any wonder that Corporations and rotten Boroughs, which are attacked and exposed, both in the First and Second Parts of *Rights of Man*, as unjust monopolies and public nuisances, should join in the cavalcade? Yet these are the sources from which Addresses have sprung. Had not such persons come forward to oppose the *Rights of Man*, I should have doubted the efficacy of my own writings: but those opposers have now proved to me, that the blow was well directed, and they have done it justice, by confessing the smart.

The principal deception in this business of Addresses has been, that the promoters of them have not come forward in their proper characters. They have assumed to pass themselves upon the Public, as a part of the Public bearing a share of the burthen of Taxes, and acting for the public good; whereas, they are in general that part of it that adds to the public burthen, by living on the produce of the public taxes. They are to the public what the locusts are to the tree: the burthen would be less, and the prosperity would be greater, if they were shaken off.

'I do not come here,' said ONSLOW, at the Surry County meeting,* 'as Lord Lieutenant and Custos Rotulorum of the county, but I come here as a plain country gentleman.' The fact is, that he came there as what he was, and as no other, and consequently he came as one of the beings I have been describing. If it be the character of a gentleman to be fed by the public, as a pauper is by the parish, Onslow has a fair claim to the title; and the same description will suit the Duke of Richmond,* who led the Address at the Sussex meeting.—He also may set up for a gentleman.

As to the meeting in the next adjoining county, (Kent) it was a scene of disgrace. About two hundred persons met, when a small part of them drew privately away from the rest, and voted an Address: the consequence of which was, that they got together by the ears,* and produced a riot in the very act of producing an Address to prevent Riots.

That the Proclamation and the Addresses have failed of their intended effect, may be collected from the silence which the Government party itself observes. The number of Addresses has been weekly retailed in the Gazette;* but the number of Addressers has been concealed. Several of the Addresses have been voted by not more than ten or twelve persons; and a considerable number of them by not more than thirty. The whole number of Addresses presented at the time of writing* this letter is three hundred and twenty, (rotten Boroughs and Corporations included) and even admitting, on an average, one hundred Addressers to each Address, the whole number of Addressers would be but thirty-two thousand, and nearly three months have been taken up in procuring this number. That the success of the Proclamation has been less than the success of the Work it was intended to discourage, is a matter within my own knowledge; for a greater number of the cheap edition of the First and Second Parts of RIGHTS OF MAN has been sold in the space only of one month,* than the whole number of Addressers (admitting them to be thirty-two thousand) have amounted to in three months.

It is a dangerous attempt in any Government to say to a Nation, 'thou shalt not read.' This is now done in Spain, and was formerly done under the old Government of France;* but it served to procure the downfal of the latter, and is subverting that of the former; and it will have the same tendency in all countries; because thought, by some means or other, is got abroad in the world, and cannot be restrained, though reading may.

If Rights of Man were a book that deserved the vile description which the promoters of the Address have given of it, why did not these men prove their charge, and satisfy the people, by producing it, and reading it publicly? This most certainly ought to have been done, and would also have been done, had they believed it would have answered their purpose. But the fact is, that the book contains truths, which those time-servers dreaded to hear, and dreaded that the people should know; and it is now following up the Addresses in every part of the nation, and convincing them of falshoods.

Among the unwarrantable proceedings to which the Proclamation has given rise, the meetings of the Justices in several of the towns and counties ought to be noticed. Those men have assumed to re-act the farce of General Warrants,* and to suppress, by their own authority, whatever publications they please. This is an attempt at power, equalled only by the conduct of the minor despots of the most despotic governments in Europe, and yet those Justices affect to call England a Free Country. But even this, perhaps, like the scheme for garrisoning the country,* by building military barracks, is necessary to awaken the country to a sense of its Rights, and, as such, it will have a good effect.

Another part of the conduct of such Justices has been, that of threatening to take away the licences from taverns and public-houses, where the inhabitants of the neighbourhood associated to read and discuss the principles of Government, and to inform each other thereon. This, again, is similar to what is doing in Spain and Russia; and the reflection which it cannot fail to suggest is, that the principles and conduct of any Government must be bad, when that Government dreads and startles at discussion, and seeks security by a prevention of knowledge.

If the Government, or the Constitution, or by whatever name it be called, be that miracle of perfection which the Proclamation and the Addresses have trumpeted it forth to be, it ought to have defied discussion and investigation, instead of dreading it. Whereas, every attempt it makes, either by Proclamation, Prosecution, or Address, to suppress investigation, is a confession that it feels itself unable to bear it. It is error only, and not truth, that shrinks from enquiry. All the numerous pamphlets, and all the newspaper falshood and abuse, that have been published against the 'RIGHTS OF MAN,' have fallen before it like pointless arrows; and, in like manner, would any work have fallen before the Constitution, had the Constitution, as it is called, been founded on as good political principles as those on which the RIGHTS OF MAN is written.

It is a good Constitution for courtiers, placemen, pensioners, borough-holders, and the leaders of Parties, and these are the men that have been the active leaders of Addresses; but it is a bad Constitution for at least ninety-nine parts of the nation out of an hundred, and this truth is every day making its way.

It is bad, first, because it entails upon the nation the unnecessary expence of supporting three forms and systems of Government at once, namely, the monarchical, the aristo-cratical, and the democratical.

Secondly, because it is impossible to unite such a discord-ant composition by any other means than perpetual corrup-tion; and therefore the corruption so loudly and so univer-sally complained of, is no other than the natural consequence of such an unnatural compound of Governments; and in this consists that excellence which the numerous herd of place-men and pensioners so loudly extol, and which, at the same time, occasions that enormous load of taxes under which the rest of the nation groans.

Among the mass of national delusions calculated to amuse and impose upon the multitude, the standing one has been, that of flattering them into taxes, by calling the Government, (or as they please to express it, the English Constitution) 'the envy and the admiration of the world.' Scarcely an Ad-dress has been voted in which some of the speakers have not uttered this hackneyed nonsensical falshood.

Two Revolutions have taken place, those of America and France; and both of them have rejected the unnatural com-pounded system of the English government. America has declared against all hereditary Government, and established the representative system of Government only. France has entirely rejected the aristocratical part, and is now discover-ing the absurdity of the monarchical,* and is approaching fast to the representative system. On what ground, then, do those men continue a declaration, respecting what they call the *envy and admiration of other nations*, which the voluntary practice of such nations, as have had the opportunity of establishing Government, contradicts and falsifies. Will such men never confine themselves to truth? Will they be for ever the deceivers of the people?

But I will go farther, and shew, that, were Government now to begin in England, the people could not be brought to establish the same system they now submit to.

In speaking upon this subject (or on any other) *on the pure ground of principle*, antiquity and precedent cease to be authority, and hoary-headed error loses its effect. The reasonableness and propriety of things must be examined abstractedly from custom and usage; and in this point of view, the right which grows into practice to-day is as much a right, and as old in principle and theory, as if it had the customary sanction of a thousand ages. Principles have no connection with time, nor characters with names.

To say that the Government of this country is composed of King, Lords, and Commons, is the mere phraseology of custom. It is composed of men; and whoever the men be to whom the Government of any country is entrusted, they ought to be the best and wisest that can be found, and if they are not so, they are not fit for the station. A man derives no more excellence from the change of a name, or calling him King, or calling him Lord, than I should do by changing my name from Thomas to George, or from Paine to Guelph.* I should not be a whit the more able to write a book, because my name were altered; neither would any man, now called a King or a Lord, have a whit the more sense than he now has, were he to call himself Thomas Paine.

As to the word 'Commons,' applied as it is in England, it is a term of degradation and reproach, and ought to be abolished. It is a term unknown in free countries.

But to the point.—Let us suppose that Government was now to begin in England, and that the plan of Government, offered to the nation for its approbation or rejection, consisted of the following parts:

First—That some one individual should be taken from all the rest of the nation, and to whom all the rest should swear obedience, and never be permitted to sit down in his presence, and that they should give to him one million sterling a year.—That the nation should never after have power or authority to make laws but with his express consent, and that his sons and his sons' sons, whether wise or foolish, good men or bad, fit or unfit, should have the same power, and also the same money annually paid to them for ever.

Secondly—That there should be two houses of Legislators to assist in making laws, one of which should, in the first instance, be entirely appointed by the aforesaid person, and that their sons and their sons' sons, whether wise or foolish, good men or bad, fit or unfit, should for ever after be hereditary Legislators.

Thirdly—That the other house should be chosen in the same manner as the house, now called the House of Commons, is chosen, and should be subject to the controul of the two aforesaid hereditary Powers in all things.

It would be impossible to cram such a farago of imposition and absurdity down the throat of this or any other nation, that were capable of reasoning upon its rights and its interest.

They would ask, in the first place, on what ground of right, or on what principle, such irrational and prepoterous distinctions could, or ought to be made; and what pretensions any man could have, or what services he could render, to entitle him to a million a year? They would go farther, and revolt at the idea of consigning their children, and their children's children, to the domination of persons hereafter to be born, who might, for any thing they could foresee, turn out to be knaves or fools; and they would finally discover, that the project of hereditary Governors and Legislators *was a treasonable usurpation over the rights of posterity*. Not only the calm dictates of reason, and the force of natural affection, but the integrity of manly pride, would impel men to spurn such proposals.

From the grosser absurdities of such a scheme, they would extend their examination to the practical defects—They would soon see that it would end in tyranny accomplished by fraud. That in the operation of it, it would be two to one against them, because the two parts that were to be made hereditary, would form a common interest, and stick to each other; and that themselves and their representatives would become no better than hewers of wood and drawers of water* for the other parts of the Government.—Yet call one of those powers King, the other, Lords, and the third, the Commons, and it gives the model of what is called the English Government.

I have asserted, and have shewn, both in the First and Second Parts of *Rights of Man*, that there is not such a thing as an English Constitution, and that the people have yet a Constitution to form. *A Constitution is a thing antecedent to a Government; it is the act of the people creating a Government and giving it powers, and defining the limits and exercise of the powers so given.* But whenever did the people of England, acting in their original constituent character, by a delegation elected for that express purpose, declare and say, '*We, the people of this land, do constitute and appoint this to be our system and form of Government.*' The Government has assumed to constitute itself, but it never was constituted by the people, in whom alone the right of constituting resides.

I will here recite the preamble to the Federal Constitution of the United States of America. I have shewn in the Second Part of *Right of Man*, the manner by which the Constitution was formed and afterwards ratified; and to which I refer the reader.—The preamble is in the following words:*

'WE, THE PEOPLE of the United States, in order to form a more perfect union, establish justice, insure domestic tranquility, provide for common defence, promote the general welfare, secure the blessings of liberty to ourselves and our posterity, DO ORDAIN AND ESTABLISH THIS CONSTITUTION for the United States of America.'

Then follow the several articles which appoint the manner in which the several component parts of the Government, legislative and executive, shall be elected, and the period of their duration, and the powers they shall have: also, the manner by which future additions, alterations, or amendments, shall be made to the Constitution. Consequently, every improvement that can be made in the science of Government, follows in that country as a matter of order. It is only in Governments founded on assumption and false principles, that reasoning upon, and investigating systems and principles of Government, and shewing their several excellencies and defects, are termed libellous and seditious. These terms were made part of the charge brought against Locke, Hampden, and Sydney,* and will continue to be brought against all good men, so long as bad government shall continue.

The Government of this country has been ostentatiously giving challenges for more that an hundred years past, upon what it called its own excellence and perfection. Scarcely a King's Speech, or a Parliamentary Speech, has been uttered, in which this glove has not been thrown, till the world has been insulted with their challenges. But it now appears that all this was vapour and vain boasting, or that it was intended to conceal abuses and defects, and hush the people into taxes. I have taken the challenge up, and in behalf of the public have shewn, in a fair, open, and candid manner, both the radical and practical defects of the system; when, lo! those champions of the Civil List have fled away, and sent the Attorney-General* to deny the challenge, by turning the acceptance of it into an attack, and defending their Places and Pensions by a prosecution.

I will here drop this part of the subject, and state a few particulars respecting the prosecution now pending, by which the Addressers will see that they have been used as tools to the prosecuting party and their dependents. The case is as follows:

The original edition of the First and Second Parts of RIGHTS OF MAN, having been expensively printed (in the modern stile of printing pamphlets, that they might be bound up with Mr Burke's Reflections on the French Revolution,) the high price precluded the generality of people from purchasing; and many applications were made to me from various parts of the country to print the work in a cheaper manner. The people of Sheffield requested leave to print two thousand copies for themselves, with which request I immediately complied. The same request came to me from Rotherham, from Leicester, from Chester, from several towns in Scotland; and Mr James Mackintosh, Author of *Vindiciæ Galliæ*,* brought me a request from Warwickshire, for leave to print ten thousand copies in that country. I had already sent a cheap edition to Scotland; and finding the applications increase, I concluded that the best method of complying therewith, would be to print a very numerous edition in London, under my own direction, by which means the work would be more perfect, and the price be reduced lower than it could be by *printing* small editions in the country of only a few thousands each.

The cheap edition of the First Part was begun about the middle of last April, and from that moment, and not before, I expected a prosecution, and the event has proved that I was not mistaken. I had then occasion to write to Mr Thomas Walker,* of Manchester, and after informing him of my intention of giving up the work for the purpose of general information, I informed him of what I apprehended would be the consequence; that while the work was at a price that precluded an extensive circulation,* the Government-party, not able to controvert the plans, arguments, and principles it contained, had chosen to remain silent; but that I expected they would make an attempt to deprive the mass of the nation, and especially the poor, of the right of reading, by the pretence of prosecuting either the Author or the Publisher, or both. They chose to begin with the Publisher.

Nearly a month, however, passed, before I had any information given me of their intentions. I was then at Bromley, in Kent, upon which I came immediately to town, (May 14) and went to Mr Jordan, the publisher of the original edition. He had that evening been served with a summons, to appear at the Court of King's Bench on the Monday following, but for what purpose was not stated. Supposing it to be on account of the work, I appointed a meeting with him on the next morning, which was accordingly had, when I provided an attorney, and took the expence of the defence on myself. But finding afterwards that he absented himself from the attorney employed, and had engaged another, and that he had been closeted with the Solicitors of the Treasury, I left him to follow his own choice, and he chose to plead Guilty. This he might do if he pleased; and I make no objection against him for it. I believe that his idea by the word *Guilty*, was no other than declaring himself to be the publisher, without any regard to the merits or demerits of the work; for were it to be construed otherwise, it would amount to the absurdity of converting a publisher into a Jury, and his confession into a verdict upon the work itself. This would be the highest possible refinement upon packing of Juries.

On the 21st of May, they commenced their prosecution against me, as the Author, by leaving a summons at my lodgings in town, to appear at the Court of King's Bench on the 8th of June following; and on the same day, (May 21) *they issued also their Proclamation.* Thus the Court of St James's,* and the Court of King's Bench, were playing into each other's hands at the same instant of time, and the farce of Addresses brought up the rear; and this mode of proceeding is called by the prostituted name of Law. Such a thundering rapidity, after a ministerial dormancy of almost eighteen months, can be attributed to no other cause than their having gained information of the forwardness of the cheap Edition, and the dread they felt at the progressive increase of political knowledge.

I was strongly advised by several gentlemen, as well those in the practice of the Law, as others, to prefer a bill of indictment against the publisher of the Proclamation, as a publication tending to influence, or rather to dictate the verdict of a Jury on the issue of a matter then pending; but it appeared to me much better to avail myself of the opportunity which such a precedent justified me in using, by meeting the Proclamation and the Addresses on their own ground, and publicly defending the Work which had been thus unwarrantable attacked and traduced.—And conscious as I now am, that the Work entitled RIGHTS OF MAN, so far from being, as has been maliciously or erroneously represented, a false, wicked, and seditious Libel,* is a work abounding with unanswerable truths, with principles of the purest morality and benevolence, and with arguments not to be controverted—Conscious, I say, of these things, and having no object in view but the happiness of mankind, I have now put the matter to the best proof in my power, by giving to the public a cheap edition of the First and Second

Parts of that Work. Let every man read and judge for himself, not only of the merits or demerits of the Work, but of the matters therein contained, which relate to his own interest and happiness.

If, to expose the fraud and imposition of monarchy, and every species of hereditary government—to lessen the oppression of taxes—to propose plans for the education of helpless infancy, and the comfortable support of the aged and distressed—to endeavour to conciliate nations to each other—to extirpate the horrid practice of war—to promote universal peace, civilization, and commerce—and to break the chains of political superstition, and raise degraded man to his proper rank;—if these things be libellous, let me live the life of a Libeller, and let the name of LIBELLER be engraven on my tomb.

Of all the weak and ill-judged measures which fear, ignorance, or arrogance, could suggest, the Proclamation, and the project for Addresses, are two of the worst. They served to advertise the work which the promoters of those measures wished to keep unknown; and in doing this, they offered violence to the judgment of the people, by calling on them to condemn what they forbad them to know, and they put the strength of their party to that hazardous issue that prudence would have avoided.—The County Meeting for Middlesex was attended by only one hundred and eighteen Addressers.* They, no doubt, expected, that thousands would flock to their standard, and clamour against the *Rights of Man*. But the case most probably is, that men, in all countries, are not so blind to their Rights and their Interest, as Governments believe.

Having thus shewn the extraordinary manner in which the Government-party commenced their attack, I proceed to offer a few observations on the prosecution, and on the mode of trial by Special Jury.

In the first place, I have written a book; and if it cannot be refuted, it cannot be condemned. But I do not consider the prosecution as particularly levelled against me, but against the general right, or the right of every man, of investigating systems and principles of Government, and shewing their several excellencies or defects. If the press be free only to flatter Government, as Mr Burke has done, and to cry up and extol what certain Court sycophants are pleased to call a 'glorious Constitution,' and not free to examine into its errors or abuses, or whether a Constitution really exist or not, such freedom is no other than that of Spain, Turkey, or Russia; and a Jury, in this case, would not be a Jury to try, but an Inquisition to condemn.

I have asserted, and by fair and open argument maintained, the right of every nation at all times, to establish such a system and form of Government for itself as best accords with its disposition, interest, and happiness; and to change, or alter it, as it sees occasion. Will any Jury deny to the Nation this right? If they do, they are traitors, and their Verdict would be null and void. And if they admit the right, the means must be admitted also; for it would be the highest absurdity to say, that the right existed, but the means did not. The question, then, is, What are the means by which the possession and exercise of this National Right are to be secured? The answer will be, that of maintaining, inviolably, the right of free investigation; for investigation always serves to detect error, and to bring forth truth.

I have, as an individual, given my opinion upon what I believe to be not only the best, but the true system of Government, which is the representative system, and I have given reasons for that opinion.

First, Because, in the representative system, no office of very extraordinary power, or extravagant pay, is attached to any individual; and consequently, there is nothing to excite those national contentions and civil wars, with which countries under monarchical governments, are frequently convulsed, and of which the History of England exhibits such numerous instances.

Secondly, Because the representative is a system of Government always in maturity; whereas monarchical government fluctuates through all the stages, from non-age to dotage.

Thirdly, Because the representative system admits of none but men, properly qualified, into the Government, or removes them if they prove to be otherwise. Whereas, in the hereditary system, a nation may be encumbered with a knave or an ideot, for a whole life-time, and not be benefited by a successor.

Fourthly, Because there does not exist a right to establish hereditary government, or in other words, hereditary successors, because hereditary government always means a government yet to come, and the case always is, that those who are to live afterwards have always the same right to establish government for themselves, as the people had who lived before them; and, therefore, all laws attempting to establish hereditary government, are founded on assumption and political fiction.

If these positions be truths, and I challenge any man to prove the contrary; if they tend to instruct and enlighten mankind, and to free them from error, oppression, and political superstition, which are the objects I have in view, in publishing them, that Jury would commit an act of injustice to their country and to me, if not an act of perjury, that should call them *false*, *wicked*, and *malicious*.

Dragonetti, in his Treatise 'on Virtues and Rewards,' has a paragraph worthy of being recorded in every country in the world—'The science, (says he,) of the politician, consists in fixing the true point of happiness and freedom. Those men would deserve the gratitude of ages, who should discover a mode of government that contained the greatest sum of *individual happiness* with the least *national expence*.'* But if Juries are to be made use of to prohibit enquiry, to suppress truth, and to stop the progress of knowledge, this boasted palladium of liberty becomes the most successful instrument of tyranny.

Among the arts practised at the Bar, and from the Bench, to impose upon the understanding of a Jury, and obtain a Verdict where the consciences of men could not otherwise consent, one of the most successful has been that of calling *truth a libel*, and of insinuating, that the words '*falsely, wickedly*, and *maliciously*,' though they are made the formidable and high founding part of the charge, are not matters for consideration with a Jury. For what purpose, then, are they retained, unless it be for that of imposition and wilful defamation?

I cannot conceive a greater violation of order, nor a more abominable insult upon morality and upon human understanding, than to see a man sitting in the judgment seat, affecting, by an antiquated foppery of dress, to impress the audience with awe; then causing witnesses and Jury to be sworn to truth and justice, himself having officially sworn the same; then causing to be read a prosecution against a man, charging him with having *wickedly and maliciously written and published a certain false, wicked, and seditious book*; and having gone through all this with a shew of solemnity, as if he saw the eye of the Almighty darting through the roof of the building like a ray of light, turn, in an instant, the whole into a farce, and, in order to obtain a verdict that could not otherwise be obtained, tell the Jury that the charge of *falsely, wickedly, and seditiously*, meant nothing; that *truth* was out of the question; and that whether the person accused spoke truth or falshood, or intended *virtuously or wickedly*, was the same thing; and finally conclude the wretched inquisitorial scene, by stating some antiquated precedent, equally as abominable as that which is then acting, or giving some opinion of his own, and *falsely calling the one and the other—Law*. It was, most probably, to such a Judge as this, that the most solemn of all reproofs was given—'*The Lord will smite thee, thou whitened wall.*'*

I now proceed to offer some remarks on what is called a Special Jury.—As to what is called a Special Verdict, I shall make no other remark upon it, than that it is in reality *not* a verdict. It is an attempt on the part of the Jury to delegate, or of the Bench to obtain, the exercise of that right which is committed to the Jury only.

With respect to Special Juries, I shall state such matters as I have been able to collect, for I do not find any uniform opinion concerning the mode of appointing them.

In the first place, this mode of trial is but of modern invention, and the origin of it, as I am told, is as follows:

Formerly, when disputes arose between Merchants, and were brought before a Court, the case was, that the nature of their commerce, and the method of keeping Merchants accounts, not being sufficiently understood by persons out of their own line, it became necessary to depart from the common mode of appointing Juries, and to select such persons for a Jury whose *practical knowledge* would enable them to decide upon the case. From this introduction, Special Juries* became more general; but some doubts having arisen as to their legality, an act was passed in the 3d of Geo. II. to establish them as legal, and also to extend them to all cases, not only between individuals, but in cases where *the Government itself should be the Prosecutor.* This most probably gave rise to the suspicion so generally entertained of packing a Jury; because, by this act, when the crown, as it is called, is the Prosecutor, the Master of the Crown-office, who holds his office under the Crown, is the person who either wholly nominates, or has great power in nominating the Jury, and therefore it has greatly the appearance of the prosecuting party selecting a Jury.

The process is as follows:

On motion being made in Court, by either the Plaintiff or Defendant, for a Special Jury, the Court grants it or not, at its own discretion.

If it be granted, the Solicitor of the party that applied for the Special Jury gives notice to the Solicitor of the adverse party, and a day and hour are appointed for them to meet at the office of the Master of the Crown-office. The Master of the Crown-office sends to the Sheriff or his deputy, who attends with the Sheriff's book of Freeholders. From this book, forty-eight names are *taken*, and a copy thereof given to each of the parties; and on a future day notice is again given, and the Solicitors meet a second time, and each strikes out twelve names. The list being thus reduced from forty-eight to twenty-four, the first twelve that appear in Court, and answer to their names, is the Special Jury for that cause. The first operation, that of taking the forty-eight names, is called nominating the Jury; and the reducing them to twenty-four is called striking the Jury.

Having thus stated the general process, I come to particulars, and the first question will be, how are the forty-eight names, out of which the Jury is to be struck, obtained from the Sheriff's book? for herein lies the principal ground of suspicion, with respect to what is understood by packing of Juries.

Either they must be taken by some rule agreed upon between the parties, or by some common rule known and established before-hand, or at the discretion of some person, who, in such a case, ought to be perfectly disinterested in the issue, as well officially as otherwise.

In the case of Merchants, and in all cases between individuals, the Master of the office, called the Crown-office, is officially an indifferent person, and as such may be a proper person to act between the parties, and present them with a list of forty-eight names, out of which each party is to strike twelve. But the case assumes an entire different character when the Government itself is the Prosecutor. The Master of the Crown-office is then an officer holding his office under the Prosecutor; and it is therefore no wonder that the suspicion of packing Juries should, in such cases, have been so prevalent.

This will apply with additional force, when the prosecution is commenced against the Author or Publisher of such Works as treat of reforms, and of the abolition of superflous places and offices, &c. because in such cases every person holding an office, subject to that suspicion, becomes interested as a party; and the office, called the Crown-office, may, upon examination, be found to be of this description.

I have heard it asserted, that the Master of the Crown office is to open the Sheriff's book as it were per hazard, and take thereout forty-eight *following* names, to which the word Merchant or Esquire* is affixed. The former of these are certainly proper, when the case is between Merchants, and it has reference to the origin of the custom, and to nothing else. As to the word Esquire, every man is an Esquire who pleases to call himself Esquire; and the sensible part of mankind are leaving it off. But the matter for enquiry is, whether there be any existing law to direct the mode by which the forty-eight names shall be taken, or whether the mode be merely that of custom which the office has created;

or whether the selection of the forty-eight names be wholly at the discretion and choice of the Master of the Crown-office? One or other of the two latter appears to be the case, because the act already mentioned, of the 3d of Geo. II. lays down no rule or mode, nor refers to any preceding law—but says only, that Special Juries shall hereafter be struck, '*in such manner as Special Juries have been and are usually struck.*'

This act appears to me to have been what is generally understood by a '*deep take in.*'* It was fitted to the spur of the moment in which it was passed, 3d of Geo. II. when parties ran high, and it served to throw into the hands of Walpole, who was then Minister, the management of Juries in Crown prosecutions, by making the nomination of the forty-eight persons, from whom the Jury was to be struck, follow the precedent established by custom between individuals, and by this means it slipt into practice with less suspicion. Now, the manner of obtaining Special Juries through the medium of an officer of the Government, such for instance as a Master of the Crown-office, may be impartial in the case of Merchants, or other individuals, but it becomes highly improper and suspicious in cases where the Government itself is one of the parties. And it must, upon the whole, appear a strange inconsistency, that a Government should keep one officer to commence prosecutions, and another officer to nominate the forty-eight persons from whom the Jury is to be struck, both of whom are *officers of the Civil List*, and yet continue to call this by the pompous name of *the glorious Right of trial by Jury*!

In the case of the King against Jordan, for publishing RIGHTS OF MAN, the Attorney-General moved for the appointment of a Special Jury, and the Master of the Crown-office nominated the forty-eight persons himself, and took them from such part of the Sheriff's book as he pleased. The trial did not come on, occasioned by Jordan withdrawing his plea; but if it had, it might have afforded an opportunity of discussing the subject of Special Juries; for though such discussion might have had no effect in the Court of King's Bench, it would, in the present disposition for enquiry, have had a considerable effect upon the Country; and in all national reforms, this is the proper point to begin at. Put a Country right, and it will soon put Government right. Among the improper things acted by the Government in the case of Special Juries, on their own motion, one has been that of treating the Jury with a dinner, and afterwards giving each Juryman two guineas, if a verdict be found for the prosecution, and only one if otherwise; and it has been long observed, that in London and Westminster there are persons who appear to make a trade of serving, by being so frequently seen upon Special Juries.

Thus much for Special Juries. As to what is called a *Common Jury*, upon any Government prosecution against the Author or Publisher of RIGHTS OF MAN, during the time of the *present Sheriffry*, I have one question to offer, which is, *whether the present Sheriffs of London, having publicly prejudged the case, by the part they have taken in procuring an Address from the county of Middlesex, (however diminutive and insignificant the number of Addressers were, being only one hundred and eighteen) are eligible or proper persons to be entrusted with the power of returning a Jury to try the issue of any such prosecution?*

But the whole matter appears, at least to me, to be worthy of a more extensive consideration than what relates to any Jury, whether Special or Common; for the case is, whether any part of a whole nation, locally selected as a Jury of twelve men always is, be competent to judge and determine for the whole nation, on any matter that relates to systems and principles of Government, and whether it be not applying the institution of Juries to purposes for which such institution was not intended? For example,

I have asserted, in the Work RIGHTS OF MAN, that as every man in the nation pays taxes, so has every man a right to a share in government, and consequently that the people of Manchester, Birmingham, Sheffield, Leeds, Hallifax, &c. &c. have the same right as those of London. Shall then twelve men, picked out between Temple-bar and Whitechapel,* because the book happened to be first published there, decide upon the rights of the inhabitants of those towns, or of any other town or village in the nation?

Having thus spoken of Juries, I come next to offer a few observations on the matter contained in the information or prosecution.

The work, RIGHTS OF MAN, consists of Part the First, and Part the Second. The First Part the prosecutor has thought it most proper to let alone; and from the Second Part he has selected a few short paragraphs, making in the whole not quite two pages of the same printing as in the cheap edition. Those paragraphs relate chiefly to certain facts, such as the Revolution of 1688, and the coming of George the First, commonly called of the House of Hanover, or the House of Brunswick, or some such house. The arguments, plans, and principles, contained in the work, the prosecutor has not ventured to attack. They are beyond his reach.

The Act which the prosecutor appears to rest most upon for the support of the prosecution, is the Act intituled, 'An Act, declaring the rights and liberties of the subject, and settling the succession of the crown,' passed in the first year of William and Mary, and more commonly known by the name of the 'Bill of Rights.'

I have called this Bill '*A Bill of wrongs and of insult.*'* My reasons, and also my proofs, are as follows:

The method and principle which this Bill takes for declaring rights and liberties, are in direct contradiction to rights and liberties; it is an assumed attempt to take them wholly away from posterity—for the declaration in the said Bill is as follows:

'The Lords Spiritual and Temporal, and Commons, do, in *the name of all the people*, most humbly and faithfully *submit themselves, their heirs, and posterity for ever;*' that is, to William and Mary his wife, their heirs and successors. This is a strange way of declaring rights and liberties. But the Parliament who made this declaration in the name, and on the part, of the people, had no authority from them for so doing—and with respect to *posterity for ever*, they had no right or authority whatever in the case. It was assumption and usurpation. I have reasoned very extensively against the principle of this Bill in the first part of Rights of Man; the prosecutor has silently admitted that reasoning, and he now commences a prosecution on the authority of the Bill, after admitting the reasoning against it.

It is also to be observed, that the declaration in this Bill, abject and irrational as it is, had no other intentional operation than against the family of the Stuarts, and their abettors. The idea did not then exist, that in the space of an hundred years, posterity might discover a different and much better system of government, and that every species of hereditary government might fall as Popes and Monks had fallen before. This, I say, was not then thought of, and therefore the application of the Bill, in the present case, is a new, erroneous, and illegal application, and is the same as creating a new Bill *ex post facto*.

It has ever been the craft of Courtiers, for the purpose of keeping up an expensive and enormous Civil List, and a mummery of useless and antiquated places and offices at the public expence, to be continually hanging England upon some individual or other, called *King*, though the man might not have capacity to be a parish constable. The folly and absurdity of this is appearing more and more every day; and still those men continue to act as if no alteration in the public opinion had taken place. They hear each other's nonsense, and suppose the whole nation talks the same Gibberish.

Let such men cry up the House of Orange,* or the House of Brunswick, if they please. They would cry up any other house if it suited their purpose, and give as good reasons for it. But what is this house, or that house, or any house to a nation? '*For a nation to be free, it is sufficient that she wills it.*'* Her freedom depends wholly upon herself, and not on any house, nor on any individual. I ask not in what light this cargo of foreign houses appears to others, but I will say in what light it appears to me.—It was like the trees of the forest saying unto the bramble, come thou and reign over us.

Thus much for both their houses.* I now come to speak of two other houses, which are also put into the information, and those are, the House of Lords, and the House of Commons. Here, I suppose, the Attorney-General intends to prove me guilty of speaking either truth or falshood; for, according to the modern interpretation of Libels,* it does not signify which, and the only improvement necessary to shew the compleat absurdity of such doctrine, would be, to prosecute a man for uttering a most *false and wicked truth*.

I will quote the part I am going to give, from the Office Copy, with the Attorney General's inuendoes, enclosed in parentheses as they stand in the information, and I hope that civil list officer will caution the Court not to laugh when he reads them, and also to take care not to laugh himself.

The information states,* that *Thomas Paine being a wicked, malicious, seditious, and evil disposed person, hath, with force and arms, and most wicked cunning, written and published a certain false, scandalous, malicious, and seditious libel; in one part thereof, to the tenor and effect following, that is to say—*

'With respect to the two Houses, of which the English Parliament (*meaning the Parliament of this Kingdom*) is composed, they appear to be effectually influenced into one, and, as a Legislature, to have no temper of its own. The Minister, (*meaning the Minister employed by the King of this Realm, in the administration of the Government thereof*) whoever he, at any time may be, touches IT, (*meaning the two Houses of Parliament of this Kingdom*) as with an opium wand, and IT (*meaning the two Houses of Parliament of this Kingdom*) sleeps obedience.'*—As I am not malicious enough to disturb their repose, though it be time they should awake, I leave the two Houses, and the Attorney General, to the enjoyment of their dreams, and proceed to a new subject.

The Gentlemen, to whom I shall next address myself, are those who have stiled themselves '*Friends of the people,*'* holding their meeting at the Freemasons' Tavern, London.

One of the principal Members of this Society, is Mr Grey, who, I believe, is also one of the most independent Members in Parliament. I collect this opinion from what Mr Burke formerly mentioned to me, rather than from any knowledge of my own. The occasion was as follows:

I was in England at the time the bubble broke forth about

Nootka Sound;* and the day after the King's Message, as it is called, was sent to Parliament, I wrote a note to Mr Burke,* that upon the condition the French Revolution should not be a subject (for he was then writing the book I have since answered) I would call on him the next day, and mention some matters I was acquainted with, respecting that affair; for it appeared to me extraordinary, that any body of men, calling themselves Representatives, should commit themselves so precipitately, or, 'sleep obedience,' as Parliament was then doing, and run a nation into expence, and, perhaps a war, without so much as enquiring into the case, or the subject, of both which I had some knowledge.

When I saw Mr Burke, and mentioned the circumstances to him, he particularly spoke of Mr Grey,* as the fittest Member to bring such matters forward; for, said Mr Burke, '*I am not the proper* person to do it, as I am in a treaty with Mr Pitt about Mr Hastings's trial.'* I hope the Attorney General will allow, that Mr Burke was then *sleeping his obedience*.—But to return to the Society—

I cannot bring myself to believe, that the general motive of this Society is any thing more than that by which every former parliamentary opposition has been governed, and by which the present is sufficiently known. Failing in their pursuit of power and place within doors, they have now (and that not in a very mannerly manner) endeavoured to posses themselves of that ground out of doors, which, had it not been made by others, would not have been made by them. They appear to me to have watched, with more cunning than candour, the progress of a certain publication, and when they saw it had excited a spirit of enquiry, and was rapidly spreading, they stepped forward to profit by the opportunity, and Mr Fox *then* called it a Libel.* In saying this, he libelled himself. Politicians of this cast, such, I mean, as those who trim between parties, and lye by for events, are to be found in every country, and it never yet happened that they did not do more harm than good. They embarrass business, fritter it to nothing, perplex the people, and the event to themselves generally is, that they go just far enough to make enemies of the few, without going far enough to make friends of the many.

Whoever will read the declarations of this Society, of the 25th of April, and 5th of May,* will find a studied reserve upon all the points that are real abuses. They speak not once of the extravagance of Government, of the abominable list of unnecessary and sinecure places and pensions, of the enormity of the Civil List, of the excess of taxes, nor of any one matter that substantially affects the nation; and from some conversation that has passed in that Society, it does not appear to me that it is any part of their plan, to carry this class of reforms into practice. No Opposition Party ever did, when it gained possession.

In making these free observations, I mean not to enter into contention with this Society, their incivility towards me is what I should expect from place-hunting reformers. They are welcome, however, to the ground they have advanced upon, and I wish that every individual among them may act in the same upright, uninfluenced, and public spirited manner that I have done. Whatever reforms may be obtained, and by whatever means, they will be for the benefit of others, and not of me. I have no other interest in the cause than the interest of my heart. The part I have acted has been wholly that of a volunteer, unconnected with party; and when I quit, it shall be as honourably as I began.

I consider the reform of Parliament, by an application to Parliament, as proposed by the Society, to be a worn-out hackneyed subject, about which the nation is tired, and the parties are deceiving each other. It is not a subject that is cognizable before Parliament, because no Government has a right to alter itself, either in whole or in part. The right, and the exercise of that right, appertains to the nation only, and the proper mean is by a national convention, elected for the purpose, by all the people. By this, the will of the nation, whether to reform or not, or what the reform shall be, or how far it shall extend, will be known, and it cannot be known by any other means. Partial addresses, or separate associations, are not testimonies of the general will.

It is, however, certain that the opinions of men, with respect to systems and principles of government, are changing fast in all countries. The alteration in England, within the space of little more than a year, is far greater than could then have been believed, and it is daily and hourly increasing. It moves along the country with the silence of thought. The enormous expence of Government has provoked men to think, by making them feel; and the Proclamation has served to increase jealousy and disgust. To prevent, therefore, those commotions which too often and too suddenly arise from suffocated discontents, it is best that the general WILL* should have the full and free opportunity of being publicly ascertained and known.

Wretched as the state of representation is in England, it is every day becoming worse, because the unrepresented parts of the nation are increasing in population and property, and the represented parts are decreasing. It is, therefore, no ill-grounded estimation to say, that as not one person in seven is represented, at least fourteen millions of taxes, out of the seventeen millions, are paid by the unrepresented part; for although copyholds and leaseholds are assessed to the land tax, the holders are unrepresented.* Should then a general demur take place as to the obligation of paying taxes, on the ground of not being represented, it is not the Representatives of rotten Boroughs, nor Special Juries, that can decide the question. This is one of the possible cases that ought to be foreseen, in order to prevent the inconveniencies that might arise to numerous individuals, by provoking it.

I confess I have no idea of petitioning for rights. Whatever the rights of people are, they have a right to them, and none have a right either to withhold them, or to grant them. Government ought to be established on such principles of justice as to exclude the occasion of all such applications, for wherever they appear they are virtually accusations.

I wish that Mr Grey, since he has embarked in the business, would take the whole of it into consideration. He will then see that the right of reforming the state of the Representation does not reside in Parliament, and that the only motion he could consistently make, would be, that Parliament should *recommend* the election of a convention by all the people, because all pay taxes. But whether Parliament recommended it or not, the right of the nation would neither be lessened nor increased thereby.

As to Petitions from the unrepresented part,* they ought not to be looked for. As well might it be expected that Manchester, Sheffield, &c. should petition the rotten Boroughs, as that they should petition the Representatives of those Boroughs. Those two towns alone pay far more taxes than all the rotten Boroughs put together, and it is scarcely to be expected they should pay their court either to the Boroughs, or the Borough-mongers.

It ought also to be observed, that what is called Parliament, is composed of two houses that have always declared against the right of each other to interfere in any matter that related to the circumstances of either, particularly that of election. A reform, therefore, in the representation cannot, on the ground they have individually taken, become the subject of an act of Parliament, because such a mode would include the interference, against which the Commons on their part have protested; but must, as well on the ground of formality, as on that of right, proceed from a National Convention.

Let Mr Grey, or any other man, sit down and endeavour to put his thoughts together, for the purpose of drawing up an application to Parliament for a reform of Parliament, and he will soon convince himself of the folly of the attempt. He will find that he cannot get on; that he cannot make his thoughts join, so as to produce any effect; for whatever formality of words he may use, they will unavoidably include two ideas directly opposed to each other; the one in setting forth the reasons, the other in praying for the relief, and the two, when placed together, would stand thus:—'*The Representation in Parliament is so very corrupt, that we can no longer confide in it,—and, therefore, confiding in the justice and wisdom of Parliament, we pray,*' &c. &c.

The heavy manner in which every former proposed application to Parliament has dragged, sufficiently shews, that though the nation might not exactly see the awkwardness of the measure, it could not clearly see its way by that mean. To this also may be added another remark, which is, that the worse Parliament is, the less will be the inclination to petition it. This indifference, viewed as it ought to be, is one of the strongest censures the public can express. It is as if they were to say, 'Ye are not worth reforming.'

Let any man examine the Court-Kalendar* of Placemen in both Houses, and the manner in which the Civil List operates, and he will be at no loss to account for this indifference and want of confidence on one side, nor of the opposition to reforms on the other.

Besides the numerous list of paid persons exhibited in the Court-Kalendar, which so indecently stares the nation in the face, there is an unknown number of masked Pensioners,* which renders Parliament still more suspected.

Who would have supposed that Mr Burke, holding forth as he formerly did against secret influence, and corrupt majorities, should become a concealed Persioner? I will now state the case, not for the little purpose of exposing Mr Burke, but to shew the inconsistency of any application to a body of men, more than half of whom, as far as the nation can at present know, may be in the same case with himself.

Towards the end of Lord North's administration,* Mr Burke brought a bill into Parliament, generally known by the name of Mr Burke's Reform Bill;* in which, among other things, it is enacted, 'That no pension, exceeding the sum of three hundred pounds a year, shall be granted to any one person, and that the whole amount of the pensions granted in one year shall not exceed six hundred pounds; a list of which, together with the *names of the persons* to whom the same are granted, shall be laid before Parliament in twenty days after the beginning of each session, until the whole pension list shall be reduced to ninety thousand pounds.' A provisory clause is afterwards added, 'That it shall be lawful for the First Commissioner of the Treasury, to return into the Exchequer, any pension or annuity, *without a name*, on his making oath that such pension or annuity is not directly or indirectly for the benefit, use, or behoof, of any Member of the House of Commons.'

But soon after that Administration ended, and the party Mr Burke acted with came into power, it appears, from the circumstances I am going to relate, that Mr Burke became himself a Pensioner in disguise,* in a similar manner, as if a pension had been granted in the name of John Nokes, to be privately paid to and enjoyed by Tom Stiles. The name of Edmund Burke does not appear in the original transaction: but after the pension was obtained, Mr Burke wanted to make the most of it at once, by selling or mortgaging it; and the gentleman, in whose name the pension stands, applied to one of the public offices for that purpose. This unfortunately brought forth the name of *Edmund Burke*, as the real Pensioner of 1,500*l.* per annum. When men trumpet forth what they call the blessings of the Constitution, it ought to be known what sort of blessings they allude to.

As to the Civil List, of a million a year, it is not to be supposed that any one man can eat, drink, or consume the whole upon himself. The case is, that above half this sum is annually apportioned among Courtiers, and Court Members of both Houses, in places and offices, altogether insignificant and perfectly useless, as to every purpose of civil, rational, and manly government. For instance,

Of what use in the science and system of Government is what is called a Lord Chamberlain, a Master and a Mistress of the Robes, a Master of the Horse, a Master of the Hawks, and an hundred other such things. Laws derive no additional force, nor additional excellence, from such mummery.

In the disbursements of the Civil List for the year 1786 (which may be seen in Sir John Sinclair's History of the Revenue*) are four separate charges for this mummery office of Chamberlain.

1st	£38,778	17	—
2d	3,000	—	—
3d	24,069	19	—
4th	10,000	18	3
	75,849	14	3

[besides £1,119 charged for Alms.]

From this sample, the rest may be guessed at. As to the Master of the Hawks, (there are no hawks kept, and if there were, it is no reason the people should pay the expence of feeding them, many of whom are put to it to get bread for their children) his salary is 1,372*l.* 10*s.*

And besides a list of items of this kind, sufficient to fill a quire of paper, the Pension lists alone are 107,404*l.* 13*s.* 4*d.* which is a greater sum than all the expences of the federal Government in America amount to.

Among the items, there are two I had no expectation of finding, and which, in this day of enquiry after Civil List influence, ought to be exposed. The one is an annual payment of one thousand seven hundred pounds to the Dissenting Ministers in England, and eight hundred pounds to those of Ireland.

This is the fact; and the distribution *as I am informed*, is as follows: The whole sum of £1,700 is paid to one person, a Dissenting Minister in London,* who divides it among eight others, and those eight among such others as they please. The Lay-body of the Dissenters, and many of their principal Ministers, have long confidered it as dishonourable, and have endeavoured to prevent it, but still it continues to be secretly paid; and as the world has sometimes seen very fulsome Addresses from parts of that body, it may naturally be supposed that the receivers, like Bishops and other Court-Clergy, are not idle in promoting them. How the money is distributed in Ireland, I know not.

To recount all the secret history of the Civil List is not the intention of this publication. It is sufficient, in this place, to expose its general character, and the mass of influence it keeps alive. It will necessarily become one of the objects of reform; and therefore enough is said to shew that, under its operation, no application to Parliament can be expected to succeed, nor can consistently be made.

Such reforms will not be promoted by the Party that is in possession of those places, nor by the Opposition who are waiting for them; and as to a *mere reform* in the state of the Representation, under the idea that another Parliament, differently elected to the present, but still a component third part of the same system, and subject to the controul of the other two parts, will abolish those abuses, is altogether delusion; because it is not only impracticable on the ground of formality, but is unwisely exposing another set of men to the same corruptions that have tainted the present.

Were all the objects that require a reform accomplishable by a mere reform in the state of the Representation, the persons who compose the present Parliament might, with rather more propriety be asked to abolish all the abuses themselves, than be applied to as the mere instruments of doing it by a future Parliament. If the virtue be wanting to abolish the abuse, it is also wanting to act as the means, and the nation must, of necessity, proceed by some other plan.

Having thus endeavoured to shew what the abject condition of Parliament is, and the impropriety of going a second time over the same ground that has before miscarried, I come to the remaining part of the subject.

There ought to be, in the constitution of every country, a mode of referring back, on any extraordinary occasion, to the sovereign and original constituent power, which is the nation itself. The right of altering any part of a Government cannot, as already observed, reside in the Government, or that Government might make itself what it pleased.

It ought also to be taken for granted, that though a nation may feel inconveniencies, either in the excess of taxation, or in the mode of expenditure, or in any thing else, it may not at first be sufficiently assured in what part of its government the defect lies, or where the civil originates. It may be supposed to be in one part, and on enquiry be found to be in another; or partly in all. This obscurity is naturally interwoven with what are called mixed Governments.

Be, however, the reform to be accomplished whatever it may, it can only follow in consequence of first obtaining a full knowledge of all the causes that have rendered such reform necessary, and every thing short of this is guess-work or frivolous cunning. In this case, it cannot be supposed that any application to Parliament can bring forward this knowledge. That body is itself the supposed cause, or one of the supposed causes, of the abuses in question; and cannot be expected, and ought not to be asked, to give evidence against itself. The enquiry, therefore, which is of necessity the first step in the business, cannot be entrusted to Parliament, but must be undertaken by a distinct body of men, separated from every suspicion of corruption or influence.

Instead, then, of referring to rotten Boroughs and absurd Corporations for Addresses, or hawking them about the country to be signed by a few dependant tenants, the real and effectual mode would be to come at once to the point, and to ascertain the sense of the nation by electing a National Convention. By this method, as already observed, the general WILL, whether to reform or not, or what the reform shall be, or how far it shall extend, will be known, and it cannot be known by any other means. Such a body, empowered and supported by the nation, will have authority to demand in formation upon all matters necessary to be enquired into; and no Minister, nor any other person, will dare to refuse it. It will then be seen whether seventeen millions of taxes are necessary, and for what purposes they are expended. The concealed Pensioners will then be obliged to unmask; and the source of influence and corruption, if any such there be, will be laid open to the nation, not for the purpose of revenge, but of redress.

By taking this public and national ground, all objections against partial Addresses on one side, or private associations on the other, will be done away. THE NATION WILL DECREE ITS OWN REFORMS; and the clamour about Party and Faction, or Ins or Outs, will become ridiculous.

The plan and organization of a Convention is easy in practice.

In the first place, the number of inhabitants in every county can be sufficiently enough known, from the number of houses assessed to the House and Window-light tax in each county. This will give the rule for apportioning the number of Members to be elected to the National Convention in each of the counties.

If the total number of inhabitants in England be seven millions, and the total number of Members to be elected to the Convention be one thousand, the number of Members to be elected in a county containing one hundred and fifty thousand inhabitants will be *twenty-one*, and in like proportion for any other county.

As the election of a Convention must, in order to ascertain the general sense of the nation, go on grounds different from that of Parliamentary elections, the mode that best promises this end will have no difficulties to combat with from absurd customs and pretended rights. The right of every man will be the same, whether he lives in a city, a town, or a village. The custom of attaching Rights to *place*, or in other words to inanimate matter, instead of to the *person*, independently of place, is too absurd to make any part of a rational argument.

As every man in the nation of the age of twenty-one years pays taxes, either out of the property he possesses, or out of the product of his labour, which is property to him; and is amenable in his own person to every law of the land; so has every one the same equal right to vote, and no one part of a nation, nor any individual, has a right to dispute the right of another. The man who should do this ought to forfeit the exercise of his *own* right, for a term of years. This would render the punishment consistent with the crime.

When a qualification to vote is regulated by years, it is placed on the firmest possible ground, because the qualification is such as nothing but dying before the time can take away; and the equality of Rights, as a principle, is recognized in the act of regulating the exercise. But when Rights are placed upon, or made dependant upon property, they are on the most precarious of all tenures. 'Riches make themselves wings, and fly away,'* and the rights fly with them; and thus they become lost to the man when they would be of most value.

It is from a strange mixture of tyranny and cowardice, that exclusions have been set up and continued. The boldness to do wrong at first, changes afterwards into cowardly craft, and at last into fear. The Representatives in England appear now to act as if they were afraid to do right, even in part, lest it should awaken the nation to a sense of all the wrongs it has endured. This case serves to shew that the same conduct that best constitutes the safety of an individual, namely, a strict adherence to principle, constitutes also the safety of a Government, and that without it safety is but an empty name. When the rich plunder the poor of his rights, it becomes an example to the poor to plunder the rich of his property; for the rights of the one are as much property to him as wealth is property to the other, and the *little all* is as dear as the *much*. It is only by setting out on just principles that men are trained to be just to each other; and it will always be found, that when the rich protect the rights of the poor, the poor will protect the property of the rich. But the gaurantee, to be effectual, must be parliamentarily reciprocal.

Exclusions are not only unjust, but they frequently operate as injuriously to the party who monopolizes, as to those who are excluded. When men seek to exclude others from participating in the exercise of any right, they should, at least, be assured that thay can effectually perform the whole of the business they undertake; for unless they do this, themselves will be losers by the monopoly. This has been the case with respect to the monopolized right of Election. The monopolizing party has not been able to keep the Parliamentary Representation, to whom the power of taxation was entrusted, in the state it ought to have been, and have thereby multiplied taxes upon themselves equally with those who were excluded.

A great deal has been, and will continue to be said, about disqualifications, arising from the commission of offences;* but were this subject urged to its full extent, it would disqualify a great number of the present Electors, together with their Representatives; for, of all offences, none are more destructive to the morals of Society than Bribery and Corruption. It is, therefore, civility to such persons to pass this subject over, and to give them a fair opportunity of recovering, or rather of creating character.

Every thing, in the present mode of electioneering in England, is the reverse of what it ought to be, and the vulgarity that attends elections is no other than the natural consequence of inverting the order of the system.

In the first place, the Candidate seeks the Elector, instead of the Elector seeking for a Representative; and the Electors are advertized as being in the interest of the Candidate, instead of the Candidate being in the interest of the Electors. The Candidate pays the Elector for his vote, instead of the Nation paying the Representative for his time and attendance on public business. The complaint for an undue election is brought by the Candidate, as if he, and not the Electors, were the party aggrieved; and he takes on himself, at any period of the election, to break it up, by declining, as if the election was in his right, and not in theirs.

The compact that was entered into at the last Westminster election* between two of the Candidates (Mr Fox and Lord Hood) was an indecent violation of the principles of election. The Candidates assumed, in their own persons, the rights of the Electors; for it was only in the body of the Electors, and not at all in the Candidates, that the right of making any such compact or compromise could exist. But the principle of Election and Representation is so compleatly done away, in every stage thereof, that inconsistency has no longer the power of surprising.

Neither from elections thus conducted, nor from rotten Borough Addressers, nor from County-meetings, promoted by Placemen and Pensioners, can the sense of the nation be known. It is still corruption appealing to itself. But a Convention of a thousand persons, fairly elected, would bring every matter to a decided issue.

As to County-meetings, it is only persons of leisure, or those who live near to the place of meeting, that can attend, and the number on such occasions is but like a drop in the bucket compared with the whole. The only consistent service which such meetings could render, would be that of apportioning the county into convenient districts; and when this is done, each district might, according to its number of inhabitants, elect its quota of County Members to the National Convention; and the vote of each Elector might be taken in the parish where he resided, either by ballot or by voice, as he should chuse to give it.

A National Convention thus formed would bring together the sense and opinions of every part of the nation, fairly taken. The science of Government, and the interest of the Public, and of the several parts thereof, would then undergo an ample and rational discussion, freed from the language of parliamentary disguise.

But in all deliberations of this kind, though men have a right to reason with, and endeavour to convince each other, upon any matter that respects their common good, yet, in point of practice, the majority of opinions, when known, forms a rule for the whole, and to this rule every good citizen practically conforms.

Mr Burke, as if he knew, (for every concealed Pensioner has the opportunity of knowing) that the abuses acted under the present system, are too flagrant to be palliated, and that the majority of opinions, whenever such abuses should be made public, would be for a general and effectual reform, has endeavoured to preclude the event, by sturdily denying the right of a majority of a nation to act as a whole. Let us bestow a thought upon this case.

When any matter is proposed as a subject for consultation, it necessarily implies some mode of decision. Common consent, arising from absolute necessity, has placed this in a majority of opinions; because without it there can be no decision, and consequently no order. It is, perhaps, the only case in which mankind, however various in their ideas upon other matters, can consistently be unanimous; because it is a mode of decision derived from the primary original right of every individual concerned; *that* right being first individually exercised in giving an opinion, and whether that opinion shall arrange with the minority or the majority, is a subsequent accidental thing that neither increases nor diminishes the individual original right itself. Prior to any debate, enquiry or vestigation, it is not supposed to be known on which side the majority of opinions will fall, and therefore whilst this mode of decision secures to every one the right of giving an opinion, it admits to every one an equal chance in the ultimate event.

Among the matters that will present themselves to the consideration of a National Convention, there is one, wholly of a domestic nature, but, so marvelously loaded with confusion, as to appear, at first sight, almost impossible to be reformed. I mean the condition of what is called Law.

But, if we examine into the cause from whence this confusion, now so much the subject of universal complaint, is produced, not only the remedy will immediately present itself, but with it, the means of preventing the like case hereafter.

In the first place, the confusion has generated itself from the absurdity of every Parliament assuming to be eternal in power, and the laws partake in a similiar manner of this assumption. They have no period of legal or natural expiration; and, however absurd in principle, or inconsistent in practice many of them have become, they still are, if not especially repealed, considered as making a part of the general mass. By this means the body of what is called Law, is spread over a space of *several hundred years*, comprehending laws obsolete, laws repugnant, laws ridiculous, and every other kind of laws forgotten or remembered; and what renders the case still worse is, that the confusion multiplies with the progress of time.[1]

To bring this misshapen monster into form, and to prevent its lapsing again into a wilderness state, only two things, and those very simple, are necessary.

The first is, to review the whole mass of laws, and to bring forward such only as are worth retaining, and let all the rest drop; and to give to the laws so brought forward a new era commencing from the time of such reform.

Secondly, that at the expiration of every twenty-one years, (or any other stated period) a like review shall again be taken, and the laws found proper to be retained, be again carried forward, commencing with that date, and the useless laws dropt and discontinued. By this means there can be no obsolete laws, and scarcely such a thing as laws standing in direct or equivocal contradiction to each other, and every person will know the period of time to which he is to look back for all the laws in being.

It is worth remarking, that whilst every other branch of

---

[1] In the time of Henry the Fourth, a law was passed, making it felony 'to multiply gold or silver, or to make use of the craft or multiplication,' and this law remained two hundred and eighty-six years upon the statute books. It was then repealed as being ridiculous and injurious.*

science is brought within some commodious system, and the study of it simplified by easy methods, the laws take the contrary course, and become every year more complicated, entangled, confused, and obscure.

Among the paragraphs which the Attorney-General has taken from the *Rights of Men*, and put into his information, one is, that were I have said, 'that with respect to regular law, there is *scarcely such a thing*.'*

As I do not know whether the Attorney-General means to shew this expression to be libellous, because it is TRUE, or because it is FALSE, I shall make no other reply to him in this place than by remarking, that if almanack-makers had not been more judicious than law-makers, the study of almanacks would by this time have become as abstruse as the study of law, and we should hear of a library of almanacks as we now do of statutes; but by the simple operation of letting the obsolete matter drop, and carrying forward that only which is proper to be retained, all that is necessary to be known, is found within the space of a year, and laws also admit of being kept within some given period.

I shall here close this letter, so far as it respects the Addressers, the Proclamation, and the Prosecution; and shall offer a few observations to the Society stiling itself 'THE FRIENDS OF THE PEOPLE.'

That the science of government is beginning to be better understood than in former times, and that the age of fiction and political superstition, and of craft and mystery is passing away, are matters which the experience of every day proves to be true, as well in England as in other countries.

As therefore it is impossible to calculate the silent progress of opinion, and also impossible to govern a nation after it has changed its habits of thinking, by the craft or policy that it was governed by before, the only true method to prevent popular discontents and commotions is, to throw, by every fair and rational argument, all the light upon the subject that can possibly be thrown; and, at the same time, to open the means of collecting the general sense of the nation; and this

cannot, as already observed, be done by any plan so effectually as a National Convention. Here individual opinion will
quiet itself by having a centre to rest upon.

The society already mentioned, (which is made up of men
of various descriptions, but chiefly of those called Foxites,)
appears to me, either to have taken wrong grounds from
want of judgment, or to have acted with cunning reserve. It
is now amusing the people with a new phrase, namely, that
of 'a temperate and moderate reform,' the interpretation of
which is, *a continuance of the abuses as long as possible. If we
cannot hold all let us hold some.*

Who are those that are frightened at reforms? Are the
public afraid that their taxes should be lessened too much?
Are they afraid that sinecure places and pensions should be
abolished too fast? Are the poor afraid that their condition
should be rendered too comfortable? Is the worn-out mechanic, or the aged and decayed tradesman, frightened at the
prospect of receiving ten pounds a year out of the surplus
taxes? Is the soldier frightened at the thoughts of his discharge, and three shillings per week during life? Is the sailor
afraid that press-warrants will be abolished? The Society
mistakes the fears of borough-mongers, placemen, and pensioners, for the fears of the people; and the *temperate and
moderate Reform* it talks of, is calculated to suit the condition
of the former.

Those words, 'temperate and moderate,' are words either
of political cowardice, or of cunning, or seduction.—A thing,
moderately good, is not so good as it ought to be. Moderation
in temper is always a virtue; but moderation in principle is a
species of vice. But who is to be the judge of what is a
temperate and moderate Reform? The Society is the representative of nobody; neither can the unrepresented part of
the nation commit this power to those in Parliament, in
whose election they had no choice; and, therefore, even
upon the ground the Society has taken, recourse must be
bad to a National Convention.

The objection which Mr Fox made to Mr Grey's proposed
Motion for a Parliamentary Reform was, that it contained
no plan.—It certainly did not. But the plan very easily

presents itself; and whilst it is fair for all parties, it prevents the dangers that might otherwise arise from private or popular discontent.

THOMAS PAINE

DISSERTATION

ON

FIRST PRINCIPLES OF
GOVERNMENT.

THERE is no subject more interesting to every man than the subject of government. His security, be he rich or poor, and, in a great measure, his prosperity, is connected therewith; it is, therefore, his interest, as well as his duty, to make himself acquainted with its principles, and what the practice ought to be.

Every art and science, however imperfectly known at first, has been studied, improved, and brought to what we call perfection, by the progressive labours of succeeding generations; but the science of government has stood still. No improvement has been made in the principle, and scarcely any in the practice, till the American revolution began. In all the countries of Europe (except in France) the same forms and systems that were erected in the remote ages of ignorance, still continue, and their antiquity is put in the place of principle; it is forbidden to investigate their origin, or by what right they exist. If it be asked, how has this happened? the answer is easy; they are established on a principle that is false, and they employ their power to prevent detection.

Notwithstanding the mystery with which the science of government has been enveloped, for the purpose of enslaving, plundering, and imposing upon mankind, it is of all things the least mysterious, and the most easy to be understood. The meanest capacity cannot be at a loss, if it begins its enquiries at the right point. Every art and science has some point, or alphabet, at which the study of that art or science begins, and by the assistance of which the progress is facilitated. The same method ought to be observed with respect to the science of government.

Instead, then, of embarrassing the subject in the outlet with the numerous subdivisions, under which different forms of government have been classed, such as aristocracy, democracy, oligarchy, monarchy, &c. the better method will be to begin with what may be called primary divisions, or those under which all the several subdivisions will be comprehended.

The primary divisions are but two:

First, government by election and representation.

Secondly, government by hereditary succession.

All the several forms and systems of government, however numerous or diversified, class themselves under one or other of those primary divisions; for either they are on the system of representation, or on that of hereditary succession. As to that equivocal thing called mixed government, such as the late government of Holland,* and the present government of England, it does not make an exception to the general rule, because the parts, separately considered, are either representative or hereditary.

Beginning, then, our enquiries at this point, we have, first, to examine into the nature of those two primary divisions. If they are equally right in principle, it is mere matter of opinion which we prefer. If the one be demonstratively better than the other, that difference directs our choice; but if one of them should be so absolutely false, as not to have a right to existence, the matter settles itself at once; because a negative proved on one thing, where two only are offered, and one must be accepted, amounts to an affirmative on the other.

The revolutions that are now spreading themselves in the world have their origin in the state of the case; and the present war is a conflict between the representative system, founded on the rights of the people, and the hereditary system, founded in usurpation. As to what are called Monarchy, Royalty, and Aristocracy, they do not, either as things or as terms, sufficiently describe the hereditary system; they are but secondary things or signs of the hereditary system, and which fall of themselves if that system has not a right to exist. Were there no such terms as Monarchy, Royalty, and Aristocracy, or were other terms substituted in their place, the hereditary system, if it continued, would not be altered thereby. It would be the same system under any other titulary name as it is now.

The character, therefore, of the revolutions of the present

day distinguishes itself most definitively by grounding itself on the system of representative government, in opposition to the hereditary. No other distinction reaches the whole of the principle.

Having thus opened the case generally, I proceed, in the first place, to examine the hereditary system, because it has the priority in point of time. The representative system is the invention of the modern world; and that, no doubt, may arise as to my own opinion, I declare it before-hand, which is, *that there is not a problem in Euclid more mathematically true,* than that hereditary government has not a right to exist. When, therefore, we take from any man the exercise of hereditary power, we take away that which he never had the right to possess, and which no law or custom could, or ever can, give him a title to.*

The arguments that have hitherto been employed against the hereditary system, have been chiefly founded upon the absurdity of it, and its incompetency to the purpose of good government. Nothing can present to our judgment, or to our imagination, a figure of greater absurdity than that of seeing the government of a nation fall, as it frequently does into the hands of a lad necessarily destitute of experience, and often little better than a fool. It is an insult to every man of years, of character, and of talent, in a country. The moment we begin to reason upon the hereditary system, it falls into derision; let but a single idea begin, and a thousand will soon follow. Insignificance, imbecility, childhood, dotage, want of moral character; in fine, every defect, serious or laughable, unite to hold up the hereditary system as a figure of ridicule. Leaving, however, the ridiculousness of the thing to the reflections of the reader, I proceed to the more important part of the question, namely, whether such a system has a right to exist?

To be satisfied of the right of a thing to exist, we must be satisfied that it had a right to begin. If it had not a right to begin, it has not a right to continue. By what right, then, did the hereditary system begin? Let a man but ask himself this question, and he will find that he cannot satisfy himself with an answer.

The right which any man, or any family, had to set itself up at first to govern a nation, and to establish itself hereditarily, was no other than the right which Robespierre* had to do the same thing in France. If he had none, they had none. If they had any, he had as much; for it is impossible to discover superiority of right in any family, by virtue of which hereditary government could begin. The Capets, the Guelphs, the Robespierres, the Marats,* are all on the same standing as to the question of right. It belongs exclusively to none.

It is one step towards liberty, to perceive that hereditary government could not begin as an exclusive right in any family. The next point will be, whether, having once begun, it could grow into a right by the influence of time?

This would be supposing an absurdity; for either it is putting time in the place of principle, or making it superior to principle; whereas time has no more connection with, or influence upon principle, than principle has upon time. The wrong which began a thousand years ago, is as much a wrong as if it began to-day; and the right which originates today, is as much a right as if it had the sanction of a thousand years. Time, with respect to principles, is an eternal NOW: it has no operation upon them: it changes nothing of their nature and qualities. But what have we to do with a thousand years? Our life-time is but a short portion to that period, and if we find the wrong in existence as soon as we begin to live, that is the point of time at which it begins to us; and our right to resist it is the same as if it had never existed before.

As hereditary government could not begin as a natural right in any family, nor derive after its commencement any right from time, we have only to examine whether there exists in a nation a right to set it up, and establish it by what is called Law, as has been done in England? I answer, NO; and that any law or any constitution made for that purpose, is an act of treason against the rights of every minor in the nation, at the time it is made, and against the rights of all succeeding generations. I shall speak upon each of those cases. First, of the minor, at the time such law is made. Secondly, of the generations that are to follow.

A nation, in a collective sense, comprehends all the individuals, of whatever age, from just born to just dying. Of these, one part will be minors, the other aged. The average of life is not exactly the same in every climate and country, but, in general, the minority in years are the majority in numbers, that is, the number of persons under twenty one years, is greater than the number of persons above that age. This difference in number is not necessary to the establishment of the principle I mean to lay down, but it serves to shew the justice of it more strongly. The principle would be equally good, if the majority in years were also the majority in numbers.

The rights of minors are as sacred as the rights of the aged. The difference is altogether in the different age of the two parties, and nothing in the nature of the rights; the rights are the same rights; and are to be preserved inviolate for the inheritance of the minors when they shall come of age. During the minority of minors their rights are under the sacred guardianship of the aged. The minor cannot surrender them; the guardian cannot dispossess him; consequently, the aged part of a nation who are the law-makers, for the *time being*, and who, in the march of life, are but a few years a-head of those who are yet minors, and to whom they must shortly give place, have not, and cannot have the right to make a law to set up and establish hereditary government, or, to speak more distinctly, *an hereditary succession of governors*; because it is an attempt to deprive every minor in the nation, at the time such a law is made, of his inheritance of rights when he shall come of age, and so subjugate him to a system of government, to which, during his minority, he could neither consent nor object.

If a person, who is a minor, at the time such a law is proposed, had happened to have been born a few years sooner, so as to be of the age of twenty-one years at the time of proposing it, his right to have objected against it, to have exposed the injustice and tyrannical principles of it, and to have voted against it, will be admitted on all sides. If, therefore, the law operates to prevent his excercising the same rights, after he comes of age, as he would have a right to exercise, had he been of age at the time, it is, undeniably, a law to take away and annul the rights of every person in the nation who shall be a minor at the time of making such a law; and, consequently, the right to make it cannot exist.

I come now to speak of government by hereditary succession, as it applies to succeeding generations; and to shew that in this case, as in the case of minors, there does not exist in a nation a right to set it up.

A nation, though continually existing, is continually in a state of renewal and succession. It is never stationary. Every day produces new births, carries minors forward to maturity, and old persons from the stage. In this ever-running flood of generations, there is no part superior in authority to another. Could we conceive an idea of superiority in any, at what point of time, or in what century of the world, are we to fix it? To what cause are we to ascribe it? By what evidence are we to prove it? By what criterion are we to know it? A single reflection will teach us, that our ancestors, like ourselves, were but tenants for life in the great freehold of rights. The fee-absolute* was not in them; it is not in us; it belongs to the whole family of man, through all ages. If we think otherwise than this, we think either as slaves or as tyrants. As slaves, if we think that any former generation had a right to bind us; as tyrants, if we think that we have authority to bind the generations that are to follow.

It may not be inapplicable to the subject, to endeavour to define what is to be understood by a generation, in the sense the word is here used.

As a natural term, its meaning is sufficiently clear. The father, the son, the grandson, are so many distinct generations. But when we speak of a generation, as describing the persons in whom legal authority resides, as distinct from another generation of the same description who are to succeed them, it comprehends all those who are above the age of twenty-one years, at the time we count from; and a generation of this kind will continue in authority between fourteen and twenty-one years, that is, until the number of minors, who, shall have arrived at age, shall be greater than the number of persons remaining of the former stock.

For example, if France at this or any other moment, contain twenty-four millions of souls, twelve millions will be males, and twelve females. Of the twelve millions of males, six millions will be of the age of twenty-one years, and six will be under, and the authority to govern will reside in the first six. But every day will make some alteration, and in twenty-one years every one of those minors who survive will have arrived at age, and the greater part of the former stock will be gone: the majority of persons then living, in whom the legal authority resides, will be composed of those who, twenty-one years before, had no legal existence. Those will be fathers and grandfathers in their turn, and in the next twenty-one years (or less) another race of minors, arrived at age, will succeed them, and so on.

As this is ever the case, and as every generation is equal in rights to another, it, consequently, follows, that there cannot be a right in any to establish government by hereditary succession, because it would be supposing itself possessed of a right superior to the rest, namely, that of commanding by its own authority how the world shall be hereafter governed, and who shall govern it. Every age and generation is and must be (as a matter of right) as free to act for itself in all cases, as the age and generation that preceded it. The vanity and presumption of governing beyond the grave is the most ridiculous and insolent of all tyrannies. Man has no property in man, neither has one generation a property in the generations that are to follow.

In the First Part of *Rights of Man*, I have spoken of government by hereditary succession; and I will here close the subject with an extract from that work, which states it under the two following heads.*

'First, of the right of any family to establish itself with hereditary power.

'Secondly, of the right of a nation to establish a particular family.

'With respect to the first of those heads, that of a family establishing itself with hereditary powers on its own authority, independent of the nation, all men will concur in calling it despotism, and it would be trespassing on their understanding to attempt to prove it.

'But the second head, that of a nation, that is, of a generation for the time being, establishing a particular family with hereditary powers, it does not present itself as despotism on the first reflection; but if men will permit a second reflection to take place, and carry that reflection forward, even but one remove out of their own persons to that of their offspring, they will then see, that hereditary succession becomes the same despotism to others, which the first persons reprobated for themselves. It operates to preclude the content of the succeeding generation, and the preclusion of content is despotism.

'In order to see this mater more clearly, let us consider the generation which undertakes to establish a family with hereditary powers, separately from the generations which are to follow.

'The generation which first selects a person and puts him at the head of its government, either with the title of king, or any other nominal distinction, acts its own choice, as a free agent for itself, be that choice wise or foolish. The person so set up is *not hereditary*, but selected and appointed; and the generation which sets him up does not live under an hereditary government, but under a government of its own choice. Were the person to set up, and the generation who sets him up, to live for ever, it never could become hereditary succession, and, of consequence, hereditary succession could only follow on the death of the first parties.

'As, therefore, hereditary succession is out of the question, with respect to the first generation, we have next to consider the character in which that generation acts towards the commencing generation, and to all succeeding ones.

'It assumes a character to which it has neither right nor title; for it changes itself from a legislator to a testator, and affects to make a will and testament which is to have operation after the demise of the makers, to bequeath the government; and it not only attempts to bequeath, but to establish on the succeeding generation a new and different form of government under which itself lived. Itself, as already observed, lived not under an hereditary government, but under a government of its own choice; and it now attempts, by virtue of a will and testament, which it has not authority to make, to take from the commencing generation, and from all future ones, the right and free agency by which itself acted.

'In whatever light hereditary succession, as growing out of the will and testament of some former generation, presents itself, it is both criminal and absurd. *A* cannot make a will to take from *B* the property of *B*, and give it to *C*; yet this is the manner in which what is called hereditary succession by law operates. A certain generation makes a will, under the form of a law, to take away the rights of the commencing generation, and of all future generations, and convey those rights to a third person, who afterwards comes forward, and assumes the government in consequence of that illicit conveyance.'

The history of the English parliament furnishes an example of this kind; and which merits to be recorded, as being the greatest instance of legislative ignorance and want of principle that is to be found in the history of any country. The case is as follows:—

The English parliament of 1688 imported a man and his wife from Holland, *William* and *Mary*, and made them king and queen of England. Having done this, the said parliament made a law to convey the government of the country to the heirs of William and Mary, in the following words, 'We, the lords spiritual and temporal, and commons, do, in the name of the people of England, most humbly and faithfully submit *ourselves, our heirs, and posterities*, to William and Mary, *their heirs and posterities*, for ever.' And, in a subsequent law, as quoted by Edmund Burke, the said parliament, in the name of the people of England then living, *binds the said people, their heirs and posterities, to William and Mary, their heirs and posterities, to the end of time.**

It is not sufficient that we laugh at the ignorance of such law-makers, it is necessary that we reprobate their want of principle. The constituent assembly of France (1789)* fell into the same vice as the parliament of England had done, and assumed to establish an hereditary succession in the family of the Capets, as an act of the constitution of that year. That every nation, *for the time being*, has a right to govern itself as it pleases, must always be admitted; but government by hereditary succession is government for another race of people, and not for itself; and as those on whom it is to operate are not yet in existence, or are minors, so neither is the right in existence to set it up for them, and to assume such a right is treason against the right of posterity.

I here close the arguments on the first head, that of government by hereditary succession; and proceed to the second, that of government by election and representation; or, as it may be concisely expressed, *representative government* in contra-distinction to *hereditary government*.

Reasoning by exclusion, if *hereditary government* has not a right to exist, and that it has not is proveable, *representative government* is admitted of course.

In contemplating government by election and representation, we amuse not ourselves in inquiring when, or how, or by what right it began. Its origin is ever in view. Man is himself the origin and the evidence of the right. It appertains to him in right of his existence, and his person is the title-deed.

The true, and only true basis of representative government is equality of rights. Every man has a right to one vote, and no more, in the choice of representatives. The rich have no more right to exclude the poor from the right of voting, or of electing and being elected, than the poor have to exclude the rich; and wherever it is attempted, or proposed, on either side, it is a question of force, and not of right. Who is he that would exclude another?—That other has a right to exclude him.

That which is now called aristocracy, implies an inequality of rights; but who are the persons that have a right to establish this inequality? Will the rich exclude themselves? No! Will the poor exclude themselves? No! By what right then can any be excluded? It would be a question, if any man, or class of men, have a right to exclude themselves; but be this as it may, they cannot have the right to exclude another. The poor will not delegate such a right to the rich, nor the rich to the poor, and to assume it is not only to assume arbitrary power, but to assume a right to commit robbery. Personal rights, of which the right of voting representatives is one, are a species of property of the most sacred kind; and he that would employ his pecuniary property, or presume upon the influence it gives him, to dispossess or rob another of his property of rights, uses that pecuniary property as he would use fire-arms, and merits to have it taken from him.

Inequality of rights is created by a combination in one part of the community to exclude another part from its rights. Whenever it be made an article of a constitution, or a law, that the right of voting, or of electing and being elected, shall appertain exclusively to persons possessing a certain quantity of property, be it little or much, it is a combination of the persons possessing that quantity, to exclude those who do not possess the same quantity. It is investing themselves with powers as a self-created part of society, to the exclusion of the rest.

It is always to be taken for granted, that those who oppose an equality of rights, never mean the exclusion should take place on themselves; and in this view of the case, pardoning the vanity of the thing, aristocracy is a subject of laughter. This self-soothing vanity is encouraged by another idea, not less selfish; which is, that the opposers conceive they are playing a safe game, in which there is a chance to gain and none to lose; that, at any rate, the doctrine of equality includes *them*, and that if they cannot get more rights than those whom they oppose and would exclude, they shall not have less. This opinion has already been fatal to thousands, who, not contented with *equal rights*, have fought more till they lost all, and experienced in themselves the degrading *inequality* they endeavoured to fix upon others.

In any view of the case, it is dangerous and impolitic, sometimes ridiculous, and always unjust, to make property the criterion of the right of voting. If the sum, or value of the property upon which the right is to take place be considerable, it will exclude a majority of the people, and unite them in a common interest against the government and against those who support it, and as the power is always with the majority, they can overturn such a government and its supporters whenever they please.

If, in order to avoid this danger, a small quantity of property be fixed, as the criterion of the right, it exhibits liberty in disgrace, by putting it in competition with accident and insignificance. When a brood mare shall fortunately produce a foal or a mule, that by being worth the sum in question, shall convey to its owner the right of voting, or by its death take it from him, in whom does the origin of such a right exit? Is it in the man, or in the mule? When we consider how many ways property may be acquired without merit, and lost without a crime, we ought to spurn the idea of making it a criterion of rights.

But the offensive part of the case is, that this exclusion from the right of voting implies a stigma on the moral character of the persons excluded; and this is what no part of the community has a right to pronounce upon another part. No external circumstance can justify it; wealth is no proof of moral character; nor poverty of the want of it. On the contrary, wealth is often the presumptive evidence of dishonesty; and poverty the negative evidence of innocence. If, therefore, property, whether little or much, be made a criterion, the means by which that property has been acquired, ought to be made a criterion also.

The only ground upon which exclusion from the right of voting is consistent with justice, would be to inflict it as a punishment for a certain time upon those who should propose to take away that right from others. The right of voting for representatives is the primary right by which other rights are protected. To take away this right is to reduce a man to a state of slavery, for slavery consists in being subject to the will of another, and he that has not a vote in the election of representatives, is in this case. The proposal, therefore, to disfranchise any class of men is as criminal as the proposal to take away property. When we speak of right, we ought always to unite with it the idea of duties; right becomes duties by reciprocity. The right which I enjoy becomes my duty to guarantee it to another, and he to me;

and those who violate the duty justly incur a forfeiture of the right.

In a political view of the case, the strength and permanent security of government is in proportion to the number of people interested in supporting it. The true policy, therefore, is to interest the whole by an equality of rights, for the danger arises from exclusions. It is possible to exclude men from the right of voting, but it is impossible to exclude them from the right of rebelling against that exclusion; and when all other rights are taken away, the right of rebellion is made perfect.

While men could be persuaded they had no rights, or that rights appertained only to a certain class of men, or that government was a thing existing in right of itself, it was not difficult to govern them authoritatively. The ignorance in which they were held, and the superstition in which they were instructed, furnished the means of doing it; but when the ignorance is gone, and the superstition with it; when they perceive the imposition that has been acted upon them; when they reflect that the cultivator and the manufacturer are the primary means of all the wealth that exists in the world, beyond what nature spontaneously produces; when they begin to feel their consequence by their usefulness, and their right as members of society, it is then no longer possible to govern them as before. The fraud once detected cannot be re-acted. To attempt it is to provoke derision, or invite destruction.

That property will ever be unequal, is certain. Industry, superiority of talents, dexterity of management, extreme frugality, fortunate opportunities, or the opposite, or the mean of those things, will ever produce that effect, without having recourse to the harsh, ill-sounding names of avarice and oppression; and, beside this, there are some men who, though they do not despise wealth, will not stoop to the drudgery of the means of acquiring it, nor will be troubled with the care of it, beyond their wants or their independence; whilst in others there is an avidity to obtain it by every means not punishable; it makes the sole business of their lives, and they follow it as a religion. *All that is required with respect to property, is to obtain it honestly, and not employ it criminally; but it is always criminally employed, when it is made a criterion for exclusive rights.*

In institutions that are purely pecuniary, such as that of a bank or a commecial company, the rights of the members composing that company are wholly created by the property they invest therein; and no other rights are represented in the government of that company, than what arise out of that property; neither has that government cognizance of *any thing but property*.

But the case is totally different with respect to the institution of civil government, organized on the system of representation. Such a government has cognizance of *every thing* and of *every man* as a member of the national society, whether he has property or not; and therefore the principle requires that *every man* and *every kind of right* be represented, of which the right to acquire and to hold property is but one, and that not of the most essential kind. The protection of a man's person is more sacred than the protection of property; and, besides this, the faculty of performing any kind of work or service by which he acquires a livelihood, or maintains his family, is of the nature of property. It is property to him; he has acquired it; and it is as much the object of his protection, as exterior property possessed without that faculty, can be the object of protection to another person.

I have always believed that the best security for property, be it much or little, is to remove from every part of the community, as far as can possibly be done, every cause of complaint, and every motive to violence; and this can only be done by an equality of rights. When rights are secure, property is secure in consequence. But when property is made a pretence for unequal or exclusive rights, it weakens the right to hold the property, and provokes indignation and tumult; for it is unnatural to believe that property can be secure under the guarantee of a society injured in its rights by the influence of that property.

Next to the injustice and ill policy of making property a pretence for exclusive rights, is the unaccountable absurdity of giving to mere *sound* the idea of property, and annexing to it certain rights; for what else is a *title* but found? Nature is often giving to the world some extraordinary men who arrive at fame by merit and universal consent, such as Aristotle, Socrates, Plato, &c.* These were truly great or noble. But when government sets up a manufactory of nobles, it is as absurd, as if she undertook to a manufacture wise men. *Her nobles are all counterfeits.*

This wax-work order has assumed the name of aristocracy; and the disgrace of it would be lessened if it could be considered as only childish imbecility. We pardon foppery because of its insignificance, and on the same ground we might pardon the foppery of Titles. But the origin of aristocracy was worse than foppery. It was robbery. *The first aristocrats in all countries were brigands.* Those of latter times, sycophants.

It is very well known that in England (and the same will be found in other countries) the great landed estates, now held in descent, were plundered from the quiet inhabitants at the conquest.* The possibility did not exist of acquiring such estates honestly. If it be asked how they could have been acquired, no answer but that of robbery can be given. That they were not acquired by trade, by commerce, by manufactures, by agriculture, or by any reputable employment, is certain. How then were they acquired? Blush, aristocracy, to hear your origin, for your progenitors were Thieves. They were the Robespierres and the Jacobins* of that day. When they had committed the robbery, they endeavoured to lose the disgrace of it, by sinking their real names under fictious ones, which they called Titles. It is ever the practice of Felons to act in this manner.

As property honestly obtained is best secured by an equality of rights, so ill-gotten property depends for protection on a monopoly of rights. He who has robbed another of his property, will next endeavour to disarm him of his rights, to secure that property; for when the robber becomes the legislator, he believes himself secure. That part of the government of England that is called the House of Lords, was originally composed of persons who had committed the robberies of which I have been speaking. It was an association for the protection of the property they had stolen.

But, besides the criminality of the origin of aristocracy, it has an injurious effect on the moral and physical character of man. Like slavery, it debilitates the human faculties; for as the mind, bowed down by slavery, loses in silence its elastic powers, so, in the contrary extreme, when it is buoyed up by folly, it becomes incapable of exerting them, and dwindles into imbecility. It is impossible that a mind employed upon ribbands and titles can ever be great. The childishness of the objects consumes the man.

It is at all times necessary, and more particularly so during the progress of a revolution, and until right ideas confirm themselves by habit, that we frequently refresh our patriotism by reference to first principles. It is by tracing things to their origin, that we learn to understand them; and it is by keeping that line and that origin always in view, that we never forget them.

An enquiry into the origin of rights will demonstrate to us, that *rights* are not *gifts* from one man to another, nor from one class of men to another; for who is he who could be the first giver? Or by what principle, or on what authority, could he possess the right of giving? A declaration of rights is not a creation of them, nor a donation of them. It is a manifest of the principle by which they exist, followed by a detail of what the rights are; for every civil right has a natural right for its foundation, and it includes the principle of a reciprocal guarantee of those rights from man to man. As, therefore, it is impossible to discover any origin of rights otherwise than in the origin of man, it consequently follows, that rights appertain to man in right of his existence only, and must, therefore, be equal to every man. The principle of an *equality of rights* is clear and simple. Every man can understand it, and it is by understanding his rights that he learns his duties; for where the rights of men are equal, every man must, finally, see the necessity of protecting the rights of others, as the most effectual security for his own. But if, in the formation of a constitution, we depart from the principle of equal rights, or attempt any modification of it, we plunge into a labyrinth of difficulties, from which there is no way out but by retreating. Where are we to stop? Or by what principle are we to find out the point to stop at, that shall discriminate between men of the same country, part of whom shall be free, and the rest not? If property is to be made the criterion, it is a total departure from every moral principle of liberty, because it is attaching rights to mere matter, and making man the agent of that matter. It is, moreover, holding up property as an apple of discord,* and not only exciting, but justifying war against it; for I maintain the principle, that when property is used as an instrument to take away the rights of those who may happen not to possess property, it is used to an unlawful purpose, as fire arms would be in a similar case.

In a state of nature all men are equal in rights, but they are not equal in power; the weak cannot protect himself against the strong. This being the case, the institution of civil society is for the purpose of making an equalization of powers that shall be parallel to, and a guarantee of the equality of rights. The laws of a country, when properly constructed, apply to this purpose. Every man takes the arm of the law for his protection, as more effectual than his own; and, therefore, every man has an equal right in the formation of the government and of the laws by which he is to be governed and judged. In extensive countries and societies, such as America and France, this right, in the individual, can only be exercised by delegation, that is, by election and representation; and hence it is, that the institution of representative government arises.

Hitherto I have confined myself to matters of principle only. First, that hereditary government has not a right to exist; that it cannot be established on any principle of right; and that it is a violation of all principle. Secondly, that government by election and representation, has its origin in the natural and eternal rights of man; for whether a man be his own lawgiver, as he would be in a state of nature; or whether he exercises his portion of legislative sovereignty in his own person, as might be the case in small democracies, where all could assemble for the formation of the laws by which they were to be governed; or whether he exercises it in the choice of persons to represent him in a national assembly of representatives, the origin of the right is the same in all cases. The first, as is before observed, is defective in power; the second is practicable only in democracies of small extent; the third is the greatest scale upon which human government can be instituted.

Next to matters of *principle*, are matters of *opinion*, and it is necessary to distinguish between the two. Whether the rights of men shall be equal, is not a matter of opinion, but of right, and, consequently, of principle; for men do not hold their rights as grants from each other, but each one in right of himself. Society is the guardian, but not the giver. And as in extensive societies, such as America and France, the right of the individual, in matters of government, cannot be exercised but by election and representation, it consequently follows, that the only system of government, consistent with principle, where simple democracy is impracticable, is the representative system. But as to the organical part, or the manner in which the several parts of government shall be arranged and composed, it is altogether *matter of opinion*. It is necessary that all the parts be conformable with the *principle of equal rights*; and so long as this principle be religiously adhered to, no very material error can take place, neither can any error continue long in that part that falls within the province of opinion.

In all matters of opinion, the social compact, or the principle by which society is held together, requires that the majority of opinions become the rule for the whole, and that the minority yield practical obedience thereto. This is perfectly conformable to the principle of equal rights; for, in the first place, every man has a *right to give an opinion*, but no man has a right that his opinion should *govern the rest*. In the second place, it is not supposed to be known beforehand on which side of any question, whether for or against, any man's opinion will fall. He may happen to be in a majority upon some questions, and in a minority upon others; and by the same rule that he expects obedience in the one case, he must yield it in the other. All the disorders that have arisen in France, during the progress of the revolution, have had their origin, not in the *principle of equal rights*, but in the violation of that principle. The principle of equal rights, has been repeatedly violated, and that not by the majority, but by the minority, and *that minority has been composed of men possessing property, as well as of men without property; property, therefore, even upon the experience already had, is no more a criterion of character, than it is of rights.* It will sometimes happen that the minority are right, and the majority are wrong, but as soon as experience proves this to be the case, the minority will encrease to a majority, and the error will reform itself by the tranquil operation of freedom of opinion and equality of rights. Nothing, therefore, can justify an insurrection, neither can it ever be necessary, where rights are equal and opinions free.

Taking, then, the principle of equal rights as the foundation of the revolution, and, consequently, of the constitution, the organical part, or the manner in which the several parts of the government shall be arranged in the constitution, will, as is already said, fall within the province of opinion.

Various methods will present themselves upon a question of this kind, and though experience is yet wanting to determine which is the best, it has, I think, sufficiently decided which is the worst. That is the worst, which, in its deliberations and decisions, is subject to the precipitancy and passion of an individual; and when the whole legislature is crouded into one body, it is an individual in mass. In all cases of deliberation, it is necessary to have a corps of reserve, and it would be better to divide the representation by lot into two parts, and let them revise and correct each other, than that the whole should sit together and debate at once.

Representative government is not necessarily confined to any one particular form. The principle is the same in all the forms under which it can be arranged. The equal rights of the people is the root from which the whole springs, and the branches may be arranged as present opinion or future experience shall best direct, As to that *hospital of incurables* (as Chesterfield calls it*) the British House of Peers, it is an excrescence growing out of corruption; and there is no more affinity or resemblance between any of the branches of a legislative body originating from the rights of the people, and the aforesaid house of peers, than between a regular member of the human body and an ulcerated wen.

As to that part of government that is called the *executive*, it is necessary, in the first place, to fix a precise meaning to the word.

There are but two divisions into which power can be arranged. First, that of willing or decreeing the laws; secondly, that of executing, or putting them in practice. The former corresponds to the intellectual faculties of the human mind, which reasons and determines what shall be done; the second, to the mechanical powers of the human body, that puts that determination into practice. If the former decides, and the latter does not perform, it is a state of imbecility; and if the latter acts without the pre-determination of the former, it is a state of lunacy. The executive department, therefore, is official, and is subordinate to the legislative, as the body is to the mind in a state of health: for it is impossible to conceive the idea of two sovereignties, a sovereignty to *will*, and a sovereignty to *act*. The executive is not invested with the power of deliberating whether it shall act or not; it has no discretionary authority in the case; for it can *act no other thing* that what the laws decree, and it is *obliged* to act conformably thereto; and, in this view of the case, the executive is made up of all the official departments that execute the laws, of which, that which is called the judiciary is the chief.

But mankind have conceived an idea that *some kind of authority* is necessary to *superintend* the execution of the laws, and to see that they are faithfully performed; and it is by confounding this superintending authority with the official execution, that we get embarrassed about the term *executive power*.—All the parts in the government of the United States of America, that are called THE EXECUTIVE, are no other than authorities to superintend the execution of the laws; and they are so far independent of the legislative, that they know the legislative only through the laws, and cannot be controuled or directed by it through any other medium.

In what manner this superintending authority shall be

appointed or composed, is a matter that falls within the province of opinion. Some may prefer one method and some another; and in all cases, where opinion only, and not principle, is concerned, the majority of opinions forms the rule for all. There are, however, some things deducible from reason, and evinced by experience, that serve to guide our decision upon the case. The one is, never to invest any individual with extraordinary power; for besides his being tempted to misuse it, it will excite contention and commotion in the nation for the office. Secondly, never to invest power long in the hands of any number of individuals. The inconveniences that may be supposed to accompany frequent changes, are less to be feared than the danger that arises from long continuance.

I shall conclude this discourse, with offering some observations on the means of *preserving liberty*; for it is not only necessary that we establish it, but that we preserve it.

It is, in the first place, necessary that we distinguish between the means made use of to overthrow despotism, in order to prepare the way for the establishment of liberty, and the means to be used after the despotism is overthrown.

The means made use of in the first case, are justified by necessity. Those means are, in general, insurrections; for whilst the established government of despotism continues in any country, it is scarcely possible that any other means can be used. It is also certain that in the commencement of a revolution, the revolutionary party permit to themselves a *discretionary exercise of power*, regulated more by circumstances than by principle, which, were the practice to continue, liberty would never be established, or if established, would soon be overthrown. It is never to be expected in a revolution, that every man is to change his opinion at the same moment. There never yet was any truth or any principle so irresistibly obvious, that all men believed it at once. Time and reason must co-operate with each other to the final establishment of any principle; and therefore those who may happen to be first convinced, have no right to persecute others on whom conviction operates more slowly. The moral principle of revolutions is to instruct, not to destroy.

Had a constitution been established two years ago (as ought to have been done) the violences that have since desolated France, and injured the character of the revolution, would, in my opinion, have been prevented. The nation would then have been a bond of union, and every individual would have known the line of conduct he was to follow. But, instead of this, a revolutionary government, a thing without either principle or authority, was substituted in its place; virtue and crime depended upon accident; and that which was patriotism one day, became treason the next. All these things have followed from the want of a constitution; for it is the nature and intention of a constitution to *prevent governing by party*, by establishing a common principle that shall limit and controul the power and impulse of party, and that says to all parties, THUS FAR SHALT THOU GO, AND NO FARTHER. But in the absence of a constitution, men look entirely to party, and instead of principle governing party, party governs principle.

An avidity to punish is always dangerous to liberty. It leads men to stretch, to misinterpret, and to misapply even the best of laws. He that would make his own liberty secure, must guard even his enemy from oppression; for if he violates this duty, he establishes a precedent that will reach to himself.

THOMAS PAINE

AGRARIAN JUSTICE,

OPPOSED TO

AGRARIAN LAW,

AND TO

AGRARIAN MONOPOLY.
BEING A PLAN FOR MELIORATING
THE CONDITION OF MAN,
BY CREATING IN EVERY NATION,
A NATIONAL FUND,

To Pay to every Person, when arrived at the Age of
TWENTY-ONE YEARS, the Sum of FIFTEEN
POUNDS Sterling, to enable HIM or HER to begin
the World!
and also,
Ten Pounds Sterling per Annum during life to every
Person now living of the Age of FIFTY YEARS, and to
all others when they shall arrive at that Age, to enable
them to live in Old Age without Wretchedness, and
go decently out of the World.

AUTHOR'S INSCRIPTION

TO THE LEGISLATURE AND THE EXECUTIVE
DIRECTORY OF THE FRENCH REPUBLIC.

THE plan contained in this work is not adapted for any particular country alone: the principle on which it is based is general. But as the rights of man are a new study in this world, and one needing protection from priestly imposture, and the insolence of oppressions too long established, I have thought it right to place this little work under your safe-guard. When we reflect on the long and dense night in which France and all Europe have remained plunged by their governments and their priests, we must feel less surprise than grief at the bewilderment caused by the first burst of light that dispels the darkness. The eye accustomed to darkness can hardly bear at first the broad daylight. It is by usage the eye learns to see, and it is the same in passing from any situation to its opposite.

As we have not at one instant renounced all our errors, we cannot at one stroke acquire knowledge of all our rights. France has had the honour of adding to the word *Liberty* that of *Equality*; and this word signifies essentially a principal that admits of no gradation in the things to which it applies. But equality is often misunderstood, often misapplied, and often violated.

Liberty and *Property* are words expressing all those of our possessions which are not of an intellectual nature. There are two kinds of property. Firstly, natural property, or that which comes to us from the Creator of the universe,—such as the earth, air, water. Secondly, artificial or acquired property,—the invention of men. In the latter equality is impossible; for to distribute it equally it would be necesary that all should have contributed in the same proportion, which can never be the case; and this being the case, every individual would hold on to his own property, as his right share. Equality of natural property is the subject of this little essay. Every individual in the world is born therein with legitimate claims on a certain kind of property, or its equivalent.

The right of voting for persons charged with the execution of the laws that govern society is inherent in the word Liberty, and constitutes the equality of personal rights. But even if that right (of voting) were inherent in property, which I deny, the right of suffrage would still belong to all equally, because, as I have said, all individuals have legitimate birthrights in a certain species of property.

I have always considered the present Constitution of the French Republic the *best organized system* the human mind has yet produced.* But I hope my former colleagues will not be offended if I warn them of an error which has slipped into its principle. Equality of the right of suffrage is not maintained. This right is in it connected with a condition on which it ought not to depend; that is, with a proportion of a certain tax called 'direct'. The dignity of suffrage is thus lowered; and, in placing it in the scale with an inferior thing, the enthusiasm that right is capable of inspiring is diminished. It is impossible to find any equivalent counterpoise for the right of suffrage, because it is alone worthy to be its own basis, and cannot thrive as a graft, or an appendage.

Since the Constitution was established we have seen two conspiracies stranded,—that of Babeuf,* and that of some obscure personages who decorate themselves with the despicable name of 'royalists.'* The defect in principle of the Constitution was the origin of Babeuf's conspiracy. He availed himself of the resentment caused by this flaw, and instead of seeking a remedy by legitimate and constitutional means, or proposing some measure useful to society, the conspirators did their best to renew disorder and confusion, and constituted themselves personally into a Directory, which is formally destructive of election and representation. They were, in fine, extravagant enough to suppose that society, occupied with its domestic affairs, would blindly yield to them a directorship usurped by violence.

The conspiracy of Babeuf was followed in a few months by that of the royalists, who foolishly flattered themselves with the notion of doing great things by feeble or foul means. They counted on all the discontented, from whatever cause, and tried to rouse, in their turn, the class of people who had been following the others. But these new chiefs acted as if they thought society had nothing more at heart than to maintain courtiers, pensioners, and all their train, under the contemptible title of royalty. My little essay will disabuse them, by showing that society is aiming at a very different end,—maintaining itself.

We all know or should know, that the time during which a revolution is proceeding is not the time when its resulting advantages can be enjoyed. But had Babeuf and his accomplices taken into consideration the condition of France under this constitution, and compared it with what it was under the tragical revolutionary government, and during the execrable reign of Terror,* the rapidity of the alteration must have appeared to them very striking and astonishing. Famine has been replaced by abundance, and by the well-founded hope of a near and increasing prosperity.

As for the defect in the Constitution, I am fully convinced that it will be rectified constitutionally, and this step is indispensable; for so long as it continues it will inspire the hopes and furnish the means of conspirators; and for the rest, it is regrettable that a Constitution so wisely organized should err so much in its principle. This fault exposes it to other dangers which will make themselves felt. Intriguing candidates will go about among those who have not the means to pay the direct tax and pay it for them, on condition of receiving their votes. Let us maintain inviolably equality in the sacred right of suffrage: public security can never have a basis more solid. Salut et Fraternité.

Your former colleague.

THOMAS PAINE.

PREFACE

THE *following little Piece was written in the winter of* 1795 *and* '96; *and, as I had not determined whether to publish it during the present war,* * *or to wait till the commencement of a peace, it has lain by me, without alteration or addition, from the time it was written.*

What has determined me to publish it now is, a Sermon, preached by WATSON, *Bishop of Landaff.* * *Some of my readers will recollect, that this Bishop wrote a book, intitled,* An Apology for the Bible, *in answer to my* Second Part of the Age of Reason. *I procured a copy of his book, and he may depend upon hearing from me on that subject.*

At the end of the Bishop's book is a list of the Works he has written, among which is the Sermon alluded to; it is intitled,

'THE WISDOM AND GOODNESS OF GOD, IN HAVING MADE BOTH RICH AND POOR; *with an Appendix, containing* REFLECTIONS ON THE PRESENT STATE OF ENGLAND AND FRANCE.'

The error contained in the title of this Sermon, determined me to publish my Agrarian Justice. *It is wrong to say that God made* Rich *and* Poor; *he made only* Male *and* Female; *and he gave them the earth for their inheritance.* *

     *

*   *   *   *   *
*   *   *   *   *
*   *   *   *   *
*   *   *   *   *
*   *   *   *   *

Instead of preaching to encourage one part of mankind in insolence   *   *   *   *
   *   *   *   *   *
   *   *   *   *   *
   *   *   *   *   *it would*

be better that Priests employed their time to render the general condition of man less miserable them it is. Practical religion consists in doing good; and the only way of serving God is, that of endeavouring to make his creation happy. All preaching that has not this for its object, is nonsense and hypocrisy.

THOMAS PAINE

AGRARIAN JUSTICE,

OPPOSED TO AGRARIAN LAW,
AND TO AGRARIAN MONOPOLY.*

BEING A PLAN FOR MELIORATING
THE CONDITION OF MAN, &c.

To preserve the benefits of what is called civilized life, and to remedy, at the same time, the evil it has produced, ought to be considered as one of the first objects of reformed legislation.

Whether that state that is proudly, perhaps erroneouly, called civilization, has most promoted or most injured the general happiness of man, is a question that may be strongly contested.—On one side, the spectator is dazzled by splendid appearances; on the other, he is shocked by extremes of wretcheness; both of which he has erected. The most affluent and the most miserable of the human race are to be found in the countries that are called civilized.

To understand what the state of society ought to be, it is necessary to have some idea of the natural and primitive state of man; such as it is at this day among the Indians of North America. There is not, in that state, any of those spectacles of human misery which poverty and want present to our eyes, in all the towns and streets of Europe. Poverty, therefore, is a thing created by that which is called civilized life. It exists not in the natural state. On the other hand, the natural state is without those advantages which flow from Agriculture, Arts, Science, and Manufactures.

The life of an Indian is a continual holiday, compared with the poor of Europe; and, on the other hand, it appears to be abject when compared to the rich. Civilization, therefore, or that which is so called, has operated, two ways, to make one part of society more affluent, and the other part more wretched, than would have been the lot of either in a natural state.

It is always possible to go from the natural to the civilized state, but it is never possible to go from the civilized to the natural state. The reason is, that man, in a natural state, subsisting by hunting, requires ten times the quantity of land* to range over, to procure himself sustenance, than would support him in a civilized state, where the earth is cultivated. When therefore a country becomes populous by the additional aids of cultivation, arts, and science, there is a necessity of preserving things in that state; because without it, there cannot be sustenance for more, perhaps, than a tenth part of its inhabitants. The thing therefore now to be done, is, to remedy the evils, and preserve the benefits, that have arisen to society, by passing from the natural to that which is called the civilized state.

Taking then the matter up on this ground, the first principle of civilization ought to have been, and ought still to be, that the condition of every person born into the world, after a state of civilization commences, ought not to be worse than if he had been born before that period.* But the fact is, that the condition of millions, in every country in Europe, is far worse than if they had been born before civilization began, or had been born among the Indians of North America of the present day. I will shew how this fact has happened.

It is a position not to be controverted, that the earth, in its natural uncultivated state, was, and ever would have continued to be, the COMMON PROPERTY OF THE HUMAN RACE.* In that state every man would have been born to property. He would have been a joint life-proprietor with the rest in the property of the soil, and in all its natural productions, vegetable and animal.

But the earth, in its natural state, as before said, is capable of supporting but a small number of inhabitants compared with what it is capable of doing in a cultivated state. And as it is impossible to separate the improvement made by cultivation, from the earth itself, upon which that improvement is made, the idea of landed property arose from that inseparable connection; but it is nevertheless true, that it is the value of the improvement only, and not the earth itself, that is individual property. Every proprietor therefore of cultivated land, owes to the community a *ground-rent*;* for I know no better term to express the idea by, for the land which he holds: and it is from this ground rent that the fund proposed in this plan is to issue.

It is deducible, as well from the nature of the thing, as from all the histories transmitted to us, that the idea of landed property commenced with cultivation, and that there was no such thing as landed property before that time. It could not exist in the first state of man, that of hunters. It did not exist in the second state, that of shepherds: Neither Abraham, Isaac, Jacob, nor Job, so far as the history of the Bible may be credited in probable things, were owners of land.* Their property consisted, as is always enumerated, in flocks and herds, and they travelled with them from place to place. The frequent contentions, at that time, about the use of a well* in the dry country of Arabia, where those people lived, shew also there was no landed property. It was not admitted that land could be located as property.

There could be no such thing as landed property originally. Man did not make the earth, and, though he had a natural right to *occupy* it, he had no right to *locate as his property* in perpetuity any part of it: neither did the Creator of the earth open a land-office, from whence the first title-deeds should issue. From whence then arose the idea of landed property? I answer as before, that when cultivation began, the idea of landed property began with it, from the impossibility of separating the improvement made by cultivation from the earth itself, upon which that improvement was made. The value of the improvement so far exceeded the value of the natural earth, at that time, as to absorb it; till, in the end, the common right of all became confounded into the cultivated right of the individual. But they are, nevertheless, distinct species of rights, and will continue to be so as long as the earth endures.

It is only by tracing things to their origin that we can gain rightful ideas of them, and it is by gaining such ideas that we discover the boundary that divides right from wrong, and which teaches every man to know his own. I have

intitled this tract *Agrarian Justice*, to distinguish it from
Agrarian Law. Nothing could be more unjust than Agrarian
Law in a country improved by cultivation; for though every
man, as an inhabitant of the earth, is a joint proprietor of it
in its natural state, it does not follow that he is a joint
proprietor of cultivated earth. The additional value made by
cultivation, after the system was admitted, became the property of those who did it, or who inherited it from them, or
who purchased it. It had originally an owner. Whilst, therefore, I advocate the right, and interest myself in the hard
case of all those who have been thrown out of their natural
inheritance by the introduction of the system of landed
property, I equally defend the right of the possessor to the
part which is his.

Cultivation is, at least, one of the greatest natural improvements ever made by human invention. It has given to created
earth a tenfold value. But the landed monopoly, that began
with it, has produced the greatest evil. It has dispossessed
more than half the inhabitants of every nation of their
natural inheritance, without providing for them, as ought to
have been done, as an indemnification for that loss, and has
thereby created a species of poverty and wrechedness that
did not exist before.

In advocating the case of the persons thus dispossessed, it
is a right and not a charity that I am pleading for. But it is
that kind of right, which, being neglected at first, could not
be brought forward afterwards, till heaven had opened the
way by a revolution in the system of government. Let us
then do honour to revolutions by justice, and give currency
to their principles by blessings.

Having thus, in a few words, opened the merits of the
case, I proceed to the plan I have to propose, which is,

*To create a National Fund, out of which there shall be paid to every
person, when arrived at the age of twenty-one years, the sum of
Fifteen Pounds sterling, as a compensation in part, for the loss of his
or her natural inheritance, by the introduction of the system of landed
property.*

AND ALSO,

The sum of Ten Pounds per annum, *during life, to every person now living, of the age of fifty years, and to all others as they shall arrive at that age.*

MEANS BY WHICH THE FUND IS TO BE CREATED.

I have already established the principle, namely, that the earth, in its natural uncultivated state, was, and ever would have continued to be, the COMMON PROPERTY OF THE HUMAN RACE—that in that state, every person would have been born to property—and that the system of landed property, by its inseparable connection with cultivation, and with what is called civilized life, has absorbed the property of all those whom it dispossessed, without providing, as ought to have been done, an indemnification for that loss.

The fault, however, is not in the present possessors. No complaint is intended, or ought to be alleged against them, unless they adopt the crime by opposing justice. The fault is in the system, and it has stolen imperceptibly upon the world, aided afterwards by the Agrarian law of the sword. But the fault can be made to reform itself by successive generations, without diminishing or deranging the property of any of the present possessors, and yet the operation of the fund can commence, and be in full activity, the first year of its establishment, or soon after, as I shall shew.

It is proposed that the payments, as already stated, be made to every person, rich or poor. It is best to make it so, to prevent invidious distinctions. It is also right it should be so, because it is in lieu of the natural inheritance, which, as a right, belongs to every man, over and above the property he may have created or inherited from those who did. Such persons as do not choose to receive it, can throw it into the common fund.

Taking it then for granted, that no person ought to be in a worse condition when born under what is called a state of civilization, than he would have been, had he been born in a state of nature, and that civilization ought to have made, and ought still to make, provision for that purpose, it can only be done by subtracting from property, a portion equal in value to the natural inheritance it has absorbed.

Various methods may be proposed for this purpose, but that which appears to be the best, not only because it will operate without deranging any present possessors, or without interfering with the collection of taxes, or emprunts* necessary for the purpose of government and the revolution, but because it will be the least troublesome and the most effectual, and also because the subtraction will be made at a time that best admits it, which is, at the moment that property is passing by the death of one person to the possession of another. In this case, the bequether gives nothing; the receiver pays nothing. The only matter to him is, that the monopoly of natural inheritance, to which there never was a right, begins to cease in his person. A generous man would not wish it to continue, and a just man will rejoice to see it abolished.

My state of health* prevents my making sufficient enquiries with respect to the doctrine of probabilities, whereon to found calculations with such degrees of certainty as they are capable of. What, therefore, I offer on this head is more the result of observation and reflection, than of received information; but I believe it will be found to agree sufficiently enough with fact.

In the first place, taking twenty-one years as the epoch of maturity, all the property of a nation, real and personal, is always in the possession of persons above that age. It is then necessary to know as a datum of calculation, the average of years which persons above that age will live. I take this average to be about thirty years, for though many persons will live forty, fifty, or sixty years after the age of twenty-one years, others will die much sooner, and some in every year of that time.

Taking then thirty years as the average of time, it will give, without any material variation, one way or other, the average of time in which the whole property or capital of a nation, or a sum equal thereto, will have passed through one entire revolution in descent that is, will have gone by deaths to new possessors; for though, in many instances, some parts of this capital will remain forty, fifty, or sixty years in

the possession of one person, other parts will have revolved
two or three times before that thirty years expire, which will
bring it to that average; for were one half the capital of a
nation to revolve twice in thirty years, it would produce the
same fund as if the whole revolved once.

Taking, then, thirty years as the average of time in which
the whole capital of a nation, or a sum equal thereto, will
revolve once, the thirtieth part thereof will be the sum that
will revolve every year, that is, will go by deaths to new
possessors; and this last sum being thus known, and the ratio
per cent. to be subtracted from it being determined, will give
the annual amount or income of the proposed fund, to be
applied as already mentioned.

In looking over the discourse of the English minister, Pitt,
in his opening of what is called in England, the budget, (the
scheme of finance for the year 1796,*) I find an estimate of
the national capital of that country. As this estimate of a
national capital is prepared ready to my hand, I take it as a
datum to act upon. When a calculation is made upon the
known capital of any nation, combined with its population,
it will serve as a scale for any other nation, in proportion as
its capital and population be more or less. I am the more
disposed to take this estimate of Mr Pitt, for the purpose of
shewing to that minister, upon his own calculation, how
much better money may be employed, than in wasting it, as
he has done, on the wild project of setting up Bourbon
kings.* What, in the name of Heaven, are Bourbon kings to
the people of England? It is better that the people have
bread.

Mr Pitt states the national capital of England, real and
personal, to be one thousand three hundred millions sterling,
which is about one-fourth part of the national capital of
France, including Belgia.* The event of the last harvest in
each country proves that the soil of France is more productive than that of England,* and that it can better support
twenty-four or twenty-five millions of inhabitants than that
of England can seven, or seven and an half.

The 30th part of this capital of £1,300,000,000 is
£43,333,333, which is the part that will revolve every year

by deaths in that country to new possessors; and the sum that will annually revolve in France in the proportion of four to one, will be about one hundred and seventy-three millions sterling. From this sum of £43,333,333 annually revolving, is to be subtracted the value of the natural inheritance absorbed in it, which perhaps, in fair justice, cannot be taken at less, and ought not to be taken for more, than a tenth part.

It will always happen, that of the property thus revolving by deaths every year, part will descend in a direct line to sons and daughters, and the other part collaterally,* and the proportion will be found to be about three to one; that is, about thirty millions of the above sum will descend to direct heirs, and the remaining sum of £13,333,333 to more distant relations, and part to strangers.

Considering then that man is always related to society, that relationship will become comparatively greater in proportion as the next of kin is more distant: It is therefore consistent with civilization to say, that where there are no direct heirs, society shall be heir to a part over and above the tenth part *due* to society. If this additional part be from five to ten or twelve per cent. in proportion as the next of kin be nearer or more remote, so as to average with the escheats* that may fall, which ought always to go to society and not to the government, an addition of ten per cent. more, the produce from the annual sum of £43,333,333 will be,

From 30,000,000	at ten per cent.	3,000,000
From 13,333,333	at ten pr. ct. with the addition of ten per cent. more }	2,666,666
£43,333,333		£5,666,666

Having thus arrived at the annual amount of the proposed fund, I come, in the next place, to speak of the population proportioned to this fund, and to compare it with uses to which the fund is to be applied.

The population (I mean that of England) does not exceed seven millions and a half, and the number of persons above the age of fifty will in that case be about four hundred thousand. There would not however be more than that number that would accept the proposed ten pounds sterling per annum, though they would be entitled to it. I have no idea it would be accepted by many persons who had a yearly income of two or three hundred pounds sterling. But as we often see instances of rich people falling into sudden poverty, even at the age of sixty, they would always have the right of drawing all the arrears due to them.—Four millions, therefore, of the above annual sum of £5,666,666, will be required for four hundred thousand aged persons, at ten pounds sterling each.

I come now to speak of the persons annually arriving at twenty-one years of age. If all the persons who died were above the age of twenty-one years, the number of persons annually arriving at that age, must be equal to the annual number of deaths to keep the population stationary. But the greater part die under the age of twenty-one, and therefore the number of persons annually arriving at twenty-one, will be less than half the number of deaths. The whole number of deaths upon a population of seven millions and a half, will be about 220,000 annually. The number arriving at twenty-one years of age will be about 100,000. The whole number of these will not receive the proposed fifteen pounds, for the reasons already mentioned, though, as in the former case, they would be entitled to it. Admitting then that a tenth part declined receiving it, the amount would stand thus:

Fund annually		£5,666,666
To 400,000 aged persons at £10 each	£4,000,000	
To 90,000 persons of 21 years, 15l. ster. ea.	1,350,000	
	5,350,000	
	remains	£316,666

There are in every country a number of blind and lame persons, totally incapable of earning a livelihood. But as it will always happen that the greater number of blind persons will be among those who are above the age of fifty years, they will be provided for in that class. The remaining sum of £316,666, will provide for the lame and blind under that age, at the same rate of £10 annually for each person.

Having now gone through all the necessary calculations, and stated the particulars of the plan, I shall conclude with some observations.

It is not charity but a right—not bounty but justice, that I am pleading for. The present state of what is called civilization, is as odious as it is unjust. It is the reverse of what it ought to be, and it is necessary that a revolution should be made in it.* The contrast of affluence and wretchedness continually meeting and offending the eye, is like dead and living bodies chained together. Though I care as little about riches as any man, I am a friend to riches because they are capable of good. I care not how affluent some may be, provided that none be miserable in consequence of it. But it is impossible to enjoy affluence with the felicity it is capable of being enjoyed, whilst so much misery is mingled in the scene. The sight of the misery, and the unpleasant sensations it suggests, which, though they may be suffocated, cannot be extinguished, are a greater draw-back upon the felicity of affluence than the proposed 10 per cent. upon property is worth. He that would not give the one to get rid of the other, has no charity, even for himself.

There are, in every country, some magnificent charities established by individuals. It is, however, but little that any individual can do, when the whole extent of the misery to be relieved be considered. He may satisfy his conscience, but not his heart. He may give all that he has, and that all will relieve but little. It is only by organizing civilization upon such principles as to act like a system of pullies, that the whole weight of misery can be removed.

The plan here proposed will reach the whole. It will immediately relieve and take out of view three classes of wretchedness. The blind, the lame, and the aged poor; and it will furnish the rising generation with means to prevent their becoming poor; and it will do this, without deranging or interfering with any national measures. To shew that this will be the case, it is sufficient to observe, that the operation and effect of the plan will, in all cases, be the same, as if every individual were *voluntarily* to make his will, and dispose of his property, in the manner here proposed.

But it is justice and not charity, that is the principle of the plan. In all great cases it is necessary to have a principle more universally active than charity; and with respect to justice, it ought not to be left to the choice of detached individuals, whether they will do justice or not. Considering then the plan on the ground of justice, it ought to be the act of the whole, growing spontaneously out of the principles of the revolution, and the reputation of it to be national and not individual.

A plan upon this principle would benefit the revolution, by the energy that springs from the consciousness of justice. It would multiply also the national resources; for property, like vegetation, encreases by off-sets.* When a young couple begin the world, the difference is exceedingly great, whether they begin with nothing or with fifteen pounds a-piece. With this aid they could buy a cow, and implements to cultivate a few acres of land; and instead of becoming burthens upon society, which is always the case, where children are produced faster than they can be fed, would be put in the way of becoming useful and profitable citizens. The national domains also would sell the better, if pecuniary aids were provided to cultivate them in small lots.

It is the practice of what has unjustly obtained the name of civilization (and the practice merits not to be called either charity or policy) to make some provision for persons becoming poor and wretched, only at the time they become so.— Would it not, even as a matter of economy, be far better, to devise means to prevent their becoming poor. This can best be done, by making every person, when arrived at the age of twenty-one years, an inheritor of something to begin with. The rugged face of society, chequered with the extremes of affluence and of want, proves that some extraordinary violence has been committed upon it, and calls on justice for redress. The great mass of the poor, in all countries, are become an hereditary race, and it is next to impossible for them to get out of that state of themselves. It ought also to be observed, that this is mass increases in all countries that are called civilized. More persons fall annually into it, than get out of it.

Though in a plan, in which justice and humanity are the foundation-principles, interest ought not to be admitted into the calculation, yet it is always of advantage to the establishment of any plan, to shew that it is beneficial as a matter of interest. The success of any proposed plan, submitted to public consideration, must finally depend on the numbers interested in supporting it, united with the justice of its principles.

The plan here proposed will benefit all, without injuring any. It will consolidate the interest of the republic with that of the individual. To the numerous class dispossessed of their natural inheritance by the system of landed property, it will be an act of national justice. To persons dying possessed of moderate fortunes, it will operate as a tontine to their children, more beneficial than the sum of money paid into the fund: and it will give to the accumulation of riches a degree of security, that none of the old governments of Europe, now tottering on their foundations, can give.

I do not suppose that more than one family in ten, in any of the countries of Europe, has, when the head of the family dies, a clear property left of five hundred pounds sterling. To all such, the plan is advantageous. That property would pay fifty pounds into the fund, and if there were only two children under age, they would receive fifteen pounds each (thirty pounds) on coming of age, and be entitled to ten pounds a year after fifty. It is from the over-grown acquisition of property that the fund will support itself; and I know that the possessors of such property in England, though they would eventually be benefited by the protection of nine-tenths of it, will exclaim against the plan. But, without entering into any enquiry how they came by that property, let them recollect that they have been the advocates of this war, and that Mr Pitt has already laid on more new taxes to be raised annually upon the people of England, and that for supporting the despotism of Austria and the Bourbons,

against the liberties of France, than would annually pay all
the sums proposed in this plan.

I have made the calculations, stated in this plan, upon
what is called personal, as well as upon landed property.
The reason for making it upon land is already explained;
and the reason for taking personal property into the calculation, is equally well founded, though on a different principle.
Land, as before said, is the free gift of the Creator in
common to the human race. Personal property is the *effect
of Society*; and it is as impossible for an individual to acquire
personal property without the aid of Society, as it is for him
to make land originally. Separate an individual from society,
and give him an island or a continent to possess, and he
cannot acquire personal property. He cannot become rich.
So inseparably are the means connected with the end, in all
cases, that where the former do not exist, the latter cannot
be obtained. All accumulation, therefore, of personal property, beyond what a man's own hands produce, is derived to
him by living in society; and he owes, on every principle of
justice, of gratitude, and of civilization, a part of that accumulation back again to society from whence the whole came.
This is putting the matter on a general principle, and perhaps
it is best to do so; for if we examine the case minutely, it will
be found, that the accumulation of personal property is, in
many instances, the effect of paying too little for the labour
that produced it; the consequence of which is, that the
working hand perishes in old age, and the employer abounds
in affluence. It is, perhaps, impossible to proportion exactly
the price of labour to the profits it produces; and it will also
be said, as an apology for injustice, that were a workman to
receive an increase of wages daily, he would not save it
against old age, nor be much the better for it in the interium.
Make, then, society the treasurer, to guard it for him in a
common fund; for it is no reason, that because he might not
make a good use of it for himself, that another shall take it.

The state of civilization that has prevailed throughout
Europe, is as unjust in its principle, as it is horrid in its
effects; and it is the consciousness of this, and the apprehension that such a state cannot continue, when once investiga-

tion begins in any country, that makes the possessors of property dread every idea of a revolution. It is the *hazard* and not the principles of a revolution that retards their progress. This being the case, it is necessary as well for the protection of property, as for the sake of justice and humanity, to form a system, that whilst it preserves one part of society from wretchedness, shall secure the other from depredation.

The superstitious awe, the enslaving reverence, that formerly surrounded affluence, is passing away in all countries, and leaving the possessor of property to the convulsion of accidents. When wealth and splendour, instead of fascinating the multitude, excite emotions of disgust; when, instead of drawing forth admiration, it is beheld as an insult upon wretchedness; when the ostentatious appearance it makes, serves to call the right of it in question, the case of property becomes critical, and it is only in a system of justice that the possessor can contemplate security.

To remove the danger, it is necessary to remove the antipathies, and this can only be done by making property productive of a national blessing, extending to every individual. When the riches of one man above another shall increase the national fund in the same proportion; when it shall be seen that the prosperity of that fund depends on the prosperity of individuals; when the more riches a man acquires, the better it shall be for the general mass; it is then that antipathies will cease, and property be placed on the permanent basis of national interest and protection.

I have no property in France to become subject to the plan I propose. What I have, which is not much, is in the United States of America.* But I will pay one hundred pounds sterling towards this fund in France, the instant it shall be established; and I will pay the same sum in England, whenever a similar establishment shall take place in that country.

A revolution in the state of civilization, is the necessary companion of revolutions in the system of government. If a revolution in any country be from bad to good, or from good to bad, the state of what is called civilization in that country, must be made conformable thereto, to give that revolution effects. Despotic government supports itself by abject civilization, in which debasement of the human mind, and wretchedness in the mass of the people, are the chief criterians. Such governments consider man merely as an animal; that the exercise of intellectual faculty is not his privilege; *that he has nothing to do with the laws, but to obey them*;[1] and they politically depend more upon breaking the spirit of the people by poverty, than they fear enraging it by desperation.

It is a revolution in the state of civilization, that will give perfection to the revolution of France. Already the conviction, that government, by representation, is the true system of government, is spreading itself fast in the world. The reasonableness of it can be seen by all. The justness of it makes itself felt even by its opposers. But when a system of government, shall be so organized, that not a man or woman born in the republic, but shall inherit some means of beginning the world, and see before them the certainty of escaping the miseries that under other governments accompany old age, the revolution of France will have an advocate and ally in the heart of all nations.

An army of principles will penetrate where an army of soldiers cannot—It will succeed where diplomatic management would fail—It is neither the Rhine, the Channel, nor the Ocean, that can arrest its progress—It will march on the horizon of the world, and it will conquer.

THOMAS PAINE

[1] Expression of Horsley, an English Bishop, in the English parliament.*

Means for carrying the proposed Plan into Execution, and to render it at the same time conductive to the public Interest.

I.

Each canton shall elect in its primary assemblies, three persons, as commissioners for that canton, who shall take cognizance, and keep a register of all matters happening in that canton, conformable to the charter that shall be established by law, for carrying this plan into execution.

II.

The law shall fix the manner in which the property of deceased persons shall be ascertained.

III.

When the amount of the property of any deceased person shall be ascertained, the principal heir to that property, or the eldest of the co-heirs, if of lawful age, or if under age, the person authorized by the will of the deceased to represent him, or them, shall give bond to the commissioners of the canton, to pay the said tenth part thereof within the space of one year, in four equal quarterly payments, or sooner, at the choice of the payers. One-half of the whole property shall remain as security until the bond be paid off.

IV.

The bond shall be registered in the office of the commissioners of the canton, and the original bonds shall be deposited in the national bank at Paris. The bank shall publish every quarter of a year the amount of the bonds in its possession, and also the bonds that shall have been paid off, or what parts thereof, since the last quarter publication.

V.

The national bank shall issue bank notes upon the security of the bonds in its possession. The notes so issued, shall be applied to pay the pensions of aged persons, and the compensations to persons arriving at twenty-one years of age.—It is both reasonable and generous to suppose, that persons not under immediate necessity, will suspend their right of drawing on the fund, until it acquire, as it will do, a greater degree of ability. In this case, it is proposed, that an honorary register be kept in each canton, of the names of the persons thus suspending that right, at least during the present war.

VI.

As the inheritors of property must always take up their bonds in four quarterly payments, or sooner if they choose, there will always be numeraire arriving at the bank after the expiration of the first quarter, to exchange for the bank notes that shall be brought in.

VII.

The bank notes being thus got into circulation, upon the best of all possible security, that of actual property, to more than four times the amount of the bonds upon which the notes are issued, and with numeraire continually arriving at the bank to exchange or pay them off whenever they shall be presented for that purpose, they will acquire a permanent value in all parts of the republic. They can therefore be received in payment of taxes or emprunts, equal to numeraire, because the government can always receive numeraire for them at the bank.

VIII.

It will be necessary that the payment of the ten per cent. be made in numeraire for the first year, from the establishment of the plan. But after the expiration of the first year, the inheritors of property may pay the ten per cent. either in bank notes issued upon the fund, or in numeraire. If the payments be in numeraire, it will lie as a deposit at the bank, to be exchanged for a quantity of notes equal to that amount; and if in notes issued upon the fund, it will cause a demand upon the fund equal thereto; and thus the operation of the plan will create means to carry itself into execution.

EXPLANATORY NOTES

ABBREVIATIONS

All references to Paine's writings not contained in this collection are either to *The Collected Works of Thomas Paine*, ed. P. S. Foner, (Secaucus, NJ, 1948), 2 Volumes, and are cited by the volume number (I or II), followed by the page; or to Moncure Conway, *Works of Thomas Paine*, 4 volumes, (New York, 1894–6), given as Conway, followed by the volume number and page.

Aldridge—A. Owen Aldridge, *Thomas Paine's American Ideology* (Cranbury, NJ, 1984).

Bailyn—Bernard Bailyn, *The Ideological Origins of the American Revolution* (Cambridge, Mass. 1967).

Doyle—W. Doyle, *The Oxford History of the French Revolution* (Oxford, 1989).

Erskine May—Thomas Erskine May, *A Treatise upon the Law, Privileges, Proceedings, and usages of Parliament* (London, 1844).

Goodwin—A. Goodwin, *The Friends of Liberty: The English democratic movement in the age of the French Revolution* (London, 1979).

Greene and Pole—J. P. Greene and J. R. Pole, *The Blackwell Encyclopedia of the American Revolution* (Oxford, 1991).

Hawke—David Freeman Hawke, *Paine* (New York, 1974).

Jones—Colin Jones, *The Longman Companion to the French Revolution* (London, 1988).

Langford (1)—Paul Langford, *A Polite and Commercial People: England 1727–1783, The New Oxford History of England* (Oxford, 1989).

Langford (2)—Paul Langford, *Public Life and the Propertied Englishman* (Oxford, 1991).

Namier and Brooke—*The History of Parliament: House of Commons 1754–1790*, ed. Sir L. Namier and J. Brooke, Volume 1 (London, 1964).

Reflections—Edmund Burke, *Reflections on the Revolution in France* (1790). Page references are given to four current editions of the *Reflections* using the following abbreviations:

   M.   ed. L. G. Mitchell (World's Classics, Oxford, 1993);

Wks. ed. L. G. Mitchell (Oxford University Press, 1991) being
      volume VIII of *The Writings and Speeches of Edmund
      Burke*, General Editor, Paul Langford.

O'B   ed. Conor Cruise O'Brien (Harmondsworth, 1968).

P.   ed. J. G. A. Pocock (Indianapolis, 1987).

Sinclair—Sir John Sinclair, *The History of the Public Revenue*
      (London, 1785).

COMMON SENSE

Thomson: James Thomson, *Liberty, A Poem* (1736), iv. 636–
7. Thomson was also the author of the words to *Rule Britannia*
(1740).

3 *laying a Country desolate . . . Sword*: after Ezek. 30: 6–8.

9 *felo de se*: one who deliberately puts an end to his own
existence, or commits any unlawful or malicious act, the
consequence of which is his own death.

10 *Charles the First*: (1600–49), king of England, tried and
executed by Parliament during the English Civil War.

as in Turkey: for colonial opposition thought, Turkey was the
epitome of despotism . . . long before the Revolution the
colonists were habituated to conceive of 'the difference between free and enslaved countries' as 'the difference between
England and Turkey.' (*Boston Gazette or Country Journal, 19
May 1755*). Bailyn, 64.

11 *from whom the children of Israel . . . custom*: 1 Sam. 8: 4–22.

12 *Gideon and the prophet Samuel, expressly . . . kings*: Judg. 8: 22–
3; 1 Sam. 8: 4–7.

Render unto Caesar . . . Caesar's: Matt. 22: 21; Mark 12: 17;
Luke 20: 25 (adapted).

Rule thou . . . son's son: Judg. 8: 22.

I will not . . . RULE OVER YOU: Judg. 8: 23.

13 *Behold thou . . . other nations*: 1 Sam. 8: 5.

But the thing . . . reign over them: 1 Sam. 8: 6–9.

14 *And Samuel told . . .* THE LORD WILL NOT HEAR YOU IN THAT
DAY: 1 Sam. 8: 10–18.

Nevertheless the People . . . fight our battles: 1 Sam. 8: 19.

I will call unto the Lord . . . TO ASK A KING: 1 Sam. 12: 17–19

15 *an ass for a lion*: the allusion is to the fable (from Aesop) in which the ass puts on a lion's skin but is betrayed by his braying. See also Joseph Addison, *Spectator* (1709) No. 13, pa. 4, and Tobias Smollett, *Roderick Random* ch. 54.

that your children ... ours for ever: Ezek. 38: 25. Compare Bill of Rights (1 William and Mary, s.2, c.2, viii) 'The lords spiritual and temporal, and commons, do, in the name of all the people aforesaid, most humbly and faithfully submit *themselves, their heirs and posterities for ever ...*' The passage is cited in Burke's *Reflections* (M. 20; Wks. 70; O'B. 103–4; P. 17–18), and is taken up by Paine in *Rights of Man*; see below.

16 *Mahomet like*: Paine's reference is obscure. It implies that Muhammad wrote the Koran solely in order to set up his own right to rule. This is, for Paine, an uncharacteristically intolerant view of another religion—although it was common for tolerance to extend only to forms of Christianity.

William the Conqueror: William I (1027–87), king of England from 1066; natural son of Robert II of Normandy. invaded England in 1066 following the succession of Harold (1022–66), Earl of Wessex, and defeated him at the battle of Hastings. Paine's description follows Voltaire's *General History of the States of Europe* (1754), 163.

Saul was by lot: there is no remit for this claim in 1 Sam. 10: 23–4.

18 *York and Lancaster*: the Wars of the Roses (1455–85).

Henry ... and Edward ... recalled to succeed him: Henry VI (1421–71), king of England (1429–71). imprisoned in the Tower of London 1465–70, restored in 1470, but imprisoned again by Edward IV in 1471 and murdered there. Edward IV (1442–83), proclaimed himself king of England in 1461. imprisoned by the Archbishop of York (1469) but released. In 1470 he was forced to flee to Holland, but he returned to oust Henry VI in 1471.

Henry the Seventh: Henry VII (1457–1509), crowned king of England after the defeat and death of Richard III at the battle of Bosworth in 1485. Head of the house of Lancaster from 1471, he married Elizabeth of York on obtaining the English crown, so bringing the dynastic conflict to an end.

18–19 *that he may ... fight our battles*: 1 Sam. 8: 20

19 *Sir William Meredith*: Sir William Meredith (d. 1790), third

baronet, M.P. Wigan 1754–61, Liverpool 1761–80. Of Meredith's various pamphlets and parliamentary speeches it is likely that what caught Paine's attention was Meredith's comment in *A Letter to the Earl of Chatham on the Quebec Bill* (1774), 35–6: 'If then, my lord, the Quebec Bill is founded in that first principle of all law, *the concurrence and approbation of the people*, and if its end is that for which all government ought to be established, *the happiness of the governed . . .*' It is this principle which Paine takes as definitional of republican government. Paine refers to the Quebec Act in his *Dialogue between Wolfe and Gage* (II, 49).

eight hundred thousand sterling: as established in the civil list, see Sir John Sinclair, *A History of the Public Revenue* (1785–90), iii. 71–2.

20   *Mr Pelham . . . last my time*: Henry Pelham (1695?–1754), Prime Minister 1743–54. The attributed quotation is most likely apocryphal (see Aldridge, 60).

nineteenth of April: the first armed clash between American militia and British troops at Lexington on 19 April 1775.

21   *Hanover's last war*: the Seven Years War, 1756–63, involved a colonial conflict between Britain, France, and Spain, conducted in North America (especially Canada), the West Indies, West Africa, and India, and a war over Silesia in which Prussia and Britain united for the protection of Hanover against France, Austria, Saxony, and Sweden.

22   *asserted in Parliament . . . each other*: in the debates on the repeal of the Stamp Act it was asserted that the colonies were independent of each other but each subordinate to the Parliament or the Crown *Parliamentary History* 1765, XVI, cols. 199–201.

23   *free port*: Paine uses the term for a situation where merchants would be free to import from or export to where they pleased. Under the various Navigation Acts passed between 1651 and 1673 colonial merchants were required to export only to England and only in English ships. For the few items they were allowed to export to other countries directly they had to pay duty at colonial ports.

25   *Boston, that seat of wretchedness . . . fury of both armies*: Boston was occupied by British troops from April 1775, and from 10 May colonial forces were encamped around Boston. The Battle of Bunker Hill on 17 June 1775 left the situation

largely unchanged, but high casualties persuaded the British forces against further direct assaults on colonial posts. The inhabitants of Boston were, as a result, occupied by a foreign force and would have been potential casualties should colonial forces attempt to seize the town.

27 *Milton . . . pierced so deep*: John Milton, *Paradise Lost* iv. 98–9. The words are Satan's!

Witness Denmark and Sweden: Paine's source is Voltaire's *History of Charles XII* and the reference to the petitioning movements concerns the reigns of Charles XII of Sweden and Frederick IV of Denmark. The citation of Sweden and Denmark as cases of corrupted republics was a commonplace in republican writing, see Bailyn, 64–5.

stamp-act: the Stamp Act of 1765 imposed a series of duties on the Colonies on playing cards, dice, newspapers, and a wide range of legal and business documents. The act provoked an imperial crisis by raising the cry amongst the colonies of 'no taxation, without representation'. The act was repealed by the Rockingham Administration in 1766 after widespread colonial opposition and non-compliance.

28 *North*: Frederick North (1732–92), second Earl of Guilford, known as Lord North, Prime Minister 1770–82, and thus regarded by many of his contemporaries as responsible for the outbreak of the American war.

a Bunker-hill price for law, as for land: 'a Bunker-hill price' means a very high price for little gain. It derives from the Battle of Bunker Hill, 17 June 1775, which was a bloody, inconclusive battle fought near Boston, in which American troops were dislodged from their position overlooking the occupied town. Very high casualties were inflicted on the British, which ensured that other emplacements were not attacked, and the British eventually evacuated Boston (17 March 1776). The battle was actually fought on the nearby Breed's Hill, above Charlestown.

32 *to sit———and to choose*: the space was left in each of the first three editions. Paine possibly intended to indicate the duration of Congress.

join Lucifer in his revolt: note the contrast between this claim and that in the quotation from Milton in the note to p. 27.

33 *Magna Charta*: the 'Great Charter' imposed by rebellious

barons on King John of England in 1215, designed to prohibit arbitrary royal acts by declaring a body of defined law and custom which the king must respect.

34   *Dragonetti on Virtue and Rewards*: Jacinto Dragonetti, *A Treatise on Virtues and Rewards*, dual Italian and English text (London, 1769). The first sentence comes from p. 155, the second adapts an earlier sentence on p. 153–5: 'Next to the virtue of sovereigns, his might deserve attention, who should discover a mode of government that contained the greatest sum of individual happiness, with the fewest wants of contribution.'

Massanello: Masaniello, a corruption of Tommaso Aniello, a fisherman's son who led a revolt in Naples in July 1647 and ruled for nine days. The grievances concerned excessive taxation and the seizure of property. Masaniello was betrayed and shot.

35   *stirred up the Indians and Negroes*: American Indians played a relatively small but complex role in the Revolution, and they were most active after the publication of *Common Sense*. In June 1776 Cherokee Indians attacked Carolina rebels, but no other tribes joined them, and in 1777 a combined force of loyalists and Indians took part in the St Leger offensive in the North. However, Indians sensed that the new republic might be less restrained in appropriating their lands than the colonial government had been. Lord Dunmore, Governor of Virginia, in November 1775, called upon slaves in Virginia to rebel against their revolutionary masters and promised them their freedom if they joined the British forces.

36   *Britain would never suffer an American man of war*: that is, the British government would not tolerate an independent American navy.

37   *Britain is oppressed ... four millions interest*: 'the Debt climbed to dizzy heights during the Seven Years War and the American War, from less than 80 million in 1757 to more than 240 million in 1783. In the same period the sum required annually to sevice the Debt rose from £2,735,925 to £9,406,406.' Langford (1), 640–1.

The first and second editions: this paragraph and the figures which follow were added in the third edition.

Entic's naval history: John Entick, *A New Naval History, or the Compleat View of the British Marine, in which the*

*ROYAL NAVY and the MERCHANT'S SERVICE
are traced through all their PERIODS and different
BRANCHES* (London, 1757), lvi.

38 *Mr Burchett*: Josiah Burchett (1666?–1746), secretary of the
admiralty, 1698–1742.

39 *Captain Death*: Captain William Death led the privateer *Terrible* (fitted out at Execution Dock, and including Lieutenant
Devil and Mr Ghost the ship's surgeon!) in an engagement
with two French privateers in December 1757 off the West
Indies, and fought a furious engagement resulting in the loss
of all but twenty-six of the crew of two hundred. A public
subscription was immediately raised for Death's widow. Smollett, *Continuation of the Complete History of England* (London,
1760), ii. 182–3.

Shipbuilding is America's greatest pride: because of the lower
cost of timber, colonial ship-builders were used extensively
by British merchants. The industry produced about £240,000
sterling worth of shipping each year; the largest producer,
Massachusetts, produced an annual average of 7,664 tons a
year between 1769 and 1771.

40 *Tories*: the partisan labels of British politics from the exclusion crisis (1679–83) and from the reign of Queen Anne
(1702–14) were appropriated by the colonists to describe
themselves and their opponents. The labels were inapt since,
unlike in England, both sides of the controversy accepted the
right to resist arbitrary government. The 'Tories', however,
refused to countenance the idea of concerted, organized opposition to British authority.

42 *non-age*: nonage, the condition of being under age, a period of
legal infancy or minority.

43 *Continental Charter*: i.e. a form of association between the
various states governing their common affairs.

44 *Associators petition . . . House of Assembly of Pennsylvania*: the
militia (known formally as the Military Association, and its
members as the Associators) in Pennsylvania in 1775 peti-
tioned the Assembly for the right to elect their officers, for
the right to vote, irrespective of other qualifications, and on
the equal participation of the wealthier classes of the community. See *Pennsylvanian Magazine or American Monthly
Museum* (edited by Paine), 1775, supplement, pp. 611–15, for
the Rules and Regulations for the Better Government of

the Military Association in Pennsylvania. The Pennsylvania Assembly, through an inequitable distribution of seats, gave control to the commercial farming counties around Philadelphia (dominated by Quakers), and under-represented the back county to the West.

Mr Cornwall: Charles Wolfram Cornwall (1735–89), Lord of the Treasury, 1774–80. Cornwall's response is recorded in *Parliamentary History*, XVIII, col. 646, 1775.

Burgh's Political Disquisitions: James Burgh, *Political Disquisitions* (1764), vol. 1, bk. II, chs. 2–7.

47   *King's Speech*: the king's speech on the Opening of the Second Session of the Fourteenth Parliament, October 26, 1775 (*Parliamentary History*, XVIII, cols. 695–7).

48   *Sir J——n D——e*: Sir John Dalrymple, *The Address of the People of England to the Inhabitants of America* (London, 1775).

the Marquis of Rockingham's: Charles Watson-Wentworth, 2nd Marquis of Rockingham (1730–82), led the government at the time of the repeal of the Stamp Act, 1765–6.

'But,' says this writer ... 'to do any thing': Dalrymple, *Address*, 31.

49   *last war*: a reference to the colonial war against France and Spain which formed part of the Seven Years War.

50   *the value of the back lands ... limits of Canada*: the Quebec Act (1774) added the Old Northwestern Territory, where many of the original colonies had land claims, to the province of Quebec.

51   *artful and hypocritical letter ... in New York papers*: possibly 'Extract of a letter from a Gentleman in London to his friend in this city, dated July 26 1775', *The New York Gazette and the Weekly Mercury*, 16 October 1775, no. 1253. Also printed in *New York Gazetteer or Weekly Advertiser*, 12 October 1775.

they are reckoning ... Host: 'He that reckons without his host, must reckon again', *Oxford Dictionary of English Proverbs*.

footing we were on in sixty-three: that is, prior to the Stamp Act and other attempts to tax the colonies (e.g. the Sugar Act, 1764). The first Continental Congress (summer 1774) sought the repeal of all legislation referring to America passed after 1763.

52 *The Rubicon is passed*: to have taken the decisive step; a reference to Julius Caesar's crossing of this stream in northern Italy, thereby beginning a war with Pompey.

54 *ANCIENT TESTIMONY ... PEOPLE IN GENERAL*: published Philadelphia, 1776, 'signed in and on behalf of a meeting of the representatives of our religious society, in Pennysylvania and New Jersey; held at Philadelphia, the 20th day of the first month, 1776'.

56 *Barclay*: Robert Barclay, *AN APOLOGY for the true CHRISTIAN Divinity As the same is held forth, and preached by the people,* called in scorn, *QUAKERS* (London, 1678). The introductory letter to Charles II from which the quotation is taken is unpaginated. The same quotation is given in M. de Voltaire, *Letters Concerning the English Nation* (London, 1733) Letter III, 22–3.

57 *When a man's ways ... at peace with him*: Prov. 16: 7

Oliver Cromwell: (1599–1658), army officer and parliamentarian active in the outbreak of the English Civil War (1642–60) and in the prosecution of Charles I (1600–49), in 1648; installed as Protector and head of the executive power, 1653.

dispersal of the Jews, though foretold by our saviour; Matt. 23: 37–9, 24: 15–20; Luke 13: 34–5, 19: 41–4.

AMERICAN CRISIS

63 *Britain ... has declared in all cases whatsoever*: see the Debate on the Resolutions of the Committee of the Whole House ... relating to the late Riots and Tumults in America, February 24, 1766, *Parliamentary History*, XVI, col. 165, and 6. Geo. 3. c. 12 (The Declaratory Act, 1766): 'Parliament has full power and authority to make laws and statutes to bind the people of the colonies, in all cases whatsoever.'

Howe: Sir William Howe (1729–1814), fifth Viscount Howe, Commander-in-Chief of the British Army in North America, 1775–8. Howe adopted a strategy of skirmishing to avoid incurring similar losses to those at Bunker Hill, where a full-scale battle was fought. He manœuvred the rebels out of Long Island, Manhattan and much of New Jersey, but the strategy foundered when his detachments were surprised at Trenton (26 December 1776) and Princeton (3 January 1777)

– only days after the publication of Paine's first Crisis Letter (19 December 1776). The spirit of the Jerseys refers to the mobilization of the militia and the opening conflict with British troops in April 1775.

64 *trembled like an ague*: a fever with hot and cold fits; a shivering fit.

a French fleet of flat-bottomed boats: French menaces of an invasion of England in 1759 included the preparation of flat-bottomed boats in different ports on the coast of France. See Smollett, *Continuation*, iii. 109–19.

Joan of Arc: the 'Maid of Orleans' (1402–31) who claimed divine inspiration and led the French army against the English, raising the seige of Orleans and inflicting heavy losses on the British. She subsequently crowned Charles king of France at Reims. She was captured by the British in 1430 and was burnt at the stake for heresy. See David Hume, *The History of England from the Invasion of Julius Caesar to the Revolution in 1688*, iii. 148–63.

Howe arrived upon the Delaware: Howe pursued Washington's troops after defeats at White Plains (28 October) and at Forts Washington and Lee (16–18 November) to the Delaware, which Washington crossed on 11 December 1776.

twentieth of November: Paine's memory is faulty; Fort Lee fell on 18 November 1776.

65 *Major-general Green*: Nathaniel Green (1742–86), Major-General in the Continental Army from 1776. Paine was Green's aide-de-camp at Fort Lee.

General Washington: George Washington (1732–99), Commander-in-Chief of Continental Army, President 1789–97.

66 *Voltaire has remarked, that King William . . . action*: Voltaire praises William the Conqueror's 'dexterity and valour' in defending himself against those who disputed his right in Normandy in *General History and State of Europe from the time of Charlemain to Charles V* (London, 1754), p. 162.

70 *Gage*: Thomas Gage (1720–87), Commander-in-Chief of the British Army whose troops suffered heavy casualties at Lexington, Concord and Bunker Hill. His army was blockaded in Boston and he was recalled (October 1775).

a peace . . . all understanding: Phil. 4: 7.

ravage the defenceless Jerseys: see note to p. 63.

71 *Hessians*: mercenary troops from the German state of Hesse.
In January 1776 the British Government entered into treaties
with several German states to provide nearly 200,000 mercenary troops.

AMERICAN CRISIS XIII

72 '*The times that tried men's souls*': The opening line of the first
Crisis, see p. 63.

73 *the cypress shade of disappointment*: cypress trees are commonly found in graveyards, hence their negative connotations.

75 *While I was writing this note*: see *Common Sense* p. 36.

76 *the states of Holland*: see *Rights of Man: Part One* p. 196.

77 *I have avoided all places of profit or office*: this is an odd
claim. Paine was certainly employed as Secretary to the For-
eign Affairs Committee of Congress, prior to the Silas Deane
affair; he also held the post of clerk to the Pennsylvania
Assembly. Moreover, he was also paid by Robert Morris's
Secret Service Fund to write in defence of the interests of the
Continental Congress in the last years of the revolution (see
Hawke, ch. 9).

78 *April 19, 1783*: The pamphlet was dated to mark the eighth
anniversary of the battle of Lexington and Concord.

LETTER TO JEFFERSON

82 *by confounding his terms*: a reference to *The Substance of a
Speech delivered by James Wilson, Esq. Explanatory of the
general Principles of the proposed Fœderal Constitution* (Philadelphia, 1787).

RIGHTS OF MAN: PART ONE

83 *being an answer to Mr Burke's attack on the French Revolution*: Edmund Burke, *Reflections on the Revolution in France,
and on the Proceedings in Certain Societies in London Relative
to that event. In a Letter Intended to have been sent to a
Gentleman in Paris* (London ... 1791).

85　*George Washington*: (1732–99), Commander-in-Chief of the Continental Army in the American Revolution, President of the United States, 1789–97. Paine later accused Washington of having colluded with Governeur Morris (American Minister in France), in denying that Paine was an American citizen when he was imprisoned in the Luxembourg Palace in 1793–4. He attacked his conduct in his *Letter to George Washington* (1796).

86　*From the part Mr Burke took*: although Burke was in favour of retaining the connection with the colonies, he was a vigorous critic of attempts to force the Americans to accept British rule.

　　violent speech last winter: Burke's Speech on the Army Estimates, 9 February 1793, in which Burke first publicly attacked proceedings in France, *Parliamentary History*, XXVIII, cols, 352–63.

　　written him, but a short time before: Paine and Burke met when Paine returned to Europe from America in 1787. They corresponded and Paine was a guest at Burke's home at Beaconsfield (see Burke, *Correspondence*, ed. Copeland, Vol. V, 3 September 1788). The letter Paine refers to is the most extensive letter extant (Burke's *Correspondence*, vi. 67–72 (17 January 1790). It is of particular interest since it provides some details of events which Burke subsequently describes in his *Reflections*.

　　experience and an acquaintance with the French Nation: in February 1778 the French had signed a Treaty of Amity with the Americans, promising not to make peace with Britain until American Independence had been recognized and confering full diplomatic status on the American Commissioners. The French also aided the American war effort financially and with supplies. Paine visited France as part of an attempt to raise more money between February and August 1781.

87　*When I came to France in the Spring of 1787*: Paine visited France from Britain on a number of occasions between 1787 and 1792, before taking up residence there in the autumn of 1792. The visits were at first related to his attempts to find funding to build a bridge he had designed, but after 1789 he went largely to stay in touch with political developments, in which he became increasingly involved.

Archbishop of Thoulouse: Étienne-Charles Loménie de Brienne, 1727–94, a careerist cleric, friend of the *philosophes*, and
Archbishop of Toulouse from 1763, he was the main opponent
of Calonne at the Assembly of Notables in 1787, and became
the king's principal minister after Calonne's fall. He introduced a series of reform measures (the May Edicts) which the
nobility opposed and he resigned in August 1788.

the private Secretary of that Minister: his secretary was the
Abbé André Morellet, a *philosophe* in his own right, who had
extensive contact with British political circles. Paine discussed
his conversation with Morellet in a letter to Burke dated 7
August 1788. See Hawke, 177 and 430.

I put this letter into the hands of Mr Burke: given Paine's
contacts with Thomas Jefferson, then American Minister in
France, and with the circle of the Marquis de Lafayette, a key
player in the early phase of the French Revolution, Paine was
valued as a source of information from Paris and he corresponded on several occasions with Burke.

91 *there was a time ... any revolution in France*: this seems an
odd claim given some of Burke's earlier comments on France,
see *Correspondence*, vi. 10, n. 2.

Dr Price: Dr Richard Price (1723–91), Welsh philosopher
and Dissenting minister whose *A Discourse on the Love of our
Country, delivered Nov. 4, 1789, at the Meeting House in the
Old Jewry, to the Society for Commemorating the Revolution in
Great Britain* (1789), provided the foil for Burke's
Reflections.

*Revolution Society, and the Society for Constitutional Informa-
tion*: the London Revolution Society was established in 1788
for the commemoration of the centenary of the Glorious
Revolution of 1688, but it enlarged its role after 1789 by
initiating a correspondence with the National Assembly of
France; its support came primarily from members of the
Dissenting community and their Whig sympathizers. The
Society for Constitutional Information was founded in April
1780 by a number of parliamentarians and other members of
the political élite to promote the dissemination of literature
advancing political knowledge and reform. It suffered a decline in the mid-1780s, but revived after 1789 and it went on
to play a major part in the dissemination of Paine's *Rights of
Man* in cheap editions. Several of its leading members were

prosecuted for treason in 1794 and, although they were acquitted, the Society collapsed.

90   *the Revolution . . . 1688*: in which James II (1633–1701) was
forced from the throne because of his Catholicism and William of Orange (1650–1703) was invited to accept the crown.
The exact character of the Revolution is a central area of
disagreement between Price, Burke, and Paine.

'The Political Devine . . . ourselves': Price's *Discourse* p. 34;
Burke, *Reflections* M. 8; Wks. 66; O'B. 99; P. 14, adapted.

'that the people of England . . . Fortunes': *Reflections* M. 16;
Wks. 66; O'B. 99; P. 14, adapted.

a declaration made by parliament . . . for EVER: Bill of Rights
1 William and Mary, s.2, c.2, viii. *Reflections*, M. 20; Wks.
70; O'B. 103–4; P. 17–18.

91   *another act of parliament . . . to the end of time*: 12–13 William
III c. 6 (1701), 'For the further securing of his Majesty's
Person, and the Succession of the Crown in the Protestant
Line; and extinguishing the Hopes of the pretended Prince of
Wales', 1701. *Reflections*, M. 24; Wks. 74; O'B. 108; P. 21.

'that if the people . . . for ever': *Reflections* M. 20; Wks. 70;
O'B. 104; P. 18.

usurpers: Burke does not use the term to describe the revolu-
tionists, but he does argue that [Sovereigns] have seen the
French rebel against a mild and lawful monarch, with more
fury, outrage, and insult, than ever any people has been
known to rise against the most illegal usurper or the most
sanguinary tyrant.' *Reflections* M. 38–9; Wks. 89: O'B. 126;
P. 34.

92   *no parent or master . . . age of twenty-one years*: a reference to
the *Habeas Corpus* Amendment Act of 1679 (31 Charles II c.
2) which allowed a writ to be issued against anyone, whether
an officer of the crown or private individual, who detained an
individual in their custody, to require that they produce the
person before a judge.

93   *In England, it is said . . .* without their consent: 'That the
levying money for or to the use of the crown by pretence of
prerogative without grant of parliament for a longer time or
in other manner the same is or shall be granted is illegal.' Bill
of Rights, 1689, 1 William and Mary, s.2, c.2; cf. John Locke,
Two Treatises of Government, II, ch. xi, 139 and 142. This

doctrine also formed a central plank in colonial opposition the British government's attempts to tax them, symbolized in the cry of 'No taxation without representation'.

shortened his journey to Rome: that is, to Catholicism. Paine relies on the common linking of Catholicism with absolutism and the doctrine of the divine right of kings.

95 *Marquis de la Fayette*: Marie Joseph Paul Roch Yves Gilber Motier, marquis de Lafayette (1757–1834), a wealthy French aristocrat who volunteered as a soldier for the American forces in July 1777 and won considerable respect and a substantial command as a result of his bravery and capacity. His exploits won him renown in France and he played a major role in the early reform movement. He was a member of the Estates-General in 1789 and was appointed commander of the new Parisian National Guard. In this capacity he played a major part in the events of 5–6 October which Burke denounces (M. 71–80; Wks. 120–9; O'B. 162–75; P. 61–70).

taking of the Bastille: following the dismissal of Jacques Necker (1732–1804), the principal minister to the king on 12 July 1789, Paris experienced popular revolt. On 14 July the crowd, together with the *Gardes-françaises*, stormed the Bastille, a symbol of the arbitrary powers of arrest of the *ancien régime*. The following day regular troops were withdrawn from Paris and Lafayette was elected as commander of the National Guard, and on 16 July Necker was recalled.

96 *Call to mind ... she wills it*: for Lafayette's proposals for a declaration of rights see *The Papers of Thomas Jefferson* (ed. J. P. Boyd and W. H. Gaines), xv. 230–33, also 255. Lafayette's speech is reported in *Journal d'Adrien Duquesnoy* (Paris, 1894), 189: 'Pour que les peuples aiment la liberté, il suffit qu'ils la connaissent, pour qu'ils soient libres, il suffit qu'il veulent l'être.'

May this great monument ... oppressed: 'May this Immense temple of freedom Ever Stand as a Lesson to oppressors, an Example to the oppressed, a Sanctuary to the Rights of Mankind.' Address to the Continental Congress (Trenton, 11 December 1784), *Lafayette in the Age of the American Revolution, Selected Letters and Papers 1776–1790*, ed. S. J. Idzerda and R. Crout (Ithaca, NY, 1983) v. 281.

Doctor Franklin: Dr Benjamin Franklin (1706–90), signatory to the Declaration of Independence in 1776, served as joint commissioner to France (1776), and later (September 1778–85) as Minister plenipotentiary. He returned to America and played a major part in the Constitutional Convention.

Count Vergennes . . . French Gazette: Charles Gravier, Comte de Vergennes (1717–87), foreign minister from 1774 until his death in February 1787. *Gazette de France*, founded 1631, was the major national domestic newspaper; it was officially financed and was censored by the government.

97 *'We have seen . . . tyrant'*: *Reflections* M. 38–9; Wks. 89; O'B. 126; P. 34.

Louis the XVIth: Louis XVI, king of France 1774–92, enjoyed national success in the American revolution, but was unable to solve the regime's financial problems. Scholarly opinion concurs with Paine's expressed view that he was well-intentioned but badly advised.

augean stable: in Greek myth one of the twelve labours of Hercules was to clean in one day the stables of Augeas, King of Elis, who owned enormous herds of cattle. The stables had never been cleaned before; Hercules achieved his task by diverting the river Alpheus through the yard.

distinction between men and principles: Paine's phrasing mimics the contrast between men and measures which Burke draws on but rejects in his *Thoughts on the Present Discontents* (1770).

98 *Charles I*: (1600–49), king of England (1625–49), who ruled for eleven years without calling a Parliament and who provoked active unrest on attempting to Anglicize the Scottish Church. Discontent led to the onset of civil war which culminated in his defeat, and eventually his trial and execution. James II was his second son (see note to p. 90).

every place has its Bastille: Paine is probably referring to the enormously complex legal structure of the old regime, especially the proliferation of *parlements, présidiaux*, Royal *bailliages* and *sénéchaussées*, seigneural jurisdictions, courts of taxation, *grandes maîtrises*, etc.

99 *Louis XIV*: (1638–1715), king of France 1643–1715, ruled as an absolute monarch from 1661.

a reign more mild: *Reflections* M. 38; Wks. 89; O'B. 126; P. 34.

'Ten years ago . . . administered': *Reflections* M. 8; Wks. 58; O'B. 90; P. 7.

100 *he is writing History, and not Plays*: the theatrical metaphor comes from Burke, *Reflections* M. 80–81; Wks. 131–2; O'B. 175–6; P. 71.

the age of chivalry . . . is gone: *Reflections*, M. 76; Wks. 127; O'B. 170; P. 66.

Quixot: from Miguel de Cervantes' *Don Quixote* (1605). Burke was portrayed in a number of satirical popular prints as a modern Don Quixote—or Don Dismallo—pursuing Marie Antoinette and fighting imaginary dangers (see Wks. 16–17).

'Othello's occupation's gone': *Othello* III. iii. 362.

101 *unfortunate Scotch in the affair of 1745*: the abortive attempt by the 'Pretender', Charles, grandson of James II, to regain the throne by an invasion assisted by the French and begun in Scotland.

Newgate: the city jail of London, extended substantially by the 'New' Newgate in 1760. *Reflections*, M. 84; Wks. 135; O'B. 179; P. 74.

We have rebuilt . . . Queens of France: M. 84; Wks. 135; O'B. 179; P. 74.

Lord G——— G———: Lord George Gordon (1751–93), an agitator associated with the anti-popery riots of June 1780 (the Gordon Riots), and prosecuted for his involvement. In 1788 he was imprisoned in Newgate after conviction for libel, where he remained until his death in 1793. He was regarded by some as mad.

two other places . . . pamphlet: first reference: M. 202; Wks. 248; O'B. 320; P. 177; second reference: M. 215; Wks. 259–60; O'B. 334; P. 187. (There is a further reference at M. 132; Wks. 181; O'B. 237; P. 116.)

bedlam: a mad-house, after Bethlem Hospital for the insane in London.

102 *pities the plumage . . . dying bird*: a reference to Burke's exaggerated portrait of Marie Antoinette, *Reflections*, M. 71, 75–6; Wks. 121–2, 126; O'B. 164, 169; P. 62, 66.

the aristocratical hand . . . purloined him from himself: a reference to the common believe that Burke had become a pensioner of the court—that is, was in the pay of the crown and had abandoned the Whig interest.

Bastille . . . two days before and after: see note to p. 95.

Bunyan's Doubting Castle and Giant Despair: John Bunyan, *The Pilgrim's Progress* (first published 1678), Oxford, Clarendon Press, 2nd ed., 1960, i. 112–9. Giant Despair is the keeper of Doubting Castle in which Christian and his friends are trapped.

103 *The National Assembly ... Versailles*: the Estates General were called to sit in May 1789 by the king at Versailles, the residence of the Court. On 17 June, the 'Commons' (the Third Estate) voted to adopt the title 'National Assembly' and agreed to vote by head rather than by estate. They were joined by the Nobility and Clergy over the next few weeks.

plot was forming ... Count d'Artois: Charles Philippe, comte d'Artois (1757–1836), a notorious figure of hate in 1789 who was suspected of involvement in the *pacte de famine*, an alleged conspiracy to starve the populace. The attack on the Bastille, and other events of this period, were motivated by the belief that the army was to be used to cut the National Assembly off from Paris so as to be able to dissolve it and re-establish Royal authority. d'Artois and other leading nobles emigrated immediately after the fall of the Bastille, confirming many revolutionaries' suspicions.

foreign troops in the pay of France: there were twenty-three foreign regiments in the French Army, including the Swiss Guards, who were permanently attached to the royal household. The build-up of troops around Versailles and Paris in June–July 1789 was rapid and drew disproportionately on the foreign, and presumably more loyal, troops.

ministry who were then in office: i.e., led by Necker (see note to p. 95).

Count de Broglio: Victor François, duc de Broglie (1718–1804) a career soldier, recalled by Louis to command troops around Versailles, then appointed War Minister after the dismissal of Necker, 12 July 1789. He resigned and emigrated after the fall of the Bastille.

an high-flying ... mischief: see Burke, *Correspondence*, vi. 70, Paine's letter to Burke of 17 January 1790. The description is attributed to Jefferson in Paine's letter and appears in a letter to Paine from Jefferson, 11 July 1789, *The Papers of Thomas Jefferson*, ed. J. P. Boyd and W. H. Gaines, (Princeton, NJ, 1958), xv. 267–8.

the devoted victims: that is, victims consigned to be sacrificed.

Archbishop of Vienne: Jean-George Le Franc de Pompignan (1715–90), Archbishop of Vienne, President of the National Assembly. The frailty of the Archbishop was of concern because the Assembly agreed, on 13 July 1789, to maintain an all-night presence for forty-eight hours to prevent a lock-out by the king's troops. Lafayette was nominated as acting president. See also note to p. 95

105   *Prince de Lambesc . . . Lewis XV*: Charles Eugène de Lorraine d'Elbeuf (1751–1825), prince de Lambesc. The place Louis XV was renamed the place de la revolution and subsequently the place de la Concorde.

106   *Mayor of Paris . . . Defflesselles*: Jacques de Flesselles (1721–9) the last *prévôt des marchands* or head of the municipal government, assassinated on 14 July 1789. Jean-Sylvain Bailly (1736–93) was the first formal mayor of Paris, appointed 15 July 1789.

Hospital of the Invalids: les Invalides, a military veterans' hospital, which was used as an arsenal—as was, to a still greater extent, the Bastille.

107   *The exiles who have fled from France*: immediately after the fall of the Bastille most of those principally involved in scheming against the Assembly fled from France, including d'Artois (see note to p. 103), Louis Joseph de Bourbon, prince de Condé, Louis François Joseph de Bourbon, prince de Conti, and the Queen's friends the Polignac family.

108   *Governor of the Bastille . . . Intendant of Paris*: Bernard-René Jourdan de Launey (1740–89), succeeded his father as governor of the Bastille in 1776; Joseph François Foulon (1715–89), given a key role in organizing the military around Paris in July. He is alleged to have said that if the people of Paris were hungry they should eat straw. His son-in-law, Louis-Benigne-François de Bertier de Sauvigny (1737–89), was, as Intendant of Paris, responsible for food supplies to the army around Paris. Both were assassinated by incensed crowds when being led to trial at the Hôtel de Ville on 22 July 1789.

Temple-bar: the point marking the city boundary at Fleet Street, London, close to the law courts and chambers.

In England . . . populace: it was possible to be sentenced to be hanged, drawn, and quartered in England, although it was not a common occurrence. None the less, punishment was in general brutal and relatively indifferent to the enormity of the crime. In May 1790 the Commons debated altering the sentence of burning alive for women convicted of certain crimes (e.g. coining); see *Parliamentary History*, XXVIII, cols. 782–4.

108 *Damien*: Robert-François Damiens (1714–57), a fanatic who attempted to assassinate Louis XV in 1757. He was tortured and hanged, drawn, and quartered.

109 *London in 1780*: a reference to the anti-popery or Gordon Riots of June 1780.

Hotel de Ville: Hôtel de Ville, the Paris Town Hall.

110 *expedition to Versailles*: Paine's account which follows is similar to standard modern accounts; see Doyle, 121–2.

111 *Declaration of the Rights of Man . . . fourth of August*: the Declaration of the Rights of Man was decreed by the National Assembly on 26 August 1789; the decrees of 4 August involved the abolition of feudal privileges. Louis refused to ratify the decrees on 15 September 1789.

Garde du Corps: the king's bodyguard.

112 *'History will record . . . melancholy repose*: *Reflections*, M. 71; Wks. 121; O'B. 164; P. 62.

Metz: a town in northern France, close to the Belgian border.

113 *President of the National Assembly*: Jean Joseph Mounier (1756–1806), President of the Assembly during the October Days, who resigned in protest at the events and in May 1790 emigrated to Switzerland (Doyle, 123; Jones, 375).

114 *trapanning the king to Metz*: trepanning him—that is, luring him into counter-revolution.

Bailley: Jean-Sylvain Bailly (1736–93), appointed Mayor of Paris by the National Constitutive Assembly in July 1789. It is possible that Paine is confusing this occasion with the visit which Louis paid to Paris, when he was welcomed by Bailly, after the fall of the Bastille, on 17 July 1789.

115 *M. Lally-Tollendal*: Tromphime-Gérard, marquis de Lally-Tollendal (1751–1830), elected by the Parisian nobility to the Estates General, was a conservative who advocated a bi-cameral legislature. He left France for Switzerland in September 1789. *Reflections*, M. 73; Wks. 124; O'B. 166; P. 64.

Tous les eveques à la lanterne: *Reflections*, M. 73–4; Wks.

123–5; O'B. 166–8; P. 63–5. Curiously, the pamphlet Burke cites as a source does not seem to exist, and no edition of Burke has identified the source of the quotation.

tout à coup et tous ensemble: all at once and all together.

magic lanthorn: the name for an optical instrument for the projection of slides and pictures (invented 1636).

Revolution de Paris: *Les Révolutions de Paris*, a weekly paper, published between 12 July 1789 and 24 May 1794, one of the most independent of the early newspapers.

116 *paltry and blurred . . . rights of man*: *Reflections*, M. 86; Wks. 137; O'B. 182; P. 75.

117 *genealogy of Christ is traced to Adam*: Luke 3: 23–38.

118 *Mosaic account*: that is, the account given by Moses in the Pentateuch, the first five books of the Old Testament: Genesis, Exodus, Leviticus, Numbers, and Deuteronomy.

And God said . . . created he them: Gen. 1: 26–7.

We fear God . . . nobility: *Reflections*, M. 86; Wks. 137; O'B. 182; P. 76.

to put in Peter: probably a reference to Peter's proverbial status as one whom God loves but neglects – that is, one who is put upon. *Oxford Dictionary of English Proverbs*.

121 *as they now march . . . European courts*: a reference to the secret influence which the Catholic church was believed to wield over Europe's Catholic monarchs.

William the Conqueror: see Paine's use of William in *Common Sense* (p. 16), and note to it.

The key of St Peter, and the key of the Treasury: that is, the key to the gates of heaven and to political power. Paine's use of synecdoche is directed against the union of Church and state. See also *Reflections*, M. 88–105; Wks. 140–54; O'B. 185–204; P. 78–92, and Burke's claim that the English have consecrated their state (M. 92; Wks. 143; O'B. 189–90; P. 81).

122 *he has signified . . . comparison*: *Reflections*, M. 164; Wks. 212; O'B. 275; P. 144.

123 *Mr Burke said . . . parliament*: Burke, *Speech on the Army Estimates: 9 February 1790*, *Works* (1808) v. 13; also *Parliamentary History*, XXVIII, col. 357.

124   *The Act by which ... in England*: triennial parliaments were replaced by septennial parliaments in the Septennial Act of 1716 (passed in the wake of an attempt on the throne by the 'Old Pretender', James Stuart (1688–1766) in 1715).

the Bill which ... Mr Pitt: William Pitt 'the Younger' (1759–1806), Prime Minister 1783–1801. Pitt introduced three bills for parliamentary reform, one on 7 May 1782; the second on 7 May 1783, and the third on 18 April 1785. All were defeated.

The constitution of France says: the pronouncements on the 'Constitution of France' which follow are references to the decrees and enactments made by the National Constituent Assembly (the title adopted by the National Assembly (the renamed Estates General, 17 June 1789) on 9 June 1789) on the recommendation of the Constitution Committee established 6 July 1789. These decrees and enactments were reviewed by the Revision Committee from 23 September 1790. Most came to be embodied in the 1791 Constitution, agreed by the National Constituent Assembly on 3 September 1791, accepted by the king ten days later (Jones 66–9). Paine's criticisms of the English system of representation were common amongst reformers in Britain and had formed a central part of the case of the Society for Constitutional Information (see note to p. 91).

tax of sixty sous: debates of 22 and 29 October 1789, and decree on primary elections of 22 December 1789.

125   *number of representatives ... elected every two years*: the markers for the new constitution were laid down in the Constitutional Act of 1 October 1789.

126   *no game laws*: 4–11 August, the abolition of feudal privileges.

all trade shall be free: 31 October–5 November 1790 abolition of internal customs barriers.

'On the Wealth of Nations': Adam Smith, *An Inquiry into the Nature and Causes of the Wealth of Nations* (London, 1776).

127   *no member of the National Assembly ... pensioner*: Decree of 7 November 1789.

Loaves and fishes: material rather than spiritual benefits. That is, Paine accuses him of sacrificing principle to venality. See *Oxford Dictionary of English Proverbs*.

the Comedy of Errors ... the pantomine of HUSH: Paine is

accusing English politicians of complicity in corruption. The reference to Shakespeare's play goes no further than its title.

128 *reside in a metaphor . . . so are the lions*: the metaphor is the crown, on display at the Tower of London. Lions, part of the king's menagerie established by Henry II, were also on display in the Tower.

Aaron's molten calf: Deut. 9. 16; Neh. 9: 18; Ps. 106: 19.

Nebuchadnezzar's golden image: Dan. 3: 1

conquering at home: a familiar republican criticism of the British government.

130 *the land that floweth with milk and honey*: a very common biblical phrase: Lev. 20: 24; Num. 13: 27, 14: 8; Deut. 6: 3, 11. 9, etc.

M. Beaumarchais: Pierre-Augustin Caron de Beaumarchais (1732–99), author of *The Marriage of Figaro* (1784); acted as a French spy and an arms dealer for the Americans in the American Revolution, when Paine may first have met him.

131 *a hard-dealing Dutchman*: a dismissive reference to William of Orange, who became William III of England in 1688.

no titles: enactments of 19–20 June 1790.

blue ribbon . . . garter: the blue ribbon is the symbol of the Order of the Garter, the most coveted order of knighthood in the gift of the Crown.

when I was a child: 1 Cor. 13: 11.

132 *rickets*: a common childhood disease involving softening of the bones, now known to be caused by a deficiency of vitamin D.

gewgaws: a bauble or showy thing without value.

133 *law of primogenitureship*: the principle (in eighteenth-century France, the law) that property and title descends to the eldest son.

134 *a corporation of aristocracy*: Paine met Lafayette frequently in the early stages of the Revolution and may have heard the phrase then.

135 *The French constitution . . . the clergy*: legislation altering the place and power of the church came thick and fast in the early phase of the revolution, beginning with the absence of its feudal fee structure and rights, 4–11 August, 1789, and culminating in the creation of a Civil Constitution of the Clergy, 12 July 1789 (see Jones, 240–2.)

That the people of England ... squire: *Reflections*, M. 103; Wks. 153; O'B. 202–3; P. 91.

Sternhold and Hopkins: Thomas Sternhold (d. 1549), versifier of the Psalms, whose metrical edition of nineteen of them appeared in 1547, followed by a second edition of thirty-seven published posthumously in 1549. A third edition with seven further Psalms appeared 1557, edited by John Hopkins (d. 1570). The collection, in the complete edition published in 1562, became known as Sternhold and Hopkins.

136 *when the dissenters bill was before the English parliament*: three applications to parliament for the relief of Dissenters from the constraints of the Test and Corporation acts were made shortly before Paine was writing, in March 1787, May 1789, and March 1790. The second application was rejected by a majority of only twenty, thus raising Dissenters' hopes, but the third application was affected by the climate of opinion over events in France and by the radicalism which Dissenters had shown by their involvement in the election of 1790. As a result, this application met considerable opposition, including the cry of 'the Church in danger'. One of the major opponents of the motion was Burke, who cited numerous documents to establish the extremism of the Dissenters, including extracts from Price's *Discourse on the Love of our Country*. The motion was decisively rejected (Goodwin, ch. 3).

abolished tythes: decree of 4 August 1789.

137 *the French constitution ... UNIVERSAL RIGHT OF CONSCIENCE*: in the *Declaration of the Rights of Man* (see pp. 161–4), decreed by the National Assembly 26 August 1789.

pope armed with fire and faggot ... traffic: a reference to the claims of the Catholic Church to its right to punish (by fire and faggot, or burning) heretics in this world (hence assuming the power of a state), and to its practice of selling or granting indulgences in the next world (a lucrative commercial activity fiercely attacked in the Reformation).

dust and ashes: Gen. 18: 27; Job 30: 19, 42: 6.

138 *tythe sheaf ... cock of hay*: although a tithe was formally a tenth of each crop produced, it could be commuted into money or taken in the form of other crops. (A cock of hay is a haycock, a temporary heap of hay.)

139 *the inquisition in Spain*: the 'Inquisition' was originally an inquiry related to the ecclesiastical jurisdiction of the Catholic Church over heresy. The Spanish Inquisition (1479–1814) was closely bound up with the power of the state and was directed initially against converts from Judaism and Islam, but spread to cover any case of suspected heresy. Suspected heretics were frequently tortured, and convicted heretics were usually burnt.

Smithfield: a 'smooth-field' originally outside the walls of the City of London, which was used for the execution, by burning, of Protestant martyrs in the reign of Queen Mary I, 1553–8.

that drove the people called Quakers: a religious sect, founded by George Fox (1624–91), whose refusal to take oaths or pay tithes and to comply with the rituals of deference to social superiors, such as removing one's hat, led to their persecution after the restoration of the Crown in 1660. The most famous group of Quaker exiles were those led by William Penn, who founded Pennsylvania in 1682. Dissenters refers in this context to Protestants who separated themselves from the communion of the Established Church. These also suffered a variety of disabilities from the Test and Corporation Acts (1663, 1661).

episcopalian: properly, a member of any church ruled by bishops. Paines' reference is to the fact that the Episcopalian Church of America is the descendant of the Anglican Church, but that is not connected to the state.

edict of Nantes: signed in 1598, bringing to an end the French wars of religion, but revoked in 1685 by Louis XIV, leading to widespread emigration by Protestants in France.

140 *places Sovereignty in the nation*: in clause III, Declaration of the Rights of Man and of Citizens, 26 August 1789.

Parliament in England ... erected by patents: the House of Commons is patented through Chancery and is formally constituted by patents; see Erskine May, 134.

141 *a king is the fountain of honour*: *Reflections*, M. 201; Wks. 247; O'B. 318; P. 175 ('in France the king is no more the fountain of honour than he is the fountain of justice').

Mr Burke ... the privilege of speaking twice: in the English Parliament 'no member may speak twice on the same issue except, i) to explain part of a speech which has been misunderstood; ii) in certain cases to reply at the end of a debate, and iii) in committee' (Erskine May, 195). Burke was a stickler for procedure, so Paine's comment should be taken as teasing.

does not ask the king ... House of Commons: freedom of speech became part of the petition of the Commons to the king at the commencement of Parliament after 33 Henry VI, 154 (Erskine May, 78).

142 *the family vault of all the Capulets*: a reference to the scene of Romeo and Juliet's deaths in Shakespeare's play. Juliet is a Capulet.

143 *there is not any description of men ... as courtiers*: cf. Montesquieu, *L'Esprit des lois* (1748), iii. 5–7.

I wrote to him last winter from Paris: Burke, *Correspondence*, vi. 67–76 (10 January 1790).

144 *He apologises (in page 241)*: *Reflections*, M. 164; Wks. 212; O'B. 274–5; P. 144.

'It looks ... in the world': *Reflections*, M. 10; Wks. 60; O'B. 92; P. 9.

145 *Louis XV ... weakness and effeminacy*: Louis XV (1710–74) was notorious for his insatiable sexual appetites, and his reign was notable for unsuccessful wars and the degradation of the court.

Montesquieu: Charles de Secondat, baron de Montesquieu, (1689–1755), author of *Lettres persanes* (1721) and *L'Esprit des lois* (1748). He also served as a magistrate in Bordeaux.

Voltaire: François-Marie Arouet, generally known as Voltaire (1694–1778), poet, historian, and philosopher.

Rousseau and the Abbé Raynal: Jean Jacques Rousseau (1712–78), political philosopher and moralist; Abbé Guillaume Raynal (1713–96) historian, *encyclopédiste*—and the target of Paine's *Letter to the Abbé Raynal* (1782).

Quesnay, Turgot, and the friends of those authors: François Quesnay (1694–1774), physician and political economist (founder of the physiocrats, a group of economists who held that land was the only source of wealth, not manufactures); Anne-Robert-Jacques Turgot (1727–81), economist and administrator, who shared the physiocrats' views. Cf. Burke's comment on Turgot, *Reflections*, M. 112; Wks. 162; O'B. 213; P. 98.

146 *The French officers and soldiers ... went to America*: the French began by providing arms, munitions, and clothing and allowing the Americans to use French ports. After the signing of the treaties of commerce and alliance in 1778, France took a more active part, mainly in the form of naval support, although a French expeditionary force (of 6,500 men) was sent to America in May 1780, and this played a decisive role in the victories of 1781.

Minister of France, Count Vergennes: Charles Gravier, comte de Vergennes (1717–87), Foreign Minister 1774–87. When America first broached the issue of aid to France in 1775–6, the French finance minister, Turgot (see note to p. 145) counselled against involvement. Vergennes was in favour, because he hoped thereby to weaken Britain's position in Europe. Paine's claim for the influence of Marie Antoinette, the French Queen, is doubtful, although it is true that she contributed to the success which Benjamin Franklin enjoyed in his period as American Minister to France (1776–1782).

147 *M. Neckar was displaced*: Jacques Necker (1732–1804), a reformist Finance Minister 1777–81 who published *Compte-rendu au Roi* (1781) which claimed that the financial situation in France was strong despite involvement in the American war, and which undermined later administrations' claims that the state was bankrupt—notably, Charles-Alexandre de Calonne (1734–1802), controller-general from 1783, and Lomenie de Brienne, who ousted him in 1787.

Pitt frequently alluded: judging by the reports of Pitt's speeches in *Parliamentary History*, the references to France were made in passing, rather than being of a substantive nature.

148 *An Assembly under this name ... 1617*: in fact, 1626.

149 *seven separate committees*: see A. Goodwin, 'The Assembly of French Notables and the Revolution Nobiliare' *English Historical Review*, (1946), 332, 343. Paine rather overstates Lafayette's role, and Lafayette's attack on Calonne was made in the Assembly, p. 361.

150 *Lettres de Cachet*: a sealed detention order, signed by the king and counter-signed by a minister, against which there was no recourse in the courts.

two new taxes: proposed by Brienne in May 1787. The Assembly of Notables declared in response that they had no authority to authorize new taxes, upon which occasion Lafayette argued for the 'convocation of a truly national assembly' (Doyle, 74). This refusal led to the dismissal of the Assembly of Notables, 25 May 1787.

Thoulouse: Brienne, see note to p. 87. He was appointed as a Cardinal as a reward for his services on his resignation in 1788.

151   *Duke de Choiseul*: Étienne François de Stainville, duc de Choiseul (1719–85), minister under Louis XV.

a bed of justice: lit de justice, called 6 August 1787. The *lit de justice* was a solemn session of the Paris Parlement in the presence of the king where the king formally registered an edict overriding parliamentary remonstrances.

and ordered the enregistering . . . illegal: 7 August 1787.

Trois: the Parlement was exiled to Troyes, 14 August 1787, at which point Brienne was appointed Principal Minister.

short time recalled to Paris: 28 September 1787.

152   *gave his word . . . States-General should be convened*: the king agreed to call the Estates General 19 November 1787.

Lamoignon: Chretien-François II de Lamoignon (1735–89), *Garde de Sceaux* 1787, was believed to have committed suicide after his fall.

153   *cour plénière*: the *cour plénière*, or Plenary Court, created 8 May 1788, was intended to be a more docile forum for registering royal edicts than the Parlement.

Duke de la Rochefoucault, Luxembourg, De Noailles, and many others . . . opposed the whole plan: the proposal for a *cour plénière* was part of a package of proposals known as the 'May Edicts' which Brienne tried to push through (8 May 1788) only to be forced to capitulate to resistance from the nobility (by 5 July 1788). Louis-Alexandre, duc la Roche-Guyon et de la Rochefoucauld d'Enville (1743–92), Member of the Assembly of Notables 1787 and the Estates General 1789. Anne-Charles-Sigismond de Montmorency-Luxembourg, 1737–1805, *Président de la chambre de la noblesse*, 12 June 1789, emigrated 1791. Louis, vicomte de Noailles (1756–1804), was Lafayette's brother-in-law.

154   *subject of convening the States-General*: in capitulating to resistance to his proposals, Brienne agreed to the convocation of the Estates General for 1 May 1789.

the last of which was in 1614: see Paine's note to p. 155.

the mode of 1614: the Paris Parlement had decreed that this should be the mode in which the Estates General met on 25 September 1788. The decision proved very unpopular and the Parlement sought to regain credibility by endorsing the principle of double representation for the Third Estate on 5 December 1788. The principle was accepted by the king's council, despite noble opposition, on 27 December 1788.

155 *he summoned again the Assembly of the Notables*: convoked 5 October 1788, and met 6 November 1788.

not a contested election: the representatives of the First Estate, the clergy, were elected in assemblies in constituencies (based on the jurisdictional boundaries of royal *bailliages*) whose membership comprised benefice-holders and indirect representation for chapters, religious communities and non-beneficed clergy. Those of the Second Estate (nobility) were elected by assemblies comprising fief-holders and male members of the nobility (purchased or inherited). The Third Estate (or Commons) was elected by a complex system of multi-stage elections, in which male taxpayers could participate. In practice this was close to manhood suffrage. (Jones, 63, also Doyle, 96–97).

L'Intrigue du Cabinet . . . i, 329: Louis Pierre Anquetil, *L'Intrigue du Cabinet sous Henri IV et Louis XIII, terminé par la Fronde* (Paris, 1780), i. 329.

156 *the Tiers État . . . declared themselves*: 17 June 1789.

Abbé Sieyes: Abbé Emmanuel-Joseph Siéyès (1748–1836), author of *Essai sur les privilèges* and *Qu'est-ce que le tiers état* (1789). He was the representative of the Third Estate of Paris in the Estates General and urged the union of the three orders in his speech to the assembly on 16 June 1789. See Murray Forsyth, *Reason and Revolution: The Political Thought of the Abbé Sieyes* (Leicester, 1987).

157 *Barons opposed King John*: baronial opposition to the rule of King John (1167–1216) compelled him in 1215 to sign the Magna Carta, whose aim was to secure the liberties of the English Church and of the baronial classes, and to restrict the power of the king.

A majority of the clergy: this refers to events of 24 June 1789, when the most of the clergy followed earlier (13–22 June) defectors who agreed to sit as one chamber with the Third Estate.

158 *The king ... held ... Bed of Justice*: Paine's chronology is slightly faulty: on 20 June 1789, the king decided to hold a *scéance royale* (a ceremonial session of the Estates General in the presence of the king) on 23 June, and closed the meeting place of the National Assembly. The deputies used a nearby tennis court as a meeting place and swore not to disperse until a constitution had been passed. At the *scéance royale* the king ordered the three estates to meet separately and over-ruled their decrees, but on his leaving the deputies reaffirmed their unity and their decrees. Recognizing defeat, the king ordered the rest of the nobility and clergy to take their place in the National Assembly on 27 June 1789. Paine's source may well have been Jefferson's letter of 11 July 1789, which refers to the circumstances surrounding the *scéance royale*.

Count D'Artois ... king would be endangered: 'the alleged danger to the Royal family was probably magnified, if not invented, by Artois as the only way of persuading the more quixotic of his colleagues to comply with the royal order.' Hampson, *Prelude to Terror* (Oxford, 1988), 48.

167 *Government is a contrivance ... wisdom*: *Reflections*, M. 60; Wks. 110; O'B. 151; P. 52.

Men have a right that their wants ... wisdom: *Reflections*, M. 60; Wks. 110; O'B. 151; P. 52. The sentence follows directly after the previous line quoted by Paine.

168 *The rights of men are their advantages ... demonstrations*: *Reflections*, M. 62; Wks. 112; O'B. 153; P. 54.

shibboleths: Judg. 12: 5–6. Shibboleth was the Gileadite test-word for an Ephraimite, here used to indicate a catch-word of a group.

Robin Hood: legendary outlaw and protector of the poor and women. His adventures have been variously assigned to reigns from that of Richard I (1189–99) to Edward II (1307–27).

169 *laboured the Regency Bill and Hereditary Succession*: in 1788, when George III suffered a temporary fit of insanity, Burke and the Foxite Whigs campaigned to secure the creation of a regency for George IV, who they believed would bring them into office. The king recovered before the attempt could succeed.

170 'The King of England ... he now wears': Reflections, M. 15; Wks. 65–6; O'B. 98–9; P. 14.

Cherokee Chief, or a Hessian Hussar: both Cherokee Indians and Hessian troops were used by the British against the Americans in the American revolution.

House of Brunswick: the house of Brunswick takes the English throne in 1714 through George I (1660–1727), great-grandson to James I (through his maternal grandmother, Elizabeth of Bohemia, James's daughter), and Elector of Hanover from 1698.

171 the then Earl of Shelburne: Sir William Petty (1737–1805), first Marquis of Landsdowne and second Earl of Shelburne, Home Secretary under Rockingham 1782 and then First Lord of the Treasury. He conceded American independence, 1783, and his administration was overthrown by the Fox–North coalition. Parl. Register XI (1783), 25.

'His Majesty's heirs ... he wears': Reflections, M. 15; Wks. 66; O'B. 98–9; P. 14.

172 'No experience has taught us ... hereditary right': Reflections, M. 25; Wks. 75; O'B. 109; P. 22.

175 the English Nation ... posterity for ever: a paraphrase of Reflections, M. 20; Wks. 70; O'B. 104; P. 18.

Fortunatus's wishing-cap, or Harlequin's wooden sword: Fortunatus is a hero of mediaeval legend who possessed, variously, a wishing cap, an inexhaustible purse, and so on. Harlequin originates from a stock character of the commedia dell'arte. He wears a spangled costume and is renowned for his cunning. He carries a light bat or lath which, in the English tradition, becomes a wand.

176 Dutch Stadtholder, or a German Elector: Paine uses the formal former titles of William of Orange and George I.

civil government is republican government: that is, conducted under the law and involving election and representation. Monarchy is here associated with hereditary succession and the right to arbitrary power.

177 when the people of England ... abandonment of Hanover: in fact, George I spent as little time as possible in England, and as much as possible in Hanover.

178 the Dutchy of Mecklenburgh ... Queen's family governs:

Charlotte-Sophia (1744–1818), of Mecklenburg-Strelitz (a German principality), queen of George III.

the animosity of the English Nation . . . ran high: George III (1738–1820), crowned 1760, was taught by Lord Bute (1713–92) fully to exercise Royal powers, but was forced in the years immediately following his accession to acknowledge the reality of party politics.

179   *an immediate coalition of the champions themselves*: a reference to the coalition between Charles James Fox and Lord North, the former a major critic of the latter's policies in North America. The government was short-lived (April 1783–December 1783) and was succeeded by that of Pitt.

180   *on the return of a new Parliament*: the election of March 1784, at which Pitt consolidated his previously weak position.

he introduced himself to public notice . . . corruption: Pitt proposed buying out thirty-six boroughs with minute electorates, for which a fund of £1,000,000 was to be created. The seats would then be redistributed. The proposal was defeated 18 April 1785.

the Dutch business . . . the national debt: the 'Dutch business' refers to Pitt's machinations over the restoration of the Stadholder in Holland, and the end of the republic; the 'sinking' of the national debt refers to the scheme which Pitt drew up, with assistance from Dr Richard Price, for the reduction of the national debt. A bill to establish a sinking fund was passed in May 1786, and a Consolidation Bill was passed in April 1787 to reform the funds which fed it.

Mr Fox had stated . . . to assume the government: Fox's speech was on 10 December 1788; see *Parliamentary Record*, XXV (1789), 24; and *Parliamentary History*, XXVII, col. 713. For Pitt's response see *Parliamentary History*, XXVII, cols. 713 and 735.

181   *making the Great Seal into a king*: the Great Seal is the chief seal used by the sovereign to authenticate state documents; it is kept by the Lord Chancellor (then Pitt). For Pitt's reference to the seal see *Parliamentary History*, XXVII, cols. 846–51.

182   *If France with a revenue . . . present debt of England*: Paine had argued for the view that France was in an economically stronger position than Britain in *Prospects on the Rubicon* (1787).

183   *Mr Burke in his review of the finances*: Reflections, M. 130; Wks. 179; O'B. 235; P. 114.

     Mr Neckar in France, and George Chalmers . . . Lord Hawkesbury: Necker (see note to p. 147); George Chalmers (1742–1825), *Estimate of the Comparative Strength of Great Britain during the present and four preceding reigns* (London, 1782). Chalmers served as a government clerk after 1786 and went on to write a hostile biography of Paine under the pseudonym Francis Oldys. See also Paine's Appendix to *Rights of Man, Part Two*. Charles Jenkinson first Earl of Liverpool and first Baron Hawkesbury (1727–1808), President of the Board of Trade 1786.

184   *increasing paper till there is no money left*: Paine expanded on this theme in his *Decline and Fall of the English System of Finance* (1796).

     Administration of the Finances . . . Vol III: *A Treatise on the Administration of the Finances of France in three volumes* (translated from the French edition of 1784 by T. Mortimer, London, 1785), 59.

186   *Mr Eden [now Auckland]*: William Eden, first Baron Auckland (1744–1814), statesman and diplomat, privy councillor.

187   *May 1777 . . . £600,000 private debts*: on 16 April 1777, Parliament voted £620,000 for arrears plus £100,000 per annum to the king. Sinclair, *A History of the Revenue*, iii. 70; also *Parliamentary History*, XIX, 211–14 and 221–34.

188   *Cast his eyes . . . once was France*: *Speech on the Army Estimates*, *Works* (1808), v. 4–5 adapted 'he did not find, on a review of all Europe, that, politically, we stood in the smallest degree of danger . . . that France had been our first object . . . [but] that France is, at this time, in a political light, to be considered as expunged out of the system of Europe.'

     sale of the monastic and ecclesiastical landed estates: this followed the nationalization of Church property on 2 November 1789, beginning 19 December 1789.

189   *the court of St James or Carlton-House*: St James's Palace, the London residence and court of the Hanoverians; Carlton House, the primary London residence of the Prince of Wales, later George IV (1762–1830), which was altered and enlarged at great expense by Henry Holland in 1788.

191   *mixed government*: government by the one, the few and the

many (of monarchy, aristocracy and democracy), paradigmatically sketched by Polybius, *The Rise of the Roman Empire*, VI, 3–10, and through Machiavelli, Harrington and Montesquieu, deeply influential on eighteenth-century British and American traditions of opposition thought. Paine's rejection of the tradition is indicative of his radicalism.

195   *Henry the Fourth ... abolishing war in Europe*: Henry IV (1553–1610), a skilled ruler, responsible for the Edict of Nantes, who is credited by Maximilien Sully (1559–1641), his finance minister, with a scheme for a federation of Europe.

196   *Holland ... an ill-constructed republic*: the Dutch republic formally rested sovereignty in the Estates of the seven provinces of the republic. The Estates were, in theory, representatives of the people, but they were, in fact, appointed by aristocratic and patrician corporations. Each province was supposed to have a veto on legislation, but the smaller provinces were often dominated by Holland, the largest of the provinces (having over half the population of the United Provinces). Each province appointed its own Stadtholder, but by the eighteenth century the practice had developed of each appointing the same, with the post becoming a herediatary office.

RIGHTS OF MAN: PART TWO

201   *if you make a campaign the ensuing spring*: on 20 April 1792, France declared war on Bohemia, Hungary, and Austria, following their tolerance of *émigré* troops on their territory and the Pillnitz Declaration of 27 August 1791, threatening combined intervention in French affairs by Austria and Prussia. The other German states made common cause against France.

203   *Appeal from the new to ... refute them*: E. Burke, *An Appeal from the New to the Old Whigs in consequence of some late discussions in parliament relative to the Reflections on the French Revolution* (1791). *Works* (1808) vi. 187–200.

204   *This will most probably ... zeal*: Burke, *Appeal ...*, *Works* (1808) vi. 200.

207   *vicinage*: the neighbourhood, or appropriate local body.

208 *all those songs and toasts ... suffocate reflection*: the publication of songs and toasts was a major feature of late
eighteenth-century popular politics. In the 1788 Westminster
by-election (see *Letter Addressed to the Addressers*, note to p.
379), a printer published his bill to George Rose, Secretary to
the Treasury, for the printing of songs and broadsheets indicating that he had provided the ministerial party with some
60,000 copies of various songs in the space of ten days. Cf. L.
Werkmeister, *The London Daily Press 1772-1792* (Lincoln,
Nebr., 1963), appendix v.

210 *Archimedes ... world*: Archimedes (*c.*287–212 BC), Plutarch,
Marcellus xiv.7, attributed to him the saying—that if he could
get to another world he could move this—on developing the
theory of leverage in mechanics.

212 *if this be monarchy ... sins of the Jews*: a reference to the
Jews' decision to appoint a king, 1 Sam. 8: 4–22, discussed in
Common Sense, 12.

a counter-revolution: the *Oxford English Dictionary* dates the
term from 1791, but in the sense of a conservative reaction to
revolution (see above, 169). Paine's usage implies a neutral
sense to the term revolution (as in Locke's willingness to use
it for both executive usurpations and popular rebellions,
Second Treatise 223, 225).

214 *As Nature created him ... ceases to act*: this contrasts with
Paine's account in the opening of *Common Sense*.

217 *The riots of 1780*: the anti-popery or Gordon riots, see note
to pp. 101 and 109.

218 *a metaphysical man, like Mr Burke*: Paine's use of 'metaphysical' suggests someone who looks for too subtle or complex
explanations, but Samuel Johnson, in his *Life of Cowley*,
para. 51–2, also used the term to identify the 'metaphysical
poets' as a race of writers whose 'whole endeavour (was to
shew their learning, who used far-fetched comparisons, and
lacked feeling,' and Paine may be adverting to this sense.

220 *a banditti of ruffians*: see *Common Sense*, 16.

curfeu-bell: curfew, the custom of ringing a bell every evening
as a signal to extinguish fires and lights. It derives from the
Norman, was instituted in 1068 by William the Conqueror
and started at the hour of 8 p.m.

221 *war is the Pharo table of governments*: Faro (or in France,

Pharaoh): a gambling game at cards where players bet on the order in which certain cards will appear.

223 *Abbé Sieyes ... I am already engaged*: Siéyès took exception to Paine's *Letter to the Authors of The Republican* (June 1791, reprinted in the *Morning Post*), and wrote to the *Gazette nationale ou Le moniteur universal* (No. 187, pp. 46–7) on 6 July 1791 asserting that there was more liberty under a monarchy than a republic: 'Je la préfère, parce qu'il m'est démonstré qu'il y a plus de liberté pour le citoyen dans la monarchie que dans la république.' Paine responded with *Letter to the Abbé Siéyès* 8 July 1791 (published 16 July, No. 197, p. 137). Siéyès replied in the same issue and denied that 'I have the leisure to enter a controversy with republican *polycrats*.' (p. 139, col. 2; but see p. 47, col. 1) Paine clearly believed that he had unfinished business, but it remained so.

224 *a levelling system*: loyalist writers sought to discredit Paine by associating him with 'levelling'—that is, demands for equalisation of property, the extension of the franchise and radical republicanism. Only the last is appropriately attributed to the Levellers of the English Civil War, from whom the term derives.

225 *If it be asked ... succession*: letter to the *Moniteur*, 16 July 1791, p. 138, col. 2.

226 *as a pensioner*: that is, in receipt of a salary from the crown and by implication suborned to that interest, a hireling from base motive.

227 *the Houses of York and Lancaster*: the Wars of the Roses (the main military conflict being 1455–85) a (partly dynastic) struggle for the English crown.

1715 and 1745: attempts to reassert the Stuart claims to the English and Scottish thrones by the son of James II by his second marriage, James (1688–1766, the Old Pretender, and by his son Charles (1719–88), the Young Pretender.

succession war for the crown of Spain: the War of Spanish Succession, 1701–13/14, involving fighting in Spain, Italy, southern Germany, the Netherlands and in the Atlantic, the Mediterranean, and the North Sea.

disturbances in Holland: concerning the restoration of the Stadtholder in 1787 in which the British, French, and Prussian governments were variously involved.

Poland ... made a voluntary essay ... to reform: a Polish convention sitting at Balia, in 1769, with doubtful authority, agreed to commission French political theorists for advice, prompting Rousseau's *Considérations sur le Gouvernement de Pologne* (1772).

228 *Homer or Euclid*: Homer (*c*. eighth-century BC), epic poet; Euclid (*c*.300 BC), Greek mathematician.

229 *the democracy of the Athenians*: established in essentials by Cleisthenes in 508 BC and lasted until 322 BC. One probable source for Paine was M. Rollin, *Ancient History*, book X, ch. 1, art. 2.

230 *What is called a republic ... the object*: see Paine's first, but essentially similar, formulations of these definitions in his *Dissertations on Government* (1786) ii. 372–3.

231 *those who have said ... countries of great extent*: Montesquieu, *L'Esprit des Lois*, book, VIII, ch. 16 and 20; Rousseau, *Du Contrat Social*, book III, ch. 4.

234 *It is better to have monarchy ... corrective*: See *Reflections ...* M. 126; Wks. 175, O'B. 230; P. 110, where Burke attributes to Bolingbroke, and endorses, the view that 'you can better ingraft any description of republic on a monarchy than any thing of monarchy on the republican forms'. However, in his speech on the Quebec Government Bill, 21 April 1791, he 'laid it down as a maxim, that monarchy was the basis of all good government, and the nearer to monarchy any government approached, the more perfect it was ... He was by no means anxious for a monarchy with a dash of republicanism to correct it.' Burke, *Speeches* (1816) iv. 21.

235 *than to any other individual member of Congress*: Paine either follows an English custom of referring to the President as the President of Congress (see P. S. Foner, i. 374), or makes a mistake in claiming that the President is a member of Congress (see H. Collins' note 21 to the Penguin edition of *Rights of Man*).

239 *Pennsylvania*: Pennsylvania's constitution (it was the eighth state to provide itself with one, and the first to do so after the Declaration of Independence), was the first to use a specially elected, rather than an already sitting, legislature to write a constitution. The legal assembly had proved unwilling to act, and the election of 1 May 1776 failed significantly to affect the balance of forces in it. Those in favour of independence

abandoned the assembly, rendering it inquorate, and the
Philadelphia Committee of Inspection called a convention of
its county committees in an attempt to bypass the assembly.
This convention met in Philadelphia and scheduled an election for 8 July 1776. The election produced a legislature
acting as a Constitutional Convention. Their deliberations
produced a constitution, adopted alongside the Declaration of
Rights on 28 September 1776. It specified a uni-cameral
legislature, with a broad suffrage, annual elections, and the
requirement that laws had to be passed by two consecutive
sessions of the legislature (see Donald S. Lutz, 'State
constitution-making through 1781', in Greene and Pole).

240   *Congress, at its first two meetings*: the first Continental Con-
gress was called for by Rhode Island in May and Massachusetts in June 1774. The Congress met in Philadelphia 5
September 1774; the second met from 10 May 1775, also in
Philadelphia. Congress worked intermittently on drafting its
Articles of Confederation from the summer of 1775 until
agreement was reached in November 1777 to submit the 13
Articles of Confederation to the states. Ratification, however,
was not completed until February 1781. Even before the
Articles came into effect problems arose concerning the right
of Congress to charge duty, indicating the need for a review
of the Articles.

242   *the state of Virginia*: James Maddison (1751–1836), who retired from Congress after the war and served on the Virginia
legislature, persuaded Virginia to invite other states to appoint
commissioners to discuss 'such commercial regulations [as]
may be necessary to their common interest and their permanent harmony'. Eight states responded favourably, but only
five appeared at the Annapolis meeting in September 1786.

243   *That though they . . . had voted for it*: Massachusetts, 6 February 1788.

244   *accepts none as President of the United States*: Foner claims
that Washington was persuaded to accept a salary of $25,000
p.a. (I, 381).

245   *Dr Johnson . . . a controuling power*: Samuel Johnson, *Taxation
no Tyranny* (1775) in *Political Writings*, ed. D. J. Greene
(New Haven, Conn., Yale University Press, 1977), 423:
'There must in every society be some power or other from
which there is no appeal . . .'

      Magna Charta . . . like an almanack of the same date: 1215.

246   *The history of the Edwards and the Henries ... Stuarts*: this is
one of the claims which is cited in the indictment of Paine for
seditious libel. Although it sounds a wild generalization, the
not notably republican *Oxford Illustrated History of the British
Monarchy* (Oxford, 1992) describes Edward I (1239–1307), as
'autocratic, short-tempered, intolerant of criticism, cruel, and
violent'; Edward II (1307–27), by 1322, as 'vindictive to the
point of cruelty'; Henry I (1068–1135), as 'cruel, lustful,
avaricious, and a stern judge; for Henry III (1216–72), it
notes that 'his naïve, foolish and deceitful actions ... created
disrespect and contempt'; Henry V (1413–1422), is described
as 'a dour, stern man, intolerant of oposition and ruthless in
the pursuit of his ends ... [although] famed for his sense of
justice'; and Henry VI (1422–61, 1470–71), as 'pious, well-
intentioned, and compassionate, but lacking shrewdness, foresight, and calculation'. This paragraph and the subsequent
two were omitted from the Symonds edition of 1792, with the
following statement by Paine: 'Here follow, on page 52 of the
original edition, four paragraphs. As those paragraphs are put
into information, and will publicly appear with the pleadings
thereon, when the prosecution shall be brought to an issue,
they are not verbally recited here, except for the first of them,
which is added in the annexed note for the purpose of shewing
the spirit of the prosecuting party, and the sort of matter
which has been selected for prosecution.' After the note,
Paine adds:'Query. Does the prosecuting party mean to deny
that instances of tyranny were acted by the Edwards and
Henries? Does he mean to deny that the Stuarts endeavoured
to pass the limits which the nation had prescribed? Does he
mean to prove it libellous in any person to say what they did?'

Bill of Rights ... right of petitioning: 1 William and Mary, s.2,
c.2 (1689). The Bill of Rights insists on 'the right of the
subjects to petition the king', but it is not the only clause in
defence of the subject.

the convention parliament: in 1689 an assembly was convened,
in essence a parliament but calling itself a convention, which
declared the throne vacant following the flight of James II to
France, and which offered it to Mary (the heir, as the eldest
daughter of James II, by his first marriage) and her husband
William of Orange (the son of the marriage of Mary, sister to
Charles II and James II, and William II of Orange), as joint
sovereigns.

the corruption introduced ... by the agency of Walpole: Sir Robert Walpole (1676–1745), who mastered the Commons during the last years of the reign of George I (1714–27) and the first fifteen years of the reign of George II (1721–60). Walpole's dominance of the Commons was engineered through the judicious use of court appointments and parliamentary corruption.

247   *bore and quoz*: the sense of 'bore' as tedious dates from the mid-eighteenth century; quoz was a mid to late eighteenth-century term for an absurd person or thing.

St James's and St Stephen's: St James's Palace was used for official receptions by George III; St Stephen's is a chapel in the Palace of Westminster, used by the Commons for its meeting place after 1547.

city of Paris paid a duty: 29 April 1790, decree on the free trade in grain. Internal custom barriers were not abolished throughout France until 31 October to 5 November 1791.

248   *America ... speech on the Canada constitution bill*: that is, the Quebec Government Bill (1791). For Burke's speech see *Parliamentary History*, XXIX, cols. 365–6.

wild beasts in the Tower: the king's menagerie was housed in the Tower of London from the reign of Henry III until the end of the eighteenth century.

Oh John Bull: from the eighteenth century John Bull was the central and much caricatured image of the Englishman. See Miles Taylor, 'John Bull and the Iconography of Public Opinion in England c.1712–1929', *Past and Present*, 134 (1992), 93–128.

Livre Rouge ... court calendar: the infamous 'red book' published in France revealing the sums paid by the crown to those attendant on the court; *The Court and City Register; or Gentleman's Complete Annual Calendar*, which included all the names of office-holders in the Royal Household, Government and Armed Services in Britain. It was a pocket-size volume bound in red leather.

251   *three or four very silly ministerial newspapers*: See, for example, *The Times*, 20 February 1792, pp. 2 and 3. The delays in publication would have allowed Paine to take account of newspaper responses to Pitt's speech on finance on 17 February 1792.

252   *In America it is generally composed of two houses*: Pennsylvania,

which Paine served as Clerk to the Assembly, was one exception, see note to p. 239.

253 *debate on engaging in the Russian-Turkish War*: a war concerning Russia's attempt to retain the port of Ochakov on the Black Sea in Bessarabia. Pitt's involvement in this complex strategic situation was debated in the House of Commons on 12 and 15 April 1791, the government holding its majorities by 253 to 173, and 254 to 162. *Parliamentary History*, XXIX, cols. 217 and 249. In the House of Lords, sixty-seven voted against the motion.

Mr Fox's bill, respecting the rights of juries: Fox's Libel Bill (32 George III, c. 60), which transferred the decision in cases of libel from the judge to the jury. The bill was passed after a year's delay in the House of Lords in May 1792. *Parliamentary History*, XXIX, cols. 551–602, 727–41, 1293–99, 1361–71, and 1404–31.

254 *to extend the duration . . . they now sit*: 2 George I, c. 38 (1716) The Septennial Act.

A general convention . . . into consideration: Paine developed this suggestion in *Letter Addressed to the Addressers* (1792) and it was adopted by several of the more radically inclined members of the reform societies, leading to their prosecution in the Treason Trials of 1794.

256 *Government, says Swift . . . heads*: Jonathan Swift, *Gulliver's Travels* (Oxford, Blackwells, 1965), 'Voyage to Lilliput', ch. 6, 59: 'Since Government is necessary to Mankind, they believe that the common Size of human Understandings, is fitted to some station or other; and that Providence never intended to make the Management of public Affairs a Mystery to be comprehended only by a few Persons of sublime Genius, of which there seldom was three born in an Age.' See also 'Voyage to Brobdingnag', ch. 7, 135–6.

257 *Duke of Richmond*: Charles Lennox (1735–1806), 3rd duke of Richmond and Lennox; Knight of the Garter and Privy Councillor from 1782. Paine's animus (see also p. 300) might derive from Richmond's apostasy—having argued for universal suffrage and annual parliaments in 1783, he strenuously opposed all reform after becoming a member of Pitt's cabinet. Richmond had patents (descended from an illegitimate son of Charles II) to the proceeds of customs duties on coal—hence Paine's comments here and below, pp. 281 and 347.

258 *Holland, by marriage ... Prussia*: the re-establishment of the Stadtholder in 1787 was secured with the assistance of the Prussians, the Stadtholder being married to the sister of the king of Prussia.

260 *figuratively taken*: Locke, *Second Treatise of Government* ch. XIII, § 151, ll. 12–21.

   the civic oath, in France: the oath to the constitution, sworn at many of the *Fêtes de la Fédération* after July 1790, and formally imposed on the clergy in November 1790.

263 *Ultima Ratio Regum*: the last argument of kings.

265 *I have been an advocate to commerce ... its effects*: see especially Paine's *Letter to the Abbé Raynal* (1782): 'Thus commerce, though in itself a moral nullity, has had a considerable influence in tempering the human mind ... the condition of the world being materially changed by the influence of science and commerce, it is put into fitness not only to admit of, but to desire, an extension of civilisation.' (*Works*, ed. Conway, ii. p. 104.)

268 *Mr Pitt ... balance of trade*: *Speeches of the Rt. Hon. William Pitt in the House of Commons* (London, 1806), i. 350–61 (12 February 1787), Speech on the treaty with France.

270 *the European Courts are plotting to counteract it*: see note to dedication.

   Three times has it ... four years of peace: Paine is referring to mobilization of the navy following Pitt's involvement in diplomatic controversies which threatened war: namely, the fall of the Dutch republic in 1787, the Nootka Sound Affair in 1790, and the Ochakov crisis of 1790–11. (See notes to pp. 227, 253 and 368.)

271 *whig and tory, or high or low*: for Whig and Tory see note to p. 40; high and low refers to different sections of the Church of England: High Churchmen upholding the authority of the Church, its sacerdotal claims and asserting the efficacy of the sacraments; Low Churchmen giving a low place to the claims of the priesthood and being closer to nonconformism than to the Catholic Church, with which High Churchmen and Tories had affinity.

272 *the Terrible ... Capt. Mendez*: see note to p. 39, and A. Barry, 'Thomas Paine, Privateersman' *Pennsylvania Magazine of History and Biography*, 101 (1977), 451–61.

273 *secretary in the foreign department*: Paine was Secretary to the Congressional Committee for Foreign Affairs (1777–9). He resigned after revealing secret documents in his attempt to demonstrate that Silas Deane (1737–89), one of the American Commissioners to France, had been involved in corruption.

pecuniary offers ... Gerard and Mirralles: Conrad-Alexandre Gérard, first French Minister to America (1778–9), and Don Juan Mirralles, the Spanish Minister. Paine did, however, accept a gift from Gérard's successor, Anne-César, chevalier de la Luzerne, in reward for Paine's *Letter to the Abbé Raynal* (1782).

affair of Arnold and Andre: Benedict Arnold (1741–1801), a General in the Continental Army, who secretly negotiated through Major John André (for the British) to surrender West Point to Clinton in return for a royal military commission and financial remuneration. When discovered, Arnold fled to the loyalists. André was captured and hanged as a spy by the Americans. Paine's comment suggests fear of reprisals against American spies. Paine discusses the case in a postscript to his *Crisis Extraordinary*, 4 October 1780.

Col. Lawrens ... son of Lawrens in the Tower: Colonel John Laurens (d. 1782), a member of Washington's staff in 1778, and a negotiator with the French after the arrival of French ships in 1778. Henry Laurens (1724–92), President of the first Continental Congress. Laurens was captured *en route* to Holland to negotiate an alliance in 1779 and was imprisoned in the Tower of London for fifteen months.

274 *charters and corporations*: these were instruments by which kings had granted rights and powers to individuals, or towns since before the conquest. The corporations, by the eighteenth century, had become synonymous with maladministration; see Langford (2) ch. 4.

276 *'Our representation ... shew the contrary'*: *Reflections* M. 56; Wks. 107; O'B. 146; P. 49.

277 *'the great ground ... to the landed interest'*: Burke, *Appeal from the New to the Old Whigs*, *Works* (London, 1808), vi. 188—a reflection interspersed between quotations from Paine.

In 1788, the amount of the land tax: Sir John Sinclair, *The History of the Public Revenue* (London, 1785), 2nd edition in three parts, each separately paginated. The land tax figures are given in iii. 154.

the land tax in 1646: the date is given in error. Paine intends to refer to 1696. See Sinclair, iii. 7.

the taxes . . . between land and articles of consumption:

	customs and excise	land tax
1688–91	4,348,264	3,171,739
1759	6,785,932	1,737,608
1788	16,172,970	1,950,000

Source: Sinclair, iii. 5–7, 29, 154.

278 *the tax on beer*: Sinclair, iii. 125 (although Sinclair does not point to the inequity of the tax).

borough traffic . . . connections: through the ownership of estates, some of which gave preponderant influence in a borough, or which were identical with the borough, members of the nobility were able to control a substantial number of seats in the Commons. Even without preponderant influence through property ownership, many constituencies had small enough electorates to allow aristocratic influence. See Namier and Brooke, i, 'Introduction'.

279 *when the vallies laugh and sing . . . rejoices*: possibly an allusion to Isaiah 44: 23, 49: 13.

'the Corinthian capital of polished society': *Reflections*, M. 139; Wks. 188; O'B. 245; P. 122.

Samson . . . temple of Dagon: Judg. 16: 22–31.

280 *a candle-holder*: names of various 'offices' in the royal household.

281 *two thousand aged persons*: that is, at £10 p.a.

not only refused offers . . . have accepted: Paine certainly turned down offers of money, but since he also turned the profits from his writings to the causes they supported he was often in financial difficulty (especially during the American War). At that time he accepted office under Congress and in the Pennsylvanian Assembly; he also received money from the French Ambassador and land from the Indiana Company, and he was paid by Robert Morris for writing for Congress. Moreover, after the Revolution he received several offers of money and land, and those he accepted left him comfortably off. But in no case can he be accused of having been bought.

'*it is the standing law . . . consequence*': *Appeal, Works* (London 1808), vi. 189.

282 *executive*: 'But because the Laws, that are at once, and in a short time made, have a constant and lasting force, and need a *perpetual Execution*, or an attendance thereunto: Therefore 'tis necessary that there should be a *Power always in being*, which should see to the *Execution* of the Laws that are made and remain in force. Locke, *Second Treatise*, ch. XII, § 144.

283 *Sir John Sinclair's History of the Revenue*: iii. xviii–xix and 113.

284 *Wat Tyler . . . Walworth . . . Richard . . . Barons . . . Runnymede*: Wat Tyler (d. 1381) is not identical to John Tyler who killed a poll-tax collector. Richard II (1377–99) was 14 at the time of the revolt. Sir William Walworth (d. 1385) was knighted for his killing of Tyler. Runnymede was the site for the signing of the Magna Carta.

285 *the amount of taxes . . . 1788*: Sinclair, iii. 154.

286 *The expence of collection . . . gross amount*: Sinclair, iii. 162, calculates the average cost of collection to be 7.5 per cent of the gross.

national debt . . . nine millions: Sinclair, iii. 264, calculates the debt at £247,981,927, with an annual interest due of £9,469,117.

France . . . possessed national domains: a reference to the nationalization and sale of the lands held by the clergy by the National Assembly (from 19 December 1789), and those held as part of the Royal domain (19 December 1789, 9 March 1790). The rules governing sales changed on several occasions in the course of 1790.

287 *popery, and wooden shoes*: the wooden shoe, or *sabot*, of the French peasant was used as a symbol of the misery and poverty of the French.

The characters of William and Mary . . . father: William III was the son of Mary, the sister of Charles II and James II; Mary II (1689–94), and Anne (1702–14) were the daughters of James II's first marriage to Anne Hyde.

bought the Dutchy of Bremin: on the transaction concerning Bremen see Sinclair, ii. 75 and his source, Henry St John, Viscount Bolingbroke, *Bolingbroke's Works* (1773) iv. 131–2, 'Some Reflections on the Present History of the Nation'.

288 *The peace establishment*: i.e., under Charles II, for the years 1675–6; Sinclair, i. 181.

war with the Dutch: the first Dutch war, Parliament voted £5,483,845; the second Dutch war, 1665–7, Parliament voted £1,238,750. Sinclair, i. 183–4.

290 *even the physicians bills ... sent to the public*: George III's numerous doctors were rewarded with pensions—£1,000 p.a. for twenty-one years in the case of the Rev. Dr Francis Willis and £650 p.a. and for his son Dr John Willis—and the London physicians were paid £10 per visit to Kew and £30 per visit to Windsor. Sir George Baker's fee amounted to £1,380. See Ida Macalpine and Richard Hunter, *George III and the Mad Business* (2nd edn., London, 1991), 95.

three offices at ten thousand pounds each: Paine is being generous: by 1792, Pitt was paid £5,622 as First Lord of the Treasury, together with some small sums as New Year's Gifts (on average £33 p.a.). As Chancellor and Under Treasurer of the Exchequer he received approximately £1,900. He also received a net income from his sinecure as Warden of the Cinque Ports of c.£3,053. Thus, even Pitt rarely netted £10,000 p.a. (J. Ehrman, *The Younger Pitt* (London, 1969), i. 595–6).

292 *poor rates are a direct tax*: poor rates were paid by householders with incomes of £40–50 p.a. or more—that is, probably by about a quarter to a third of the population. The amount paid fluctuated according to the needs of the parish.

Sinclair ... £2,100,587: iii. 163–4.

Birmingham is said to contain: W. Hutton, *An History of Birmingham*, 2nd edn. (Birmingham, 1783) gives a figure of 48,252; Paine's source is obscure.

taking two millions ... national amount: the inquiry into poor-rate expenditure conducted in 1786 calculated that about £2 million per annum was spent on average for 1783–5.

293 *reduction of ... the national debt*: Paine appears to mean that four million would service a debt of one hundred and twenty million—a similar ratio as obtained in 1762; Sinclair, ii. 88.

294 *At fifty*: Paine was 54 in 1791.

295 *thrown off from the revolutions of that wheel*: the wheel of fortune, a commonplace of medieval and renaissance literature.

296 *six pounds ... ten pounds per ann.*: in 1777 it was calculated that a lowly manual labourer and his wife were likely to be earning about £22 p.a. Moreover, the purchasing power of this wage had declined gradually over the previous twenty years. Langford (1), 458.

tontine: a financial scheme by which the subscribers to a loan each receive an annuity for life, the value of which increases proportionately as their number is gradually reduced by death.

let George ... Saib: the kings of Britain and France; Leopold II, Emperor of Austria (1747–92); Frederick II the Great of Prussia (1740–86); Catherine II the Great of Russia (1762–96); Charles Cornwallis (1738–1805), first Marquis, second Earl, second-in-command under Clinton in the American war, then Commander-in-Chief and Governor-General in India; Tipu Saib (d. 1799), Sultan of Mysore, a thorn in the flesh of British policy in India, and a victim of cultural stereotyping in the British imagination.

298 *relieving parishes from this charge*: the fact that a parish bore directly the costs of any poor person resident within its boundaries, together with the high cost of poor relief in some parishes, sometimes led parishes to police their territory and eject those likely to become a burden to the rates.

Public schools do not answer: schooling took place either in institutions established under charters and statutes which restricted their options, or in charity schools established in the first half of the eighteenth century. In both cases the numbers educated were limited.

302 *Chelsea College pensioners*: inmates of Chelsea Royal Hospital for old or disabled soldiers, founded 1682.

303 *the tax on houses and windows*: by acts of 1766 and 1779, cf. Sinclair, iii. 136.

commutation tax: established in the Commutation Act of 1784, which sharply reduced the tax on tea and increased the window tax as a way of reducing the incentives for the smuggling of tea. Sinclair, iii. 138–46.

307 *tax on beer brewed for sale under Charles II*: Sinclair, i. 186.

309 *reports on the corn trade*: average corn prices in the inland and maritime counties, and average prices for exportation, were printed regularly in the *London Gazette*.

310 *Several laws are in existence . . . workmen's wages*: between the
1720s and 1790 almost forty acts had been passed forbidding
'combinations' or unions in particular trades, although these
were not very effective.

312 *the condition of the inferior revenue officers . . . twenty years
ago*: Paine acted for his fellow excisemen in 1772, writing his
Case of the Offices of Excise in defence of their claims for
higher wages.

314 *news of the coalition*: the Fox–North coalition, 1783; see note
to p. 179.

he ransacked Europe and India for adventures: Paine is referring to Pitt's involvement in various alliances and strategic
interventions designed to maintain Britain's position in
Europe, and to Cornwallis's campaigns in India. (On Pitt's
European activities see Paine's *Prospects on the Rubicon*
(1787).)

317 *Holland . . . Brunswick*: William III; George I; Zell is probably a reference to Zeeland, a province of Holland on the
border with Belgium.

318 *Rebellion consists . . . by a government*: cf. Locke, *Second Treatise*, ch. XIX, § 227: 'when either the Legislative is changed,
or the Legislators act contrary to the end for which they were
constituted; those who are guilty are *guilty of rebellion*.'

320 *the horrid scene that . . . East-Indies*: a reference to the brutality of British military conduct in India.

321 *the Age of reason*: also the title of Paine's attack on Christianity, the first part of which was published in 1793.

the oppressed soldier . . . the tortured sailor: references to the
very poor conditions faced by both soldiers and sailors, and
to the forced methods of recruitment used. Both suffered
from a traditional reluctance to allow a standing army of any
size, lest it be used to consolidate the power of the king
against the people and parliament.

322 *sowered*: obsolete form of soured.

323 *The Algerine piracy may . . . cease*: piracy by Algerian ships
against those of Europe and North America was common.
The attacks were seen as made possible by a failure of co-
operation between those victim to them; Paine, and others,
particularly blamed the British for this.

the former National Assembly: the Legislative Assembly, replacing the National Constituent Assembly, formally opened on 1 October 1791.

325   *the present Bishop of Landaff*: Dr Richard Watson (1737–1816), scientist and theologian, who was known for his latitudinarian views, but who answered Paine's *Age of Reason* with *An Apology for the Bible* (1796).

On a certain occasion three years ago: probably during the Regency Crisis.

327   *Mr Pitt's Speech . . . 31*: *Parliamentary History*, XXIX, cols. 786–7 (31 January 1792); see also 17 February 1792, cols. 816–38.

328   *Address and Declaration of the Thatched House Tavern*: *Address and Declaration of the Meeting of the friends of Universal Peace and Liberty, held at the Thatched House Tavern, St James Street, August 20, 1791*, signed by John Horne Tooke, but written by Paine; Foner, ii. 534–7.

intended to be published before the meeting of Parliament: that is, before 31 January 1792. It appeared 16 February 1792.

printer's hands: Thomas Chapman, who subsequently testified against Paine at his trial.

330   *a ministerial bookseller*: John Stockdale of Piccadilly printed Francis Oldys's *Life of Thomas Pain* (London, 1792). Oldys was a pseudonym for George Chalmers, who was a clerk in Hawkesbury's office—indeed, Paine refers to him in *Rights of Man: Part One*, p. 183.

LETTER ADDRESSED TO THE ADDRESSERS

335   *late Proclamation . . . and Addresses*: Royal Proclamation against Seditious Writings and Publications, 21 May 1792, *Parliamentary History*, XXIX, cols. 1476–7; *London Gazette*, nos. 13418–24. The *Gazette* had noted 220 Addresses to the king by the end of June 1792.

336   *afraid to whistle, lest they should increase the wind*: 'The seamen will not endure to have one whistle on shipboard: believing that it rayses winds', *Oxford Dictionary of English Proverbs*.

the Outs as well as the Ins: those in opposition and those in political office.

337   *Lord Stormont*: David Murray (1727–96), Viscount Stormont, and from 1793, second Earl of Mansfield. Keeper of Scone was a formal title referring to an ancient Scots region. For Stormont's speech see *Morning Chronicle* 1 February 1792, or *Parliamentary History*, XXIX, cols. 749–50.

338   *captivating eulogium . . . by Lord Bolingbroke*: Henry St John Bolingbroke, *Dissertation on Parties* (London, 1735), Letter XIII, 153–4.

339   *Grenville*: William Wyndham, Baron Grenville (1759–1834), created a peer 1790. In 1792 he was both President of the Board of Control and Foreign Secretary.

341   *the Statutes at Large of the Jews*: that is, the Old Testament and an allusion to *Statutes at Large: From the Magna Carta to George III*, 10 vols. (London, 1786).

341   *Saul gave the most convincing proofs*: 1 Sam. 9: 3 and 20.

342   *exasperated, at the proposal of the Jews*: 1 Sam. 8: 6 (see *Common Sense* pp. 11–19)

      Paternoster-row: Paternoster Row, a street close to St Paul's cathedral in London, allegedly where monks in procession to the cathedral said the Pater Noster (Lord's Prayer); by the eighteenth century it was a centre of publishing and bookselling. Joseph Johnson, who set but did not publish Part One of the *Rights of Man*, had his premises on the Row.

      Amen Corner: at the west end of Paternoster Row, purportedly where the monks finished the Pater Noster in their procession on Corpus Christi.

      Antiquarian Society: from the 1730s to 1777, the Antiquarian Society met at the Mitre, Fleet Street.

      1 Samuel, chap. 8: verses 10–18.

343   *Are our young men . . . sailors*: Paine's irony is directed against the impressing methods used to man the army and navy.

      every man may sit under his own vine . . . fig tree: 1 Kings 4. 25.

      Is the tenth of our seed: a reference to the payment of tithes on the produce of the land to the Church.

      Is not the G. R. or the broad R. stampt upon everything: the royal stamp was used to indicate that the 'Stamp Tax' had been paid on the articles in question. Stamp Tax was payable on gold, silver, hats, gloves, newspapers, etc.

344   *the Lord Chancellor*: Edward Thurlow (1731–1806) first
Baron Thurlow, Lord Chancellor 1778–83 and 1783–92. Thurlow's relationship with Pitt deteriorated after 1788, breaking
out in public conflict in May 1792. On 16 May Pitt informed
the king that he could not sit in the same council with
Thurlow, and Thurlow was dismissed—but allowed to leave
in June. Since the Regency Crisis, Thurlow had been closer
to George, Prince of Wales, than to Pitt. Paine's reference to
York (Frederick Augustus, 1763–1827), and Clarence (William IV, 1765–1837), the two younger sons of George III,
implies a cabal against the king.

   Mr Dundas: Henry Dundas (1742–1811), Home Secretary,
1791–4, and thus principally responsible for domestic order.

345   *Cæsar in the Tyber, crying to Cassius*: *Julius Caesar*, I. ii. 113.

346   *having announced their arrival in the Gazette*: that is, the
London Gazette, an official government journal.

   hic jacet: literally, 'here lies'. Paine uses it to mean their
obituary.

347   *Onslow, at the Surry County meeting*: see Paine's two letters
to Cranley Onslow, 17 and 21 June, 1792 in Foner, ii. 457,
460. The Meeting was reported in *The Times*, 19 June 1792.
In the first of his letters Paine accuses Onslow of trying to
influence in advance the jury who were to try him for *Rights
of Man*.

   Duke of Richmond . . . at the Sussex meeting: see 'To the
Sheriff of the County of Sussex', 30 June 1792, ii. 463.

348   *got together by the ears*: to fight together—Butler, *Hudibras*
'When hard words, jealousies and fears, set folks together by
the ears.' What Paine says of Kent was also replicated
elsewhere.

   number of Addresses in the Gazette: *Annual Register for 1792*,
34/2, 37 noted 341 addresses by 1 September; Eugene Black,
The Association (Cambridge, Mass., 1963), 232 suggests that
over 360 addresses were received before the end of the summer.

   at the time of writing: Paine's *Letter* was composed in the
summer of 1792, most likely in late July, or August. Paine
arrived in France in September and the *Letter* was published
in England in October.

   a greater number of the cheap edition . . . one month: the
number of copies sold is the subject of much debate. A

recent, moderate suggestion gives a figure of 10, 000 copies of part two being sold per week in 1792, with 100, 000 of each part being in circulation by 1793. See Gregory Claeys, *Thomas Paine: Social and Political Thought* (London, Unwin Hyman, 1989), 112.

done in Spain . . . Government of France: in pre-revolutionary France, and in Spain, the Chruch exercised extensive powers of censorship, as did the state. In France a book had to be awarded the 'privilege' of being printed by a board of censors. In practice, there was latitude, and when books were banned they generally enjoyed considerable success after their production was moved to Holland.

349   *meetings of the justices . . . General Warrants*: in 1763 John Wilkes and others involved in the publication of *North Briton* No. 45, which had directly criticized the king in connection with the Peace of Paris, were arrested and imprisoned under a 'general warrant', which permitted the arrest of anyone involved in the publication (i.e. there was no requirement to name the offender in the warrant). This produced a public outcry, and the courts eventually ruled such warrants illegal although they had been used against Jacobites earlier in the century).

garrisoning the country: in May 1792 the government ordered new barracks for cavalry to be built at or near Sheffield, Manchester, Nottingham, Coventry, and Norwich, with a view to policing the country more effectively.

350   *France . . . absurdity of the monarchical*: on 10 August 1792, the monarchy was overthrown in France and the creation of a National Convention was agreed (to which Paine was elected in September).

351   *George . . . Guelph*: i.e. George III, Guelph being the name of the ruling family of Hanover and Brunswick.

hewers of wood and drawers of water: Josh. 9: 21, 23.

353   *The preamble is in the following words*: cited correctly, apart from minor differences in punctuation, and the omission of 'and' prior to 'secure'.

354   *part of the charge . . . Locke, Hampden, and Sydney*: John Locke (1632–1704), philosopher, active in the 'exclusion crisis' of 1679–81, when parliamentary Whigs sought to force on Charles II a bill excluding his Catholic brother James

from the succession. Following their failure in 1681, some close to Locke were involved in the Rye House Plot to assassinate the king. On discovery, Locke became a fugitive. Algernon Sydney (1622–83) was arrested after the plot, and his manuscript for his *Discourses Concerning Government* was used by the prosecution to demonstrate his treason. He was executed on Tower Hill. Had Locke been detained with his *Two Treatises of Civil Government* he would undoubtedly have shared Sydney's fate. John Hampden (1656?–96), who was also connected with the Rye House Plot, was in 1685 condemned to death for high treason following the Monmouth rebellion (an attempt to overthrow James), but was subsequently pardoned.

Attorney-General: Sir Archibald Macdonald (1747–1826), Attorney-General 1788–92.

James Mackintosh: (1765–1832). His *Vindiciae Gallicae* (London, 1791) was a philosophically sophisticated reply to Burke's *Reflections*. Mackintosh renounced his former opinions in the later part of the decade.

355 *Thomas Walker*: (1747–1817). Manchester cotton merchant, founder member of the Manchester Constitutional Society (1790), tried for conspiracy in April 1794 and acquitted.

a price that precluded an extensive circulation: Johnson's never-published first edition was to have sold for two shillings and sixpence; Jordan sold both the first edition of part one and that of part two for three shillings each.

356 *Court of St James*: that is, the Crown.

a false, wicked and seditious libel: 'a certain false, scandalous, malicious and seditious libel'; *State Trials* (London, 1817), xxii. col. 360.

357 *The County Meeting for Middlesex . . . 118 addressers*: *London Gazette*, No. 13450, 633: but see the *Morning Chronicle* for 10 August 1792, which gives an account of a divided meeting at which seventy-five voted against the Address.

359 *Dragonetti . . . national expence*: Paine quotes exactly the same passage in *Common Sense* (pp. 33–4), where he refers to it as 'extracts'—a more accurate description since the quotation is made up of two phrases separated by a page in the original.

360 *The Lord will . . . wall*: Acts 23: 3 'Then said Paul unto him [the judge who had ordered that he be struck on the mouth], God shall smite thee, *thou* whited wall.'

361   *special juries*: as established by 3 George II, c. 25 (1730), although the broad intention of the Act was to prevent the packing of juries (see *Parliamentary History*, VIII, col. 803), the sections of the Act on special juries (xv–xviii) seem to have had a different intent, concerning the rights of courts to strike juries.

362   *Esquire*: those legally entitled to use this were mainly the younger sons of peers and knights and their eldest sons; those so created or by office, as judges, justices, officers, and barristers. By the early nineteenth century it was clearly a courtesy title for all those considered gentlemen.

363   *a deep take in*: that is, a hoax or swindle.

364   *Temple-bar and Whitechapel*: the west and east bounds of the City of London.

365   *a bill of wrongs and of insult*: *Rights of Man: Part Two*, p. 246.

366   *House of Orange*: a Dutch royal house, supporters of Charles II in his exile, and the house from which William III descended.

     For a nation to be free: see *Rights of Man: Part One*, p. 96 where Paine quotes Lafayette's remark in full.

     Thus much for both their houses: by implication, a plague on both, *Romeo and Juliet*, III. i. 112.

367   *the modern interpretation of Libels*: probably a reference to the changes consequent on Fox's Libel Bill (32 Geo. III, c. 60) which transferred the decision as to whether the content of a publication was libellous from the judge to the jury (which had previously been asked to assess only whether or not the person was guilty of publication). However, Paine's comment implies the old dispensation, as if the Attorney-General need only prove to the jury that Paine was the author of the book, not that what he wrote was libellous. The Act was passed by the Lords on 21 May 1792, the same day that proceedings against Paine were launched.

     the information states: the quotation is a compilation of a number of claims made in the indictment; see *State Trials*, cols. 358–62.

     With respect to . . . sleeps obedience: *Rights of Man*: Part Two, p. 253.

     Friends of the people: a political association comprising mainly parliamentarians and aristocrats sympathetic to moderate reform launched with the *Declaration at the Freemasons Tavern* on 26 April 1792 (published in *Parliamentary History*, XXIX, cols. 1303–9). Charles Grey (1764–1845), a young opposition MP, played a leading role. James Mackintosh was secretary of the society for a period.

368   *the bubble broke forth about Nootka Sound*: Nootka Sound, on the north-west coast of America, was a source of concern in January 1790 when news reached the government that the Spaniards had seized a British ship and were proclaiming Spanish possession of the territory. The events as seen from the British captain's point of view were published in May 1790, leading to the mobilization of the British Fleet; war seemed inevitable. It was averted when Spain backed down in July 1790. See John Ehrman, *The Younger Pitt*, i. 554–64.

  the day after the King's Message . . . I wrote to Mr Burke: the king sent a message to Parliament concerning Nootka Sound on 5 May 1790. No correspondence between Paine and Burke from this time is extant, but there is no reason to doubt Paine's word.

  Mr Grey: Charles Grey (1764–1845), second Earl, a leading aristocratic Whig in favour of moderate reform.

  I am in treaty with Mr Pitt about Mr Hastings's trial: Burke was the major force behind the impeachment proceedings against Warren Hastings (1732–1818), Governor General of India, for which he required the co-operation of Pitt.

  Mr Fox then called it a Libel: *Parliamentary History*, XXIX, col. 1315 (30 April 1792).

369   *declarations of this Society, of the 25th of April, and 5th of May*: see *Parliamentary History*, XXIX, cols. 1303–9.

  the general WILL: a rare reference by Paine to Rousseau's formulation of popular sovereignty, *Du contrat social* (1762) bk. 2, chs. 1–4 (see also below, p. 376).

370   *for although copyholds . . . the holders are unrepresented*: as opposed to forty shilling free-holders in the counties. See Sir L. Namier and J. Brooke, (eds.), *The History of Parliament: House of Commons 1754–1790*, Vol. 1 (London, 1964) 'Introduction'. On the Land Tax see Sinclair, *History of the Public Revenue*, iii. 106–15.

371   *Petitions from the unrepresented part*: one means of redress for grievances from areas without parliamentary representation was the petition. It was not notable for its success in the

1790s, and its failure (for example in the spring of 1793, when radical societies organized petitions in support of bill for the reform of Parliament introduced by Grey) encouraged radicals to take the route of conventionism, which led to their being tried for treason in 1794.

372 *Court-Kalendar*: that is, the register of those in receipt of Crown patronage.

an unknown number of masked Pensioners: In the Civil List, in the sixth class, the sum of £107,404–13s–4d is marked for unnamed pensions. Most other pensions are earmarked to particular offices. See Sinclair, *History of the Public Revenue*, iii, App. 1, vi. Paine cites this figure below, p. 374.

the end of Lord North's administration: 1770–82.

Mr Burke's Reform Bill: a bill for reforming the Civil List and establishing parliamentary control of Crown estates 1780: Burke's Establishment Act (22 George III. 82).

Burke became himself a Pensioner in disguise: Burke was formally granted a pension in August 1794, of £1,200 p.a., with a further grant in September 1795 to the value of an additional £2,500 p.a. There is no evidence to support Paine's claim that Burke was in receipt of a pension before this date.

373 *Sir John Sinclair's History of the Revenue*: iii, App. 1, vi–xi. The four separate charges Paine identifies are variously listed: 1. Bills in the Lord Chamberlain's Department; 2. the Lord Chamberlain at the Exchequer; 3. salaries payable in the office of the Lord Chamberlain; 4. the Lord Chamberlain's gate alms and Maundy money. The Master of Hawks is listed on p. ix.

374 *£1,700 . . . to Dissenting Ministers*: see Sinclair, iii, App. 1, xi.

377 *Riches make themselves wings, and fly away*: Prov. 23: 5. The chapter begins, 'When thou sittest down to eat with a ruler, consider diligently what *is* before thee and put a knife to thy throat, if thou *be* a man given to appetite . . .'

378 *disqualifications, arising from the commission of offences*: the most famous recent case was in 1784, when following his success in the Westminister election, Charles James Fox, leader of the Whigs, was not returned to parliament because the high bailiff had granted a scrutiny on the grounds of accusations of corruption and false votes (see Ehrman, *The*

Younger Pitt, i. 217–21). But it is acknowledged that corrupt practices were commonplace in fiercely contested elections.

379 *the compact that was entered into ... Fox and Lord Hood*: Westminister returned two candidates, Fox and Samuel Hood (1724–1816) in 1784, with the second ministerial candidate, Sir Cecil Wray, being defeated. In 1788 Hood was offered a lordship at the Admiralty and convention required that Members accepting office had to stand for re-election in their constituency. This caused an equally vigourously fought by-election, won by the Foxite, Sir John Townshend (1757–1833). So expensive was the contest, that in 1790 an agreement between Pitt and Lord Lauderdale led to the seats being uncontested, with Fox and Hood being returned. See D. Ginter, 'The Financing of the Whig Party Organisation', *American Historical Review* (1966), 71(1), 421–40; and Namier and Brooke, vol. 1.

381 *Henry IV ... to multiply gold or silver*: 2 Henry IV, c. 4: the Act was directed against alchemists 'multiplying' gold and silver (not mathematicians).

382 *with respect to regular law, there is scarcely such a thing*: *Rights of Man: Part Two*, p. 249.

DISSERTATION ON FIRST PRINCIPLES OF GOVERNMENT

388 *mixed government, such as the late government of Holland*: 16 May 1795, the Treaty of the Hague transformed the United Provinces into the Batavanian Republic, ending the mixed government established at the overthrow of the republic in 1787.

389 *Euclid*: Greek mathematician, who lived in Alexandria, *c.*300 BC, and who became synonymous with geometry.

390 *Robespierre*: Maximilien-François-Isidore [de] Robespierre (1758–94), a member of the Estates General, a Jacobin, and a member of the Paris Commune in the time of the Legislative Assembly (October 1791—September 1792). He was elected to the convention in 1792, urged the execution of the king and subsequently acted as a key agent in the revolutionary terror, which ended with his overthrow and execution in July 1794.

Capets, Guelphs, Robespierres and Marats: Louis Capet and

George Guelph are Paine's common names for Louis XVI and George III. Jean-Paul Marat (1744–93) was a democrat and ideologue, whose journal *L'Ami du peuple* won him notoriety. A member of the Paris commune, and elected to the Convention by Paris, he was instrumental in the downfall of the Girondins and was assassinated by Charlotte Corday in July 1793 for his part.

392 *fee-absolute*: the holder of the fee-absolute is the absolute owner of the land, in contrast to fee-simple, which is an estate held on condition of homage and service to a superior lord.

393 *First Part of Rights of Man*: see pp. 173–4.

395 *Act of Settlement and Bill of Rights*: see note to pp. 90–1.

the Constituent Assembly of France: on 9 July 1789, the National Assembly (constituted from the Estates General) adopted the title of the National Constituent Assembly, which was disbanded in September 1791 to make way for the Legislative Assembly. Hereditary succession was accepted with the establishment of a constitutional monarchy in October 1790.

401 *Aristotle, Socrates, Plato*: Greek philosophers, Socrates (469–399 BC) was Plato's (427–347 BC) teacher, who in turn taught Aristotle (384–322 BC).

great landed estates . . . plundered at the conquest: a common claim in radical circles and part of a view of the legacy of the conquest as a Norman yoke, on a previously free people.

Jacobins: members of the Société des Jacobins, which acted as a parliamentary pressure group, agreeing on the line which should be followed in the Assembly. From late 1792 the club was dominated by the left, and became intimately associated with the Terror. The term 'jacobin' was deployed by British loyalists as a slur on English radicals from early in 1793.

403 *apple of discord*: a golden apple, inscribed 'to the most beautiful', said to be thrown among the gods by Eris (the personification of strife) at the wedding of Peleus and Thetis. The apple was awarded to Aphrodite by the judgement of Paris, who had promised he would have the most beautiful (mortal) wife. They carried off Helen, thus inaugurating the Trojan war.

405 *hospital of incurables, as Chesterfield refers to it*: Philip Dormer Stanhope, 4th Earl of Chesterfield (1694–1773), who wrote in his character of Mr Pulteney that he was fixed in the House of Lords, that hospital of incurables. *Miscellaneous Works,*

Letters to his Friend, Characters . . ., ed. J. Bradshaw (London, 1905), III, 1416.

AGRARIAN JUSTICE

AUTHOR'S INSCRIPTION

412 *the present Constitution of the French Republic*: that is, the Constitution of Year III (1795), a liberal republic, designed to separate rather than concentrate powers, and including a property suffrage. The executive to be a Directory of five members, elected by the upper house from lists of names presented by the lower house.

Babeuf: François-Noel Babeuf, 1760–97. A radical critic of the Convention and the Directory, he organized a 'Conspiracy of Equals' and planned a *coup d'état*. Arrested in May 1796, he was executed the following May.

'royalists': in January 1797, André-Charles Brottier (1751–98) was arrested with Thomas-Laurent-Madelaine Duverne de Presle (1763–1844), for plotting against the Directory in the hope of establishing a constitutional monarchy.

413 *the execrable reign of Terror*: traditionally understood as the period from the purge of the Girondin faction through to the overthrow of Robespierre; that is, from *c.*5 September 1793 (when the Convention announced that terror was to be the order of the day), to 9 Thermidor II (27 July 1794, when Robespierre was executed).

PREFACE

414 *present war*: 20 April 1792 saw the opening of the Revolutionary Wars, with France declaring war on Austria. War was declared on Britain on 1 February 1793, and Britain reciprocated ten days later. France remained at war with Britain until the brief Peace of Amiens (1801–3).

Watson: Dr Richard Watson (1737–1816), a divine and scientist, who wrote *An Apology for the Bible in a Series of Letters Addressed to Thomas Paine* (1796).

inheritance . . . Instead . . . insolence . . . it would be: the deletions appear in the 1797 English edition, to which this Preface was added. There is no record of Paine's original version.

416   *Agrarian law ... Monopoly*: originally a Roman law for the division of conquered lands, which in the republican tradition came to mean a law which divided land in equal parts amongst the citizenry of a state. Agrarian Monopoly is Paine's term for all property in land being held in the hands of a few.

417   *Man, in a natural state ... ten times the quantity of land*: the argument is exactly that of Locke, *Second Treatise*, ch. 5, §37, lines 14–27, and §40.

condition ought not to be worse: Locke's proviso of 'good and enough for all', ch. 5, §34, makes a similar point.

earth ... the common property of the human race: see Locke, ch. 5, §26.

418   *ground-rent*: the rent paid to the owner of land which is let for building upon.

neither Abraham, Isaac, Jacob nor Job ... were owners of land: according to the Bible they were members of nomadic tribes.

contentions ... about the use of a well: Gen. 26: 14–34.

421   *emprunts*: borrowing or loans.

My state of health: Paine nearly died from illness contracted in the Luxemburg and was unwell for more than a year after his release.

422   *the English Minister Pitt ... for the year 1796*: December 1796 *Parliamentary History*, XXXII, col. 1256–64. Philip Foner dates this pamphlet to Jan–Feb 1796, which is in keeping with when Paine first wrote it. However, it seems clear that he revised it subsequently (taking Pitt's speech into account) before it was published in 1797.

the wild project of setting up Bourbon Kings: that is: the son of Louis XVI, Louis XVII (Louis Charles, 1785–95, unproclaimed accession in 1793); and the brothers of Louis XVI: Louis XVII (Louis-Stanislav-Xavier, 1755–1824, accession 6 April 1814); and Charles X (Charles Philippe, comte d'Artois, 1757–1836, accession 16 September 1824).

Mr Pitt states the national capital ... Belgia: Belgium was occupied by French forces in 1792–3 and 1794–5, and formally annexed to France in October 1795. It is not clear on which sources Paine is making his claims about the national incomes of other states.

the event of the last harvest ... England: Britain suffered poor harvests and food rioting in 1795; France also suffered from virtual famine conditions in 1795, but dramatically improved production in 1796–8.

423   *collaterally*: that is, to the side, or indirectly.

      escheats: in feudal law, where a fief reverted to a lord if a tenant died without heir; forfeited property more generally.

425   *as odious as it is unjust ... it is* necessary that a *revolution should be made in it*: these two phrases were replaced by ***** in the English and American editions.

426   *property, like vegetation, increases by off-sets*: short, lateral off-shoots from the stem or root of a plant which could be used in propagation were known as off-sets.

429   *what I have, which is not much, is in the United States*: Paine's only capital was a small farm in America, given him for his services to the American Revolution.

430   *Horsley . . . in the English Parliament*: Samuel Horsley, (1733–1806), Bishop of Rochester, *Parliamentary History*, XXXII, November 1795, cols. 258 and 267.

INDEX

JANE AUSTEN	Emma
	Persuasion
	Pride and Prejudice
	Sense and Sensibility
ANNE BRONTË	The Tenant of Wildfell Hall
CHARLOTTE BRONTË	Jane Eyre
EMILY BRONTË	Wuthering Heights
WILKIE COLLINS	The Woman in White
JOSEPH CONRAD	Heart of Darkness
	Nostromo
CHARLES DARWIN	The Origin of Species
CHARLES DICKENS	Bleak House
	David Copperfield
	Great Expectations
	Hard Times
GEORGE ELIOT	Middlemarch
	The Mill on the Floss
ELIZABETH GASKELL	Cranford
THOMAS HARDY	Jude the Obscure
WALTER SCOTT	Ivanhoe
MARY SHELLEY	Frankenstein
ROBERT LOUIS STEVENSON	Treasure Island
BRAM STOKER	Dracula
WILLIAM MAKEPEACE THACKERAY	Vanity Fair
OSCAR WILDE	The Picture of Dorian Gray

*The
Oxford
World's
Classics
Website*

www.worldsclassics.co.uk

- Information about new titles
- Explore the full range of Oxford World's Classics
- Links to other literary sites and the main OUP webpage
- Imaginative competitions, with bookish prizes
- Peruse *Compass*, the Oxford World's Classics magazine
- Articles by editors
- Extracts from Introductions
- A forum for discussion and feedback on the series
- Special information for teachers and lecturers

www.worldsclassics.co.uk

American Literature

British and Irish Literature

Children's Literature

Classics and Ancient Literature

Colonial Literature

Eastern Literature

European Literature

History

Medieval Literature

Oxford English Drama

Poetry

Philosophy

Politics

Religion

The Oxford Shakespeare

A complete list of Oxford Paperbacks, including Oxford World's Classics, OPUS, Past Masters, Oxford Authors, Oxford Shakespeare, Oxford Drama, and Oxford Paperback Reference, is available in the UK from the Academic Division Publicity Department, Oxford University Press, Great Clarendon Street, Oxford OX2 6DP.

In the USA, complete lists are available from the Paperbacks Marketing Manager, Oxford University Press, 198 Madison Avenue, New York, NY 10016.

Oxford Paperbacks are available from all good bookshops. In case of difficulty, customers in the UK can order direct from Oxford University Press Bookshop, Freepost, 116 High Street, Oxford OX1 4BR, enclosing full payment. Please add 10 per cent of published price for postage and packing.